Core Resource

Managers of Virtue

MANAGERS
of VIRTUE

Public School Leadership
in America, 1820–1980

DAVID TYACK

&

ELISABETH HANSOT

Basic Books, Inc., Publishers

NEW YORK

"Dream Deferred" on page 214 is reprinted from *The Panther and the Lash*, by Langston Hughes, by permission of Alfred A. Knopf, Inc. Copyright © 1951 by Langston Hughes.

Library of Congress Cataloging in Publication Data

Tyack, David B.
    Managers of virtue.

    Includes bibliographical references and index.
    1. School management and organization—United States
—History.   2. Educational sociology—United States—
History.   3. Leadership—History.   I.   Hansot, Elisabeth.
II.   Title.
LB2805.T9   371.2'00973   81-22923
ISBN 0–465–04376–3 (cloth)   AACR2
ISBN 0–465–04375–5 (paper)

For Samuel, Mary, and John Tyack
A wise and loving family

For David and Ruth Wolf
From whom I have learned much
about leadership and friendship

CONTENTS

PART III

Managers OF Virtue

Prologue

At the turn of the century the British educator Michael Sadler observed that "the American school is radiant with a belief in its mission, and it works among people who believe in the reality of its influence, in the necessity of its labors, and the grandeur of its task." Americans have long had faith in the power of education to shape the future. The architects of public schooling took literally the motto on the Great Seal of the United States, *Novus Ordo Seclorum,* believing that their crusade for common schools was part of a providential design to make America a new order for the ages.[1]

After the American Revolution a deep vein of millennial thought in religion became suffused with republican aspirations. Many of the public-school promoters of the mid-nineteenth century were convinced that America was literally God's country, the land He had chosen to bring about the redemption of mankind. The version of millennialism they most commonly shared was not that of an apocalyptic Second Coming, but rather the gradual creation of the Kingdom of God on earth and the triumph of Christian principles in government and society. This process of redemption was not passive or deterministic, however; the common-school crusaders regarded themselves as God's chosen agents. This sense of being part of a larger providential plan infused even ordinary tasks with a larger meaning. In the Progressive era, school leaders retained much of this earlier moral earnestness and sense of mission, but they lost much of the specifically religious content of millennialism. Instead, they drew on a newer aspiration to control the course of human evolution scientifically through improving education. Each group had a firm sense of its place in the trajectory of human events. Each felt qualified, in different ways, to be managers of virtue.

Today both a sense of the past and hopes for the future are in disarray in public education. Few would now affirm that the teacher is "the prophet of the true God and the sharer in the true kingdom of God" or would recall that John Dewey wrote those words in *My Pedagogic Creed.* Today the media focus on pathologies: violence in classrooms, falling test scores, warring interest groups, tax revolts, and discord within the educational profession itself. Public education, traditionally an expanding enterprise based on a consensual ideology, has begun to constrict and become litigious. Older histories portraying the emergence of the common school as the result of providential design or progressive evolution of a unified profession have given way to revisionist accounts that stress the gaps between aspirations and achievements. People are uncertain about the forms and direction that educational leadership should take or even whether leadership is possible.[2]

In the present period of disarray, conflict, and diminished sense of potential, we think it worthwhile to understand how leaders of public education thought and acted in the past, especially with regard to the social meanings they and their contemporaries brought to the work of building and reconstructing public schools. An institution like public education gains coherence not only from organizational forms but also from the social meanings that people attribute to it. The study of history provides insight into how these forms and meanings emerged in the past and how they may continue to shape the present and future.

The public-school manager of today resembles an heir receiving a handsome legacy from a distant relative whose purposes now seem unclear or even quaint. Both nineteenth- and twentieth-century educational reformers shared an evangelical confidence in their mission, their certainties grounded in either the revelation of God's will or the assurance of expert knowledge. Today the only certain people are critics who know what is wrong with public schools. School officials are likely now to keep a low profile, out of the crossfire of conflicting demands.

Traveling across the United States one can find school buildings that exemplify diverse legacies from the turning points in our educational history. In a country landscape, the one-room school, with its steeplelike bell tower, remains the symbol of the common-school movement of the nineteenth century, reflecting its chiefly rural character, its affinity with the family farm, its unbureaucratic nature, and its Protestant-republican ideology of creating the nation in the hearts and minds of individual citizens. Like a church with its Bible, the rural school with its McGuffey Readers was to be a small incubator of virtue. Today many of the founders of the fundamentalist Christian Day Schools yearn for the certainties of their evangelical forebears.

In the heart of the older cities is the quintessential legacy of the early twentieth-century professional managers: the urban high school, often looking like a hard-edged factory with pilasters, visually representing the union of an attenuated traditional culture with a dominant utilitarianism. Planned and staffed by specialists, sorting students into programs that would profoundly influence their life chances, the high school was an archetype of the ideal of social efficiency that dominated the thinking of the new professional managers. Inside one would have found in 1915 an imposing office for the principal, secretaries busy typing memos and filing reports, a gymnasium and assembly hall, counselors talking with students, and young people in classrooms studying algebra or metalwork or domestic science. The school conveyed an air of certainty then; one knew that it was a portal. Today, run-down and often full of students who have no desire to be there but no jobs beckoning them either, it resembles a fortress overrun by the very people it was meant to arrange in serried ranks.

And moving to an expanding suburb today, one is not quite sure whether that new, sprawling one-story complex is going to be a shopping and service center or a school. Soft-edged, divided into segments, united mostly by a common parking lot and heating system, both school and shopping center are eclectic in offering something to everybody, blurred in purpose, adapted to the anomic consumerism and possessive individualism of a postindustrial middle class. The complex of buildings articulates individual tastes and interests clearly, but what does the whole add up to?

Like the architecture of the schools, the tasks that educational leaders faced and the social order within which they worked changed dramatically from the early nineteenth century to the present. The central challenge for common-school crusaders of the mid-nineteenth century was to mobilize the people in support of public education and to construct an educational system. They worked within an overwhelmingly rural nation. State departments of education were small and weak, and the federal government exerted little influence over public schools. Schooling was largely unbureaucratized and unprofessionalized. For the most part, these leaders did not devote their entire careers to education, but treated it as one among several occupations and causes that engaged their attention. They saw public schooling as crucial to the development of the United States as a capitalist nation and were themselves often members of local elites, but the economy they knew was mostly small-scale and decentralized. Largely Protestant in religion and Anglo-Saxon in ethnic background, they shared a common religious and political conception of the role of public education in shaping a Christian nation. Because the school promoters tended to see themselves linked by a common moral earnestness and civic activism, we have called them an "aristocracy of character." Although they turned to state governments for assistance in carrying out their educational plans, they relied heavily on the consciousness-raising and institution-building activities of voluntary associations. These school reformers associated in regional and even national networks. We suggest that a useful way to conceptualize their leadership is to see it as mobilizing a vast institution-building social movement akin to the religious movement that spread Protestant churches across a far-flung rural nation. We discuss this phase of leadership in Part I of this book.

By contrast, the educational leaders of the period 1890–1954, described in Part II, were social engineers who sought to bring about a smoothly meshing corporate society. In some respects their optimism about the potential of education was as utopian as that of the earlier crusaders, but their version of a millennial society was far more secular. Their task was not to create but to redesign the public-school system, not to arouse public participation in education but to constrain it, not to campaign for a common denominator of education so much as to differentiate it according to the needs of a complex society (as *they* interpreted those needs). Most of these leaders made education a life-long career and were pioneers in its professionalization. They wished the state to take an active role in transforming public education.

Their lives encompassed a period of rapid consolidation of corporate capitalism and concentration of wealth among urban elites. It was also a period when work in America was being transformed and class divisions were intensifying. Workplaces were growing sharply in size, the planning of production was increasingly being divided from its execution, the nonproduction sector was growing at a fast pace, and the "visible hand" of management, as Alfred Chandler has shown, was revolutionizing the way in which American business was controlled. At the same time, strikes, labor turnover, and other forms of working-class unrest were threatening the new order. To complicate the social equation, immense numbers of immigrants, from southeastern Europe in particular, were pouring into the cities and augmenting the industrial work force. The new social division of labor transformed the character of decision making in education as in many other domains, substituting administrative discretion for governance by elected lay representatives.[3]

The members of the "educational trust" (as the administrative progressives were sometimes called) embraced the new managerial models developed in business. Rarely self-conscious about their cultural assumptions, they incorporated many of the values of their small-town pietist upbringing into what they regarded as an objective "science of education." They sought legitimacy through expertise rather than through deference to character or through broad public participation in policy making. Linked in networks that combined university leaders with influential superintendents and foundation officials, these leaders sought a form of private power: they gained, as did leaders in other occupations, authority to define what was normal or desirable. Transmuting numbers into norms, they shaped their preferred policies into a standard template of reform which they applied to state after state, district after district, in their school surveys and legislative proposals. They successfully changed the structures of decision making and sought to turn political issues into matters for administrative decision, confident that the schools could rise "above politics." They believed that school leaders could do their part in shaping the smooth and conflict-free evolution of a complex urban-industrial society. This was their own version of managing the millennium.

Whereas school leaders in the nineteenth century tended to see themselves as constituting an aristocracy of character, in the twentieth century they began to regard themselves as a distinct group of experts, certified by specialized training, linked into exclusively professional associations like the American Association of School Administrators (AASA), sponsoring and being sponsored by fellow experts, elaborating legal and bureaucratic rules, and turning to science and business as sources of authority for an emergent profession.

The earlier religious legacy, with its sense of providential purpose to reform society, was not abandoned, however. Local leaders, like district superintendents, often continued to regard schools as "museums of virtue," to use sociologist Willard Waller's phrase. The nineteenth-century social movement for the common school had given educational leaders much of their moral capital, a lasting fund of metaphors, an overarching sense of purpose to animate work that was often mundane. Yearbooks of the AASA reflected this blend of science and missionary zeal. In 1933 the yearbook said that the task of the educational leader was nothing less than "to mold character and to ameliorate the whole intellectual, moral, social, civic, and economic status of their fellows." Such incantations, like inspirational speeches at conventions, may sometimes have been soothing background music for harried bureaucrats. But until the last generation the rhetoric of moral charisma and millennial hope complemented the dream of professionalism and the language of science and evolutionary social efficiency.[4]

Since 1960 much of this composite ideal of educational leadership has come under attack for being a "closed system" of governance by educational experts. Traditional leaders have been assaulted by dispossessed groups and delegitimized by competing elites. Educational policy making has become politicized and fragmented. Beginning with blacks and their white allies in the civil-rights campaign, successive groups—feminists, Hispanics, the handicapped, native Americans, and many others —have mounted powerful protest movements to win practical and symbolic gains. Within the educational system, an older professional consensus has eroded and internecine battles have erupted. Many factions have found the law a ready instrument of challenge and reform, and, as a result, a new kind and degree of litigiousness has emerged. Federal and state governments have created a kaleidoscope of new programmatic reforms, each with its own regulations and accounting system.

One result of these changes—most of them long overdue attempts to achieve social justice—has been fragmentation and discord in educational governance. Leaders have lost the ability to command securely either as aristocrats of character or as experts. Indeed, amid the litigiousness, the competing claims of protest groups, the infighting within a once united educational profession, the confusing and sometimes conflicting requirements of the new paperwork empire of categorical programs, people have sometimes wondered if *anyone* was in charge. Amid the claims of single-issue reformers it has been hard to find a common ground, a belief system that could make the parts of public education coherent. The older notion of the common school as a public good has come to seem as antiquated as the one-room school.

Both the common-school crusaders and the administrative progressives believed in public education as an instrument of progress. In retrospect, the belief systems that undergirded their optimism may appear to be merely myths, but myths are not the same as falsehoods. Organizational myths are a way of making vivid a sense of what institutions can be; by elaborating a heroic past, they direct people toward an equally potent future. Embedded in myths are images of potentiality.

Myths change, and the sacred beliefs of one generation may simply become mystifications to the next, to be dismissed with polite incredulity or angry polemics. The revisionist historians of the past generation have been more angry than politely incredulous, for they have seen earlier myths as barriers to social justice and excuses for not engaging in basic societal change. They have termed their predecessors' views of educational policy "elitist" and "self-serving," designed to blur fundamental class, racial, sexual, and ethnic divisions in American society and, in so doing, to obscure the role schools have played in perpetuating inequalities.

In recent years some radical historians have written a version of the educational past almost diametrically opposed to the traditional interpretation. They have sought to demystify public education, to scatter the fog of sentiment that covered harsh realities. They have argued that its basic structure was hierarchical and elitist, not democratic; that its operation was class-biased, racist, and sexist; that it was imposed by elites, not created democratically by educational statesmen and their allies; that its ideology was suffused with notions of social control, often covert; that tinkering with minor improvements would not set it right; and that, most important, its claim of being able to right the basic inequities of American life was a legend.

The radical attack on the traditional and optimistic faith has made both historians and policy makers wary of grandiose claims. People who desire basic social change will not be likely now to think that it can readily be accomplished through schooling. Revisionism has clearly raised new issues for analysis (although some of these had earlier been raised, in somewhat different form, by such scholars as Merle Curti and George Counts). Many people (ourselves included) have become newly aware, thanks to the radical analysis, of ideological frameworks and class interests too much taken for granted.[5]

It would, of course, be a serious mistake to suppose that the loss of faith in schools—and in other key institutions—is primarily the result of critical scholarship about education, including the work of revisionist historians. Such national traumas as the Vietnam War, assassinations, Watergate, ghetto riots, and the oil squeeze have altered the perceptions and expectations of Americans and dashed hopes for peace and prosperity shared by all. David Cohen and Bella Rosenberg wrote in 1977 that it was in the previous decade that Americans began to suspect that their faith in the mythology of "the redeeming power of science, formal learning, and modernity" might have been misplaced. Americans witnessed in the media

extraordinary visions of the destructive power of things modern and American: visions of massive technological and scientific warfare on innocent peasants; visions of the democratic American state become devious and oppressive, its effectiveness enhanced by electronic technology; visions of modern industry and technology out of control, wreaking havoc on the countryside; and visions of angry poor and minority youth for whom stories about the power of knowledge and the economic fruits of schooling had become a frustrating trick—a great promise which the very institutions of hope seemed incapable of redeeming.[6]

The disarray of earlier ideals and a related feeling of powerlessness and lack of leadership arose from many sources, some of them far from public education.

Now that conflicts arising in the larger society have turned public schools into a more obvious battleground of contending social and political forces, leaders in education often find themselves ill-equipped by training and professional ideology to cope with the new conditions. Those who shaped public schools in the past would have regarded the conflict of the recent years as pathological, for they believed that the common school should be "above politics," a noncontroversial and integrative institution. The builders of Horace Mann's generation sought a common denominator of belief as a means of persuading citizens to create the system, while the experts of the Progressive era tried to buffer schools from lay influence, to keep the politician's nose out of the professional tent. Although public education has in fact always been an arena where different groups have contended for benefits, it has never developed a consistent ideology to justify such conflict. Both lay and professional leaders have sought common ground and accommodation and regarded conflict as abnormal and undesirable.

In this respect public education has differed from other sectors of society where competition and conflict have been taken for granted and treated as part of the natural order. Religious denominations, for example, confident that their own version of truth and virtue would triumph in the end, have competed freely for souls and funds. The market system of capitalism has relied in theory on economic competition, however imperfect actual competition has been. Clashes of interest between organized labor and management have been based on adversarial principles. Political parties have fought one another with ritualistic regularity.

With few exceptions, public educators have believed in the basic soundness of the American social order and the belief systems supporting it, including the value of controlled competition in such domains as politics, religion, and the economy. Within public education, however, they have sought to prevent organized opposition by stressing consensus, by claiming schools should be "above politics," or by absorbing, co-opting, or deflecting outside forces. A sign of their success in defusing conflict has been that the major American political parties, unlike, for example, their counterparts in England or Germany, have rarely differed substantially about educational policy. Another sign has been the fact that competing Protestant sects have generally called a truce at the schoolhouse door. The genius of the public-school establishment, like that of the Roman Catholic Church during much of its history, has been its ability to absorb dissidence and to accommodate demands from influential groups, ruling only a few claims beyond the pale (and those usually stemming from groups that lacked power). Some leaders have actually believed their own claims that schools were apolitical, while others have simply regarded the rhetoric as a smart policy strategy.

One reason that schools have been able to absorb outside demands for change is that they have been steadily expanding during most of their history and could reform by accretion. This kind of incrementalism has made it possible to smother conflict by acquiescence—to say, yes, we'll have that, too. Educators such as Ellwood P. Cubberley wrote histories glorifying the system's ability to accommodate the constant addition of new structures and functions. People who opposed incrementalism could be dismissed as ignoramuses or opponents of the democratic mission of public education.

In a time of retrenchment and hard choices, declining consensus, and open conflicts, the old habits of reform by accretion, of dealing with conflicts by absorption, and of blurring basic social cleavages no longer offer an easy way out. But if the older myths of the origin and destiny of public schools no longer seem persuasive, Americans still need to find a common ground of thought and action that does not deny the validity of conflict or the pluralism of values and interests.

Although we believe that it is important to recreate a community of commitment to public schooling, we do not propose a remystification or bogus consensus. We believe that it is possible to move beyond simple celebration or recrimination. A history of public-school leadership that is simply a tale of injustice and elite imposition and not also a story of generous ideals and common effort lacks the complexity and texture of actuality. The present fragmentation of belief and governance endangers what Michael Walzer calls "civism, the citizen's sense of being a participant in a common enterprise." As Walzer notes, the term "civism" can mean to conservatives "little more than the ideology through which self-restraint is to be taught to the working class." That, he says, "is a lesson that won't be learned and shouldn't be. The resulting social order would not have the form of a common enterprise. Civism depends on equality, or, at least, much greater equality than we have today." It was, in fact, to such an egalitarian ideal that recent protest groups appealed and on which they based their claims for social justice. Revisionist history has taught much about how schools failed to fulfill ideals of equality and inculcated a noninclusive civism. But without civism in Walzer's sense it is hard to see how citizens can weather a time of scarcity without resorting to a narrow privatism, a possessive individualism.[7]

Of the many possible approaches to writing a book on the history of educational leadership, we have chosen to focus on the people who created, managed, and reshaped the public-school system. Our study is on three levels: that of individuals and the personal networks they formed; of the institutions they built; and of the transformations in the larger society that acted as preconditions and precipitants of change in public education. Since our intent is exploratory, we first develop a general argument in each of the major parts of the book and then send out historical probes in the form of case studies of individuals and organizations.

By looking at the work of individuals within the broader matrix of organizations and societal change we are rejecting both the great-man theory that sees leaders essentially as unconditioned actors, and a deterministic viewpoint that argues that individuals are simply pawns of vast historical forces. We argue that there have been effective leaders in American education who achieved much in one period but would have been misfits or failures in another. Horace Mann's evangelical style was well suited to his era, for example, but could have appeared stiff-necked and priggish in a later time. We agree with Karl Marx's aphorism that "men make their own history, but they do not make it just as they please; they do not make it under circumstances chosen by themselves, but under circumstances directly encountered, given, and transmitted from the past." Those conditions are always specific to time and place —that is, historical and particular.[8]

We take a broad view of the kinds of circumstances that shaped educational leadership. We blend different modes of interpretation— the economic with the cultural, the biographical with the organizational. We seek to integrate different ways of seeing. History has split into separate compartments called "intellectual" or "social" and into topical specialties like "church history," "family history," "business history," and "educational history." Such specialization tends to obscure the actual coherence of experience of, say, a person in a Michigan town in 1880 who was a Presbyterian lawyer, a major property holder, a temperance reformer, a father of two daughters, a Republican, and a school board member.

We believe that the study of broadly held and influential ideologies is one way to erase the boundaries separating the intellectual, political, and social history of public schooling. Such belief systems, John Higham writes, "give large bodies of people a common identity and purpose, a common program of action, and a standard for self-criticism." They give resonance and meaning to the ordinary work of ordinary people. In this book we examine such widespread belief systems rather than writings of sophisticated theorists or avant-garde experimenters (there is already a rich vein of scholarship on such intellectual leaders and pedagogical pioneers). Focusing on leaders who built and transformed the operation of institutions, we seek to understand two related but separable issues: how they made sense of their lives, and what sense we as historians, looking backward, can make of their work. We take seriously, for example, the millennial Protestant-republican beliefs of the common-school crusaders, since it formed an essential part of their world view and is a key to their success in persuading their fellow citizens to build schools. But this does not mean that we must take at face value their claims that they were creating classless and universally acceptable institutions. Similarly, it is useful to understand the assumptions, goals, and methods of the administrative progressives without accepting their belief system as an accurate transcription of social reality. Ideologies do not float in the air; they are rooted in complex ways in the social structure. They reveal social strains and serve the interests of particular groups (normally those dominant at the time). Groups compete with each other to have their particular ideology accepted as authoritative.[9]

Initially drawn from belief systems that were powerful in the larger society, rationales for public education became institutionalized over time as organizational creeds or professional litanies. This narrowing gave stability and a sense of common purpose to educators, but the dampening of public debate about education and the avoidance of conflict that attended the rise of expertise in management gradually eroded an earlier common ground of support for the common school. A broad-based public philosophy of education may be regarded as a community of commitment linking the people and their schools, articulated by leaders but giving citizens a strong voice. We believe that a central task of leaders today is to reformulate the common purposes of public education in a manner tough-minded enough to encourage controversy and broad enough to foster pluralism.

PART I

An Aristocracy of Character, 1820–1890

Through costly experiments, splendid failures, and baffled hopes, we make our way toward the Augustan age. As the Israelite awaits the readvent of the lost glory of his race, the Christian the dawn of the millennial day, and the millions the coming of that good time when the earth shall be greener and the skies brighter, so we believe in the golden age of schools and teachers. But for this inspiring hope, this vague but indistinguishable faith and longing for something worthier and better, who of us would not be at times ready to drop the oar and in hopelessness to drift any whither?

Newton Bateman
Illinois state superintendent of public instruction
Addresses and Proceedings of the NEA

1. THE PILGRIM'S PROGRESS

"Educate the rising generation mentally, morally, physically, just as it should be done," Senator Henry Blair told his colleagues in the capitol in 1882, "and this nation and this world would reach the millennium within one hundred years." Across the nation in a white schoolhouse planted among the hills of Ashland, Oregon, Alice Applegate sat writing a theme: "Addam was the first man that looked out upon the face of the earth and he was then in the garden of eden. Around him were all kinds of fruits and flowers and in the center of the garden grew the tree of the Knowledge of Good & Evil To be continued." To Alice, to the teacher (her brother Oliver Cromwell Applegate), and to her schoolmates the Bible explained and ordered the universe. Twice daily they read the Scriptures aloud. In their textbooks Christianity merged imperceptibly with Americanism. A generalized Protestantism was part of the accepted wisdom of the common school, and both were part of a divine plan that led from Eden to a millennial future.[1]

Many of the educational leaders of the nineteenth century found meaning for their labors in this larger providential conception which looked both backward and forward. Consciously or unconsciously, many educators who wrote autobiographies echoed *The Pilgrim's Progress* (John Bunyan's tale was the second most popular book, after the Bible, in the childhood homes of school superintendents). Like Christian tangling with Apollyon in the Valley of Humiliation, schoolmen wrote of contests with bullyboys in one-room schools. They told of the Pliables or Obstinates who lost faith when they encountered the pedagogical Slough of Despond. Mr. Worldly Wiseman often appeared in the guise of textbook salesman in the autobiographies. The city school board sometimes resembled the jury in *Vanity Fair*, with its Mr. Blindman, Mr. Nogood, Mr. Malice, and Mr. Hate-light. Fiery darts came from the wicked in every quarter, while deceptive bypaths distracted School-man from his quest for the Celestial City. One superintendent spoke of his fellow pioneers who had pursued their pilgrimage "thru devious ways, against tremendous obstacles, and over the trail . . . with vigorous opposition, in contest and in conflict to the end. One and another languished, fell, died, and are buried by the side of the road." But the goal was clear, the dream of common schooling announced by the evangelist Horace Mann.[2]

For many years the Department of Superintendence of the National Education Association (NEA) printed "necrologies" or brief biographies of its departed pilgrims. Here one finds important clues to the self-image of nineteenth-century school leaders, for certain key words recur: "earnest," "Christian character," "pure," and "true scholar." A fitting inscription for most of them would have been Longfellow's "Psalm of Life": "Life is real! Life is earnest!/ And the grave is not its goal!" Here was an aristocracy of character whose worth was certified by church membership and social service. Rarely did biographers dwell on educational background or professional training; the age of specialization and certification did not come until the twentieth century. Rather, leadership in public education was often seen as a *calling* similar to that of church missionary, and in teachers' institutes superintendents were sometimes as interested in converting to religion as in evangelizing for schooling. Their belief in an "All-Seeing Eye"—God witnessing all human behavior—invested even the commonplace with cosmic significance.[3]

The Pilgrim's Progress

It takes some effort of historical imagination to reconstruct the context—both material and ideological—within which Americans of the mid-nineteenth century embarked on their most ambitious and successful social movement, the crusade to create a common-school system. Today, when people take for granted the complex organizational structures of schooling, large government bureaucracies, big cities, an immense industrial base, intense division of labor, and pluralism of values, it is easy to forget that mid-nineteenth-century America was four-fifths rural, had a minuscule government, possessed only a rudimentary industrial system composed mostly of small firms, and had only begun the bureaucratization that would later mark a mature corporate society. It is even harder to understand the world view that gave coherence to the decentralized campaign for public education. Much of the rhetoric of the school builders—the millennial hopes, the Bunyonesque self-conceptions—strikes readers today as quaint, like the illustrations and evangelical diction of the McGuffey Readers. Yet this social movement produced by the end of the century more schooling for more people than in any other nation and resulted in patterns of education that were remarkably uniform in purpose, structure, and curriculum, despite the reality of local control in hundreds of thousands of separate communities.[4]

The mainstream of American public schooling during most of the nineteenth century was rural, chiefly unbureaucratic in structure, exhibiting only rudimentary professionalism, and dependent on the actions of hundreds of thousands of lay promoters and school trustees.

The model nineteenth-century school was a small one-room building. Nineteenth century America had a predominantly rural and dispersed population. In 1860, 80 percent of Americans lived in places defined by the census as rural (under 2,500), and as late as 1890, 71 percent were rural. Rural enrollments typically were higher than urban. One-room schools dotted the landscape from Maine to Oregon. The census of 1850 reported about 80,000 public schools and only 90,000 teachers; the census of 1890 tallied more than two times more school buildings than existed almost a century later in 1970, despite the vast increase in the numbers of pupils. This indicates that in 1890 schools were mostly small in size.[5]

Teachers in such rural schools could hardly be considered members of a profession or even bureaucratic employees. They were young, poorly paid, and rarely educated beyond the elementary subjects. Hired and supervised largely by local lay trustees, they were not members of a self-regulating profession, however much school reformers tried to make it such. Turnover of teachers and administrators was extremely high. In Massachusetts, for example, which was a leader in the campaign to make teaching a stable occupation, there was such high mobility out of teaching that in 1860 one out of five adult women had at one time been a teacher, according to one estimate. Even the most notable school promoters and administrators tended to pursue education as only one among several careers. Until the end of the century there was little formal training for educational specialties beyond "normal" (or teacher training) classes; in 1890 a survey of education departments in twenty leading universities, for example, uncovered only two courses in educational administration. The major national professional association, the National Education Association, never had more than 355 members until 1884. Its conventions took on the character more of an evangelical camp meeting for education than of a specialized and powerful professional agency.[6]

Federal and state governments exercised little direct control over public education, unlike educational agencies in many other nations. The United States Office of Education, founded in 1867 with a staff of six and a budget of $13,000, did little more than collect statistics and diffuse information. As late as 1890 the median size of state departments of education was two, including the superintendent—or roughly one state official per 100,000 students enrolled in public schools. State officers complained that they had little power to compel local districts to do anything, even though states did provide funding and sought to encourage and standardize education.[7]

In this part of our study of educational leadership we focus on the middle of the nineteenth century and seek to analyze how public schooling spread so quickly and then developed in such uniform ways. We concentrate on what we take to be the mainstream: rural, unbureaucratic, locally created schools, controlled by lay people and permeated with a Protestant-republican ideology. Much recent scholarship on the history of education has stressed instead the origins of urban schools, the processes of bureaucratization, incipient professionalization, the enlarging role of the state in educational affairs, and the relationships between schooling and the new social relationships of production in mercantile and industrial capitalism. We have written on these themes ourselves and believe them to be important both in themselves and for understanding how schooling developed in the twentieth century. It is surely valuable to analyze such major transformations in society during their formative stages, when their structure and dynamics were not yet obscured by decades of accumulated rhetoric and vested interests. Thus, Michael Katz, for example, has argued that bureaucracy can best be understood by examining its emergence when it was only one among several competing forms of school organization. According to this view, it is justifiable to focus on industrial states like Massachusetts, or on cities, since in such places one can find harbingers of the future.[8]

Historians know how things turned out. This is both an advantage and a disadvantage. It is an advantage, because hindsight makes it easier to distinguish between the basic, underlying forces of change and the ephemeral. The disadvantage is that concentrating on developments that *later* became crucial may obscure the mainstream of past experience as seen through the eyes of contemporaries.

Although we are interested in harbingers of future developments—and deal with them in section 8— we argue that the mainstream public schools of the mid-nineteenth century were the product of an institution-building social movement led by men and women who shared a similar ideology and interests and who helped to build a common-school system by persuading and mobilizing their fellow citizens, mostly at the local level. In many respects the common-school movement resembled the institution-building crusade that dotted the land with Protestant churches. It was not government, but the actions of voluntary groups and individuals that prompted the phenomenal growth of church membership during the nineteenth century. Uniting both movements was a common belief that the United States was a redeemer nation entrusted with a millennial destiny. Schools and churches were institutions designed to produce a homogeneous moral and civic order and a providential prosperity.[9]

The voluntary and decentralized character of institution-building in America fascinated European visitors accustomed to the large government bureaucracies of continental nations, their established churches, their surviving feudal institutions, and their police and standing armies. Arriving here after his unsuccessful efforts in the revolution of 1848, the German immigrant Carl Schurz said: "Here in America you can see how slightly a people needs to be governed. In fact, the thing that is not named in Europe without a shudder, anarchy, exists here in full bloom." The Swedish observer Per Adam Siljestrom wrote in 1853 that just when old-world governments were becoming more centralized and were attacking the rights of voluntary associations, in America local self-government and private groups were flourishing. He cited public education as a case in point, for here leaders relied not on the force represented by the state so much as "upon the power of persuasion and on the activity of the people itself, when it shall have been raised to consciousness." "Being raised to consciousness" was the key, he believed. While ministers of education in Europe wrote their fiats in "Egyptian darkness," American reformers worked in the broad daylight of public opinion, visiting schools, talking with local school boards, addressing groups wherever they might be found, and gathering and disseminating information. The result of all this activity was not thirty different state systems, nor prodigious variation in local districts, but instead a great uniformity, said Siljestrom, for "nothing is more common in America than imitation and repetition, carried so far as to give a character of monotony to the public institutions, viewed as a whole." A quarter of a century later an English educator still found local control the most conspicuous feature of schooling in the United States and resistance to central supervision still strong.[10]

Although the common-school movement was decentralized, it would be a mistake to see it as some sort of bucolic grass-roots event in a stolid and unchanging rural society. Increasingly, even remote family farms were becoming part of a worldwide capitalist market system. People in nineteenth-century America were highly mobile geographically, and communication between like-minded groups was rapid and extensive. School reformers were in touch with one another and formed associations that shared the latest pedagogical ideas and political strategies. Benevolent societies—such as the American Sunday School Union, which we shall examine—developed highly sophisticated methods of operation. The reformers inextricably mixed religion, politics, and economics in their vision of a redeemer nation.[11]

The consciousness sought by school promoters was not the separatist mentality of a sect, but a consensus that could lead to common action. The reformers of Horace Mann's generation did not believe that they were so much discovering new truths as that they were reminding their fellow citizens of convictions they all shared. What distinguished the educational reformers was that they took these ideals more seriously and worked harder than most people to put them into effect, to square the society with its professed articles of faith. Like William McGuffey, they believed that their world view was one that could be shared by all right-thinking people, properly reminded (in the case of adults) or instructed (in the case of the young). Their task was didactic, to make sure that all citizens acknowledged the practical dictates of a common value system.[12]

The consensus behind the creation of public education in the nineteenth century was based in large part on a belief system that John Higham has called a Protestant-republican ideology, a source of unity in a highly decentralized nation. It had strong millennial elements shared by many of the Protestant sects, a conviction that God had selected America as a redeemer nation: "By giving the millennium a temporal and secular character," Higham has observed, "the Protestant clergy identified the Kingdom of God with the American Republic; and the Protestant ideology thereupon attached itself to American nationalism." Just as Protestants located salvation in the individual's relationship with God, most school reformers saw good citizenship as individual righteousness. Their conception of the polity was atomistic. Lord Bryce noted this when he wrote in 1888 that "Americans conceive that the religious character of a government consists in nothing but the religious belief of the individual citizens, and the conformity of their conduct to that belief. They deem the general acceptance of Christianity to be one of the main sources of their general prosperity, and their nation a special object of the Divine favour."[13]

Although the millennial vision of the Protestant-republican ideology gave coherence and resonance to the rhetoric of the common-school crusaders, they freely mixed economic arguments with the religious and political case for public education. They were confident that within the consensual vision of a providential universe there could be little incongruity among patriotism, godliness, and prosperity. Out of this confidence, the contagious certainty of the institutions builder, grew an aversion to conflict and controversy. Many of the leaders in the common-school crusade were only part-time educational reformers, earning their livings as ministers, lawyers, farmers, businessmen, editors, politicians, and college presidents and professors. They were skilled rhetoricians who cast their arguments not in narrowly professional terms but in broadly persuasive language. Their contemporaries considered oratory not only an important art form and common-place entertainment, but also a source of civil unity, a means of discovering harmony amid apparently discordant parts. No small part of the consensus in favor of public education grew from the rhetoric of speakers like Horace Mann whose secular sermons called for a large loyalty that could dissolve apparent conflicts.[14]

School promoters were typically British-American in origin, Protestant in religion, and entrepreneurial in economic outlook. Although they tried to speak for all Americans, they wore the blinders of their class, religion, and ethnic background. They were intolerant of the

Roman Catholic Church and so alienated Catholics that they hastened the growth of a separate parochial-school system. They wanted to assimilate foreigners to their own version of Americanism. As citizens near the economic apex of their local communities, attuned to the values and economic interests of a burgeoning capitalism, they praised the United States as a land of economic opportunity and justice and tended to blame the poor for their plight. The majority of the leaders took their own values for granted, assuming them to be the basis of a righteous moral order.

Conflicts did arise despite the quest for consensus. While all groups shared a commitment to formal education and moral training of the young—to character formation through schools—they differed over the content or orientation of that education. Precisely because most groups did believe that education was vital, they fought over whose values would be legitimized, whose views would prevail. Conflicting groups generally did not cast issues in economic terms, though clearly the controversies had class overtones. A lawyer in the Cincinnati Bible case described such "status-group competition" succinctly: "In my judgment, the contest is not about religious education at all. It is about denominational supremacy, the right to be higher, to be better, to be more powerful than your neighbor; the right to say to one: 'You are nothing but an unbelieving Jew,' and to another, 'You are the slave of a Roman bishop,' and to both, 'What rights of conscience that a Protestant need to respect have you?'" The issue in Cincinnati was the use of the Bible as the basis of moral instruction in public schools. Other issues provoking conflict at the time were the use of public funds to support Catholic schools and instruction in languages other than English in schools serving immigrant children.[15]

In reading the debates over such issues one is struck by how much both sides talked past one another, perhaps because the values they expressed were so deeply embedded in their own cultures that they believed them to be the only ones reasonable people could hold. Ethnocultural conflicts in education entered the courts for adjudication; they were widely debated in educational and religious associations; they sometimes split political parties; but rarely were they settled authoritatively during the nineteenth century. Few people saw them at the time as issues of constitutional rights. Rather, they were typically regarded as questions of who had the most power. Educators were most apt to accommodate demands when protesters, like Germans or French, had political and economic clout.[16]

Because the common school so rapidly became the mainstream of

American education in the nineteenth century, it is tempting to assume that its hegemony was inevitable and hence to lose a sense of surprise at its triumph. But one can easily imagine a counterfactual history in which the divisions that marked education early in the nineteenth century persisted unabated, and schooling remained as separatist as Protestant churches. Before the common-school crusade of the mid-nineteenth century, educational institutions had often reflected differences of class, ethnicity, and religion. To the crusaders themselves it was by no means a foregone conclusion that they would be able to attract rich and poor, Baptists and Unitarians, Germans and Yankees to the same common school. Free schools in cities had often been designed for the lower classes and carried a pauper taint. Groups like the Germans in Pennsylvania had kept apart in their own schools for generations. In other English-speaking nations, Protestant denominations had created their own elementary-school systems, much as Catholics did in this country. In the South the common school did not become established until after the Civil War, and then was supported only grudgingly: before Reconstruction, blacks were denied formal education, while whites who could afford private schools generally preferred to attend them.[17]

Separatism is one way to avoid conflict. The absence of an established church in the United States had permitted each new group of dissenters to withdraw to form its own new denomination. Ethnic groups have often preserved their distinctiveness and avoided conflict with other subcultures by creating their own neighborhoods and even separate communities. People had different tastes in education as in other domains and had been accustomed to buying the kind of schooling they wanted for their children if they had the money to do so. Why should a *common* school for people in all walks of life have become the dominant form of education? How did the school promoters persuade Americans to support *public* education?

As we have said, the common-school movement was led mostly by citizens who were notables in their communities, people who both shaped and represented a widespread ideology that stressed civic and moral values that they claimed could only be maintained through public education. The nation could fulfill its destiny only if each rising generation learned those values together in a common institution. This was the dominant theme in the rhetoric of consensual persuasion. But the leaders of the movement also were canny about framing their arguments and programs to bring possible dissenters into the common school. By stressing the similar elements of faith among most Protestant denominations, they persuaded Protestants to cooperate. By playing on the fears of the prosperous about social instability and by building palatial high schools for their children in cities, they tried to demonstrate that public education was respectable and a guarantee of order. They assured the common people that public schools were a portal to economic opportunity and a right of citizenship.

Closely integrated with the religious and political case for the common school was the economic folklore of nineteenth-century capitalism. Public education was designed to do more than produce moral citizens. By training children to be literate, temperate, frugal, hardworking, and good planners it also taught them to make their way in the small-scale capitalism idealized in the textbooks. The same virtues that made a young person a good employee could, with appropriate modifications, be translated into entrepreneurial assets. Long before economists developed their theories of "human capital" American citizens believed that investment in education paid off both in individual and collective economic benefits.[18]

Historians have analyzed the relationship between bureaucratic schooling and the new hierarchical social relationships of production in large-scale industrial and commercial capitalism. What is sometimes forgotten in such analyses is that during the mid-nineteenth century most schooling took place in one-room or small-town schools and that the economy was composed mostly of small-scale enterprises. In many parts of the nation the family farm was the chief system of economic production, while in many industries old work techniques and shop cultures persisted. Thus in looking at the connection between capitalism and public schooling it is useful to focus on more than the new social relationships of production in large-scale industry. Capitalism not only entailed new and exploitative relations between employer and employee, important though these were; it also meant an unbound and mobile labor system, a complex system of markets, protection of private property, and a supportive ideology.[19]

It was through inculcating this ideology—and a related set of behavioral traits—that public education of the mid-nineteenth century probably contributed most to American capitalism. By making the republican political system seem inextricable from a system of free labor and open markets, by rationalizing wealth or poverty as the result of individual effort or indolence, and by making the political economy seem to be not a matter of choice but of providential design, the common school buttressed capitalism. A large proportion of twentieth-century economic leaders—like the school managers of that era—grew up in rural communities where they learned the folklore of capitalism taught in text-books like McGuffey's. It is perhaps no accident that one of the industrialists who did most to change the organization of production, Henry Ford, so idealized the one-room school and McGuffey that he enshrined them in a museum near Detroit.

In the public schools of small communities in nineteenth-century America no sharp lines separated religion, citizenship, and economic enterprise. In one such school Alice Applegate sat unself-consciously writing about Eden.

The World According to Oliver Cromwell Applegate

The one-room school in Ashland, Oregon, was more palatial than most rural schools in the state. The balloon-frame building measured 28 by 32 feet, was painted white on the outside, sheathed with boards on the inside, and had several windows looking out on steep brown hills and rolling valleys. Its master, Oliver Cromwell Applegate, was no ordinary teacher. The son and nephew of prominent trailblazers and men of political and social influence in southern Oregon, Oliver was equally at home in the drawing room as on the bear hunt. Witty, a talented artist, knowledgeable about politics, a humorous rhymer if not a poet, a skilled penman in an age when elegant script was a mark of refinement, Applegate was able to raise the cultural horizons of his students at the same time that he knew firsthand their rustic life. One of the boys in his class envied "a gun that would shoot fifteen times like Mr. Applegate has."[20]

The Ashland school in 1865 had thirty-three pupils ranging from ages six to eighteen. There were four Applegates, four Grubbs, four Helmans, three Millions, six Walkers, and two Smiths—all in all, a family affair. School began with reading and geography, arithmetic and spelling, and, for the older scholars, recitations in history and natural philosophy. Applegate posted a list of school rules on the wall and apparently enforced them, if a pious essay by his sister Alice is to be taken seriously:

ORDER IN SCHOOL

There is nothing like Order in School. Students should always be orderly, and when any one is Speaking, they should pay strict attention to all that is said and be as quiet as possible. They should sit facing their teacher and not be turning around and looking at those behind them, and doing things to attract their attention and make them laugh. They should try to get their lessons and if they do not get them very well, what more can they do but try. . . . They should try to obey all the rules and be able to answer perfect every evening.

All was not grim propriety in the Ashland School. Applegate emulated the young literati of Santiam Academy, Willamette University, and other cultural centers by writing and staging plays and helping the students to write ambitious manuscript newspapers. Frequently the children performed for their parents and neighbors, declaiming the themes they had written (or sometimes copied). In these themes and newspapers the pupils reflected what the textbooks and Mr. Applegate were teaching them about the world beyond the village of Ashland. In Ashland, as in other rural schools, pupils read books written by men from afar who told of distant lands, who painted gaudy panoramas of virtue and vice, who talked in language never heard on the playground or in the country store. For millions of children who would migrate to cities, the Sunday School or the weekday school was the first taste of life outside their small circle. There they might study the geography of the Holy Land, the Hanging Gardens of Babylon, the character of George Washington, or scenes from Shakespeare's plays.[21]

The incongruity between the correct diction and monumental morality of the textbooks and the actual life of rural communities was the source of humor in a comic play called *The Country School*, which was written to be performed in settings like the Ashland school. The play revealed what the ideal graduate of a rural school was *not*. The roles of the linguistic delinquents and n'er-do-wells "should be played," said the author, "by prominent citizens of your town, if such can be prevailed upon to appear—the more dignified, staid, and incongruous in years and bearing the better. Dignified professors, judges, doctors, lawyers, teachers, etc., should be prevailed upon to forget their present greatness, don the costumes and revive the scenes of their youth." The men who never escaped Aunt Sally became Huck Finns—truants, ignoramuses, liars, and dunces—when judged by the official standards of the school. Underlying the drama was the clash of the provincial ways of the countryside and the highfalutin culture of the curriculum. "Next, tell me the meaning of excruciating," asked a committeeman of a girl: "Excruciating means that natural and peculiar prohibition of undulatory and molecular attraction which encompasses the plausibility of capillary promulgation and gelatinous hyperbole, while giving an enallage of paradigms," she glibly replied. Education, the play seems to say, may seem unreal and even ridiculous; but moral instruction and linguistic propriety may fit one for the world outside—for the city, for success, for greatness as represented in those figures who condescended in the play to return to their youth in the country school.[22]

Above all, the textbook writers were careful not to confuse the pupils with wishy-washy morality. Schools were to be what Willard Waller would later call "museums of virtue." The rules were always clear: *Never Drink, Never Smoke, Work Hard, Tell the Truth, Obey Authority, Trust Providence.* And the message got across, at least in the official themes of Applegate's students:

IDLENESS

Idleness is a sin, yet there are a great many who will idle away their time; and what do they gain? What kind of men and women will boys and girls make if they give themselves up to idleness? I will tell you what I think: They will be lazy good-for-nothing men and women. The men the boys will become, will sit in the Bar room while their families are left in dark cellars to starve. Think of it. Thousands have perished in this way. I warn you to guard against this evil, hoping that you will never spend your precious time at the gaming table. For remember "time flies on Eagle's wings," and if you lose it once, you can never catch it again. A great many have written on this subject, but I do not think too much can be said about so great a sin as Idleness.

That rule was absolute: no loafing. Another rule was equally firm: "to be happy you must never taste strong drink it is very wrong to taste strong drink always take water in the place of it and you will feel much better."[23]

Follow the rules, work hard, be temperate, be frugal—these were simple enough. But what about ambition—was it a good quality? Here the Ashland scholars were ambivalent. One of the boys greeted "Friends, Teacher and Parents" at the Friday declamation by saying: "I have determined to be *somebody* when I come to be a man. I don't think I can ever consent to be tied down to a yard stick or watch the tiresome motions of a sawmill. I'll clime the ladder of fame. I may go away up, and then come down 'kerspat.' But what of that, we are bound to have our ups and downs in this world any way." If it was fine to be a self-made man, it was not fine to be one of the haughty rich: "If a man is rich," wrote one pupil, "he is no better than a poor man. Some folks think if they are wealthy they are the wisest and do not notice the poor."

All agreed that there was work to do, a continent to be conquered, fortunes to be made. Despite his flowery diction, the scholar who declaimed on the "Resources of Our State" saw hard cash ahead and lost no sentiment over mastered nature:

Oregon is yet young. Her 'shadow scarce reaches to her father's knee.' Her resources are undeveloped, her mighty accomplishments of the future are 'veiled in obscurity.' But they must become known. Who that has beheld the rising magnificence of the states, presided over by the Godess of Liberty, can doubt for an instant the grandeur she will attain. . . . Every land however barren or unsightly it may appear, will unfold to the industrious laborer, whose deeds are presided over by freedom, the rich fruits of glory and glow with grandeur and sublimity. . . . Ere long, when our youthful state shall behold the unfolded wings of time, mighty changes will meet our gaze on every hand. . . . And the whole land will glow with the smile of plenty and satisfaction.

These mid-century themes suggest how deeply the absolutist morality of the evangelical movement became interwoven with a work ethic and ideology favoring the development of capitalism. Just as Christianity was inseparable from Americanism, so the entrepreneurial economic values seemed so self-evidently correct as to be taken for granted. The school gave everyone a chance to become hardworking, literate, temperate, frugal, a good planner. From then on, success was up to the individual, and in America the potential for the person "to be *somebody*" was almost infinite. Or so it seemed in the millennial future the schools predicted for the righteous.[24]

Americans had rarely lacked enthusiasm for education. What the common-school crusaders did was to translate that quest for enlightenment, economic opportunity, moral improvement, and a new kind of citizenship, into support for a particular institution, the common school. Not separatism, but a consensus based on schooling as a common and public good became an enduring legacy of that millennial faith.

2. THE ASCENDANCY OF THE COMMON SCHOOL

The American faith in education did not originate with the common-school movement of the mid-nineteenth century, nor did widespread popular schooling begin with what we would now recognize as public education. After the Revolution the majority of the early state constitutions expressed a common conviction, that education was essential to civil peace and prosperity as well as to individual morality. Hence education was in the public interest, and many forms of schooling deserved the favor of government. Alexis de Tocqueville was only one of many foreign observers who commented on the zeal of Americans for diffusing knowledge. It has been estimated that at the time of his visit in the 1830s about one-third of children from ages five to nineteen were attending some sort of school.[1]

One sign of the effectiveness of the many forms of education in the United States was that Americans were among the most literate people in the world. In the 1840 census, about 90 percent of white adults were listed as literate. A recent study of a sample of the 1860 census shows that 94 percent of free males were literate, and among these the older men were only slightly less literate than the younger ones, indicating that instruction had been widespread even early in the nineteenth century.[2]

What was the pattern of education that produced such results? It was highly diverse. In the early nineteenth century citizens tended to have an attitude toward education that Americans today have toward religion: attend the school of your choice. The choices largely reflected differences of class, religion, ethnicity, race, sex, and regional tastes and needs. They not only reflected these differences, but also perpetuated them, often deliberately. One prominent kind of education was the private school run as a business by a teacher who would instruct pupils in whatever parents would pay to have them learn. In such ventures the controls were those of the market—the same as a cobbler's shop, for example—because the private teacher either satisfied the customers or went out of business. Parents and students who could afford to do so also patronized the rapidly multiplying academies and colleges, schools that were usually chartered by the state and more permanent in form and structured in program than the proprietary schools. Benevolent societies and churches, sometimes aided by governments, established charity schools for children whose families were too poor to afford schooling. In settled parts of the Northeast there were also forerunners of the common school, "district schools" that were supported by local taxation or state school funds and governed by locally elected trustees.[3]

The line between "public" and "private" was blurred in the early nineteenth century, however. State governments and cities gave public funds to many kinds of institutions from Harvard University to church schools for street urchins. Parents in "public" district schools often had to supplement public funds with private tuition for their children—called "rate bills." Students in academies—especially those planning to teach—sometimes received scholarships from the state. Americans thought education a worthy cause, but they did not have united opinions about who should control or pay for it. All sorts of motives impelled

Americans to found schools: the desire to spread the faith, to retain the faithful, to maintain ethnic boundaries, to protect a privileged class position, to succor the helpless, to boost the community or sell town lots, to train workers or craftsmen, to enhance the virtue or marriageability of daughters, to make money, even to share the joys of learning. However effective the hodge-podge of schools may have been, at least for those who had the resources to make choices, its unsystematic and nonuniversal character troubled the common-school crusaders.[4]

During the middle decades of the nineteenth century the common-school crusaders like Horace Mann sought to translate Americans' diffuse faith in education into support for a particular institutional form, the public school. In their vision the common school was to be free, financed by local and state government, controlled by lay boards of education, mixing all social groups under one roof, and offering education of such quality that no parent would desire private schooling. The common school was to be moral and religious in impact but it was not to be sectarian; it was to provide sound political instruction without being partisan. Perhaps more than any other reformers in a seedtime of social change, the mid-century evangelists for public education succeeded in their campaign. So sharp were the outlines of public education by 1875 that Francis Adams could call his book *The Free School System of the United States,* for *system* it was. Funds spent on public schools comprised only 47 percent of total expenditures for education on all levels in 1850, but by 1900 they had become 79 percent. By 1890 the portion of rural elementary students in public schools had risen to 98 percent, while in the cities the only major competitors to public grammar schools were the growing Roman Catholic parochial schools. Free education became almost entirely a monopoly of public schooling.[5]

To a surprising degree, given the contentiousness of party politics and the competition of religious sects, the leaders of the common-school movement succeeded in making public education appear to be not only nonsectarian but also politically nonpartisan. Although disputes did arise among political parties over Bible reading in the public schools and over issues like the use of foreign languages in elementary classrooms, in general the parties did not have separate educational platforms or different educational principles, as did conservative and liberal parties in England.

And although public education was often so Protestant in orientation that it repelled Catholics, its pan-Protestant compromise of teaching the Bible without comment encouraged most denominations to support a common school. "Strength in unity" was the motto of the American

The Ascendancy of the Common School

Institute of Instruction. In contrast with the bitter Protestant contention found in other English-speaking societies such as Canada and Australia, Protestants in the United States were unified in support of the common school, for it embodied important elements of the "culture religion" described by Winthrop Hudson. The system of public education expressed an ideological coherence represented by established churches or centralized governments in other nations.[6]

Common-school crusaders faced quite different tasks in the developed states of the Northeast than they did in the expanding new states of the West or the slave culture and caste system of the South. School enrollments in Massachusetts and New York had already been high before the 1840s, especially in rural areas. About 60 percent of children up to the age of nineteen years old were enrolled in schools in New York state from 1820 to 1850, while in Massachusetts in 1826 an astonishing 80 percent of the same age group were listed on school registers in towns of under 2,500, according to Carl Kaestle and Maris Vinovskis. It was thus not quantity of enrollment but standardization and quality of schooling that reformers in Massachusetts were seeking. There was actually a decline in the percentage of school-aged children enrolled in Massachusetts schools from 1840 to 1880 following the establishment of the state board of education; this decline reflected a deliberate policy to limit the number of very young children in the public schools, but it was also a result of new employment opportunities for older youth, especially in industrial cities. Educational leaders in the Northeast were eager to improve regularity of attendance, lengthen the school term, professionalize teaching (in part by creating normal schools to train teachers), improve schoolhouses, introduce structural innovations like the graded school and supervision of teachers, eliminate rate bills, and unify and improve the curriculum by standardizing textbooks and introducing new subjects and methods. Above all they were concerned about effective moral and civic training.[7]

For Horace Mann the main challenges to a standardized common school were private education and the enormous variability in decentralized district schools. The percentage of pupils attending private schools did decline from 14 to 8 percent between 1840 and 1880 in Massachusetts. But traditions of local control in Yankee towns remained strong despite attempts to strengthen the role of the state by coupling fiscal support with state standards and by enacting a compulsory attendance law in 1852. As we shall indicate, the formal powers of state leaders were relatively weak.[8]

Leaders in public education in the expanding West and South tried not so much to improve and elaborate existing schools as to build new ones. Despite some success in states such as North Carolina and Tennessee, the South as a whole did not significantly expand the common schools. The 1840 census reported only 16 percent of southern school-aged children enrolled in all schools, a figure that increased only to 31 percent by 1860. The elites who dominated the economy and politics of the South had little interest in educating poor whites and forbade teaching slaves to read. Prosperous parents sent their children to private schools. The southern failure to create a system of universal public schooling similar to that in the North did not stem from poverty. The region spent almost double the national average on pupils actually enrolled and had more surplus wealth than did the West in 1850. But by 1860, on the eve of the Civil War, the South was paying for only 10.6 days of schooling for each white child of school age, compared with 63.5 days in New England. The ideology and institutional form of the common school did not match either the economic interests or the cultural values of the planter class, and it was only in a few cities and piedmont areas that the public school took hold.[9] (We shall explore the postwar development of southern public education in section 8.)

The story was far different in the West. In the North Central states enrollment of school-aged children swelled from 29 percent in 1840 to 69 percent in 1860. Beginning with the comparative figures first issued by the United States Office of Education (USOE) in 1870, the North Central states consistently outperformed the North Atlantic states in enrollments throughout most of the century, while the enrollments in the Far West jumped from 55 percent in 1870 to 73 percent in 1890. The common school became almost the only form of elementary schooling in rural areas of the West, while western cities rapidly emulated the urban reforms pioneered in the East. During the latter half of the nineteenth century regional variance in enrollment declined markedly in the East and West, while the South began its long slow climb toward parity.[10]

Statistics agregated by region or state do not reveal an important set of distinctions, however. Enrollments in northern rural schools were generally higher than in urban schools, and patterns of public education in the two environments were different. The one-room common school was a practical form of education for scattered populations. The facts of demography render another alternative hard to imagine, whatever the religious, ethnic, or class diversity of rural people, for sparse settlement made it almost impossible to have schools segregated by religion, ethnicity, class, or sex. Indeed, the dual racial

The Ascendancy of the Common School

system of the rural South enormously retarded its postwar educational development.[11]

Accounts of rural education indicate that the common school was generally an important source of social cohesion for communities, a place not only where the young received instruction but also where families gathered for entertainment, for religious services, for political meetings, and to hear news of the outside world, whether of agricultural prices in Europe or the evil doings of railroad magnates. Despite the many purposes it served, the rural school was cheap. The school calendar complemented the seasonal farm labor of children so that parents would not miss them when they needed them most. Rural schools enrolled a wider age range of students than did urban, in part because they offered older children a sociable way to spend long winter months. A local man or woman could be hired cheaply in the off-season as teacher. Although rural schools enrolled over 70 percent of the children in 1890, only 43 percent of the dollars spent on public schools went to rural education. County superintendents of schools complained incessantly about the parsimony of rural patrons.[12]

Urban schools presented contrasting patterns. There pupils encountered a far more structured form of education in graded classrooms. Educators insisted on daily attendance and punctuality. Because school terms were longer in cities and average daily attendance was higher, urban children generally received more days of schooling than their rural counterparts. While rural pupils attended schools over a longer range of years, starting younger and continuing into late adolescence, urban children concentrated their attendance during the years from seven to thirteen. After thirteen, students (especially of the working class) began to leave school for work, unable to alternate school and work as could their rural counterparts because of the long school term and the nonseasonal character of most city jobs.[13]

The direct costs of educating children in cities and in the countryside differed sharply, as did expenditures by state. Urban schools often cost two or three times more per pupil than did rural. But beyond the direct costs of paying for buildings, teachers, and other necessities, Americans demonstrated their support for schooling by what economists call "opportunity costs," or the potential income lost to the family when children attended school. Such a subsidy by families constituted 58.2 percent of the total costs of schooling in 1880; it is an eloquent testimony to the conviction of Americans that education did matter.[14]

By 1880 attending a public school had become a standard part of the life cycle of all but a small proportion of American children. Merely one among several forms of educational institutions at the beginning of the century, public schools became the standard means for educating the young in nearly all American communities. There was no federal ministry of education to structure schooling by fiat. The tiny state departments of education could do little to police compliance at the local level. The creation of common schools and everyday decision making rested with hundreds of thousands of local people, but the result of their actions was what could be regarded as a "national system."

3. THE BUREAUCRATIZATION OF REDEMPTION

Protestant activists were a driving force in the common-school crusade, especially on successive frontiers. Missionaries, settled ministers, and devout men and women took a prominent place in the ranks of school promoters and regarded public education with proprietary interest as a pan-Protestant establishment. Fired with the enthusiasm of the proselytizer, they saw the common school as only one among many agencies to carry out God's will. Distrustful of ephemeral party politics, they were nonetheless profoundly political in their conception of society. They wanted nothing less than to bring about God's government on earth.

European visitors were puzzled, John Higham notes, that Americans "could be so intensely religious in a setting that seemed so largely secular. In actuality, secular life was suffused with a pan-Protestant ideology that claimed to be civic and universal. . . . It infused a generalized piety in school textbooks and civic oratory." This outlook gave Protestant activists a feeling of "praetorian responsibility for the whole society," for they "identified the kingdom of God with the American Republic" and saw its destiny as "manifest."[1]

The religious awakening of the early nineteenth century and a continuing series of revivals released great social energy, much of which became channeled into educational reform movements. This evangelical quickening in the mainstream northern Protestant churches—notably the Presbyterian, Congregational, Baptist, and Methodist—not only stimulated concern for personal salvation through an experience of conversion but also inspired social activism designed to purify society. Not all denominations or factions within churches shared this sense of "praetorian responsibility," of course, and members of nonevangelical sects like the Unitarians were also prominent in social reform. But the quickening of religious faith produced a powerful impulse to educate Americans to carry out their millennial destiny. As a result, individual churches and interdenominational voluntary associations created a host of agencies that became forerunners of the public-school system.[2]

Of these institutions, perhaps the most revealing was the Sunday School. At first there was little difference either in ideology or practice between the nondenominational Sunday School and the "public" but actually pan-Protestant common school (often called the "weekday school"). The American Sunday School Union (ASSU), founded in 1824, illustrates the purposes and methods of the evangelical educational reformers. Although Sunday Schools later became sectarian agencies to train children in the doctrines of particular faiths—as they typically are now—at first the ASSU had a broader purpose. The early Sunday Schools often reached adults as well as children and frequently taught illiterates to read. They were pan-Protestant rather than denominational. Similar in their purposes and even in their curriculum to many of the "public" schools of the time, they were often held in the same building as the free "weekday" public schools and were taught by "weekday" teachers on Sundays. The purposes of the ASSU were "to concentrate the efforts of existing Sabbath-school societies in the different sections of our country; to strengthen the hand of the friends of religious instruction of the Lord's Day; to disseminate useful information, circulate moral and religious publications in every part of the land, and to endeavor to plant a Sunday-School wherever there is a population." In spreading the gospel the ASSU used whatever means were necessary, including teaching people to read and stimulating the founding of churches, but it saw its program as an auxiliary to the public school and the various Protestant denominations. Its main concern was to reach the neglected, those who had not the means of grace, the unchurched and untaught wherever they might be found, in city slum or in the open countryside. It was a missionary enterprise that united rather than divided the lay leaders of evangelical denominations. Such interdenominational cooperation in founding a "union" of nonsectarian Sunday Schools prepared the way for similar Protestant cooperation in founding public schools.[3]

The ASSU was an extraordinarily efficient enterprise. By 1828 it had branches in most states and enrolled about one-seventh of all children aged five to fifteen. This was just the beginning, for in 1829 the Union vowed to place a Sunday School "in every destitute place" in the Mississippi Valley from Michigan to Louisiana, from the Alleghenies to the

Rockies. Its promoters did not think small. Designed by prosperous merchants and lawyers in eastern cities, the Union was a complex bureaucracy of redemption and a marketing system as well as a decentralized missionary enterprise. The headquarters in Philadelphia housed an elaborate organization consisting of a lay board, president and vice-president, and several "managers" each responsible for tasks broken down by function and geographical regions. The managers supervised agents in the field who were each assigned to particular territories and who numbered 322 by 1854. The staff conducted research and kept accounts of souls reached: surveys of the churched and unchurched, questionnaires collected from local Sunday School superintendents, records of how many miles the missionaries traveled, the audiences they addressed, and the numbers of books and tracts they distributed. Such records helped them to plan their strategies and win funds from hardheaded businessmen. Financier Jay Cooke was a fiscal manager at the Union before he went on to bigger things in the 1860s.[4]

Before any business firm in America had a middle manager, the Union had its own intermediate officials and had pioneered a national marketing system. Charles Foster writes of the lay trustees and paid leaders who designed this advanced organization: "Their objective was not merely to produce and distribute religious material efficiently but to bring the Kingdom of God to the United States—by driving every other form of literature off the market by price competition." They used methods far "in advance of current business practice. It was undoubtedly the first American experience of mass production for a national market at the lowest possible price; it was not merely production at a low profit but at a deliberate, calculated loss to be made good by the faithful." The Sunday School books and other tracts were standardized in appearance and price, allocated through warehouse managers, and promoted by salesmen (missionaries) all over the nation. Later the Union developed uniform lessons to be used on the same day all over the world. Because of its centralized corporate structure, the ASSU was far more bureaucratized in operation than any state public-school system, at least until the Progressive era. Indeed it anticipated the bureaucratization of city schools in the latter part of the nineteenth century.[5]

Standardization proceeded quickly at the local level. Long before public-school systems acquired their superintendents, the Sunday School superintendent was a familiar male authority figure organizing the work of his unpaid, mostly female teachers. One of the best known of these was the merchant John Wanamaker, who superintended the largest Sunday School in North America, using the latest techniques of advertising and management of large groups of people. "When Wanamaker was appointed Postmaster General by President Harrison in 1889," wrote Robert Lynn and Elliott Wright, "he was willing to let others run the store but not to give up a weekly trip to Philadelphia to supervise activities at Bethany." John D. Rockefeller ran a Sunday School in Cleveland. To such men there was nothing contradictory about amassing wealth and being pious, between the hectic pace of industrial expansion and the salvation of souls. A Sunday School hymn ran thus:

> As you roll across the trestle,/Spanning Jordan's swelling tide,
> You behold the Union Depot/Into which your train will glide;
> There you'll meet the sup'rintendent,/God the Father, God the Son,
> With the hearty, joyous plaudit,/"Weary pilgrim, welcome home."[6]

The elite architects of the Sunday School movement had definite notions of what a standard American Christian should be like, and from their positions of power in the metropolis they tried to shape the mentality of people in the countryside to this design. There was nothing haphazard or decentralized about their technology or their ideology of reform. But when one looks at the experience of the missionaries in the field, one sees that even such a businesslike Christian venture finally depended on local people who shared a common evangelical ideology. Many were the barren and stony fields, and tales of the ordeals of Sunday School missionaries often rivaled those of evangelists in foreign lands; not all barbarians lived across the ocean, nor did all Americans agree about the terms of God's government. Crossing icy streams or brushy mountain passes was not so trying as encountering frontier families who seemed to revel in their ignorance, their Sabbath-breaking, and their corn whisky.[7]

The ASSU fieldworkers, like those of the tract and Bible societies, worked in ways quite similar to the county and state public-school superintendents who traveled about on horseback from community to community trying to rouse the consciousness of the local people about educating their children. An ASSU missionary would usually seek out an influential local person as an initial contact, perhaps sending him tracts or some promotional literature in advance. This local notable would assist in calling a meeting of his fellow citizens at which the missionary would exhort the congregation to set up Sunday Schools or improve the ones they had (improvement usually included buying

ASSU school books and a predigested curriculum). If the residents were poor, often the rich merchants in the metropolis would donate the tracts. After all, said one enthusiast, Francis Scott Key, it was a bargain if the Union "gives a child a testament and teaches him to read it for 37 cents." Many of the books provided by the ASSU and the tract societies found their way into public schools in parts of the country where reading matter was scarce. And in 1859, of the 50,000 libraries that were classified as "public," 30,000 were in Sunday Schools. The ASSU advanced toward its bluntly stated goal of being "dictators to the consciences of thousands of immortal beings." That was a far better way to achieve God's government than to trust to political parties. Not far beneath the surface of "voluntary" societies lurked an impulse to coerce.[8]

Alexis de Tocqueville expressed the difference between the coercive but "voluntary" moral consensus sought by the evangelicals and the tumultuousness of secular politics: "In the moral world, all is classified, coordinated, foreseen, decided in advance. In the political world, everything is agitated, contested, uncertain; in the one, passive obedience, although voluntary; in the other, independence, mistrust of experience, and jealousy of all authority."[9]

Cooperation in the pan-Protestant Sunday School movement and in similar campaigns gave Protestants in the united evangelical front a precedent for supporting a similar "nonsectarian" public school rather than competing with one another in establishing separate denominational schools. There were, of course, other reasons for creating a *common* school at public expense. One was the dispersion of the rural population, which would have made separate church schools almost impossible to support. Public-school advocates also believed that the democratization of the suffrage made it desirable for the young to undergo the same civic indoctrination in school at an impressionable age. But schools were not to be "political" in a partisan sense, at least in theory, for they were part of God's government, above secular contests and devoted to producing individuals worthy of a redeemer nation. American Protestants united in support of the common school, for it embodied important common elements of a shared millennialism.*

One of the groups with the clearest mandate to found common schools was the corps of home missionaries sent West to the new territories by groups like the American Home Missionary Society (AHMS).

---

*In section 6 we discuss ethocultural opposition to the political-religious common denominator prompted by the united evangelical front.

The Bureaucratization of Redemption

Indeed, the influence of these missionaries illustrated the seminal work of evangelical schoolmen in the institution-building that was taking place in public education. This role was epitomized in many respects by the career of George Atkinson, an AHMS missionary who went to Oregon to work for the Lord in 1848.

In Search of Huck Finn: George Atkinson

Nancy Atkinson sat alertly in her Boston rocking chair as Indians rowed her and her missionary husband, the Reverend George Atkinson, up the Willamette River from Fort Vancouver to Oregon City. Remembering the fate of other missionaries (the Whitmans, who had been murdered recently in Washington), the Atkinsons were entering a new and possibly threatening world. They had no doubts about their task, however. It was to recreate on the distant Oregon frontier the kind of Protestant civilization they had known in New England. A graduate of Dartmouth College and Andover Theological School and a Congregational minister, Atkinson knew that his native New England should be "a model" for the West. He and his wife had never left New England in spirit. With the stubborn ethnocentrism of an Englishman donning his dinner jacket nightly in the tropics, Atkinson carried an elm tree around Cape Horn and planted it in his yard amid giant firs—the first in Oregon. He preferred dried cod to fresh salmon and brought along $200 worth of Yankee school books. A neighbor watching Atkinson clearing the brush and decaying logs from his front yard, warned him that "if you have as great a work to do in the moral world in Oregon as you have in the natural world, you have a great work before you."[10]

So he did. When Atkinson arrived in Oregon there were only a few struggling private schools. When he died in 1889, public education was flourishing, and for his arduous crusading he became known as the father of the common school in the state. His commission by the AHMS had instructed him to attend to common schools as part of the missionary program to create "churches, schools, whatever would benefit humanity—temperance, virtue; the industrial, mental, moral and religious training of the young, and the establishment of society upon sound principles by means of institutions of religion and learning." Accordingly, Atkinson called on Governor Lane in March, 1849, to plead the cause of public education. Lane asked Atkinson to draft the substance of his legislative message on education. On 5 September 1849, the legislature passed a law also largely designed by Atkinson. Somewhat revised by subsequent legislation, this law remained in force during Atkinson's lifetime. It provided for a "uniform and general system of common schools" and a hierarchy of school directors, commissioners, and a superintendent, as well as a common-school fund. Atkinson was appointed first school commissioner for Clackamas County and promptly drew the school district boundaries. The law's reach exceeded its grasp: some of the school districts in that vast county had no inhabitants.[11]

Sparseness of settlement handicapped the founding of churches as well as of schools. Like township land speculators, ministers often tried to predict where the population would settle in order to occupy the strategic sites of future cities. Men like Atkinson sensed that the river towns in Oregon, like those in the Ohio and Mississippi River Valleys, would soon dominate the commercial and transport system of the territory. In such accessible settlements one might rapidly transplant civilized institutions. "Settlements are the foundations of our social and moral edifice," wrote Atkinson. "Roving teachers and roving ministers make moving schools and wandering churches, and these produce a people of like disposition."[12]

If frontiersmen were individualistic, skeptical, barbaric, ignorant—so many Huck Finns who had lit out for the territories—then this simply increased the need to civilize them. Atkinson recalled that when the western fever hit Vermont "a distinguished clergyman spoke disparagingly of the movement, and remarked that those who left their eastern homes and churches, could well be spared, as they were an unstable class, who could not be relied upon." Unstable they were, and powerful means had to be devised to bring them to Christ. Scattered settlers were bereft of "all educational and religious privileges." Uninstructed parents felt that "they have got on well enough and their children can," thereby tending "to lower the standard of education and convert the children to *barbarism.*" Fathers went hunting on the Sabbath, young men lurched down the streets of the town, cheeks flushed by "the intoxicating cup," and children ran wild. Many pioneers were willing to practice total abstinence—from church and school.[13]

The missionaries hoped they could at least reach the children. "Multitudes of children and youth, some orphans, need to be rightly trained in S. Schools and in week schools and Academies," Atkinson commented. Parents must be taught "the advantage of disciplining and storing the minds of their children." This reconstruction of the family and through it the redemption of the society was no easy task. Atkinson lamented that parents had no religious training "and therefore . . . no capacity, purpose or desire of giving it" to their own children. "We have a class who have no attachments, religiously or hardly in family or society, who will not assume responsibility unless they are made to feel their obligations."[14]

Ministers in Oregon feared that settlers would fall prey to Roman Catholics who were rapidly building schools and churches. Through their correspondence runs a common note of anti-Catholic hysteria, which was also a staple item in the fund-raising literature of the missionary societies. The minister who had preached Atkinson's ordination sermon in Vermont had warned of the wicked ways of the "mother of abominations," of "crowds of Catholics, of priests and bishops, sent out by the Pope and emptied upon our shores, their institutions of learning—their monasteries and nunneries—their churches and cathedrals scattered over the land . . . even upon the shores of the Pacific." Did not Oregon City demonstrate the fact? Since the arrival of two priests in 1838 the Catholic establishment had grown until the province included three bishops, twenty-seven priests, thirteen sisters, and two schools. Atkinson glumly recorded that Catholics were building a girls' school right next to his house and that fickle Protestants were sending their daughters there. He became obsessed with the idea that "by education . . . the Catholics will get their influence." Ezra Fisher, a Baptist missionary who was trying to build a school in Oregon City, implored eastern donors to send a Protestant bell to clang in competition with the papal bells; "the Romans regulate the time of our city," he wrote in despair.[15]

For ministers like Atkinson who depended on support from eastern missionary bureaucracies, founding schools—both public and private—was a vital way to justify the funds poured into their work. Partly because he had such high standards of piety for admission to church membership, after fifteen years of laboring in the Oregon vineyard Atkinson had only about twenty active church members (he did not compute the per capita cost of conversion). But setting up academies and colleges, establishing Sunday Schools, selling Bibles and textbooks, and above all establishing public-school systems helped to persuade eastern donors that the missionaries were earning their keep. In explaining why they admired their minister, the trustees of Atkinson's congregation chose this order of priorities: "the labors of our pastor have been greatly instrumental in advancing the cause of education in our midst; in maintaining a firm and consistent opposition to intemperance; in laying the foundations for moral, religious and intelligent community; and in dissemination of sound piety." They saw, as he did, that

Atkinson and his fellow ministers had a unified strategy of creating a Protestant *paideia,* a gathering of people into communities in which family, church, and school could reinforce each other.[16]

Most of the Protestant institution builders did not draw sharp distinctions between public and private education except for Roman Catholic schools. Ministers were eagerly sought as teachers of public as well as sectarian schools and welcomed as leaders in teachers' associations. In communities that had chosen to support public elementary schools, they rarely tried to duplicate the common school with religious schools. Instead they concentrated on founding academies and "colleges" (mostly secondary schools at best), often in rural areas where there was no alternative to boarding schools. In order to attract pupils these denominational schools were largely pan-sectarian in practice, trying to appeal to all Protestant families.[17]

Atkinson saw little difference between public education and Protestant schools open to all children. His experience illuminates this easy shifting from private to public education. Although he had written the public-school bill and was superintendent of schools for Clackamas County, he did not hesitate to establish the Clackamas Female Seminary when he realized that the citizens of Oregon City would procrastinate about starting a public school. After a decade Oregon City purchased the seminary's building and used it as a public school, hiring Atkinson and his wife as teachers. They graded the school on the model of Boston's Quincy School. Later, Atkinson's daughter taught in an Episcopal parochial school in Portland. At the very time that Atkinson was defending the Portland public high school from attacks by private schoolmen and other enemies, he was founding sectarian academies in the Washington territory. Moreover, he was a trustee of sectarian institutions while serving as a public-school superintendent.[18]

His description of the role of county school superintendent resembled his own later work as general missionary in the Northwest for the American Home Missionary Society:

> No office has proved more important to our public schools than this. Its direct and frequent contact with the people in personal speech and by the press, enables the faithful officer to watch every feature of the school system in its practical working in every district, and to flash the light of the best experience and the warmth of earnest conviction upon every little company of co-workers, to stimulate their interest and cheer their progress. It is just to say that the office of County Superintendent can be the local inspiration of the system or the dead weight upon its vitality. It can be the radiant light of full reports for all the people, or the center of darkness.

The Bureaucratization of Redemption

The formal duties of the county superintendents were simply to examine and certify teachers, to disburse school money, and to visit and report on the schools. Those familiar with Atkinson's work testified that he was "the local inspiration of the system," a person who persuaded citizens to put their ideals into practice. As superintendent in Clackamas and Multnomah counties, he visited remote corners of the county where log schoolhouses nestled among Douglas firs. He advised teachers about the best textbooks. He preached to the public about the need for good schools and wrote hortatory articles about "school morals and discipline, primary instruction, the selection of teachers, and other subjects" in the newspaper. He persuaded "several young men of good education who were out of employment or disheartened, to teach, and in this way several successful teachers were made." He helped grade Portland schools and examined the achievement of the scholars. On his trips East he studied educational improvements and publicized this information on his return to Portland. A leader among teachers in the county, he was chosen president of the Multnomah County Teachers' Association when it was formed in 1871. He wrote a history of public education in Oregon for the 1876 International Centennial Exhibition in Philadelphia and regularly reported on education in Oregon and Washington to John Eaton, United States Commissioner of Education.[19]

In 1888, shortly before his death, George Atkinson spoke at the National Education Association's convention in San Francisco, urging educators to use the Bible as a textbook in the public school. He argued that "the right training of . . . future citizens takes precedence of every other question." The school must reach those whom home and church do not train and "compel . . . youth to be law-respecting and law-abiding citizens." As the influence of family and minister diminished, the public school had to take over an increasing share of moral indoctrination. There was a "pressure of *necessity* upon the guardians of the public welfare *now*" to avert catastrophe. Secular history and civics were not enough; the school must teach Christian sanctions that buttressed rectitude. "These principles are axioms, self-evident truths," he said, "needing only to be stated in order to be admitted."[20]

Reconciled to—indeed proud of—the voluntary system in their churches, many Protestant ministers, like Atkinson, saw no incongruity in urging the majority to make the common school a pan-Protestant establishment. People of proper conscience would recognize the need for public education; others must have the chance to acquire a proper conscience.

Atkinson's intense concern for the afterlife and religious doctrine did not preclude strong interest in worldly affairs. He was an enthusiastic promoter of the economic development of the Northwest. He advocated the planting of wheat in Washington's "Inland Empire" and welcomed commerce and the railroads. He spoke to the New York City Chamber of Commerce about investment opportunities in the West. It was said of him that "he spoke of commerce as a merchant might speak, of railroads like a corporation president, of resources like a capitalist." Like his fellow missionary Josiah Strong, he had no doubt that the Anglo-Saxons held the key to ordered liberty and were the keepers of the American political tradition. In him the Victorian trinity of entrepreneurial economic outlook, evangelical Protestantism, and Americanism found characteristic expression.[21]

4. LEADERSHIP IN A DECENTRALIZED SOCIAL MOVEMENT

Social movements are deliberate attempts to modify the social order by mobilizing opinion and action. Joseph Gusfield defines them as "socially shared activities and beliefs directed toward . . . change." The leaders of the public-school movement sought to excite a sense of common purpose among their fellow citizens in order to renew or build a system of common schools. In the settled regions of the East their task was not so much to *create* as to reinvigorate a system of public schools. In the West and South they sought to build new systems.[1]

Their strategy was in a sense a didactic one, for they generally lacked strong official power or the sanctions of bureaucratic authority. As Robert Wiebe has written, the educational "reformers believed that they spoke for the nation rather than to it. They assumed that community leaders everywhere shared the same ethical system, the same dedication to public service and the same aspirations to unity." For that reason, they endeavored "not to convince people but simply to rouse them, and like-minded legions across the land, community by community, would translate their dream into practice." Not all could be easily aroused to consciousness, of course, but the movement was predicated on the belief that citizens could recognize their duty if properly reminded. "It was fitting that Victorian opinion leaders should place such a premium on persuasion rather than strong government," writes Daniel Walker Howe, for with the proliferation of voluntary groups and inexpensive printing "they possessed far greater access to the opinions of multitudes than had ever been possible before."[2]

Who were the reformers? How did they proceed to promote the common school? By and large the prominent educational reformers resemble the more general picture Howe has given of Victorian opinion leaders: they were of British origin, Protestant, and professionals or small-scale entrepreneurs. There were, of course, common-school crusaders who were German-American or black, not British-American; there were working-class educational reformers who shared some similar values with their bosses; there were Catholics or Jews who helped to build a common-school system even though it generally had a pan-Protestant ethos. But the roster of names of the best-known leaders is mostly British, their religious backgrounds mostly Protestant, and their status comfortably middle class.

Most of the prominent school crusaders of the mid-century had very fluid careers, moving from one occupation to another. Very few picked education as a lifelong calling. Their alternate occupations give some clue to their location in the economic and social structure. Consider the occupational histories of the fourteen educational leaders singled out by Ellwood Cubberley and Lawrence Cremin as key reformers: Henry Barnard, Robert Breckinridge, James Carter, Isaac Crary, Ninian Edwards, Samuel Galloway, Samuel Lewis, Charles Mercer, Caleb Mills, John Pierce, Calvin Stowe, John Swett, and Calvin Wiley. Collectively they paralleled Mann's multi-faceted career as lawyer, state and federal legislator, secretary of the Massachusetts Board of Education, president of Antioch College. Eleven of the fourteen were elected to political office; nine were lawyers; ten (like Mann) edited journals; six were college presidents or professors; and four were ministers (almost all, like Mann, were deeply religious men). Only Swett was a career educator, and even he went in and out of school work as a result of changing political fortunes.[3]

Using a larger sample of seventy-four prominent state leaders in education in the years from 1840 to 1890, compiled from John Ohles's *Biographical Dictionary of American Educators*, Michael Imber found similar multiple career patterns. Thirty-four percent were also ministers; 40 percent were lawyers or judges; 30 percent were college presidents and 22 percent college professors; 18 percent were businessmen; 14 percent were farmers; and a number of them worked at other jobs, including physician, diplomat, and journalist. (Because the same individuals had several jobs, the totals exceed 100 percent.) In that group of 74 leaders, only 12 percent were educators all their lives and only 41 percent of the 74 had ever been teachers and/or principals.[4]

For many of the educational leaders—as for Mann—their real *career* was promoting reforms. It was that intensity of concern that gave coherence to occupational histories that to twentieth-century eyes might appear haphazard or even dilletantish. And the diversity of their skills as preachers, writers, politicians, scholars, and lawyers proved to be valuable resources in their work as reformers in multiple causes.

In addition to the career fluidity of educational promoters, many were highly mobile geographically. Nine of the fourteen men we named above—who pursued their educational campaigns in seaboard states ranging from Massachusetts to North Carolina—came from New England. Seventy-three percent of Imber's 1840–1890 sample came from New England and the Middle Atlantic states but worked all over the nation. In 1842 Henry Barnard traveled to every state but Texas, "preaching the gospel of common school reform," writes Vincent Lannie, "to eleven legislatures and sixty municipalities." Horace Mann, likewise campaigned for public education in states ranging as far west as Iowa, where he helped to write a new school law.[5]

The obituaries of pioneer educators published in the NEA *Proceedings* gave dozens of examples of similar Johnny Appleseeds of the common-school movement. One active superintendent, Francis Parsons, was born in New York in 1840 and ran schools in Wisconsin, Illinois, Kansas, Missouri, Nebraska, Texas, and Alabama before he died in 1889. Joseph Baldwin, born in 1827 in Pennsylvania, taught in public schools and normal schools in Missouri, Pennsylvania, Indiana, and Texas, actively promoting public education in each state. Such habits of transiency were by no means unusual. Americans were a migratory people in the nineteenth century as in the twentieth. From a variety of census studies of American cities, towns, and rural areas, Stephan Thernstrom estimates that 40 to 60 percent of residents moved away each decade, and, in newly opened farming areas in the West, only about one-third of the people remained in the same place from one census to the next.[6]

Migratory as many of the common-school promoters may have been, most of them had a distinct image of their task as bearers of civilized order and morality. The NEA obituaries, as we have suggested, laid far more stress on indices of character—such as coming from Puritan New England stock, active church membership, superintending Sunday Schools, or promoting causes like temperance—than on pedagogical expertise or specialized training. In the eulogies the school leader was an expert mainly in the formation of moral character. Such traditional qualities legitimized his leadership, as they would that of a minister. It was hardly accidental that many of the eulogized leaders had either been clergymen or had intended to enter the ministry. Coming largely from respectable but hardly affluent middle-class families—like the twentieth-century school superintendents who succeeded them—they saw themselves as upholders of stern standards of individual morality and a common denominator of civic virtue in a mobile, rapidly changing economic and social order.[7]

In many ways, Newton Bateman exemplified the type. Migrating from New Jersey to Illinois at the age of eleven, he attended Illinois College, and under the powerful religious influence of its founders he intended to become a minister. When his health failed, he turned instead to education and became principal of the high school in Jacksonville, Illinois. For fourteen years, beginning in 1859, he was state superintendent of public instruction for Illinois. It was a turning point in the state's history, wrote a eulogist: "The history of the world is marked by significant epochs, decisive crises. If the right work is done at such times, then follows great prosperity or happiness to the individual or the state; if the right work is not done, the progress of the individual or the state is hindered." Bateman, he said, had the vision to translate weak laws into effective institutions and the power to persuade a conflicting and confused public sentiment to support a public system of common, high, normal, and higher schools. Recognized as "by divine right the leader of the educational army," Bateman expressed a characteristically millennial hope in his last address to the state teachers' association: "In the rapt visions that come to me, as they come to all, I sometimes seem to see the apocalyptic gate swing open, and far down the aisles of the future, brightly revealed in the soft clear light, there stands the incarnate idea of the coming teacher."[8]

How did such reformers win support for public education? Preachers, teachers, lawyers, politicians, businessmen, professors—these aristocrats of character who spearheaded the common-school movement used a variety of means to arouse consciousness and to form networks of peers and supporters. Drawing on the full resources the culture provided, they employed the tested methods of revival religion, the ideological marketing techniques of the ASSU and Bible and tract societies, the nationalistic appeals of the Fourth of July convention and political campaigns, and the communal logrolling mode of institution-building common in rural America. They made full use of the voluntary associations by which Americans transacted so much of their civic business. They edited dozens of educational journals to spread their ideas both within their states and outside. Those who moved geographically kept in touch with developments in other parts of the nation and sought to reproduce familiar institutions in new settlements or to introduce innovations pioneered elsewhere. Corresponding with one another, exchanging journals and school reports, they quoted one another freely and felt themselves part of the difficult but achievable quest for Bateman's "golden age of schools and teachers." Mann voiced the conviction of many of his peers when he wrote to Barnard: "You and I and others have to work . . . with harassment and obstruction, but when I look into the future and see the beautiful and glorious development it shall have in other hands, I find not satisfaction in my toils, merely, but I feel a pride, in being stationed at this more honorable post of labor." Public education, he wrote his friend, "is the greatest of earthly causes. It is part of my religion to believe that it must prevail."[9]

The religious revival provided one important model in spreading the gospel of education, a technique used by state and county superintendents as well as home missionaries. Like the itinerant ministers or Sunday School agents, education officials in the early stages of school-building traveled about from community to community to energize the local citizens. They would typically try to find local supporters—notable citizens sympathetic to the cause—who would help them set up public meetings to inspire the faithful and convert the dubious. Often using a cadre of influentials organized into informal local networks, school promoters set up and advertised their talks on school improvement well in advance. In a letter to Mann, Barnard described the work of one such "school missionary" in Connecticut:

> I write you at the request of Mr. W.L. Baker, a teacher who on my invitation has spent the last four or five months in visiting schools, selling and distributing books on education, addressing assemblages of children, of teachers & parents, & in every way in his power promoting the improvement of education in this state. . . . He is anxious to enter in the same work—of school missionary—in Barnstable County—to visit schools, hold meetings in each town, dispose of books, get subscribers to your Journal, & will do so at the rate of $30 a month. . . . He makes himself very acceptable to the people.[10]

An important part of the work of early state and county superintendents was to conduct "teachers' institutes" or short-term conventions to train teachers. These often followed the format of religious revivals, not the primitive frontier camp meeting with its hellfire sermons and writhing sinners, but the more dignified denominationally sponsored revivals of the 1830s and 1840s. Carefully planned and publicized in advance, as Paul Mattingly notes, these "educational revival agencies" not only focused on pedagogy, but also sought to weld "a congregation of individuals into a conscious moral body with its own special tone and spiritual goal." Institutes often began and ended with prayer and hymns, and ministers were often employed as "conductors" or instructors. Sometimes, as in Wisconsin, the teachers attending experienced a religious as well as a pedagogical conversion.[11]

Educational associations, those serving educators, lay "friends of education," as well as those more exclusively composed of professional state teachers, were an important means of carrying on the crusade for common schools. One of the earliest and most prestigious of these voluntary groups was the American Institute of Instruction. Founded in 1830, this organization helped to give direction to a national movement of school reform, although its membership was overwhelmingly from New England (180 of its 250 founding members were from Massachusetts). Most of these Massachusetts members were teachers, but not from the rank and file of district school instructors, who were young, female, and with only modest training. Instead, they were all men, almost all were college graduates, and a majority taught in academies—a group that regarded itself as expert in the training of character and as the elite of the educational profession. A clan with a similar concern for traditional morality was the large contingent of ministers in the Institute, people who supported the common school from their pulpits, as they did temperance and other reforms. Public-school teaching, said one of these minister members, was clearly "a domestic field of labor, which promises . . . much for the advancement of the Redeemer's kingdom." Many of these ministers and lay reformers were also active in the other evangelical agencies such as the ASSU and tract societies; indeed, some of them sponsored a system of public-school agents that closely paralleled the work of the ASSU, traveling about as circuit riders to hold educational revivals and to give training sessions to district school teachers in New England, New York, Ohio, and Illinois.[12]

In their speeches and journal the members of the Institute sounded the themes that dominated the rhetoric of school promoters during the Victorian era. They worried about the alleged decline in parental discipline, the alien beliefs and habits of immigrants, the prevalence of poverty and crime, the insolence of the rich and the violence of the mob, and the danger of an uneducated electorate.

Similar associations cropped up elsewhere to inspire both lay people and educators to support educational reform. In the early stages the state educational associations tended to be dominated by the state superintendents, who used them to extend their own influence in standardizing educational practice. One prominent regional society was the Western Literary Institute and College of Professional Teachers in Cincinnati, which boasted such luminaries as William Holmes McGuffey, Lyman Beecher, and Calvin Stowe (husband of Harriet Beecher Stowe).[13]

Educational journals tended to follow the same pattern as the state and regional associations. At first, the periodicals devoted to education bore titles like the *Free School Clarion* or the Illinois *Common School Advocate* and advanced arguments designed to appeal to citizens in general. Eighteen journals had the word "advocate" in the title. The *Monthly Advocate of Education,* for example, announced that education was "the sheet anchor of our political hopes as a Nation . . . the great lever to be employed, under Providence, for the political and moral regeneration of the world." General and inspirational in content, drawing on history and European experience for rationales for reform, their purpose was to mobilize public opinion in favor of free schooling. Over time, however, as the common school became institutionalized, the educational periodicals became more narrowly professional: some stressed how-to-do-it classroom procedures; some were organs of state superintendents in which the officials passed on new state regulations to school boards and teachers; and some offered news of the activities of county or state teachers reminiscent of the fare of small-town newspapers. With the important exception of Barnard's scholarly *American Journal of Education,* few journals during the nineteenth century were aimed at sophisticated audiences or provided specialized knowledge. Such journals would await the growth of the field of education as a university study, which did not flourish until the turn of the century.[14]

Although Barnard, like others, dreamed of creating a national center for school reform—what he called a "Central Agency for the Advancement of Education in the United States"—and wished to use his journal as the national exchange network of ideas on education, no periodical or educational association won preeminent national influence during the mid-nineteenth century. School reformers were more loosely linked together, less subject to bureaucratic controls, than were the agents and missionaries of the ASSU or the missionaries sponsored by fund-raising associations. While the National Education Association tried to become the arbiter of national policy, its real influence in the early years was hortatory and social; it was a place where the pilgrims could gather to share ideas and to comfort one another.[15]

Typically, the early state superintendents of schools had little formal power, low pay, and a status that depended heavily on their qualities of character and personality. Often they had no staff and worked only part-time. Like the Sunday School missionaries, they often became circuit riders, traveling from place to place to give speeches to citizens, visit schools, conduct institutes for teachers, and collect and diffuse information. Their leadership in state educational associations and editorship of state education journals gave them some influence over teachers. Their location in the state capital and their access to information usually helped them to shape school legislation, particularly if they were astute politicians. But they had almost no real leverage over the elected county superintendents, who usually did the job part-time while pursuing another main occupation. State leaders also frequently complained that local boards of education complied with legislation only when they agreed with it. Energetic and eloquent state superintendents could and did make a difference—John Swett in California, for example, did much to raise the standards of training and certification of teachers—but the most successful reformers relied most heavily not on the authority of their official position but on alliances with local supporters in the communities of their states.[16]

Sometimes state laws or directives about public schools operated not as a stimulus to local effort but as a drag on it. Lloyd Jorgenson writes that such was the case in Wisconsin, where local educational reformers chafed under the spending limitations imposed on school districts by the territorial lawmen: "The movement for free schools was essentially a local one. Tax-supported schools were not created by the territorial legislation; it would be much nearer the truth to say that they developed in spite of the legislation." Indeed, many local communities in Wisconsin moved aggressively to create schools. Samuel Luce, a Vermonter who became a newspaper editor and county school superintendent in Galesville, Wisconsin, reported that in one week the families of a district had organized themselves politically, hired a teacher, erected a school, and started enrolling pupils. He observed that settlers had much work to do in clearing land, planting crops, and building shelters, but he believed that many of the pioneers feared a loss of familiar standards of education and civilization and hence worked hard to arrest a possible slide into Dogpatch. German immigrants to Wisconsin, coming generally from places where literacy and school attendance rates were high, typically tried to reproduce the educational standards of the old country and had longer school terms and paid teachers better than did the average Wisconsin district. Places where evangelical influences were strong also tended to have well-developed schools as well as churches and other agencies of Protestant socialization. Often it took some time for leaders at the state or territorial level to bring state standards up to the level of these local communities.[17]

The career of Michael Frank, sometimes called the "father" of public education in Wisconsin, illustrates how school promoters moved back and forth between the local and state levels of reform. Frank was born in New York, the son of a German immigrant, and became editor of the *Southport Telegraph* in Kenosha County, Wisconsin, in 1839. An advocate of temperance and free soil as well as public education, he worked successfully to secure a territorial school law. He later returned to Southport to organize meetings of residents to promote a local free-school system. Succeeding there after much controversy, he returned again to the state level when Wisconsin held a constitutional convention. With the help of Henry Barnard and other reformers, Frank helped to write the clauses that embedded a system of public schools in the constitution of the state. There was little opposition to the principle of the common school. The Racine *Advocate* expressed a widely held conviction: "Assure the gradual progress of solid and enlightened education, and take no other heed for the morality of the people."[18]

In a study of the role of local newspapers in promoting the growth of public schooling in Ohio, Edward Stevens notes that newspapermen like Frank and Luce were catalysts in arousing public interest in the common school. While attuned to local events and tastes, they were often sophisticated men aware of what was happening in the rest of the world, and they provided vital communication links for people in geographically isolated communities. They had a vested interest in literacy, for it helped them to sell their product; the number of newspapers and circulation rates increased dramatically during the first half of the nineteenth century. In 1810 there were 359 papers and an annual circulation rate of 3.81 per capita of the total white population; by 1850 the number had grown to 2,526 and a circulation of 21.81. Newspaper publishers frequently sold school textbooks, too. Newsmen published speeches given by the reformers, covered state legislation on education, and argued for improved local schools. Frequently, to prick local pride, they described the advances made elsewhere. The geographically mobile and entrepreneurial leaders who joined the westward movement wanted to stay in touch with the politics, the markets, and the intellectual life of the rest of the country. Newspapers in Ohio, for example, give vivid accounts of the educational reforms sweeping the nation. To be out of contact with the outside world was to subject oneself to scorn, to be a hick. In 1853 the Michigan state superintendent said that the only places in his state where common schooling was not established were a few communities "not favored with conveniences for the speedy transmission of news, and where people are still voting for General Jackson."[19]

Every time people moved into new regions to establish settlements, leaders among them emerged to prompt the building of churches and schools, bridges and roads, banks and land offices, and a host of other community needs. Stanley Elkins and Eric McKitrick argue that this recurring process of institution-building and the election of public officers helps to give "a meaning for Turner's frontier," namely that the formation of new settlements did call forth "wide participation in public affairs, a diffusion of leadership, a widespread sense of personal competence to make a difference." New communities in the midwestern frontier had to develop their own cadres of leaders. Local influentials rallied their townspeople through voluntary associations and sought their votes for public office. Often one person moved easily from venture to venture. James Lathrop of Canton, Ohio, for example, became a lawyer, was the town's first librarian, led a campaign to start an academy, turned to banking, became town president, and then was elected to the Ohio legislature, where he was chairman of the committee that wrote the state's first law requiring school taxation.[20]

While these local leaders had to prove themselves to their fellow citizens, it would be questionable to assume that they were a cross section of the population. In analyzing twenty-six leaders of early Trempeauleau County, Wisconsin, Merle Curti found that they were considerably wealthier than other settlers, that they were almost all old-stock Yankees (nineteen were born in New England and New York), and that they continued to predominate in county affairs even after non-English-speaking immigrants had become a majority of the citizenry. Patricia Graham discovered that school board members in the midwestern communities she studied were generally prosperous and prominent citizens. And Frederick Wirt found that school board elections in nineteenth-century Illinois were rarely contested and showed very low rates of voter turnout. Such conclusions are consistent with twentieth-century studies of school boards and other forms of small-town leadership that show that "notables" or "contributors" tend to come from the upper reaches of the social structure of their communities.[21]

Although the governance of education was largely decentralized and the task of creating or reforming schools was largely the responsibility of local leaders and their co-workers, it is important to recall that the notables in these local communities were linked together with state and national leaders in many ways: through religious associations and churches; through participation in regional or national market economies; through printed media; through geographical mobility; and through similar political interests, ideologies, and organizations.[22]

The arguments for public education advanced by reformers suggest the complexity of their motivations and interests. We have already suggested how the crusade reflected the fears and aspirations of Protestants. Revival religion provided much of the social energy and some of the motivational and organizational techniques used by school promoters. Robert Wiebe suggests a pattern to be found in the ritualistic sermons of sin, possible damnation, and potential salvation preached by many of the educational leaders: "Both speaker and listener knew that they could walk the edge of damnation in the early part of the ritual with assurance that the path would ultimately lead them to safety."[23]

Political arguments were also a salient part of the case for the common school, both among those who pointed out the dangers of an uneducated mob and among those who argued that political equality demanded trained intelligence in order to protect the rights of the common man. Of special concern were the immigrants who needed, thought the reformers, to be taught Anglo-American political values and institutions. The metaphors and similes the promoters used for the process of political incorporation betrayed their biases toward the various streams of immigrants. Thus Calvin Stowe in Cincinnati, on the favored Germans: "Let us, then, make the most of the German mind that is among us; and from the mixture produce a compound, which, like the Corinthian brass, shall be more precious than the purest gold." By contrast, a writer in Massachusetts regarded the Irish as similar to the muddy Missouri that polluted the pure upper Mississippi of Protestant Yankees.[24]

Whether by blending strengths of immigrant and native groups or by purifying the children of the newcomers of their parents' imperfections, the common school was expected to inculcate the Protestant-republican ideology in the newcomers. Nothing less was at stake, thought the reformers, than the perpetuity of the republic. Only by reaching the young and shaping their individual characters could God's government survive the vagaries of secular politics. The French visitor Ferdinand Buisson declared that the political case for education was made both by those who hoped and those who feared: "The optimists, those who are still too proud of their country to let anything shake their confidence in the great destinies of the Union, see in the public school one of the glories of America which it is of importance to preserve in its splendor. Others, who feel anxious for the fate of the Republic, also take an interest in the school; it is the last cherished hope they will part with."[25]

Common-school promoters also used a variety of economic arguments designed to appeal to different constituencies. Conservatives fearful for the security of their wealth claimed that schooling was a defense against mobs and thieves, a better and cheaper cure than heavy locks and policemen. Such arguments were voiced during the years following the Panic of 1837 and were resurrected in the depression years of the late 1870s. In 1877 the president of the National Education Association quoted a citizen who said that " 'it was the good sense of an immense majority of working people, created, fostered, and developed by public education, that saved us from the terrors of the French Commune.' "[26]

Horace Mann advanced arguments similar to those elaborated by economists of the human-capital school in the twentieth century, attempting to prove by questionnaires that educated workers were more productive and better paid. To employers he claimed that schooling made workers more industrious, obedient, and adaptive, thereby increasing their output; to working people he held out the hope of increased earnings. Buisson observed that Yankee families were acutely aware of the cash value of education in a complex market economy:

> Education has a double value: it has besides its real value a kind of surplus value, resulting from its practical and commercial usefulness. The whole political economy of the United States takes this for granted. . . . We sometimes think that the eagerness of Americans to support and improve schools is a kind of national pride, vanity, or show. Not at all. It is a calculation, and a sound one; enormous advances are made, but it is known that they will be returned a hundredfold.

In addition to socializing workers to their tasks, protecting property, and creating collective wealth and individual earnings, promoters claimed that building schools in new communities would raise property values and attract settlers. Local boosterism was also a potent force in spreading the common school, part of the contagion of land speculation that penetrated most of the nation.[27]

These and other arguments reflected the diverse purposes of leaders in the common-school movement. Idealistic rationales intersected with private motivations and class interests of school reformers in ways almost impossible to disentangle. Indeed, the vision of a providential universe shared by many educational crusaders blurred the lines of distinction between religious, political, and economic concerns. As we have seen, the career of George Atkinson illustrates such overlapping values. He saw the common school as the creator of moral character, "the local educator in the principles of self-government," and an acclerator of economic development. A newspaper obituary summed up his life thus: "In all the industries and activities of life Dr. Atkinson saw forces that contributed to the growth of the kingdom of God." Alexis de Tocqueville remarked of such missionaries that when you met a minister, you encountered "a politician where you expected to find a priest." And perhaps it would be equally true to say that if one scratched a politician, one might have found an entrepreneur. The local booster was often an avid social reformer. Industrialists no doubt expected to increase their profits and to obtain dependable workers by supporting the common school, but many of them were also inspired by the millennial visions of evangelical Protestantism. Public-school teachers and administrators had a vested interest in persuading legislators to increase tax support and to upgrade educational standards, but educators promoted the Protestant-republican ideology of schooling with as much conviction as did the home missionaries.[28]

No one better expressed the range of arguments for public education or better symbolized the idealism of the social movement for the common school than did Horace Mann. Crusades require heroes that personify their values. In the ranks of the aristocrats of character of public education Mann occupied the premier place.

The Celestial City of Horace Mann

Horace Mann's career mirrored the tensions of the Victorian era. A lawyer who glorified railroads and economic development, he also recognized some of the negative results of industrial capitalism, especially the growth of class conflict and extremes of poverty and wealth. Both optimistic and fearful, he claimed that America started out a thousand years ahead of European nations, freed from the tyranny and vice of old-world feudalism, yet he depicted vivid panoramas of the social evils he saw around him. Both a panegyrist and a prophet of doom in politics, he saw the republic as a noble yet precarious experiment in self-government. Converted to Unitarianism after years of paralyzing religious anguish and doubt, he retained most of the moral absolutism and sense of cosmic drama he inherited from his Calvinist upbringing. Earnest, certain of his values, ready at any instant to battle his foes, he sought to be "a fluid sort of man," a pragmatist in reaching his goals.

Convinced that fragmentation—religious, economic, professional, racial, and political—threatened American society, he was a bitter polemicist against those who disagreed with him. A person who believed that moral suasion and voluntary action were mainsprings of social reform, he led a movement that eventually expanded the role of the state in everyday life and prepared the way for the bureaucratization of the public school. A compulsive worker for the public interest, he prized the ideal of domestic quiet and childhood play while driving himself to labor fifteen hours a day.[29]

Mann's early years profoundly shaped his personality and later career, even though intellectually he rejected many doctrines he learned then. Son of a farmer in the town of Franklin in western Massachusetts, his earliest recollections were of endless labor in the fields in summer and braiding straw hats with his sisters in winter. "Industry, or diligence," Mann recalled, "became my second nature; and I think it would puzzle any psychologist to tell where it joined on to the first. Owing to these ingrained habits, work has always been to me what water is to a fish." Both his parents and his teachers in the one-room school regarded play as suspect and "a snare to virtue." One day young Horace wrote ornately in his school copybook that "when the devil catches a man idle, he generally sets him to work."[30]

The Mann's family pastor, Reverend Nathaniel Emmons, had strong and precise opinions about the devil and God, for he was a latter-day advocate of the strictest "willing to be damned" version of Calvinism. Not only in the pulpit on Sunday, but also in the weekly catechetical sessions in the schoolhouse, Emmons impressed his theological views on people. "He expounded all the doctrines of total depravity, election, and reprobation, and not only the eternity, but the extremity, of hell-torments, unflinchingly and in their most terrible significance," Mann recalled, "while he rarely if ever descanted upon the joys of heaven, and never, to my recollection, upon the essential and necessary happiness of a virtuous life." As a child, Horace believed it all, and his faith "spread a pall of darkness" over his whole life, for he did not know whether he or those he loved were saved. He could not bear the thought of souls destined by an unforgiving God to live forever in "the bottomless and seething lake filled with torments."[31]

At the age of twelve, after countless sleepless, sobbing nights of mental anguish bordering on insanity, he finally broke with Emmons's doctrines. Two years later Mann's brother drowned while swimming in a pond on the Sabbath. Emmons preached a funeral sermon on the evil of "dying unconverted." In rebellion against God as the Infinite Malignity who took pleasure in others' pain, Horace chose to suffer instead with the damned. As time went on he sought to make "a heaven of society around him," but the effect of the Puritan teachings on his nerves and moral absolutism never totally disappeared. For Mann the world would always be composed of a fixed right and wrong, of an ethical calculus that was not for mortal stakes.[32]

Mann's career as an educational reformer started in 1837 after he had already established a promising reputation as a lawyer and Whig legislator in Massachusetts. As assemblyman and later as president of the state senate he had argued that the state should assist both in economic and moral development (his perception of the two domains as closely related is shown in a temperance pamphlet he wrote arguing that grocers would make more money if their customers did not drink alcohol). He pressed not only for favorable charters for railroads but also for state and municipal support for their construction. Active in the voluntary temperance organizations and believing that moral persuasion was the best way to correct alcohol abuse, he nonetheless sponsored a license law to shut Boston grogshops catering to the working class. He was a pioneer in improving prisons and mental hospitals. An ardent humanitarian, later an abolitionist, he believed that both voluntary action in associations and state intervention were essential for effective social reforms. Like many other Whig politicians he believed it a virtue to mind other people's business.[33]

When the Whig legislature created the state board of education, it was by no means clear how the new body was to operate. Massachusetts citizens valued their decentralized control of schools, and Democrats stood ready to attack the new agency as yet another instance of Whig bureaucracy. The ten-man board—composed of the governor; lieutenant-governor; and eight ministers, businessmen, and legislators (including Mann)—had power only to gather information on the public schools and recommend changes to the legislature. It was clear that this group, like voluntary associations, needed an able executive secretary in order to have any impact on policy. Despite the claims of others to priority in advancing the cause of the common school—notably the educator and legislator James Carter, also a member of the board—Horace Mann was selected, for he had become known for his political skill, his determination, and his ability to rouse the unconverted.[34]

When Mann began his career as secretary, he admitted that he knew little about the schools of the state—or about education, for that matter. After a month's reading of books on the subject, he entered upon his campaign of visiting schools, addressing teachers, and trying to persuade communities to support a common-school system of instruction that could train moral citizens for a world being transformed by railroads, the red brick factories next to river falls, the influx of Irish immigrants, and new networks of transportation and communication radiating from the growing cities. As he went about the state, riding more than 500 miles by horseback on his circuit, he tried to reassure his audiences that he and the state board of education did not want to replace local initiative but to stimulate it. All over the state he urged local citizens to create their own local committees to improve the schools. The board had no authority "as to the amount of money to be raised," he declared, "the teachers to be employed, the books, apparatus, or other instruments of instruction to be used, the condition of the houses in which the schools are taught, nor, indeed, as to any subject which can, in the slightest degree, abridge the power or touch the property of towns or districts" where the responsibility has always rested, "and where, it is to be hoped, it always will rest."[35]

The key to improvement of schooling, then, lay with public sentiment at the local level, and Mann approached the task of rousing opinion as a trial lawyer might convince a jury ("Let the next generation be my client," he said on assuming the position); as a muckraking journalist, exposing child labor or poor school buildings or incompetent teachers; as a pioneer political economist, collecting statistics on the cash value of schooling to the state and to individuals; and, above all, as a minister, taking his congregation to the brink of a social hell and then pointing the way to the celestial city by the path of universal education. A bureaucrat in the modern sense he was not, for he had no staff, he had obscurely defined roles and powers, and he relied mostly on force of personality rather than rules and organizational sanctions. Mann and other reformers liked to use the language of self-sacrifice, even martyrdom, seeing themselves as passively driven by duty rather than acting through ambition.[36]

Although from Mann's point of view he and the board had too little power and posed no threat to local control, some disgruntled Whigs and most Democrats in the legislature thought otherwise. A Democrat was elected governor in 1839, partly because the Whig legislature had enacted a bill that prohibited the sale of spirituous liquors in quantities less than fifteen gallons. This temperance law was aimed at saloons and was widely seen as class legislation, the kind of elite moral interventionism by the state that said it was fine for the rich to enjoy their drinks at home but not right for the poor man to take his whiskey at the local grogshop. Popular animus against this law and against Whig use of the state to accelerate economic development spilled over into opposition to the state board of education as a Prussian-inspired "system of centralization and of monopoly of power in a few hands, contrary, in every respect, to the true spirit of our democratical institutions." A committee of the legislature recommended abolition of the board, saying the new state normal schools were unnecessary since academies and high schools furnished adequate teachers and arguing that responsibility for directing education should rest with the parents in each district. "District schools, in a republican government, need no police regulations, no systems of state censorship, no checks of moral, religious, or political conservatism, to preserve either the morals, the religion, or the politics of the state. 'Let them ever be kept free and pure.' " Opponents of the board were committed to improving the common school, but the way to do this, they insisted, was to subdivide the responsibility: "Diffuse and scatter this interest far and wide . . . not only into towns and districts, but even into families and individuals."[37]

The legislature voted 245 to 182 to retain the board, but the debate did raise issues of great significance for the future governance of public education. Characteristically, Mann dismissed his protagonists as *"political* madmen," but in hindsight their prediction that the "power of recommendation" might one day be turned into "a power of regulation" was to prove accurate, first in the crowded states of the Northeast in the nineteenth century and then more generally in the American states during the twentieth. Massachusetts became a pioneer in the use of state power in education, passing the first compulsory attendance law in 1852 and slowly proceeding to more minute regulation by legislative or administrative law.[38]

But this lay in the future, after Mann's twelve-year tenure as secretary. Actual enforcement of state laws on education remained haphazard in most places, partly because of minuscule state departments of education. In fact, *democratic localism* (to use Michael Katz's useful categories) was more prevalent in most parts of the nation than was *incipient bureaucracy,* except in the larger cities (a point to which we shall return). As late as 1889, most state superintendents of public instruction said that compulsory schooling laws, for example, were dead letters unless local public opinion supported them.[39]

Mann, of course, did not disagree with the basic belief that obedience to laws depended in large measure on public opinion. In his report on the enforcement of the 1836 law on child labor he found that some communities and employers, particularly the ones who employed large numbers of workers, like the Boston Manufacturing Company, carefully obeyed the law while others flagrantly ignored it. Prominent among the lawbreakers were transient private individuals or small corporations that sought quick profits in rented quarters. Such people, Mann wrote, "may be supposed to feel less permanent interest in the condition of the people who are growing up around them . . . and . . . are less under the control of public opinion in the vicinity." Much of the state legislation of moral interventionism and social reform was merely hortatory in its effect. It attempted to put sanctions of majority rule behind those who sought to preserve a social consensus on right action in local communities. This seems especially to have been the case with respect to causes like temperance and compulsory education.[40]

Indeed, one of Mann's key goals, as Jonathan Messerli has noted, was to prevent fragmentation of the society through improvement of common schooling. Mann worried about signs of social disintegration: mob violence on the streets, bitter political partisanship, sectarian strife (especially between Catholics and Protestants), ill will and rivalry between the native-born and the immigrants flocking to Yankee cities, and economic conflict between rich and poor, employers and employees. Mann told a friend that "as population increases, and especially as artificial wants multiply, and temptations increase, the guards and securities must increase also, or society will deteriorate." He believed that public education was equal to all these challenges, but that to win the support of all citizens it must not reflect or contribute to the fragmentation of the larger society. This meant that it must bypass all sectarian quarrels, all partisan issues in politics, and instead concentrate on just those moral and civic values that all Christian republicans could support.[41]

Naturally most Catholics, some Protestant leaders, and a scattering of nonbelievers could not accept Mann's version of pan-Protestant teaching—reading the King James Bible and prayers without comment—as actually neutral. And in practice, as Ruth Elson has shown, the actual teaching of political and moral principles through common-school textbooks showed a marked conservative and often nativist bias. But in order to win public support for this presumed consensus, Mann was willing to ban controversy from the public school. Though against slavery himself, he even condemned a normal-school principal for taking future teachers to an abolitionist meeting and withheld his own support for desegregation of the Boston schools for fear it might damage the common-school cause. His doctrine of neutrality beyond the realm of commonly approved opinions, while seductive and politically apt, would prove a dubious legacy for future leaders, while his version of civic morality contributed to turning the common school into a place where teachers preached virtues that few adults cared to practice.[42]

Mann's taut, earnest personality and absolutist cast of mind drove him into fierce encounters with his opponents, despite his counsel to himself when he took the job: "I must not irritate. I must not humble, I must not degrade any one in his own eyes. . . . I must be a fluid sort of man, adapting myself to tastes, opinions, habits, manners, so far as this can be done without hypocrisy or insincerity, or a compromise of principle." Indeed, Mann did appeal to all sorts of motives: shame, humanitarian concern, desires of employers for profits and workers for higher wages, status anxieties of an older middle class, national pride, and fear of social disorder. He did adapt to his audience, as when he sent an ingeniously propagandistic questionnaire to manufacturers asking them about the economic benefits of schooling. But on some subjects his temper flared.[43]

One of these, not surprisingly in the light of his traumatic Calvinist upbringing, was sectarian dogma. When attacked by preachers for abandoning sound religious instruction, or for favoring books of Unitarian bias, he retorted violently with pamphlet after pamphlet and speech after speech. The same overkill—Theodore Parker compared it to shooting a mosquito with a 64-pound shot—characterized Mann's attack on Boston schoolmasters who objected to his approving report on mild discipline in Prussian schools and saw it as an assault on themselves. Mann objected to corporal punishment of children, but he verbally flailed orthodox ministers or stick-in-the-mud teachers. Primed by his childhood terror that there was a satanic fiend behind every bush, Mann was incapable of taking Benjamin Franklin's advice that the best response to criticism was to let the spot on one's coat dry and then dust it off.[44]

Mann lacked an ability to put his values in perspective, to see the world with a sense of humor, to lose a few battles gracefully. But his extraordinary moral energy and commitment made him the great proselytizer for public education. When he looked back on his twelve years as secretary he could take pride in the founding of state normal schools to train teachers, on the creation of school libraries, on improved schoolhouses, on more regular school attendance, on enlarged public expenditures for education, on the beginning of graded classrooms in cities, on more responsible supervision by local committees. Above all, he could see about him a new sense of purpose, a stabilized ideology and a model of public schooling. Whether he would have approved of the ways in which these reforms became institutionalized in the decades to come is open to question. Whether his overselling of the benefits of education was to prove a boon or a bane is still debated. But he remains the archetype of the mid-century school reformer.

5. FEMALE NETWORKS AND EDUCATIONAL REFORM

Thus far we have been discussing male leadership in the common-school movement. In the nineteenth century—and since—men have received most of the credit for creating and running public education. In part this resulted from the widespread assumption that leadership in the public sphere was a male prerogative. In part it also stemmed from the fact that the very important ways in which women contributed to the common school were less apparent because they were largely confined to women's sphere. But networks of women leaders and their widening circles of co-workers were central forces in the rapid spread of public schooling in America. In the campaigns of leaders such as Catharine Beecher, Emma Willard, Mary Lyon, and Zilpah Grant appeared many of the central themes that characterized Victorian educational leadership more generally: a fervor for moral homogenization, an effective use of oratory and writing to mobilize voluntary action, a blend of apocalyptic fear and millennial hope so characteristic of religious and political evangelism, and a commitment to use nongovernmental associations to promote "national" purposes.

Because of the constraints on women's public activity, female leaders devised their own strategies of influence. They drew on their access to other women through the bonds of sorority, the resources of time and (through their families) funds available to middle-class women, and a common commitment to bringing about a millennial future through the proper upbringing of the young. Essentially what most female leaders did was to enlarge women's sphere rather than to question it, using the moral authority and social prestige accorded to women, but not directly challenging the view that power in the public domain belonged to men. Among women the female leadership was direct and powerful, but when they moved among men they took care to preserve the appearance, if not the reality, of deference. Even the most ambitious and effective female leaders often needed men to front for their activities and to persuade males to grant the resources of money and power they required to pursue their work.[1]

In the churches men preached while women filled the pews. In religious benevolent associations men generally held the paid jobs and positions of official leadership, while women taught the Sunday School classes and formed "auxiliary" associations that provided logistic support. In public schools women rapidly became the majority of teachers, but men continued to run the system as school board members and superintendents. There were some exceptions—a few female school board members or superintendents—but they were rare except in the far western states that were the first to permit women's suffrage. Women pioneered in the professional preparation of teachers, but men typically received the credit for instituting normal schools.[2]

The most prestigious educational associations at first banned women members and then reluctantly admitted them when membership began to erode; but women rarely achieved prominent positions in such groups. Ella Flagg Young, who became the NEA's first woman president in 1910, recalled that when she first attended a meeting in 1867, women were simply "permitted to sit in the gallery and listen to discussions carried on by the men." The typical attitude of the male leaders, who persisted in addressing their mixed audiences as "gentlemen," appeared in this resolution of the NEA: "That we are encouraged in our work by the approving smiles and encouraging words of women, and that we regard her as the most accomplished and successful teacher; that we hail as honored co-laborers every 'Lady Pilgrim' who with 'High and Holy aims and Calm and Happy mind' produced 'by the perusal of God's Holy Word' and 'with healthful and robust body' devotes her powers to the noble work of education."[3]

Lady Pilgrims were to be seen and not heard; they were to appreciate and not criticize. Rare were the women who openly protested male dominance of professional associations and public leadership of the educational crusades. One such outspoken feminist was the Quaker teacher Susan B. Anthony. In a teachers' convention in 1853 she listened with rising anger as men debated for three days about why teachers lacked the respect accorded doctors, lawyers, and ministers. Finally she asked to speak. The men argued for half an hour about whether to hear her and then, while she stood waiting, reluctantly gave her permission. "It seems to me, gentlemen," she said,

> that none of you quite comprehend the cause of the disrespect of which you complain. Do you not see that so long as society says a woman is incompetent to be a lawyer, minister, or doctor, but has ample ability to be a teacher, that every man of you who chooses that profession tacitly acknowledges that he

has no more brains than a woman? . . . Would you exalt your profession, exalt those who labor with you.[4]

A few radical feminists confronted the assumptions of patriarchy head on, as did Anthony. Encountering sexual discrimination in salary and power helped to radicalize a number of women teachers and to convert them to the cause of women's rights. A far more common strategy for women educational leaders, however, and one that conformed with their values and belief, was not openly to question the dominant ideology that woman's true vocation was to be wife and mother, but rather to seek to enlarge woman's sphere to encompass the entire education of children. They argued that women should take an active interest in common schools because their role as "mothers of the republic" and shapers of the Christian character and civic virtue of future citizens required it. They claimed that women were destined by God to be teachers of the young because they were more moral, patient, understanding, inventive, and nurturing than men. Teaching in district schools was not a substitute for motherhood, they argued, but an ideal preparation for it. The most famous of the women educational leaders—Emma Willard, Catharine Beecher, Mary Lyon, and Zilpah Grant—rooted their campaign to train women teachers and uplift public education in a deeply held Protestant world view, that in fact expanded women's functions in society. God had designated crucial roles for women to play in the school, as in the family, to bring about the regeneration of the world.[5]

Though these leaders sometimes chafed at the restrictions on their actions posed by the narrow stereotypes of proper female behavior, they generally avoided antagonizing traditional males, for they depended on them for funds and political support in their enterprises. Sometimes, as in the case of Beecher, they chose complaisant males to be public spokesmen for their voluntary groups while pulling the strings behind the scenes. Willard, an excellent speaker, typically asked a man to read her public lectures or talked to mixed groups sitting down, so as to create the atmosphere of a conversation rather than a public address. They often achieved power through indirection. Emma Willard traveled about the country to organize in many communities the "Female Association for the Common Schools" that she had established as school superintendent in Kensington, Connecticut. To legitimize the work of the mothers—often former teachers—she proposed that there be two resolutions signed by the friends of education. The first was for men only:

> Resolved: That we will forward the cause of the common schools by inviting the ladies of the districts to which we severally belong—as we may have opportunity—to take such action in the common schools of each district, as may seem to us, that they are peculiarly fitted to perform; and such as we regard as properly belong to their own sphere in the social system.

The second was for the women:

> Resolved: That if the men, whom we recognize, as by the laws of God and man, our directors, and to whose superior wisdom we naturally look for guidance, shall invite us into the field of active labor in the cause of common schools—that we will obey the call with alacrity, and to the best of our abilities fulfill such tasks as they may be judged to be suitable for us to undertake.

As Anne Firor Scott observes in her perceptive essay on Willard, "having thus taken care of the social mores, she urged the women to take responsibility for everything having to do with the schools."[6]

Willard, Beecher, Lyon, and Grant chose to work chiefly through networks of women created among alumnae of the seminaries they founded and the women's associations they helped to build. Long before Horace Mann and Henry Barnard discovered the virtues of women teachers and advocated public normal schools, these women had designed highly effective curricula to prepare young women to be teachers and efficient networks to place them in jobs. The demand for their graduates as teachers far exceeded the supply, a demand stimulated partly by local ministers who applauded the religious zeal of the alumnae. The female seminary founders had made a conservative case for employing women rather than men, stressing that the virtues God had given women in their special sphere as mothers also adapted them to teaching young children. Just as evangelical religion justified missionary adventure for those women who went as ministers' wives and helpers to foreign parts or to the unchurched frontier, so teaching provided a secret passageway to greater autonomy for many young women committed to the gospel of the common school.[7]

As a pioneer in the systematic formal education of women, Willard generated a network of graduates who went all over the country establishing female seminaries and building up the common-school system. As Scott has shown, Willard deliberately organized and kept alive a network composed of a "series of concentric circles," with herself at the center and formalized in the Willard Association for the Mutual Improvement of Teachers, which had 200 members in the year of its founding, 1837, and many more "honorary members" who supported the purposes of the organization. The hub of the group was the small circle of faithful teachers at Troy Female Seminary; next came the women who had themselves founded or taught in girls' academies; and, finally, there were thousands of former students, scattered across the nation and often active in common-school associations in their local communities while raising families or pursuing careers. A woman of great social energy as well as brilliance, Willard kept in close touch with her band of disciples by correspondence and travel. In 1846 she traveled 8,000 miles and visited almost every state, staying with former pupils, organizing common-school associations, and lecturing on education. In this, she was a female Henry Barnard, quite as effective in her organizational talents as he.[8]

The best female seminaries—places like Ipswich, Troy, Abbot, Mount Holyoke—gave young women a strong sense of the strength of their minds, the duties imposed on them by religion, and the empowering ideal of sisterhood. The women who ran them were models of one kind of effective leadership, a style that sought to extend the scope of women's contributions to society and to employ their talents wisely while still preserving Victorian notions of women's sphere. That this task was rarely easy is illustrated in the career of Catharine Beecher.

Domesticating the Nation: Catharine Beecher

A friend of Horace Mann, Catharine Beecher had much in common with him. Although raised in a New England Calvinist family, she questioned much of its austere theology and never had the experience of spiritual conversion her father thought essential to salvation. Like Mann, she remained convinced, however, that there was a "true standard of rectitude," and that it was her duty to spend her life teaching it to others. In common with Mann, she was brilliant, articulate, energetic, doughty, and dogmatic. As did many Victorian reformers, both tended to project their own anxieties outward and to treat their fears as objective characteristics of society. Both educators realized that an ability to define social reality gave an eloquent person great influence upon the behavior of others. They mastered the revivalistic technique of alternating apocalyptic visions of social doom with millennial rhetoric of national salvation through schooling. Both thought that a major way to improve public education was to recruit and produce and train women teachers. They based reform on the heightened consciousness of the individual, family, and voluntary group more than on the bureaucratic action of the state. While they talked of a "national" system of schooling, it was to result from emulation of a common model, repeated over and over again in local communities. Both ended their careers as institution builders in the West, Mann as first president of Antioch College in Ohio and Beecher as founder of Milwaukee Female College. Both were convinced that they were helping to civilize a culturally barren western territory that one day would shape the destiny of the nation.[9]

But there was an important difference: Catharine Beecher was a woman. This meant that she could not become a politician like Mann or follow the normal vocation of the formidable Beecher male clan, the ministry. It meant that she had to struggle all her life to defend her role as an independent, unmarried woman in a culture that denigrated women who did not become wives and mothers. It meant that she had to disguise her assertiveness, often asking men to front for her in ventures that she designed and led.

Since she did not reject the central values of Victorian culture, she was forced to bargain with the men who held power. If women could not vote, they could at least create the character of future citizens as mothers and teachers. If they could not run the government or the economy, they could be "prime ministers" of the home (at times in her scheme the father seemed to be a figurehead king). They could assure the stability of society by fulfilling their supreme roles as wives and mothers. What they might fail to gain by confrontation, they could win by indirection.[10]

To Beecher the creation of careers for women could be reconciled with the general interests of society as well as with the special concerns of women. Writing to the former governor of Vermont about her project to train teachers for western common schools, she asserted that it would appeal to "all patriots," because it would promote "popular education as the only means of saving our nation from ruin," would interest those of religious persuasion because it was "a missionary effort to save not only from temporal evils but from perils of the future life," and would satisfy "those who are laboring to secure women's rights and remedy her wrongs" since it was "the shortest, surest, and safest method" of uplift. What was good for women was also good for the country.[11]

As Kathryn Kish Sklar shows in her biography of Beecher, the key influence in her early life and on her later style as an educational leader was her father, the charismatic Lyman Beecher, a Calvinist preacher who was the sulphurous superintendent of beliefs and behavior in the town where she spent her childhood. He called her his "best son." Even Horace Mann, foe of orthodoxy in religion, was impressed with the restless spontaneity and drama of Lyman's sermons, his compelling tale of social decline. Catharine Beecher shared her father's vigor, his high spirits and moments of deep depression, his knack for acquiring power over people's thoughts and actions. But she was not able to experience the spiritual awakening Lyman thought essential to the salvation of her soul. She could not find in herself the agonized sense of sin, the repentance, and emotional submission to God that true conversion required, and this led first to discord within her family and then to her lifelong interest in metaphysics and moral philosophy as well as her quest for a moral regeneration of *this* world.[12]

At the same time that she was undergoing this religious trauma, Beecher also became engaged to a professor of science at Yale, Alexander Fisher. Unable to submit to the will of God, she was also reluctant to submit to matrimony. Her suitor seemed at first to be a cold fish—lacking "sensibilities of the heart," as she put it—compared to her own affectionate and lively family. But pressed by her father's insistence and Fisher's determined attentions she changed her mind and set a date for the marriage. Shortly thereafter Fisher died in a shipwreck. Beecher never married, but public knowledge of her tragic engagement helped to shield her against the popular prejudice of the time against spinsters.[13]

Beecher's religious crisis and the loss of her fiancé "instilled in her a strain of resistance to her inherited cultural patterns," Sklar observes, "and forced her to begin the search for alternative social forms." One of these forms she developed when she moved to Hartford in 1823 at the age of twenty-three and founded the Hartford Female Seminary. Forbidden by her gender to be a minister or a politician, constrained in her influence on the larger society, she created a small society composed mostly of women—teachers and pupils—which provided her with a supportive community where she exercised social influence comparable to that of her father in the broader community. She insisted that girls should acquire not only polite accomplishments but also solid knowledge comparable to that taught in the best schools for boys. She developed a course in moral philosophy and a program to prepare young women to become teachers. She even led religious revivals within the circle of the all-female community, making sure that the socially prominent were among the first to be saved. Finding that the elite men of Hartford thought her ambitions farfetched, even ridiculous (she had designed an elegant new structure for her endowed seminary), she turned successfully to their wives for support. It was a pattern of school founding and female sponsorship that she would repeat in other communities. To both the students and to mature women in her circle she became the model of a self-sufficient, independent, unmarried woman, while their admiration, friendship, and financial support fulfilled her own needs.[14]

But the sphere of a small seminary proved to be too small for a woman of her aspirations and talents. She became a prolific writer on moral philosophy (including a moral primer for children), domestic economy, and education. She believed that the nation was beset by "vice, infidelity and error" and that only women could save it. They could do this partly by being pious and effective mothers. But equally important, she believed, God had "designed woman to be the chief educator of our race" and thus women teachers could redeem a fallen nation. Teaching would also provide them an honorable profession, "a respectable alternative to marriage," as Sklar writes, in case they remained single.[15]

Beecher believed teaching children to be distinctly a female role, one in which a woman "need not outstep the prescribed boundaries of feminine modesty." It was also an occupation that would make women better mothers, their chief destiny. Replying to Beecher's plan to recruit women in the East to teach in the West, Mary Lyon, founder of Mount Holyoke, wrote that it was especially important to seek "young ladies scarcely out of their teens whose souls are burning for some channel into which they can pour their benevolence, and who will teach two, three, or four years and then marry and become firm pillars to hold up their successors" as educational missionaries to the West. Lyon's plea underlined an important fact about the status of women in the nineteenth century. There were precious few ways in which respectable women could leave the confines of Victorian family life and venture alone to the frontier. In the case of sending women teachers to the West, however, both religion and national need sanctioned an independent, humanitarian adventure. Ideally, the adventure was to end in matrimony; in fact, it usually did.[16]

It was while she was in Cincinnati with her family, where she founded the Western Female Institute, that Beecher developed her plan to uplift the common school throughout the nation by educating female teachers. Cincinnati was a center of educational reform in the Ohio and Mississippi Valleys. But its Western Literary Institute and College of Professional Teachers was closed to women (though men might on occasion publicly read essays women wrote), and Beecher found their views on the education of women tame and unimaginative. Instead she turned to elite women in the East to support her ambitious goals of saving the nation.[17]

Female Networks and Educational Reform

Like her father in his fiery *Plea for the West,* Catharine Beecher decried the frontier's moral and educational degeneracy, which she described in lurid terms. Multitudes of children were growing up without schooling, without religious influences, prone to "insubordination, anarchy, and crime." Lower-class youngsters ran wild; "degraded foreigners, and their ignorant families are pouring into this nation at every avenue." It was idle to hope that men could be hired to teach in the thousands of classrooms needed, for they had other, more lucrative opportunities. The only way to stem the tide of ignorance and vice was to recruit women to seminaries where they could learn the principles of instruction and become teachers. "Moral and religious education must be the foundation of national education," she asserted. The way to accomplish this herculean task was to appeal to private donors, by hiring an agent "to arise and awaken the people."[18]

Although little came from this early plan, Beecher revived it a decade later in the mid-1840s and added arguments to appeal to Protestants. Quoting school reports that told of degenerate teachers, dilapidated schoolhouses, and neglected western children, she saw that there was a challenge for self-denying and idealistic Protestant women. If they had been Catholic they could have been nuns and served the needy, but as Protestants they had few outlets for their religious and humanitarian sentiments. Would not teaching provide a worthwhile career for poor women exploited in factories and prosperous young ladies whose souls were starved by elegant leisure? Their task as teachers would be nothing less than to build a Christian nation. As well-trained and dedicated teachers took up their stations in the one-room schools of the West, they would teach the young the "principles of morality," the three Rs, and religious truths. This would destroy sectional feelings and frontier isolation and create truly national feeling.[19]

Sending out circulars in Calvin Stowe's name, lecturing in most major eastern cities, securing endorsements from leading educators such as Mann, gaining the local sponsorship of the most prominent citizens, Beecher was a consummate propagandist for her cause. She raised enough money to hire Governor William Slade as a permanent agent, and together they successfully recruited and placed 450 women in teaching jobs in the West. Beecher herself gave normal school training to 70 women in 1847, telling them how to cope with inadequate books and facilities, how to deal with sectarian squabblings yet provide moral instruction, and how to serve as exemplars of virtue. These missionary teachers sent her vivid letters about their experience with people who spent the Sabbath hunting and fishing, about boarding in families with eight children living in two small rooms, about illiterate parents so eager for their children to read that they built a schoolhouse for the teacher. "The people seem to like me," wrote one, "say their children never behaved so well before, visit the school, were present at my examination, and like the Eastern way of keeping school."[20]

Although 450 teachers were a tiny cadre dispersed far and wide across a vast frontier, these women, like Beecher, were adventurous, committed people who exemplified the self-sufficiency and moral influence she advocated. Siljestrom was impressed with the "firmness of character," the "superior degree of independence and decision" of American female teachers in comparison with women in Europe. The result was a "combination of manly earnestness and womanly gentleness" that he found exceptionally effective. Although Beecher's plans to reform the nation's schools through women teachers were grandiose, the practical results went well beyond the small cadre she trained and sent out. She publicized teaching as a career that prepared women for marriage and thereby made it compatible with Victorian ideals of domesticity. She also gave moral sanction for a policy of feminization that was financially advantageous to taxpayers, since women were paid only about half of the salary of male teachers. The effect of women on the expansion of public schooling, not to mention the effects of teaching on them, was a drama in which Beecher played a leading role.[21]

Sklar has pointed out that in Beecher's old age, in the 1870s, some of her "millennial glow" changed into a more professional view of women's work and social roles, as she responded to "society's increasingly specialized" occupations and organizational complexity. Whether as moral reformer or as professional, Beecher's experience had taught her that gender was a dividing line in American society, more pervasive and important, in her opinion, than divisions based on class or religion or ethnicity. Even within the enlightened, comfortable, influential upper reaches of Victorian society, life was bicultural: male and female. It had been her life's work to make education a means for creating new social definitions and sources of power for women within their own sphere.[22]

6. DISCORD AND DISSENT

In the middle of the nineteenth century the chief goal of common-school crusaders was to *attract* citizens to support and send their children to public schools. They sought to adapt their arguments to many groups and to avoid alienating people. Thus they sought a common denominator of values and interests. In this task they succeeded with one major exception: Catholics decided to form their own common-school system, the only major competitor to the public school by the end of the nineteenth century. But in a society that was ethnically very diverse, split by religious contention, divided by partisan political loyalties, and rent by deep divisions of class, conflicts did arise. No one ideology was broad enough or set of interests so universally compelling that consensus on them could smother protest arising from social divisions. Public-school leaders and their opponents often failed to understand differences of opinion, for their values were so self-evident to themselves that they took them for granted. Accordingly, much of the controversy is a study in noncommunication.

Apart from local squabbles over the location of school buildings or the level of tax support, most of the arguments concerned questions of ethnicity and religion—that is, debate over whose cultural values would be legitimized in the public schools. On the surface there was little explicit class conflict, though that did emerge in some places. Rather, issues of class, religion, and ethnicity were crosscutting and intertwined in complex ways. The growth of commercial and industrial capitalism produced an intense concentration of wealth and power in the advanced sectors of the economy, created new and conflicting relationships between employers and employees, and disrupted traditional patterns of social interaction. When entrepreneurs and workers discussed the meaning of the emerging political economy, however, they more often used a language of religious and ethnic division than of class.

In education as in other domains ethnocultural conflicts often crossed class lines. Group consciousness based on common religion or ethnicity frequently allied employer and employee, the prosperous and the poor. It is likely that the working-class people who most enthusiastically supported educational reform were those who shared the Protestant-republican ideology of the school promoters. In a study of conflicts in Philadelphia, David Montgomery has argued that "the political behavior of workingmen in the 1840s was fashioned not so much of the economic impact of industrialization as by the workers' reactions to the political demands made by evangelical Protestantism: the moral content of education, liquor licensing and prohibition, Sabbath closing and the suppression of 'lewd and tumultuous' conduct." Many Protestant workers joined forces with middle-class and elite reformers who demanded the use of the King James Bible in schools and the prohibition of alcohol. By contrast, temperance and Bible reading were red flags to Irish Catholic workers who wanted religious and ethnic autonomy.[1]

To say that different ethnocultural world views energized the politics of the mid-nineteenth century is not to deny the importance of economic issues. Rather, the evangelists who promoted religious revivals and the reformers who fought intemperance or immorality had their program for responding to the problems induced by the new forms of capitalism. Basically they were saying that social evils were an aggregation of individual sins. Those on the top of society bore a responsibility to purify society by giving individuals the means of self-improvement. As Paul Johnson notes, this form of radical individualism, in which "every man was spiritually free and self-governing," enabled employers to deny an older Christian ideal of communal interdependence. And for the worker who accepted the evangelical vision, the key to personal advance as well as to salvation was self-control and self-help. Methodist Sunday School books exemplified this approach. Contained in the religious ideology was a vision of an ideal political economy.[2]

The members of those denominations that Paul Kleppner and Richard Jensen have called pietist believed that individual conversion was not enough, however. It was also necessary to mobilize against sin and ignorance in all their forms. The major Protestant denominations—Baptist, Methodist, Presbyterian, and Congregationalist—fell mostly into the evangelical pietist camp. By contrast, liturgicals—Roman Catholics and certain branches of Protestantism, such as the confessional Lutherans—believed, Kleppner says, that "salvation was imparted . . . through the mediation of the church and the sacraments." Such beliefs led pietists to try to create the Kingdom of God on earth by aggressive reformism, while liturgicals were more concerned with the preservation of their own corporate integrity. The political result was a "crusading moralism" among pietists as opposed to tolerance of cultural pluralism among liturgicals. The major issues of contention between the two groups were matters like temperance, Sabbath observance, Bible reading in the public schools, and the use of foreign languages in the common school. For the most part, pietists were active in the Whig and Republican parties, while the Democrats reflected the tolerant pluralism of the liturgicals.[3]

Public-school leaders were overwhelmingly of the pietist persuasion. The NEA enthusiastically supported Bible reading, temperance, and moral training based on the knowledge that there was an All-Seeing Eye. The forerunner of the NEA, the National Teachers Association, resolved in 1869 that "the Bible should not only be studied, venerated, and honored as a classic for all ages, people, and languages . . . but devotionally read, and its precepts inculcated in all the common schools of the land." Immediately thereafter they voted "that the teaching of partisan or sectarian principles in our public schools, or the appropriation of public funds for the support of sectarian schools is a violation of the fundamental principles of our American system of education." The membership seemed unaware of any contradiction between the two resolutions, probably because it was a fairly homogeneous middle-class Protestant group to whom Horace Mann's solution of letting the Bible "speak for itself" was self-evidently nonsectarian. Indeed, one of Mann's successors as secretary of the Massachusetts State Board of Education ridiculed the "croakings" of the men who would "turn all the Christianity of the Bible out of the schools." Anyone opposed to "nonsectarian" religion in public education was automatically on the defensive at NEA sessions.[4]

The very people who made the public-school leaders nervous in the first place about the state of the nation—Catholic and Jewish immigrants in particular and urban "politicians" in general—led the assault on religion in public education. Priests and party bosses catering to the new immigrants sought to dampen controversy by eliminating all religious teaching from the schools. Joining the battle were the secular advocates of evolution who would cull "the conscience of a saint from the pleasant titillations of contiguous lumps of jelly at the bottom of a preadamite sea."[5]

Either explicitly or implicitly, Catholics were the target of several NEA speakers. In 1889 John Jay attacked the Roman Church, accusing its hierarchy of a conspiracy to defraud the common school, aided in its dirty work by "the foreign element, uninstructed in American civilization." When Archbishop John Ireland, a liberal Catholic, addressed the NEA the next year, he felt he had to preface his remarks by saying that he was not and never had been un-American or an enemy of public education. More genteel than the pornographic pamphleteers of the Know-Nothing days of the 1850s or the street vigilantes of anti-Catholicism, the NEA spokesmen nonetheless believed with missionary Josiah Strong that America was *Our Country*—that is to say, Protestant.[6]

Although school leaders who spoke at NEA meetings were dogmatic in their demand for biblical sanctions for moral education, they were somewhat evasive in describing actual practice in the schools. In a number of cities—as in Cincinnati in 1869—Catholics and liberals campaigned against the use of the King James Bible in schools, thereby undermining the consensus sought by the school promoters. By 1880, however, a speaker could observe that the tide of "ultra-secularism in public instruction" had turned. Seven years later one schoolman estimated that 80 percent of public schools used the Bible. But a county superintendent wanted to keep the matter out of the public eye: "As a fact the Bible *is* in the classroom. . . . We want no legislation on the subject." Clarence Darrow recalled that in his boyhood school in Ohio, religion "was taught to us children in the same and direct way" as was good conduct. Far from Ohio, in Portland, Oregon, a final examination in the high school asked students to "write and punctuate the Lord's Prayer."[7]

From the 1840s onward many Catholic leaders—especially in cities with large numbers of immigrants—protested the use of the King James Bible, the slurs against their religion or ethnic groups in school readers, and the added injustice of being forced to pay taxes for pan-Protestant schooling while being denied public funds for their own parochial schools. In turn, Protestants accused Roman Catholics of trying to destroy the common school by demanding the ejection of the Holy Scriptures and the division of the school tax.[8]

Such bitter arguments were not limited to big cities, although it was in pluralistic districts that opponents of pan-Protestantism had their greatest successes. Even in Kansas, where Catholics never exceeded 8 percent of the population during the nineteenth century, the sectarian battle over the common schools raged for decades. Comments by citizens in the local newspapers showed how deeply ingrained were the pietist millennial assumptions about education. A resident of Atchison, Kansas, wrote in *Freedom's Champion* that "this age is purely American. . . . Americanism is Protestantism. . . . Protestantism is Life, is Light, is Civilization, is the spirit of the age. Education with all its adjuncts, is Protestantism. In fact, Protestantism is education itself." The state superintendent expressed the conventional wisdom of his peers when he wrote that the Bible was the "best textbook on moral instruction ever published." Kansas educators deplored controversy over religion in other states and vowed to defend their little red schoolhouses from infidels and papists. Catholics, in turn, argued that justice demanded the division of the school fund since sending their children to public schools would endanger their faith. They failed to win public funds, and in 1904 the Kansas Supreme Court upheld the constitutionality of Bible reading without comment.[9]

The campaign to enforce a pan-Protestant morality through the common school moved to the national level in the 1870s and 1880s and divided the Republican and Democratic parties. In 1875 President

Ulysses S. Grant declared that "if we are to have another contest in the near future of our national existence, the dividing line will not be Mason and Dixon's, but it will be between patriotism and intelligence on one side and superstition, ambition, and ignorance on the other." He went on to urge "that every child in the land may get a common school education unmixed with atheistic, pagan, or sectarian teaching." Catholics did not doubt that they were the target of Grant's remarks. Democrats retorted that the Republicans were raising an emotional anti-Catholicism in the Congress as a new kind of bloody shirt.[10]

In 1875 Republican presidential hopeful James G. Blaine introduced a constitutional amendment in the House of Representatives banning the use of state funds for sectarian schools. It passed the House, but by the time it reached the Senate a new clause had been added saying that the article "shall not be construed to prohibit the reading of the Bible in any school or institution." A fierce debate ensued in the Senate, continuing into the early hours of the morning, pitting the Republicans, who saw pluralism as a threat, against the Democrats who defended decentralized political decision making and portrayed the new amendment as an attack on Roman Catholics. The vote on the Senate versions of the amendment followed party lines, the Republicans for and the Democrats against, and failed to achieve the two-thirds required.[11]

This defeat did not deter Henry Blair, senator from New Hampshire, where the state constitution until the twentieth century urged "the support and maintenance of public Protestant teachers of piety, religion, and morality." Blair saw Jesuit conspirators everywhere. In 1888, supported by the pietist press and self-announced "leading citizens," he submitted a new and unsuccessful constitutional amendment forbidding public funds to sectarian schools but requiring instruction "in the common branches of knowledge, and in virtue, morality, and the principles of the Christian religion." He used the old logic: an embattled society needed moral education; morality depended on religious sanctions; only the common school could reach all future citizens; therefore, religious instruction in the public school. "The preservation of the State demands it," said Blair, "and self-preservation is the first law of nature to the State as to individuals." Blair was the chief friend of public education in the Congress of his time, trying again and again to pass a law granting federal aid to the common schools of the nation.[12]

To Blair, to the majority of public-school people, and to pietist ministers and lay people, the common school was a symbol of patriotism, an emblem of a government rooted in the virtue of free individuals. The place of education in the Catholic liturgical world view was quite different. For Catholics, wrote the prominent editorialist, Isaac Hecker, in the *Catholic World* in 1871:

> The education needed is not secular education, which simply sharpens the intellect and generates pride and presumption, but moral and religious education, which trains up children in the way they should go, which teaches them to be honest and loyal, modest and unpretending, docile and respectful to their superiors, open and ingenuous, obedient and submissive to rightful authority, parental or conjugal, civil or ecclesiastical; to know and keep the commandments of God and the precepts of the church; and to place the salvation of the soul before all else in life.[13]

Only the Catholic church could give such education, he added. Agreeing with Protestants about the need for moral instruction, Catholics differed about its content and form, in particular the importance of church doctrine versus individual conscience, the sacraments versus individual experience of conversion, and the maintenance of the corporate life of the Catholic community versus the redemption of the whole society. Rightly, Catholics rejected, Hecker said, the attempts of evangelicals in Congress and outside to train "our children up in the way of Evangelicalism" and to mold "the whole American people into one homogeneous people, modelled . . . after the New England evangelical type."[14]

For a majority of the pan-Protestant school promoters and Catholic leaders, compromise on religion in public education proved impossible. Despite some experiments in public funding of parochial schools, Catholics failed in their attempts to gain tax money. Even when school districts banned all Bible reading, Catholic clergy and prelates were instructed to require parents to send their children to parochial schools —though in fact many Catholic children did, of course, attend public schools, in part because of the enormous effort required for working-class parishes to build their own schools while paying taxes. The parochial-school system that emerged by the second half of the nineteenth century—reaching a total enrollment of 626,496 by 1890—was the largest "alternative school system" in the United States and testified to the inability of contending groups to meet halfway on such fundamental differences of educational and religious outlook.[15]

Public-school leaders were, for the most part, more willing to compromise on ethnic differences than on religious, though they preferred an education in American principles conducted in the English language. They had to respond to demands from prosperous, politically self-conscious and educationally advanced concentrations of immigrants like the Germans who insisted on using their native language in the schools their children attended and who retained great pride in their ancestral culture. The issue arose not only in cities—such as Cincinnati, Cleveland, Baltimore, St. Louis, and Chicago, where Germans settled in large numbers—but also in rural areas of the Midwest, where Germans or Scandinavians often predominated.

State laws in Wisconsin indicated that English should be the language of instruction but permitted, by implication, the teaching of another language as an additional "branch of education." De facto if not de jure, immigrants dominated public schools where they constituted sizable enclaves in Wisconsin. There were 15,000 Belgians across three Wisconsin counties who effectively controlled their own rural schools with French-speaking teachers only. In many German settlements only German was used in the classroom, in school board meetings, and in keeping records—a practice that persisted in some places down to World War I. As late as 1893 the German-born made up 37 percent of the population of Wisconsin.[16]

When English-speaking families moved into such districts, they sometimes withdrew their children from the public school. Forcing communities to conduct public schools in English would have been an impossible task, many leaders concluded; it would simply have driven immigrants to a private alternative. One Wisconsin county superintendent wrote in his annual report that "public money may be sometimes appropriated for a school that might not be exactly a legal school" because it was not conducted in English, but should not the Germans be indulged?

> Knowing as I do that these Germans keep more school than the Americans, that their children attend more days and that they take greater interest than do our countrymen, the question presented itself in this manner to me; shall I, by my action, kill these schools, create a feeling against the common school system and cause the establishment of private schools; or shall I take what I can get, knowing that the next generation—after the old stock is out of the way, and they come to associate more with us—will work into the English schools entirely?

By the late 1880s eight states had statutes permitting bilingual instruction in public schools; in 1872 Oregon legalized monolingual German schools.[17]

School boards and superintendents in cities with large numbers of Germans generally followed a similar course of action. They feared that public education would be endangered if this politically and economically potent group could not be included in the common school. They were willing to compromise with this powerful, respected ethnic group, to include German in some schools as the language of instruction or as a separate subject; and they developed elaborate pedagogical arguments and cultural rationales to justify their decisions. They claimed that bilingualism did not impede the learning of common-school subjects, but advanced it. They proclaimed the glories of German scholarship and culture. Respecting the ancestral culture, they argued, would strengthen families and ease the long-term assimilation of Germans into American society. City school boards were not generally so ready, however, to make concessions to other less numerous or prosperous groups who protested the attention given to Germans. In St. Louis, for example, angry Irish demanded that if the Germans could use their language in the public school, the Irish should learn in Gaelic. The board regarded that as a rhetorical gesture. Typically, except in a few politically pluralistic cities like San Francisco and Milwaukee, school teachers ignored the language maintenance claims of groups less politically powerful and socially favored than the Germans. But in ethnically monolithic small communities, diverse languages continued to be used in the common schools.[18]

When states attempted to eradicate foreign languages as a medium of instruction in public and private schools, such laws led to great conflict and generally proved to be political donnybrooks for their proponents until the avid patriotism of World War I and the fear of internal fifth columns created a xenophobic climate sufficiently strong to carry the day for nativism. The Republican party was generally in the forefront in pushing legislation banning foreign languages in elementary schools during the nineteenth century. In Massachusetts anti-Catholic and anti-immigrant elements of the party focused much of their attention on the parochial schools founded by French-Canadians and taught in their native tongue. In 1888 some legislators introduced a bill requiring all private schools to be approved by local school committees, one requirement for approval being that "teaching shall be in the English language." The next year a new bill added a provision to punish by fine anyone hindering parents from sending their children to public schools "by any threats of social, moral, political, religious, or ecclesiastical disability."[19]

The first person to testify at a hearing on the bill was an ex-Catholic newsman who claimed that priests coerced parents to send children to parochial schools by telling them that "teachers in the public schools were mistresses of the school committee," that public-school graduates were "imps of hell," and that families would be denied the sacraments if their children went to common schools. The superintendent of the Haverhill Public Schools complained that Father Boucher, leader of the French-Canadian community, "was not an American citizen and knew nothing of the Massachusetts school system" but instead "would teach his school in his own way and in his own language." In their schools the immigrant children studied a French history of Canada but no history of the United States; little wonder was it that a French newspaper reported that French Canadians should owe no allegiance to George Washington " 'who began his career by the massacre of a French officer in Ohio.' " The Republican candidate for governor in 1891 declared that "the public school is needed to Americanize our youth. It is the great digestive apparatus by which the many nationalities in our state will become assimilated."[20]

Republican anti-popery and opposition to the French-Canadian schools boomeranged, however. Enough of the French-Canadians shifted their votes to the Democrats (whom they had formerly distrusted since the party was dominated by the Irish) that the Republican gubernatorial candidates lost in 1890, 1891, and 1892. Although it was tempting to Republican politicians to draw on the deep reservoirs of anti-Catholic and antiforeign sentiment that lay close to the surface of the political consciousness of evangelical nativists, the Massachusetts experience demonstrated that this strategy had its dangers. Both Republicans and Democrats endorsed public education, but their styles of promoting it differed. Republicans favored homogenization while Democrats embraced a tolerance for cultural differences.[21]

In two other states, battles to eliminate foreign languages in elementary schools overturned Republican rule. Both the Bennett Law, passed in Wisconsin in 1889, and the Edwards Law, passed in Illinois that same year, required pupils to attend "some public or private day school" and defined an acceptable school as one in which English was the language of instruction. The legislatures themselves were predominantly Republican, but the measures had bipartisan support and their passage hardly stirred debate.[22]

When the laws began to be enforced, however, the Democrats attacked them in a campaign designed to arouse voters against the Republicans. German Catholics and Lutherans alike—joined by vigorous ethnic secular associations—denounced the Republicans as paternalists who invaded family prerogatives and the German heritage, endangering their religious and ethnic autonomy. Democrats portrayed themselves as the defenders of cultural autonomy and religious liberty.

In turn, Republican leaders argued that their opponents were enemies of that potent symbol of patriotism, the "little red school," and foes of assimilation. Republican Governor William Hoard of Wisconsin told teachers that "unprogressive elements" were conspiring "against poor, ignorant, and defenseless children." There was only one way to save these "poor German boys," he said: "that unrivalled, that invaluable political and moral institution—the New England system of free schools." Appropriately, his Democratic opponent was George Peck, author of *Peck's Bad Boy*. Republican professionals quickly saw that disaster lay ahead at the polls for true believers who, like Hoard, thought that extremism in defense of nativist virtue was not vice. After the Republican routs at the polls in Wisconsin and Illinois, one of them wrote a friend that "defeat was inevitable. The school law did it—a silly, sentimental and damned useless abstraction, foisted upon us by a self-righteous demagogue."[23]

Educators were bewildered and outraged by the ethnic and religious opposition to these two laws. Ambitious "bi-lingual politicians" were fomenting dangerous, un-American ideas, complained school leaders. In Illinois the state teachers' association passed a resolution declaring that the Edwards Law "was a measure calculated to promote intelligence, humanity, and liberty" and vowed to defend it "against the assaults of demagogues and dogmatists." The assertion that *compulsion* to attend schools in which the language was English could be a guarantee of *liberty* sounds Orwellian. The assumptions underlying that belief, however, become clear when one reads the discussions of Americanization in the self-appointed policy-making body of the NEA, the National Council of Education in 1891. A committee had just reported to the council that the idle and vicious were filling the jails of the nation, corrupt men were getting the ballot, and "foreign influence has begun a system of colonization with a purpose of preserving foreign languages and traditions and proportionately of destroying distinctive Americanism. It has made alliance with religion."[24]

The committee was really saying that there were two classes of citizens, we and they. An educator in the audience asserted that "the report assumes that when the people established this government they had a certain standard of intelligence and morality; and that an intelligent and moral people will conform to the requirements of good citizenship." Things have changed, he added: "People have come here who are not entitled to freedom in the same sense as those who established this government." The question was whether to raise those inferior newcomers to the standards of the Anglo-Saxon forefathers or to "lower this idea of intelligence and morality to the standard of that class" of new immigrants. Republican liberty depended on a homogeneity of virtue and knowledge that only compulsion could create in those who did not fit the mold.[25]

Almost without exception native-born and Protestant, NEA leaders in the nineteenth century took naturally to the notion that real citizens were those who fit the American pietist mold. Part of the dominant culture themselves, they could not see their own clannishness. In a society growing more and more heterogeneous, they could not so easily count on a similar "consciousness" to rouse. Failing to persuade, they turned finally to laws to compel attendance, harbingers of a new corporate order to come in public education.

7. THE SPECIAL CASE OF THE SOUTH

The South was a Protestant land, a seedbed of revivalism. Most southern states prior to the Civil War had a tax base as strong as those in the old Northwest. In Thomas Jefferson it had a great spokesman for public schooling. Like northern rural states, it had a dispersed population that might have been served more economically and efficiently by a *common* school than by institutions segregated by class, religion, or race. Yet the South was the great exception to the patterns we have described thus far. In public education as in so many other domains it was another country, at least during most of the nineteenth century. In 1859 about one-fifth of the whites in slave states were illiterate, compared with about one in twenty in the North. School attendance rates in the South were far lower as well. More than nine out of ten blacks were then illiterate—hardly surprising in view of the widespread laws making it a crime to teach slaves to read. In certain cities and in a few states —notably North Carolina, Kentucky, and Louisiana—educational leaders succeeded in founding rudimentary networks of public schools. But throughout the antebellum South education was mostly a private matter, not a civic concern, and only those who could pay received much schooling. Until 1870 the majority of all the pupils enrolled were in private schools.[1]

The people who did finally create and reform public education in the South were a strange mixture: ex-slaves mobilized in a vast social movement to educate themselves, northern soldiers and federal bureaucrats, missionary teachers paid by Yankee benevolent societies, southern moderates who shared many of the goals of the northern school promoters of Mann's generation, foundation officials, and rich northern capitalists. As a colony of the North, first political, then economic, the postwar South experienced a series of upheavals in its social structure that produced waves of educational change. The history of southern educational leadership is a complex interweaving of the familiar northern themes—religious enthusiasm and economic self-interest, private power and public action, millennial political hopes and everyday work —with the South's tortured racial history, its glorification of its "feudal" past, and its peculiar economic structure.

Here we shall focus on a few shifting patterns of educational leadership: on the small minority of antebellum crusaders who tried to create public schooling in a political economy in many ways hostile to the northern concept of the common school; on the grass-roots social movement of blacks after emancipation striving to educate themselves to the full meaning of freedom, and the whites who helped them; on the southern white leaders after Reconstruction who tried to refashion a nascent public-school system to serve their interests in a poor, rural society sharply divided by caste; and finally, on leaders in the educational awakening at the turn of the twentieth century that transformed white schools while it starved those for disenfranchised blacks—an odd mixture of southern educators, politicians, and ministers allied with northern capitalists and their philanthropic agents.

The antebellum South was barren ground for promoters of the common school. Those few crusaders who did succeed to a degree, like Calvin Wiley of North Carolina or Robert Breckinridge of Kentucky, were men similar to their northern counterparts: religious, committed to the Protestant-republican ideology, eager to empower their fellow citizens through enlightenment of the kind that Jefferson had said was essential to self-government. A large proportion of these were ministers or academy teachers and graduates of Presbyterian seminaries and colleges. They were most successful among the white yeomen of the Piedmont—people whose economic circumstances and religious world views were more similar to those of northern rural populations than they were to those of prosperous slaveholders. But the men who controlled the political economy of the slave South for the most part had patrician values and different economic interests from those of the school promoters.[2]

In the debate that took place from 1830 to the Civil War about the proper nature of southern education it was the ideology of the slave owners that triumphed. Afraid of attacks on slavery and the undermining of their privilege, eager to construct a special southern form of education to defend their orthodoxies, patricians looked on public schooling more as a threat to the social order than as a buttress of it, especially when the textbooks and teachers came from the North. The public school of the North was predicated on the notion that all men might be citizens, part of the campaign to create the millennial Kingdom of God. The South, by contrast, had a class of noncitizens—the slaves—and large slaveholders had doubts about the value of education even for whites, if they were poor and powerless. The southern reformers who shared Horace Mann's vision and turned to him for advice and support came increasingly to feel like outcasts in their own land.[3]

When regional hostility increased in the 1840s and 1850s, William Taylor writes, the debate over schooling moved

> away from a commitment to education as a matter of public responsibility, as a matter of general concern to the states in question, toward the definition of education as a private, or, at best, a local question. . . . One can say with a good deal of justice that the prevailing view changed from regarding education as providing an electorate that could control the machinery of democratic government, to regarding it as providing an electorate that the machinery of government could control.

The southern brand of Protestantism reinforced this conservative political stance, for the evangelical leaders of the South stressed individual salvation far more than collective action to improve society.[4]

Emancipation of the slaves and the radical phases of Reconstruction opened a new and tumultuous chapter in the history of American education. Both the freedmen and the Yankee missionary teachers who flowed South after the Civil War saw schooling as a badge of freedom, a means of asserting political identity. "Freedom and school books and newspapers, go hand in hand," announced the New Orleans *Black Republican* in 1865. "Let us secure the freedom we have received by the intelligence that can maintain it." As Carter Woodson established long ago, free blacks before the Civil War made enormous sacrifices to establish schools for their children and to win their admission to public schools in the North. New research by James Anderson and Herbert Gutman demonstrates how central emancipated slaves were in establishing systems of Sunday Schools and universal public education in the South during Reconstruction. Churches and ministers in the black community were often the nucleus from which such campaigns spread in a social movement that took in all of the former Confederate states. By 1868 the African Methodist Episcopal Church had already enrolled 40,000 pupils in Sabbath Schools; the numbers swelled to 200,000 children by 1885, instructed almost entirely by black teachers not only in church doctrines but also in basic literacy. Such schools represented a grass-roots system of popular education hardly distinguishable from the "public" schools of the time.[5]

Booker T. Washington gave a classic description of this social movement in his autobiography, describing the excitement of "a whole race beginning to go to school" and the envy his neighbors felt for the accomplishments of a young Ohio black who could read the newspaper. John Alvord, who was "inspector of schools" for the Freedmen's Bureau, found that all over the South the ex-slaves were engaging in "self-teaching" in what he called "Native schools." When the Freedman's Bureau cut off funds it had given to a large number of such schools created by blacks in Louisiana, the black families protested bitterly. "I saw one [petition] from plantations across the river," Alvord wrote, "at least 30 feet in length, presenting 10,000 negroes. It was affecting to examine it and note the names and marks (x) of such a long list of parents, ignorant themselves, but begging that their children might be educated, promising that from beneath their present burdens, and out of their extreme poverty, they would pay for it." Similarly, urban blacks pressed hard politically for adequate schools and urged school boards to hire black teachers. Giving political expression to such hopes, black and white Reconstruction legislators did more to establish the legal principle of universal education in a few years than the southern states had accomplished in the previous five decades.[6]

The Union Army, the Freedmen's Bureau, and northern missionary associations gave vital assistance to southern blacks in this crusade, believing that education was an essential means of remaking the South along the familiar lines of the Protestant-republican ideology that had shaped nation building in the North. Northern evangelical ministers and educators of abolitionist leanings had long believed that the Civil War might have been averted and the South redeemed had it enjoyed a Yankee-style educational system. After the war, the American Missionary Association and several individual denominations joined the federal government in pouring money into efforts to educate the freedmen. These groups sent teachers to the black common schools and founded dozens of secondary schools and colleges designed especially to train black teachers.[7]

Northern teachers, most of them women, went South full of zeal for the gospel and their task of helping blacks to achieve full citizenship. They held evangelical revivals in their schoolrooms and sought to help blacks reverse the effects of decades of slavery. Here is the transcript of a lesson in one of these early "Freedom schools" of 1866:

> Now children, you don't think white people are any better than you because they have straight hair and white faces?
> No, sir.
> No, they are no better, but they are different, they possess great power, they formed this great government, they control this vast country. . . . Now what makes them different from you?
> MONEY. (unanimous shout)
> Yes, but what enabled them to obtain it? *How* did they get money?
> Got it off us, stole it off we all![8]

Put in the long perspective of history, the educational achievement of the southern blacks and their white allies (both northern and southern) was little short of revolutionary. In 1860 according to the United States census, fewer than 2 percent of all blacks of school age were enrolled in school, in 1870 about 10 percent, in 1880 about 34 percent, and in 1910 about 45 percent. The illiteracy of blacks dropped from 82 percent in 1870 to 30 percent in 1910. Considering the extreme poverty of the group, the starvation diet of schooling, the oppressiveness of the caste society within which most of them lived, and the low job ceiling, this is a triumph without parallel in the history of American education. This educational revolution did little to lessen, however, the racial structuring of opportunity in the economy or to create the political and social equality that schooling was theoretically designed to foster.[9]

Until well into the twentieth century, southern blacks were able to obtain secondary or higher education chiefly in the private institutions created by northern missionary associations and in the private schools founded by their own black churches. W. E. B. DuBois wrote that "the teachers in these institutions came not to keep Negroes in their place, but to raise them out of the defilement of the places where slavery had wallowed them. The Colleges . . . were social settlements; homes where the best of the sons of the freedmen came in close and sympathetic touch with the best traditions of New England." In time, as James McPherson has shown, blacks began to take control of these schools. From the black colleges came a large proportion of the leaders of the race in education, the professions, in business, and in civil-rights organizations (although the approach of most of them to race relations tended to be accommodationist in the mold of Booker T. Washington).[10]

After the brief experiment of radical Reconstruction, southern white Redeemers took over the state governments and mostly starved the nascent public schools. This group—primarily men "of middle-class, industrial, capitalist outlook" and with close ties to railroad interests—found ways to "compose their differences amicably and to rule by coalition" with the old planter class, C. Vann Woodward observes. Even had they been deeply committed to effective public schools, the southern political leaders would have faced severe problems, for the South's tax base after emancipation of the slaves and wartime destruction of property was skimpy, its public credit in disarray, its population widely dispersed, and its ratio of children to adults larger than in other sections of the country, thereby increasing the burden on adults of working age. Reconstruction legislators and educational leaders had fallen short of their ambitious goals of providing free schooling to both blacks and whites (in segregated schools). But the Redeemers generally put a low priority on public education, were determined to create a rigid caste system, and tried to economize in government. They redesigned the governance of schools to delegate most important decisions to the county level, replaced the mostly Yankee state superintendents with southerners (often former Confederate officers), and generally required that blacks and whites fund their schools separately from their own property tax bases. Where schools for either race thrived—and they did in some places—it was often the result of the efforts of dedicated state and county superintendents and concerned parents and teachers, sometimes aided by agents of northern philanthropists.[11]

Table 7.1 ignores important variations among communities—the great urban-rural differences, for example—but indicates the degree to which the South remained educationally distinct from the rest of the nation well into the twentieth century. Considering the inaccuracies of educational statistics in the nineteenth century—great discrepancies between census and USOE figures are only one sign of the problem—the comparisons can only be gross at best. But the results of southern parsimony were appalling: in 1900 there were 1,198,774 white illiterates and 2,637,774 black illiterates in the South, not surprising in a region that at that time was providing instruction in public "schoolhouses costing averages of $276 each, under teachers receiving an average salary of $25 a month," and "giving the children in actual attendance 5 cents worth of education a day" for three months a year.[12]

At the turn of the twentieth century, southern educators, ministers, and political leaders joined forces with northern capitalists and philan-

The Special Case of the South

TABLE 7.1

School Attendance, Per-Pupil Expenditures, and Pupil Enrollment in the North and South, 1870–1910

	1870	1880	1890	1900	1910
Mean length of school term (days)					
North and West	131	140	142	152	168
South	86	76	89	97	121
Mean expenditures per pupil (in current $)					
North and West	10.8	10.2	15.8	18.1	36.7
South	5.8	3.3	4.2	4.5	11.2
Enrollments as percentage of school age group					
North and West	76	75	73	78	79
South	29	45	57	63	68

SOURCES: United States Commissioner of Education, *Reports,* and adopted from a table in Meyer et al., *Public Education as Nation-Building,* pp. 594, 597.

thropists to bring about a massive educational awakening. The pattern for this North-South collaboration had already been set in the work of the Peabody Education Fund and its agents. Founded in 1867 with a gift of $1 million (later augmented to about $2 million), the Peabody staff sought to stimulate the growth of public schooling in the South largely through exhortation, dissemination of information, and small matching grants to schools. As for the ministers and teachers who went South to teach the freedman during Reconstruction, the South was missionary territory to the agents of the Peabody Fund, but with a difference: they accepted the racial caste system and sought to rouse the consciousness of white southerners in terms they could appreciate and make their own.[13]

The first Peabody agent was Barnas Sears, Mann's successor as secretary of the Massachusetts State Board of Education and previously a professor of theology, but the most influential agent was a southerner, Jabez Lamar Munroe Curry. A man of great zeal and eloquence, he declared that "my life is a ministry of public education." Traveling all over the South, speaking in churches and courthouses and to legislatures, he and his disciples addressed the people in the language of a revivalist. "The free school supported by all the people was carried before the people as the Ark of the Covenant," school reformer Charles Dabney wrote of Curry. The new gospel preached was summéd up in the utterance, "Every child has the same right to be educated as he has to be free; the one right is as sacred as the other." One of Curry's listeners in a North Carolina town described his impact:

> Curry . . . pleaded with passion and power for the children of the community. I remember how he seized a little child impulsively, and with dramatic instinct placed his hand on his curly head, and pictured to the touched and silent throng the meaning of a little child to human society. It was the first time I had ever heard a man of such power spend himself so passionately in such a cause. I had seen and heard men speak in that way about personal religion and heaven and hell, and struggles and wrongs long past, but never before about childhood. It seemed to me, and to all the young men who heard him, that here was a vital thing to work for, here indeed a cause to which a man might nobly attach himself, feeling sure that, though he himself might fall, the cause would go marching grandly on.[14]

The revival pattern pioneered in the South by Curry was repeated over and over again, community by community, as the campaign gained momentum after 1900. Missionaries converting the people to education had to seek out citizens in rural areas. Governor Charles Aycock of North Carolina told his fellow school reformers: "When a man is hungry, he will come to you for bread, but the ignorant man will not come. We have to go to him and insist that he educate his children." Dabney agreed that schools should grow from the grass roots: "the schools should be born out of the home, grow out of the community which they are intended to serve, and be the result of local effort and local work." But where folk were unconverted, there the educational evangelist had to bring the gospel so that the awakening could proceed. In 1902, under Aycock's direction, speakers held over 350 rallies over North Carolina, where families arrived at the courthouse or town square, their wagons muddy from arduous treks over country roads, ready to listen to orators and to respond as to a traveling evangelist in their plain churches.[15]

Much of the educational revival in the South stemmed from the initiative of state and local leaders, but northern capitalists, like merchant Robert Ogden, railroad man William Baldwin, and Standard Oil's John D. Rockefeller, also promoted the movement both by funding the chief propaganda agency—the Southern Education Board—and by planning strategies with southern educators, ministers, and politicians. A large number of the board members of the Southern Education Board were also directors of a foundation created by Rockefeller called the General Education Board and to which he gave $53 million between 1902 and 1909. This philanthropic agency funded many new ventures in public schools in the South. Earlier eastern elites had supported the missionary associations that sought to Christianize and civilize the West, in part to bring it more into the ideological orbit of the Northeast. Now, on a grandiose scale, northern entrepreneurs took an active interest in improving the education of southerners. They chartered trains to bring together their capitalist friends, educators, and ministers to confer about strategy; opened their mansions to meetings of the Southern Education Board; and held meetings at the Waldorf Astoria Hotel. Individual philanthropists such as Julius Rosenwald, John F. Slater, Anna Jeanes, and Andrew Carnegie poured millions into southern schools.[16]

Economically, the South had become in many respects a colony of northern business interests. Baldwin took a special interest in training blacks so that they would be more efficient and docile railroad workers. His mentor in such matters, General Samuel Armstrong of Hampton Institute, encouraged him to support industrial schooling, saying that "an able-bodied student represents a capital of perhaps a thousand dollars ... [but] when they learn a trade, they are worth three-fold more in the market." Baldwin concluded that "in the Negro is the opportunity of the South." Rockefeller and other investors built company schools in the iron and coal regions of Alabama. They played black and white workers off against each other, hoping to forestall unionization. The broader campaign for schools enlisted their interest and support, for it promised to modernize a population that was increasingly important to the national economy and to their profits. The Du Pont family gave funds sufficient to build and equip a school in every black community in Delaware. But their motivation was also religious. Rockefeller and Ogden both ran Sunday Schools and were ardent churchmen who preached "business idealism." They believed that they were doing the Lord's work as well as serving their own interests.[17]

Thus the movement combined the capital and organizational skills of northern entrepreneurs with the evangelical rhetoric and grass-roots revivals of southerners. The chief propaganda arm of the Southern Education Board, its Bureau of Information and Advice on Legislation and School Organization, reflected a mixture of efficiency and revivalism, incongruous in hindsight but natural to an industrious Protestant of the era, such as Dabney, its director. One of the bureau's pamphlets noted why:

The campaign of education, as being conducted, has already awakened in many communities educational enthusiasm amounting to religious fervor.

But unless this emotion can be transformed into quiet intelligent interest it cannot last, neither can it construct efficient schools unless it be guided by sane educational statesmanship. This statesmanship cannot be adequately supplied by a few minds capable of taking the larger view, for in a democratic community schools and school systems must, in the last resort, be constructed by the people.

What the South needed, he argued, were both "missionaries" to reach the isolated population and superior leaders of schools who could be sophisticated "educational engineers." Thus in its publications the bureau made statistical studies of southern education, disseminated information about new conceptions of schooling in the North as well as the South, and sought to build an economic case for investment in public education, including estimates about how much more productive educated citizens were than ignorant ones.[18]

But the potent religious themes by no means disappeared. At annual summer schools for thousands of teachers from all over the South, held at the University of Tennessee and designed to "fill them with our gospel and make them missionaries for the cause," its director gave talks on the social teachings of Jesus, bringing to the Gospel a more collective interpretation than was common in the individualistic revivalism of southern Protestantism. And on 4 July, 1902, a day to reaffirm the millennial character of the nation, the 1,700 teachers in attendance at the summer school declared: "Conscious of our dependence upon the God of our fathers, and believing that the highest and truest civilization can be attained only by following the precepts of the great teacher, Jesus Christ, we favor the recognition of the Bible in our public schools."[19]

The strategists for the crusade to improve southern education—educators, entrepreneurs, and ministers—agreed at their third conference in 1900 that "the best way to provide training for the Negroes was first to provide adequate schools and training for the neglected whites." And helping whites, but not blacks, was what happened, as Louis Harlan has abundantly documented. The Christian logic was hard to follow, but the political pragmatism was clear enough. By the time the southern crusade to upgrade the public schools began in earnest, in the early twentieth century, blacks had been effectively disenfranchised and restricted by Jim Crow laws in most southern states. Thus they could not fight inequality at the ballot box. The resulting distribution of school funds was predictable. In Alabama, for example, the annual reports of the state superintendent ceased reporting expenditures by race at just about the time when whites were pressing to deny blacks the vote, in

1891–92. Before then the per capita expenditures per year for teachers' salaries had been roughly equal—and low, ranging from $.82 to $1.30—blacks typically receiving a dime to a quarter less. When the superintendent resumed reporting by race, in 1907, whites were receiving $5.05 per capita and blacks $.89. The allotment for whites continued to climb rapidly, while blacks were frozen at very low levels. In 1930, for example, whites had $19.66 and blacks $4.80.[20]

An observer of the southern scene wrote in 1907 that "passionate and rapidly developing enthusiasm for white education is bearing sharply and adversely upon the opportunities of the negro. There is not only no chance to help the situation of the negro educationally, but it is steadily growing worse." White county superintendents appointed "good Negroes" (sometimes faithful house servants) to principalships; school boards in the black belt systematically deprived black communities of rightful funds in order to give white schools the latest improvements; and "public" education gave once-hopeful blacks yet another lesson in their powerlessness, a feeling not alleviated by the need to appeal for help to northern philanthropists who sent agents to instruct them and funds to build schoolhouses. "Deep down we distrust the schools that the Lords of the Land build for us," wrote Richard Wright, "and we do not really feel that they are ours. In many states they edit the textbooks that our children study, for the most part deleting all references to government, citizenship, voting, and civil rights. . . . They say that 'all the geography a nigger needs to know is how to get from his shack to the plow.'" In studying a rural community in Alabama, Charles Johnson discovered that those black farmers who had more than five years of schooling fared worse than those who were barely literate. The white man's arithmetic at the store or cotton gin was always right, his guidance on other matters absolute. Too much schooling was of questionable value to blacks "in the shadow of the plantation."[21]

But for whites the educational awakening at the turn of the twentieth century was their own version of the crusade that had swept the rest of the country a half-century earlier. Private power and public purpose, industrial productivity and godliness, grass-roots support generated by the agents of New York millionaires, talk of universal education and democratic purpose in a caste society—these seem contradictory if not hypocritical in retrospect. But in the special millennialism of the day in the South, the awakening brought to whites a dream of Progress that combined a Protestant social evangelism with the promise of modern efficiency, a union of missionaries and social engineers.

8. HARBINGERS OF A NEW EDUCATIONAL ORDER

The relationships between the material conditions of life and culture are complex and constantly shifting in modern societies. People screen "facts" through the culture of their societies, and it is thus that facts acquire significance. As Herbert Gutman reminds us in his studies of working-class cultures, traditions of thought and patterns of class culture often persevere even when outward patterns of life change abruptly. Cultural consciousness is normally continuous for groups, changing slowly as does memory for an individual.[1]

Thus far we have examined the interplay between the spread of a decentralized but fairly uniform common-school system and the actions and ideology of nineteenth-century leaders. We have stressed the connections between religious, political, and economic elements of that ideology, believing that the millennialism of the crusaders cannot be dismissed simply as atavistic, quaint, or a cover for "real" economic interests. We have not argued that their world was composed of isolated primordial communities, but rather that they were mobile, well-informed people who saw the United States as part of a world economy and a dynamic Western civilization. The Protestant belief in voluntarism in religion matched a political faith in decentralized power and balanced spheres of governmental action. Both the religious and political visions presented the nation as redemptive. Indeed, it is perhaps more accurate to talk of a civil religion rather than a separate religious and political conception of the nation. Both focused responsibility on the individual. The common school, like the Fourth of July oration, inaugural address, or revival sermon, provided symbols and rituals that strengthened patriotism and pan-Protestant piety.[2]

As this religious-political ideology waned, however, harbingers of another system of integration gradually emerged. Higham calls this new system "technical unity," by which he means "a reordering of human relations by rational procedures designed to maximize efficiency. Technical unity connects people by occupational function rather than by ideological faith. It rests on specialized knowledge rather than general beliefs." He points out that this new system of integration transformed most sectors of life. "As a method of production, technical integration materialized early in the factory system. As a structure of authority it has taken the form of bureaucracy. As a system of values, it endorses a certain kind of interdependence, embodied in the image of the machine. Technical relations are machinelike in being impersonal, utilitarian, and functionally interlocking." As we have seen, even evangelical voluntary groups of the 1820s like the ASSU showed some of these features, and as we shall suggest, much of the Protestant-republican ideology persisted well into the twentieth century. But slowly the older foundations of belief and action in education began to shift in reaction to changes in the economic system and the reorganizing of relationships in other spheres of society during the late nineteenth century.[3]

The growth of cities and industrial organizations, the development among some educators of a consciousness of belonging to a distinct national occupation, the conception of scientific study and expert management in education, and a willingness to use the state to regulate and expand the domain of public schooling—these elements of technical unity shaped the theory and practice of educational leadership. In this section we will discuss some harbingers of the educational order that became dominant during the twentieth century: the bureaucratization of urban schools, an early argument for scientifically trained superintendents, pioneer efforts of leaders in the NEA to set professional standards and arbitrate conflicts, and attempts by Republican politicians to use the federal and state governments in new ways to support and control schooling.[4]

Big-city school systems, like police departments, were among the first examples of hierarchically organized public bureaucracies in the United States. As the studies of Michael Katz, Stanley Schultz, and Carl Kaestle have documented, Boston and New York were leaders in creating complex school systems with distinct roles and rules, standardized curricula and procedures, and an administrative ideology of efficiency, rationality, precision, continuity, and impartiality. Initially, most cities had small, relatively uncoordinated schools controlled by lay board members. But reformers became fascinated with the possibility of applying to education some of the norms of technical unity they observed in factories where one "superintendent" and a few foremen supervised the work of hundreds of operatives. Would it not be possible to hire such a superintendent to oversee and rationalize the process of teaching the thousands of children crowded into heterogeneous city schools? The district superintendent began as a hired agent of the school board in a few cities in the 1830s, and the practice of hiring such administrators rapidly spread across the nation in most sizable communities after mid-century. This was the origin of a group of educational leaders that probably came to have more impact on the everyday management of education than any other set of individuals—the local superintendents of schools.[5]

In practice, however, the real powers and performance of city superintendents often fell far short of the bureaucratic ideal. Typically they had few or no supporting staff members, save in the largest or most advanced districts. They were the agents and factotums of the boards they served and performed a vast array of tasks such as arranging pupils into age-graded classrooms, examining them for promotion to the next class, supervising teachers, arranging repairs, setting clocks, compiling statistics, writing reports, and buying supplies. Essentially they were the hired hands of the boards, often subject to ouster as newly elected members gave the spoils of office to their friends. Turnover was high, and superintendents came from and went to a variety of occupations. Their powers were obscure since lay board members were accustomed to deciding substantive questions and even details like the choice of desks. Typically, school boards divided themselves into subcommittees that dealt with such functions as the hiring of teachers, the budget, or the shaping of the curriculum. The pattern of governance was often labyrinthine in large cities; there might be a large central board of dozens of members, local ward boards added as the city expanded into outlying areas, and a further division of responsibility among these groups and city councils and boards of public works. Opportunities for graft as well as administrative confusion abounded. Superintendents frequently shared information with one another, but there were no training programs or uniform management techniques. Often administration was primitive: in Los Angeles in the 1890s, for example, the superintendent of schools assembled his teachers at the end of the month, gave them a peptalk, and handed each a paper bag containing a month's salary.[6]

The educational press of the nineteenth century resounded with complaints about the faults of chaotic and unprofessional urban school governance. How could the city superintendency become a profession rather than a procession? A first step would be to allow school leaders, armed with the appropriate skills, to achieve clear authority.[7]

But did the actual superintendents of the day *deserve* greater authority? Charles Francis Adams, grandson and great-grandson of U. S. presidents and a railroad executive, favored expertise in school administration, for he had seen the dramatic improvement in the schools of Quincy, Massachusetts, after Francis Parker became superintendent there. But he had a low opinion of the general run of school superintendents, who tended to be (he thought) grammar school teachers gone to seed or ministers and politicians out of a job.[8]

Adams was one of a post-Civil War generation of leaders George Frederickson describes as having largely abandoned the expansive style of reform of the prewar period and having turned instead to science and specialized expertise as the best means to reform and control society. Believing that "the future of our country is in the hands of our universities, our schools, our specialists, our scientific men, our writers," Adams urged that such an elite was more to be trusted than centralized power in the federal government. To him, the process of evolution, which he defined (following Herbert Spencer) as "the tendency of things to pass from lower and simpler to higher and more complex forms of organization," had outmoded the early phases of school supervision and demanded a new stage in which universities would prepare scientific experts who alone should have the authority to administer schools.[9]

In 1880 Adams explained his plan for educational reform through expertise in a speech to the NEA. He had already irritated many school people by his attacks on the alleged inefficiency of the common school and obtuseness of its leaders. His address did little to soothe feelings, for his history of the first two stages of the superintendency was hardly flattering. At first, he said, the task of the untrained school administrators was simply to improve the school plant, and their monument was "the four-square school-hous and the separate desk."* School boards were suspicious of their power and tended to make them "mere purchasing agents and superintendents of—repairs." The second phase he called the "pseudo-intellectual," one which still reigned. Its dominant characteristic, like that of the American people generally, was organization: "As everyone knows if two Americans meet together for the transaction of business they instinctively, as it were, organize;—one of them is appointed chairman and the other secretary, and they make a record of their proceedings." The result of this "drill-sergeant stage" in urban schooling was mindlessness, an educational machine that combined "the principal characteristics of the cotton-mil and the railroad with those of the model state's prison." Knowledge was chopped up into portions to be memorized by students and regurgitated at examinations. Pupils and teachers alike were tyrannized by a superintendent who prized himself on rigid ad-

*As the quotations from Adams illustrate, the NEA was then in the grip of a phonetic spelling craze.

herence to his timetable and program, smugly and ignorantly pleased with his pedagogical machine.[10]

What was wrong with this was not only the "prison chil" it induced in the schoolchildren but also the fact that students did not learn anything useful. Adams was no anarchist, however, nor one who would advocate a return to an unsupervised and loose kind of schooling. Rather, he believed that the only correct principle of authority for the common school was *science*, that is the study of how children actually learned, and that a new breed of superintendent should be trained in leading universities in this science, just as modern lawyers or doctors were educated in rigorous postgraduate study. He berated Harvard and Yale for bypassing the study of pedagogy, pretentiously assuming that anyone could teach. "We thus turn over our children to those whom we would never dream of entrusting with our potato patch." Only when universities take the science of education seriously, he argued, can "a higher walk of the profession" be created, a new "class which shall be to the teacher what the staff officer is to the line officer,—what the jurist is to the attorney,—what the physician is to the pharmacist. They must be imbued with the science of their calling."[11]

Adams stated an ideal which was to become highly influential at the turn of the century, but during the nineteenth century few took his advice seriously. Only a relative handful of institutions created professorships in education, and none a full-fledged program in school administration until Teachers College, Columbia, began one in 1905. Not until the 1930s was it common for states to require specialized credentials and substantial training for administrators.[12]

During the 1880s, however, a number of leaders in the NEA worried about a disarray in the ranks of school people which made it difficult to develop an authoritative consensus—or to reply to lay critics such as Adams. Insofar as there was any national center of influence in American education during the nineteenth century, it was probably the NEA, an organization in which city and state superintendents and normal-school and college people predominated. The membership was tiny: in 1870, 170; 1880, 354; 1890, 5,474; and 1900, 2,332. NEA members gathered yearly to hear earnest speeches on such topics as moral education, supervision, curriculum, and a smattering of educational theory. Religious beliefs provided an important source of authority and group cohesion. It was a place for educators to meet their peers and to exchange information, but it lacked effective professional sanctions, political clout, and ways to counteract decentralization of governance and conflicting lay and professional opinions about education.[13]

Harbingers of a New Educational Order

Thomas Bicknell was an energetic entrepreneur who had been Rhode Island commissioner of schools and was editor of the *Journal of Education*. He decided in 1879 that what the NEA and American education needed was a policy-forming group. He appealed to his colleagues in the Department of Superintendence to set up an inner sanctum within the NEA, a National Council of Education. He argued that the "hurried reading of essays" to "a restless audience" at the NEA hardly provided the "consistent and weighty discussions" needed for "valuable conclusions on many of the complex questions and interests of modern education." Since universities had not taken "the science of didactics" seriously, little help could be expected from them "to reach and control the teaching profession." Teachers stayed in the occupation only a short while, and nine-tenths of them were "in no way professionals." Yet schooling was in their hands and subject only to the control of local "school committees . . . whose fitness to form a consistent system of education and supervise its workings is not asserted by anybody."[14]

The contrast with Europe was striking, he said, for, there, government supervises higher education and "through boards of experts, elaborates the methods of organization and instruction and enforces compliance with all the weight of centralized power." Local autonomy and mobility in America had its advantages, he admitted. "Every year a swarm of energetic teachers is transferred from the old fields of routine work to newly settled communities of active-minded people, where the new foundation of the school can be laid by the help of all previous experience, and every aspiration for superior work have full opportunity for experiment." As a result, "within the past twenty years, a vast system of instruction has come up in the new states between the Alleghenies and the Pacific, in which the most advanced ideas and effective modes of instruction from all countries have often been incorporated with remarkable success." But this very experimentation also produced "furious pedagogic partisans," people of small vision and large egos, who urged their particular innovations as panaceas for all to adopt and who failed to appraise their work in broad, scientific perspective. What was needed was a national elite, a sort of pedagogic supreme court, which could decide disputed educational issues, assess the merits of reforms, and discipline members of the profession prone to "heated controversy" and "undignified intrigue."[15]

The members of the Department of Superintendence in the NEA had mixed reactions to this idea. William T. Harris, aware of political realities as superintendent in St. Louis, reminded his colleagues that Americans were "jealous of any centralization of authority" and that beleaguered schoolmen hardly had time to spend in long philosophical discussions, so likely were they to be hit by a "backhanded blow" from the state legislature or city council when they returned home. The secretary of education in Pennsylvania asked what value its deliberations would have since it had no authority to enforce its decisions. But others thought it might help to neutralize upstart critics writing in the newspapers and might overthrow "heresies and false notions of education." On balance they thought it worthwhile and created the National Council of Education in 1880.[16]

As Edgar Wesley has observed, the Council "was founded to a considerable extent upon a belief in authority and also upon a widespread and persistent faith in eternal verities. The prevailing assumption was that there were such entities as good taste, trust, correct thinking, right answers, and "the best that has been thought and said." It was the task of members, with their Prince Edward coats and impressive beards, to declare these principles to the country. It irked some of them that the group was merely advisory and not authoritative, for "here lies the weakness of our educational and of our political system," said one would-be panjandrum; "there is need of a spinal column somewhere." But a fellow educator admitted that "the authority of the council at first would be only such as the *character* of its members and the *wisdom* and *justice* of its conclusions would give it." Although they longed for the final word, for a centralization of doctrine, most of them still conceived of the leader as an aristocrat of character, not a scientific expert.[17]

The Council probably had its greatest impact on its own membership, who could go home from meetings with a confirming glow of consensus on basics. One superintendent welcomed an important report of the Council on high schools as "the cloud by day and the pillar of fire by night that is to lead us into the promised land." Then, changing the metaphor significantly, he called the report "the superintendents' armor, offensive and defensive." It was useful back home to be able to say that the experts agreed on what constituted a good secondary-school program. As Prince Edward coats and Victorian homilies in the style of McGuffey went out of fashion, and as a new university-based science of education gained influence, the Council endured slow decline and finally death. But in its desire to regulate practice and dictate taste this agency was a harbinger of the much larger and more powerful American Association of School Administrators of the twentieth century.[18]

During the latter half of the nineteenth century an increasing number of Americans began to lose faith in the voluntary and decentralized approach to solving problems and turned to the federal and state governments to enforce their vision of a redeemer nation. Some thought that the problems posed by immigration, industrialization, and the reintegration of the conquered South into the Union were beyond the reach of the old voluntaristic groups. As an earlier consensus eroded, they believed, reform by persuasion should perhaps give way to coercion by the state.

No one expressed the new mood of government intervention better than Senator Henry Wilson of Massachusetts, the Republican national party chairman. In an essay in 1870 on "New Departure of the Republican Party," he recounted the story of the previous decade of war and turbulence, the emancipation and enfranchisement of millions of slaves, the rise of a new "money power" which manipulated government at all levels, the influx of crowds from Europe, the rush to the western territories, the degradation of workers in factories and mines, and the increasing employment of young people. These all were creating a crisis for the nation that could not be solved by old familiar voluntary means: "those scattered efforts of individuals, churches, and voluntary association for the public good, which have hitherto so grandly illustrated and adorned American history, and which have, through home missions, tract, Bible, and Sabbath-school associations, and aid to colleges and schools, done so much for civilization and republicanism on this continent." No, the old work of public betterment is now so vast that "the government should . . . recognize a responsibility of its own which it has heretofore left entirely to others. . . . The two great necessities of the country, at the present time, are UNIFICATION and EDUCATION." These should be central planks in the Republican platform. Americans should learn the value of compulsory schooling from the victory of Prussia in the recent war. Republicans should unite in strengthening the United States Bureau of Education and in supporting "the establishment of a system of national education."[19]

Wilson's remarks were not mere campaign rhetoric, although they were that too. Both in the national government and in the states, numberous Republicans sought to centralize public policy in education. In 1864 Congress passed a law to make school attendance compulsory in the District of Columbia. Prodded by like-minded educators, Republican congressmen passed a resolution in 1865 saying that the Civil War was traceable "in a great degree, to the absence of common schools" in the South and calling for an inquiry into forming "a national bureau of education, whose duty it shall be to enforce education, without regard to race or color, upon the population of all such States as shall fall below a standard to be established by Congress." Education was a vital element in the Radical Republican campaign to reconstruct the southern people, both white and black. The use of national power during the war encouraged Republicans to use compulsion by the states to spread schooling where local people did not build common schools and send their children to them. In 1867 Congress created the Department of Education (later demoted to Bureau) on the model of the Department of Agriculture, as an agency to collect data and diffuse information about new educational developments.[20]

Because of fears of centralization of power and the political and administrative weakness of the first commissioner, it soon became clear that the Bureau would not have influence except as gatherer and dispenser of information about schooling. During the 1870s and 1880s, however, Republican congressmen from New England advocated granting federal aid for public schools under different plans of federal accountability. In 1870 George Hoar introduced a bill into the House that would not only have granted money to states but would have given the federal government authority to set standards and inspect schools, supervise production of textbooks, and even run schools where states were delinquent. It went too far even for most of his Yankee Republican colleagues and was condemned by the NEA as well.[21]

Later bills concentrated on allocating aid to states with a minimum of federal control and proposed grants in proportion to illiteracy in the states. Several of these passed either the House or the Senate, but none passed both; Gordon Lee attributes this defeat to Democratic legislators responsive to southern and Catholic opposition to federal aid. Since funds for schools would have come largely from revenues from the tariff, opponents of the tariff tended to vote against aid to public education. Whereas Democrats had platform planks attacking Republican policies in education as undue centralization, Republicans repeatedly called for federal aid, arguing that "the free school is the promoter of that intelligence which is to preserve us as a free nation." President Grant even advocated a constitutional amendment requiring states to establish enough public schools for all the children and making "education compulsory, so far as to deprive all persons who cannot read and write from becoming voters after the year 1890."[22]

In the states as well as the federal government, Republicans often took the lead in using government to coerce those who disagreed, departing from the older tradition of reform by persuasion. During the last three decades of the nineteenth century almost all northern states passed compulsory attendance laws. From data compiled by Walter

Harbingers of a New Educational Order

Dean Burnham on the party composition of state governments we have found that Republicans usually were governors and constituted a majority of legislators in both houses in those years when individual states passed compulsory schooling legislation. During the most active period of passage of such laws—from 1874 to 1892—the governorships were nearly equally divided between Republicans and Democrats, but twice as many compulsory schooling laws were passed under Republican governors as under Democratic. Republican-dominated legislatures passed over five times as many compulsory schooling laws as did Democratic. While only close study state by state could untangle the specific contributions of the two parties, it is highly likely that compulsion was predominantly a Republican initiative. In California, for example, there was a straight party vote in 1874 on a compulsory schooling law, the Republicans for and the Democrats against. By contrast, the only repeals or vetoes of compulsory schooling laws we have been able to find were carried out by Democratic governors or legislatures.[23]

It is important to put the Republican actions in perspective, however, for they were at most a foreshadowing of a new state-dominated and bureaucratic educational order. The laws for federal aid did not pass. States had no effective ways, generally, to enforce the compulsory attendance laws; in fact, most superintendents said they were dead letters, at least until the 1890s in most states. But by invoking the state, political leaders hastened the time when a member of the later "educational trust"—Ellwood P. Cubberley, in 1909—could say that "each year the child is coming to belong more to the state, and less and less to the parent."[24]

The men and women who created the new educational order of the twentieth century were the children of the mid-century leaders. As Gregory Singleton has observed, there was no abrupt discontinuity between the outlook and mode of operation of the Victorian leaders—who accomplished reforms through voluntary associations, who used evangelical rhetoric, and who operated on a simpler and smaller scale—and their children who came to maturity at the turn of the twentieth century, a time of organizational revolution when historians discern a vast growth of corporate power and government regulation and a period when "technical unity" became the dominant pattern. The parents developed new forms of association that gave Americans a national perspective and scope, while many of the older pietist attitudes persisted into the Progressive era. "To assume that there is no important relationship between the world of the voluntaristic fathers and the social and economic world of the corporate sons," Singleton writes, "is to introduce an ahistorical notion that a child is nurtured by the social trends of his adulthood rather than by the existing social world of his parents."[25]

To that world of the corporate sons and daughters we now turn, aware that much of the culture they shared was still continuous with that of the mid-nineteenth century, even though the material conditions of life had changed greatly. It will be no surprise to find that in a group of superintendents who were asked in the late 1920s what they did to improve themselves professionally, three-quarters wrote that they read religious literature weekly (this was number eight in frequency in a long list in which number nine was participation in national professional meetings). Nor is it surprising that a leading urban educator should tell his colleagues in 1899 that "it is left to you to be the only true superintendents, superintendents of the moral well-being of the universe." For it was such a millennial conception that gave their ordinary work extraordinary significance.[26]

PART II

Schooling by Design in a Corporate Society, 1890–1954

Through the knowledge of the science of human nature and its work in the industries, professions and trades, the average graduate of Teachers College in 1950 ought to be able to give better advice to a high school boy about the choice of an occupation than Solomon, Socrates, and Benjamin Franklin all together could give.

Edward L. Thorndike
"The University and Vocational Guidance"

9. ENGINEERING A NEW ORDER

Frank Whitney was superintendent of schools in Collinwood, Ohio, in 1908 when a terrible fire claimed the lives of 162 elementary-school children and two teachers. The tragedy did not dim his faith, however, that the public school was "at the heart of all progress. It was the key to the future. It was the focus of all those wild and entrancing dreams of what seemed the coming golden age, no longer dim and remote but just around the corner." He reflected that "just to be alive in that period and to have a sense of sharing even in some small way . . . in the great adventure called education was a privilege beyond price."[1]

Superintendent William Maxwell of the New York Public Schools faced staggering problems at the beginning of the twentieth century, but his optimism was no less sturdy than Whitney's. Steamers every week discharged thousands of immigrant children who turned up at the doors of schools already overcrowded. Inside the classroom teachers tried to instruct as many as seventy pupils who spoke dozens of different languages, who often arrived without having had breakfast, and who lacked facilities to bathe in their fetid tenements. In fifteen years the number of students swelled by 60 percent. Beset by scanty financing and conflicting political pressures, Maxwell nonetheless tried to expand and systematize what he regarded as a chaotic collection of schools. He created a whole new range of services: special classes for the handicapped, school lunch programs, medical inspections, vocational training, vacation schools, and rooftop playgrounds for children. Truculent and grouchy by temperament, still he believed that education's role in social evolution was ineluctably progressive: "The trials to which public education has been subjected are doubtless the means by which the system will be moulded to better and nobler things. . . . The Wheels of Progress can no more stop than the earth can stand still."[2]

By the turn of the twentieth century leadership in American public education had gravitated from the part-time educational evangelists who had created the common-school system to a new breed of professional managers who made education a lifelong career and who were reshaping the schools according to canons of business efficiency and scientific expertise. These new leaders—whom we shall call administrative progressives or (in a term of the time) the "educational trust"—believed that they lived at a critical juncture in the evolution of American society and of public education. Though more secular than the earlier crusaders, they had their own images of a millennial future and their own sources of certitude. The reformers of Mann's generation had believed that they were the chosen agents of a providential deity. The administrative progressives were certain that they possessed the instruments of scientific progress that would enable them to shape society toward "ever nobler ends."

By a selective interpretation of the history of the public school, the educators of the Progressive era were able to create a sense of inspiring tradition for the new generation of full-time professional leaders. They were building, they thought, on foundations laid down by the generation of Horace Mann. Indeed, they did share many concerns with the Victorian school promoters, especially their interest in moral and civic training, their passion for efficiency, their earnestness, their desire to combine new bureaucratic techniques with traditional ideals of character. But there were significant differences in the outlooks and strategies of the later educational leaders. Whereas the educational evangelists of the mid-nineteenth century aroused the citizenry against *evils*, the administrative progressives talked increasingly of *problems* to be solved by experts. The rhetoric of reform shifted slowly from a revivalist Protestant-republican ideology to the language of science and business efficiency. Instead of trying to mobilize local citizens to act, the twentieth-century managers sought to "take schools out of politics" and to shift decision making upward and inward in hierarchical systems of management.[3]

Believing that the basic structure of society was just and progressive, the new leaders thought they knew how to bring about a smoothly running, socially efficient, stable social order in which education was a major form of human engineering. Society would control its own evolution through schooling; professional management would replace politics; science would replace religion and custom as sources of authority; and experts would adapt education to the transformed conditions of modern corporate life. One day, in this dream, political conflict over education would become as futile and unnecessary as witch trials; the experts would run everything to everyone's benefit. This was their own version of a millennial future.

The ideal of a society planned by experts and run by scientific managers rested on assumptions not only about how to govern but also about who should govern. It was a conception of leadership designed to consolidate power in large and centralized organizations, whether steel mills, large department stores, or city school systems. The process of concentrating decision-making power and delegating it to a manager in public education is most apparent in the campaign of the administrative progressives to alter the governance of urban education. There the new advocates of professional management and their allies among elite business and professional groups waged political battles to destroy the old ward-based and lay management of schools and to replace it with a new corporate model of decision making. Under that corporate model, small central school boards elected at large from the city and composed of "successful men" were expected to act as policy-making bodies that delegated actual management to trained superintendents. When administrative progressives succeeded in doing this by changing city charters—which they usually did—they often blocked the political channels by which the cities' working-class and ethnic communities had traditionally expressed their political interests in education. In the process they also enhanced the power of cosmopolitan elites.[4]

The goal of such structural changes in urban school governance was to turn controversial political issues—formerly decided by large numbers of elected representatives on ward and central committees—into matters for administrative discretion to be decided by experts claiming objectivity. This was, of course, not depoliticization at all; it was another form of politics, one in which authority rested not on representativeness or participation but on expertise.

The decline of lay participation in school governance—creating buffers between the people and their schools—was part of a much larger transformation in the way Americans conducted their public business. As Walter Dean Burnham has shown, the high rates of voter turnout common in the United States in the late nineteenth century dropped sharply during the first three decades of the twentieth century, the period when the administrative progressives were seeking to "take schools out of politics." Despite much talk about democracy, an increasing number of citizens, the bulk of them at the bottom of the social system, were sufficiently apathetic or alienated to stay away from the ballot box—or were actually disenfranchised, as in the case of southern blacks. Contributing to this decline in participation was a sectional realignment of the parties in 1896 that gave, says Burnham, "immense impetus to the strains of anti-partisan and anti-majoritarian theory and practice. . . . By the decade of the 1920s this new regime and business control over public policy in this country were consolidated . . . the functional result . . . was the conversion of a fairly democratic regime into a rather broadly based oligarchy."[5]

The decline in voting and party competition and the submergence of older forms of ethnocultural conflict was accompanied by a significant increase in the size and complexity not only of local and state school bureaucracies but also of federal, state, and local governmental agencies, increasingly managed, as were businesses, by university-trained people. Samuel Hays has observed that there was an upward shift in levels of responsibility for educational decision making in states and counties: "professionals with cosmopolitan rather than local perspectives were extremely influential in shifting the scope of interest and level of decision making."[6]

In seeking to depoliticize education, in moving the regulation of education upward and inward in urban and state bureaucracies, in basing legitimation for new authority on scientific expertise, the new managers in education were following patterns of action and thought pioneered in the corporate sector of business and in the politically influential professional and trade associations. Within such functional groups there emerged, as Corinne Gilb has observed, "hidden hierarchies" of established influentials who did much to shape both private and public policies in their domains. Through the interaction of key educational policy circles in the universities, the foundations, and in key city and state superintendencies there emerged what was called at the time the educational trust.[7]

Members of this educational trust were acutely aware of how changes in the economy had transformed American society. They were worried about the potential for class conflict and eager to use schooling to preserve—but improve—the existing social order. One of their number, Ellwood P. Cubberley of Stanford, wrote in 1909 that the last decade had been "a period marked by the concentration of capital and business enterprise in all fields . . . 'trusts', combinations, and associations were formed in all lines of business; the specialization of labor and the introduction of labor-saving machinery took place to an extent before unknown." As urbanization accelerated, "a more cosmopolitan attitude began to pervade our whole life." Small-scale capitalism gave way "to large mercantile and industrial concerns. No longer can a man save up a thousand dollars and start in business for himself with much chance of success. The employee tends to remain an employee . . . the worker tends more and more to become a cog in the machine and to lose sight of his place in the industrial process." As a result of "the ever increasing subdivision and specialization of labor," he warned, "the danger from class subdivision is constantly increasing."[8]

Recent scholarship has confirmed Cubberley's contemporary portrait of the changes in the economy. Alfred Chandler's detailed studies of the managerial revolution in the leading sectors of corporate capitalism, Daniel Nelson's analysis of changes in the scale of factories and in the organization of work, Harry Braverman's critique of the deskilling of labor and the divorce of the planning of work from its execution, Daniel Rodgers's tracing of the tortured course of the work ethic under these new conditions, and Samuel Haber's study of scientific management—these have probed the far-reaching changes in the social relationships of production.[9]

So concentrated was ownership of industry that by 1920 the top 5 percent of all industrial corporations earned 79 percent of total corporate income. The major beneficiaries of this were the wealthy; in 1910 the top 1 percent of the population received 33.9 percent of all personal income in the United States, while the bottom 20 percent earned only 8.3 percent. By very high rates of turnover, by absenteeism, strikes, and record-breaking votes for Socialist candidates in 1912 and 1920, industrial workers protested the degradation of work into mindless routines and the loss of control over the work process.[10]

How did the new professional school managers respond to this revolutionary transformation of the economy? How did business influence public education? The linkages between educational and business elites and the nature of "influence" are both complex, all the more so since both groups worked within a larger culture and took for granted many of its values and structural arrangements. As Thomas Cochran has observed, "on the fundamental level the goals and values of a business-oriented culture established the rules of the game: how men were expected to act, what they strove for, and what qualities or achievements were rewarded." This does not mean total consensus or absence of conflict. It does mean that what was not on the agenda—what was not discussed or decided—was often as important as what was. Norms of "scientific management" became a basis for a new consensus, in education as in other domains.[11]

From 1890 to 1930, no other lay group had as much an impact on public education as did businessmen. Charles E. Lindblom has shown that American business was not simply another "interest group" contending pluralistically with other organized segments of society; it was a predominant force. Businessmen were active in the political movement to abolish ward school boards and to refashion urban systems on the corporate model; they and their wives pushed hard for such reforms as vocational schooling and the kindergarten; they served—together with professional people—disproportionately on city school boards; they lavishly supported educational research and educational campaigns, such as the movement to upgrade education in the South; and their language, techniques, and ideology permeated the new "science" of educational management.[12]

In the nineteenth century, ministers and evangelical lay leaders had provided public education with a justification and with networks of followers in the common-school crusade, thereby tapping into the great reservoir of social energy unleashed by revivalism. In similar ways, businessmen in the early twentieth century promoted education and reform by investing them with their prestige and power and by publicizing the need for change through such organizations as the National Association of Manufacturers and the National Civic Federation.

The textbook teachings of the nineteenth-century common school had undergirded the small-scale capitalism of the time with an ideology that taught that hard work, loyalty, and good character led to success, while poverty and failure were the results of personal defects. The individual and not the social order were on trial. A modest amount of schooling would prepare all for equality in the race of life. In the twentieth century, by contrast, most educators and businessmen agreed that character and the three Rs were not enough; extended schooling (often through the university) led to extended career ladders.[13]

All children, according to the theory of the administrative progressives, should be given through public education a fair chance to acquire the knowledge and skills necessary for success in a specialized, credential-oriented society. Hierarchy and inequality in the economy were justified by the twin notions of equality of opportunity and meritocracy. If all had equality of initial access to schools, then the doctrine of meritocracy—that the best made it to the top—assured the justice of hierarchy. Although many educators were aware of actual inequalities of opportunity in schooling and sought to correct them, they had a vested interest, as did their professional and business colleagues, in advocating the concept of "contest mobility" through education. This form of individual competition was legitimate; other forms of conflict stood outside a consensus that denied differences of class interest.

The literature on vocational education is a fascinating index of the way in which the new educational managers could perceptively diagnose the severe problems created by the new forms of corporate capitalism and then provide paltry remedies. It also exemplifies their faith in the power of public schooling to correct structural inequities by improving individuals, to reform the society not by direct means but by teaching youth. Advocates of vocational schooling wrote study after study documenting the ill-paid and deadening character of the subdivided and routinized work available to those on the bottom of the system. They argued that it was so exploitative that child labor should be forbidden by law. But at the same time few suggested any fundamental changes in the character of work for adults or thought of altering the balance of power between workers and employers in industries. They placed their hopes on a better system of vocational training that would help workers to be more productive and to understand the larger significance of the work they performed.[14]

A particularly revealing reform was the "continuation school," a plan whereby youthful workers would attend schools for four or five hours during their workweek. Its proponents made extravagant claims for the power of the continuation school to improve the lives of young workers and to give them opportunities for social mobility and self-help. It was to do this by improving the individual, by providing skills, knowledge of the industrial system, and stronger motivation—not by changing the structure of the workplace.[15]

This behavior developed into a quintessentially American pattern of postponing immediate reform by improving the next generation. Although the impetus for reforms often came from business and other groups outside the schools, faith in schooling was flattering to educators and provided jobs for hosts of new experts. It enabled them to redefine problems in such a way that they could engineer solutions. And it gave concerned citizens the reassuring feeling that something was being *done*—however symbolically—about real problems. As new demands were made upon the schools by different constituencies, educators could and often did respond by simply adding yet another function. In the process, schools became pedagogical conglomerates, again paralleling the business sector.

Educators were aware of conflicts and cleavages in the larger society in the years from 1890 to 1920. The most dramatic were those induced by the rapid change in the nature of work, by a surge of immigration (especially from southeastern Europe), and by social problems in the teeming cities. School leaders wanted to buffer the schools politically and ideologically from these conflicts, confident that they, as experts, were the best persons to devise solutions. For the most part they were enthusiastic Americanizers who believed that they understood the principles of American society well enough to impose them on immigrants. Finding businessmen useful allies in their plans for reform—though sometimes also critics of public education—the new professional managers enthusiastically emulated what they understood to be "business efficiency," assuming that it served all people impartially.

In the mid-nineteenth century, ethnic and religious conflict had threatened the consensus that educators sought to achieve. At the turn of the twentieth century, religion had diminished as a source of contention because Catholics had created a separate system, and changes in school governance had restricted the influence of immigrant groups. But the revolutionary transformation of the economy had sharpened antagonisms between workers and owners, threatening a political split along class lines. Cubberley believed the public school could meet this challenge: "The task is thrown more and more upon the school of instilling into all a social and political consciousness that will lead to unity amid diversity." This was, he insisted, "a social consciousness as opposed to class consciousness." Cubberley and most of his colleagues in the educational trust believed that the existing political economy was natural and proper and that it was the schools' duty to convey this message. If left free to develop their science of education and program of social efficiency through schooling, educators might one day bring about a nearly conflict-free society. Education was too important a matter to leave to parents or politicians. It was "a phase of political science—that of a study of means of improving the state and of advancing the public welfare." Politicians, with their penchant for conflict, need not apply. It was a job for experts—for the educational trust.[16]

We will examine the backgrounds and ideology of those new leaders and analyze how they carried out their work in a corporate society. Most of the lay members of the educational trust came themselves from small-town pietist backgrounds and thus experienced personal continuity with the experience and values of an earlier American society. They were pioneers, however, in creating a new kind of career for scientific managers in education. Closely linked in private networks, they were enthusiastic entrepreneurs and gained an awesome influence: the power to define what was normal and desirable in education. They developed programs to train managers and carved out regional or national spheres of influence as sponsors of their graduates. Through the survey movement they spread their reforms, measuring actual district or state programs of schooling against a template of approved practice. Deliberately they chose to do "research" on precisely those matters that could most quickly make a practical difference, such as school finance, governance, or curricular differentiation; they also believed that an important part of their task was to persuade others to adopt the innovations such applied research highlighted. They saw themselves as problem-solvers, not philosophers, but they subtly transmuted their numbers into norms. They were interested in the what and how, and in examining their work we also concentrate on *how* they influenced American education, for we believe that they had more impact than many other educators whose thought was more profound or whose practice was more subtle.

In school districts the individual leaders who exerted the most influence on public schools were the local superintendents. In their professional training or reading or in association meetings most of these administrators came in contact with the program of the educational trust, and it was the superintendents who served as conduits for the new professional norms in communities scattered across the nation. Some of the more prominent superintendents—especially in the big cities— were themselves members of the inner circle of administrative progressives, or were at least their students and allies. The converging set of practices and professional norms of "educational executives" in the twentieth century owed much, wrote Jesse Newlon, to "a small group of educational thinkers" who created "revolutionary changes in the schools" as a result of emulation of their ideas by local superintendents.

But the work of local administrators also reflected their social backgrounds, their occupational socialization in the schools, and the local demands of the communities they served. Thus they were both carriers of a cosmopolitan set of professional standards and also persons who had to respond to local constituencies. We examine these aspects of educational leadership in our group biography of local superintendents.[17]

While our focus is on the work of the educational trust and the local superintendents, it is important to recall that people both inside and outside the educational system challenged the new cadre of leaders and their programs. Organized teachers protested the undemocratic and hierarchical quality of the "reforms" they advocated and protested the separation of the management of education from classroom practice. At times opposition to the trust took on the character of a war between the sexes as women claimed their share of administrative jobs and demanded more democratic decision making. Lay groups objected to innovations such as intelligence testing. And thinkers like John Dewey proposed philosophies of education quite different from those advocated by the administrative progressives.

Such dissent was important, but to a large degree the educational trust was successful in persuading other educational leaders to accept their definition of what was normal and desirable in education. As the school leaders of the early twentieth century tinkered toward their particular version of utopia, they were not so much conscious servants of corporate power as they were unself-conscious celebrants of the small-town values of their youth, emulators of the most successful models of the age—businessmen—and people hard at work building systems of schooling while they created their own new careers as scientific educational entrepreneurs.

10. NEW CAREERS: THE BLENDING OF SMALL-TOWN PIETISM AND SCIENCE

When Ellwood P. Cubberley applied for the superintendency of schools in San Diego in 1896, the chairman of the school board was worried about his qualifications for the job. Cubberley had never had a course in education, but that was not the problem. He did not have a graduate degree, but that was not the problem either. The sticking point for the chairman was the question of Cubberley's piety, his religious orthodoxy, for he was a scientist who had written about geology and was known to be a believer in evolution. What was his view of religion, the chairman wanted to know, and what were the guarantees of his good character? Cubberley replied to this inquiry with a strong testimonial from his Indiana minister and his own affirmation that "I believe firmly in God and the principles of the Christian religion." He continued, "I am in the strongest sense a harmonizer of Religion and Science; there is no conflict in my mind between the two." For most of the leaders of Cubberley's generation it took no contortions of intellect or conscience to graft scientific conceptions of education onto the evangelical but nonsectarian legacy of Horace Mann's generation. While he, like many others, turned away from the doctrinal content of Protestantism (diluted as it had become in the late nineteenth century) and rarely used explicitly religious language, the implicit values he took for granted as the basis of individual character and social morality were largely those he learned in his childhood and youth in pietist small-town America. Science gave him and many others a new source of certainty that sat comfortably alongside the old.[1]

This self-assurance about their values gave many members of the educational trust much of their energy. Robert McCaul writes of Charles Judd—dean of the School of Education at the University of Chicago—that "his moral and intellectual world contained no shadows or dark places; his mind, his attention, his temperament, his views were always in sharp, hard focus . . . throughout his life he exhibited a professional militancy and fervor that betrayed his evangelical, pietistic upbringing." Judd was only one of a cadre of leaders in education whose fathers were Protestant clergymen; so, too, Edward Thorndike, Leonard Ayres, Sydney Pressey, William Kilpatrick, Paul Monroe, Lewis Terman, and Bruce Payne. Like G. Stanley Hall, Judd had originally planned to become a minister before shifting to psychology. Many other key educators testified to the importance of their early evangelical training in their later careers, whether they remained as church members or abandoned formal religion. Once at a convention some scholars were debating the sources of the ideology of George Counts. A distinguished old man in the back of the audience stood up to say that it had been an interesting session but that the historians had missed the major inspiration, indeed the one true religion. Puzzled, the chairman asked what that might be. The white-haired visitor—George Counts himself—replied "the Methodist Church and its social gospel."[2]

The first dean of Teachers College, who served for thirty years from 1897 to 1927, understood the pietist frame of mind very well. "I was brought up in the strictist sect of the Pharisees," he wrote, "a Scotch Presbyterian community in upstate New York." In his work he sought "the modern significance of the old theological doctrines of original sin and salvation by grace." Man, he wrote, "is the only animal capable of being converted by the stimulation of new ideals. . . . His pedagogical savior is the teacher who understands his personal problems, who has a personality that embodies high ideals, who exhibits in his daily contacts attitudes that are contagious, and who has the knowledge and skill —in a word, the saving grace—to bring forth works meet for repentance." He believed that Teachers College could "have no greater mission than to equip its students for such missionary service" and that it had been under a "providential guidance."[3]

Protestant churches and families, of course, conveyed different messages to children as they grew up in the late nineteenth century. Some stressed social justice and charity, some individual uprightness, some a duty to rise on the ladder of success, some a blend of these and other lessons. The young men who became the movers and shakers of education in the twentieth century responded to the messages in different ways. By and large the part of their religious upbringing that seems to have left the deepest mark on them was the conventional stress on hard work, duty, order, thrift in time and money, and a pietist imperative to set the world straight. When the new leaders admired efficient organization, "scientific" facts, methodological planning, they were not turning away from religious values but selectively emphasizing certain parts of their heritage. As we have shown, as early as the 1820s Protestant benevolent associations were already using highly sophisticated organizational techniques, collecting detailed statistics, and demanding accountability from their missionary employees. In *Our Country,* Josiah Strong emblazoned his pages with census figures and exalted social science and public schools as means of creating the Kingdom of God in America.[4]

Jean Quandt has shown how much the earlier millennial character of Protestantism became fused with the evolutionary thought of many social scientists, imparting to the latter group a continuing faith in moral absolutes, an optimism about social destiny, and an energizing call to action. "The process of secularization," she observes, "entailed a partial transfer of redemptive power from religious to secular institutions." In the case of the new educational scientists, the older providential view of redemption became subtly transmuted into a view of social evolution which held that people could control and improve their world by conscious means, notably through education. Interdependence coupled with the rational planning of experts might soon usher in a new form of social order. Such a vision saw piecemeal reforms as part of the crusade to redeem society.[5]

Growing up almost entirely in small towns, exposed to the pietism of public school and Sunday School readers, the educators of Cubberley's generation absorbed clear-cut standards of individual and civic virtue that they rarely questioned. Clyde Griffen has observed of the middle-class political progressives that they "grew up with a moral consensus so clear and unquestioned that they tended to assume this consensus was characteristic of human nature wherever it was permitted to develop freely." Assuming these standards to be the norm, they had little hesitation in using powerful agencies to shape others to their mold. Cubberley and his colleagues often wrote nostalgically of the older village patterns of child raising—the cohesive families, the churches, the powerful force of public opinion that kept the young "in the path of rectitude." They believed that changes such as urbanization, immigration, and industrialization required public schools to devise effective patterns of socialization for those not favored by growing up in an Anglo-American village. It was precisely their confidence in the older norms—largely unquestioned—that encouraged them to use the strong hand of the state to enforce their values. Since the new immigrants were, wrote Cubberley, "illiterate, docile, often lacking in initiative, and almost wholly without the Anglo-Saxon conceptions of righteousness, liberty, law, order, public decency and government," they must be compelled to adapt to American ways.[6]

No one expressed the small-town Protestant norms more clearly than Frank Spaulding, a prominent member of the educational trust who held five city superintendencies before becoming a professor of educational administration at Yale University. He agreed with his teacher and fellow New England farm boy, G. Stanley Hall, that "the best education we can now give in industry, civics, physical culture, economics, morals and the rest, does not begin to equal that afforded by the old New England farm as it existed a few generations ago." Growing up on a hilltop farm in Dublin, New Hampshire, in the 1870s, Spaulding learned to hoe and hill potatoes, to scythe hay and lift it to the barn loft, to care for the animals, to bank the farmhouse against the winter winds. In school he learned to read and write and cipher, though work at home left little time to practice his skills. He came to know every boulder and woodlot within walking reach of Spaulding hill. On Sundays he attended church and Sunday School with his parents and prayed and read the Bible at home; the Scriptures gave clear lessons about right and wrong, echoed by both his parents and his teachers. He learned about politics by attending town meetings and reading newspaper accounts of Republican victories. Images of the outside world came from visiting uncles: one had traveled to Louisiana and described slaves working on plantations (for Spaulding had never seen a black); another was a jeweler in distant San Francisco. Spaulding's was a coherent, homogeneous world that taught him his "most important ideals, objectives, values, ambitions," a set of habits and beliefs that guided him and a great majority of his peers in educational leadership: independence, thrift, self-reliance, foresight, obedience to authority, self-confidence, industry, ambition, and "belief in the religion of right conduct."[7]

Nostalgia for the virtues of country life was a recurring theme in the writings and speeches of educators at the turn of the century, as William Bullough has shown. A superintendent at the NEA meeting in 1896 declared that the strong and individualistic leaders of America had been "born and bred in village and rural homes, away from the turmoil of city life, in quiet communion with nature in her grand and ennobling forms." Many urban educators self-consciously devised ways to expose the city child to nature and to the discipline provided by rural nurture, whether through school kitchen gardens, nature study, or manual training. Henry Canby recalled of his schooldays in Wilmington, Delaware, that the moral principles taught "were agrarian ethics, and we town dwellers already felt their frequent inapplicability and, without realizing the cause, wearied of similes drawn from agriculture."[8]

At the same time that they glorified rural childhood, few educators wanted to spend their professional lives in the countryside. City school systems lured ambitious men like Cubberley and Spaulding, for there one could find career ladders, decent pay (for administrators, at least), and prestige. Ambitious educators at the turn of the twentieth century were more and more coming to treat school work as a lifelong occupation, not one in a series of jobs; they saw it, in other words, as a *career* with a distinct trajectory, one that required training, planning, specialization, and identification with a cohort of peers. Indeed, the generation of Cubberley, Spaulding, and George Strayer created the specialty of educational administration in the same way that men like Thorndike, Terman, and Judd created the discipline of educational psychology. Like so many other occupational groups at the time, leaders in education sought to professionalize their work.[9]

No one better expressed the mixture of personal ambition and public service, efficiency and uplift, of these village-bred educational entrepreneurs than did Cubberley. Invited to become a professor of educa-

New Careers: Small-Town Pietism and Science

tion at Stanford University, he exclaimed to a friend on the faculty that "the department should strive to have an ennobling influence" on the whole state. "I will be the happiest boy in California," wrote Cubberley, school superintendent and ex-college president. "It will be my ambition to make the Department of Education at Stanford famous, and this I believe I have the power in time to do." Cubberley's biographer, fellow country boy and colleague of many years, Jesse Sears, observed of this letter: "How American the tone of it is: Where is there a grown-up boy from farm or village in this country who has not felt something like it and who would not understand the drive behind its words?" Educational leadership was a career that could bring out the best in noble men "with red blood in their veins," Cubberley would say in 1907. He wanted leaders who "know the world, its needs, and its problems," who had "largeness of vision, and the courage to do and to dare," and who could "train the youth with whom they come in contact for useful and efficient action." Boyish vigor and trained expertise, muscular Christianity and entrepreneurial zeal—these merged easily in the age of Theodore Roosevelt and in the dreams of success of the new generation of educational leaders.[10]

The educational entrepreneurs who sought to create these new careers and to refashion American education in the process, the leaders we call the administrative progressives, came to maturity at a time of enormous structural changes in the economy, the polity, and the society as well as in the ideologies by which people explained their lives. The small-scale capitalism of the nineteenth century was changing to a nationwide and large-scale corporate capitalism. Public bureaucracies were growing rapidly in size and influence as government came to be used increasingly as a coordinator of private interest groups and functional associations (for example, business and professional groups). More and more issues were defined as matters for expert adjudication rather than "political" settlement. Society was becoming more urbanized, more ethnically diverse, and more sharply divided into distinct occupational groups.

Undergirding these structural changes, as Magali Sarfatti Larson argues, were "new forms of the legitimation of power" which appealed "to the rationality of science—science as a method and as a world view, more than as a body of knowledge—and to the rationality of scientifically trained experts who act in the bureaucratized institutions of the new social order." Such an appeal to science and to scientific management of both private and public business obscured the conflict generated by basic economic changes, and it justified the increasing power of elites in various domains to set the terms of public debate and to make critical decisions affecting the public interest.[11]

It was on scientific expertise—coupled with new notions of business management—that the new administrative progressives in education placed their chief reliance for professionalizing their careers, consolidating their power, and influencing public schooling. The prestige and objectivity of science promised them a claim to status as experts similar to those in other fields, an opportunity to raise schooling above political conflicts, and an end to armchair theorizing and neighborhood disputes that seemed to make everybody an authority on education. Furthermore, to base educational leadership on science would link it closely, as in other professionalized bureaucratic occupations, to the universities that increasingly guarded the gates to specialized, high-paying work.

What did these new leaders in the administration of public education mean by "science"? In brief, they saw educational science as applied social science, the systematic collection of facts for the purpose of policy formation. Many founders of systematic training in school administration—for example, George Strayer at Teachers College, Columbia; Paul Hanus at Harvard; Edward Elliott at Wisconsin; and Cubberley at Stanford—had been teachers of natural science before turning to education as a field of study. They sought to develop an applied technology of decision making similar to the technologies of production and management that were transforming the bureaucratized corporate economy. Insofar as their science of education dealt at all with questions of values and political power, it reflected the evolutionary presuppositions of the new—and avowedly scientific—fields of educational history and educational sociology. Dorothy Ross has noted that one way social scientists attempted to reconcile science and value conflicts was

> to root values directly in scientific evolutionary laws. Within an evolutionary framework, the disparate ideals of the older, agrarian and commercial society and the newer heterogeneous, urban one, and the countercurrents of emotional expression and rational control that the Victorian culture had organized into sexual and class roles—all these could be hierarchically arranged and pinned down on a scale of races, classes, sexes, and historical stages, rooted in nature itself and organized to display the future triumph of traditional virtues.[12]

In his own career and evolutionary view of history, Cubberley exemplified the traditional virtues of the small town in which he was raised, the lure of science, the tendency to accept the new social order as natural and proper (including its arrangement of "races" and classes), and the romance of scientific management—all of which linked him with his colleagues in the educational trust.

The Gospel of Efficiency: Ellwood Patterson Cubberley

"Those knowing Dr. Ellwood Patterson Cubberley, or 'Dad Cubberley' as he is known to all the boys who studied with him at Stanford, think of him first of all as a delightful friend whose chief characteristic is his unbounded enthusiasm for education." So wrote the president of the Colorado State Teachers College at the time of Cubberley's retirement in 1932. The New York commissioner of education saw him as a "real educational evangelist" on his "gospel tours to the East." Others testified in *School Executives Magazine* that he had changed their lives, converting them to careers in education rather than in law or other fields. At the age of twenty he had won a prize for oratory with a speech that declared, with the conventional rhetoric of Protestant-republican ideology, that "if we are to live as a nation, the people must be intelligent, the people must be virtuous, the people must be free. This involves a conquest for the teacher." Converted to a view of education as a means of directing social evolution when he studied with biologist David Starr Jordan, he joined what he and others saw as a deliberate movement to remake the school through the use of science and business efficiency in administration. He was both a symbol and catalyst of the managerial and ideological revolution that took place during his lifetime.[13]

Cubberley was one of a small band of leaders who professionalized school administration, a field that hardly existed as a specialization in 1900. Linked into a network, these men tended to share common social backgrounds, similar views of what constituted good training and good school programs, and similar reform strategies. At the time of his retirement he was himself so much an institution that it was hard not to see his achievement as foreordained: at his retirement dinner he claimed that he represented a cause rather than a person. When he began, however, the shape of things to come was uncertain to say the least. Out of a nearly nonexistent field and an inchoate occupation Cubberley and his peers created, with enormous energy and entrepreneurial talent, a conventional wisdom and numerous professional empires.

Like the majority of educational leaders of his lifetime—both university professors in education and city superintendents—Cubberley was raised in a rural community. He was glad to have escaped the petty moralisms, muddy streets, and constricted tastes of the small town when he entered the cosmopolitan world of higher education, but to a large degree he still accepted the Protestant, Anglo-Saxon, middle-class perspectives of his upbringing as quintessentially normal and hence American. This extraordinary entrepreneur lacked a sense of the relativism of cultural values, and his understanding of educational science did little to make him more self-conscious about those value assumptions.

Growing up in Andrews, Indiana, Cubberley worked in his father's drugstore, attended the local high school (the upper three grades in a one-building school system), and entered the college preparatory department of Purdue University. His parents hoped that he would study pharmacy and come home to run the family business. In 1886, however, a talk by David Staff Jordan, then president of Indiana University, gave Cubberley a vision of an exciting world of scholarship and service, of scientific idealism, of actually shaping the evolution of society, that made small-town life and the drugstore seem narrow and parochial. Jordan became his freshman advisor and later employed him as his assistant in giving stereopticon slide lectures across the state. Cubberley took Jordan's course in "bionomics"—a blend of natural and social science with old-fashioned pietist religion—and had many opportunities to talk with the dynamic president when they rode together in trains or shared hotel rooms. Jordan became his mentor and sponsor, recommending him for three positions and eventually inviting him to the new university he created at Stanford. Cubberley majored in physics and received his degree in 1891, after spending a year teaching in a one-room school.[14]

Cubberley remained in Indiana for the next five years. After teaching briefly at a Baptist college in Ridgeville, he became professor of physical science at Vincennes University, where despite a heavy teaching load he found time to publish two papers on geology. In 1893, at the age of twenty-five, he became president of Vincennes. He was already demonstrating the focused energy and powers of organization that would make him a legend.

In 1896, through Jordan's influence, he received an offer to become superintendent of schools in San Diego, California. He accepted and immediately found himself in the midst of a political controversy; several board members had wanted to hire a local person and saw no reason why a businessman was not preferable to an educator. It was the board rather than the superintendent that controlled the school administration through subcommittees that determined the hiring and firing of teachers, the choice of curriculum, and the management of finances. Aggressive and hardworking, Cubberley tried with only partial success to convince his superiors that the board should delegate the running of the schools to him.

The San Diego experience persuaded him that urban school boards should be "nonpolitical," small committees elected at large rather than by wards. The same logic demanded that county and state educational officials should not be elected but rather "appointed solely with regard to educational and executive ability." The best person should be hired, regardless of geography: "Local pride is too often used as a shield for incompetence." Throughout his career Cubberley advanced these ideas, drawing on his experience in San Diego. And in his inspirational talk to Stanford students on how to become a superintendent—later included as a chapter in his *Public School Administration*—he was largely autobiographical.[15]

The superintendent, he was to say, "must seize intelligent hold of the conception that education stands for the higher evolution of both the individual and the race." The job offered great scope "to men of strong character, broad sympathies, high purposes, fine culture, courage, exact training, and executive skill" who were willing to prepare themselves for the cause. In a footnote he said that the male pronoun was used "for the simple reason that nearly all of our city superintendents are men," but of course what he said was "equally applicable to women." That the latter was dubious became clear when he said that "manliness" was an essential virtue and pointed out the "dangerous pitfalls" that lay in the path of the ambitious schoolman. "On the streets the men call him 'Professor', and pretty grade teachers and women with marriageable daughters seek him out and flatter his vanity. His daily work in superintending women and children, who usually accept his pronouncements as law, perhaps give him an added importance in his own eyes." Being a big frog in a small puddle, being "spoiled by too easy, too small, and too early successes" could endanger his ascent up the long ladder, as could "local social obligations, which are wasteful of time and energy and have little in them of permanent profit." No, "he must learn to lead by reason of his larger knowledge and his contagious enthusiasm," an educational Teddy Roosevelt, energetic, honorable, square, mixing with men of affairs, a person who displays "the manners and courtesy of a gentleman, without being flabby and weak."[16]

In 1898 Cubberley decisively shaped his future by accepting an appointment as assistant professor of education at Stanford University, where his mentor Jordan was president. In his letter of acceptance to Professor Edward Griggs, a friend of student days at Indiana, he expressed some self-doubts about his ability to "do work satisfactorily at first," for he had no training in education. But he asserted his belief in his own "potential strength" and his conviction that the field of education would give him far more scope than geology, where "one must specialize with all his power, if he wishes to do anything great." Already, he told Griggs, he had in mind a dozen courses he could teach on such subjects as "school administration, school problems, school organization, school statistics, secondary schools, history of education, relation of ignorance and crime to education, etc."[17]

When Cubberley arrived at Stanford, however, he found that the faculty did not share his sanguine hopes for the field. Indeed, shortly after he arrived, Jordan called him into his office and told him that the faculty wanted to abolish the department. You have three years to make the field respectable, he warned; if you fail, you and the department will be dropped. "That was a challenge that called upon all the fighting blood in me," Cubberley later recalled, "and I told him I was very glad to accept the appointment on those terms." Over the years, he reminisced, "I may have had to carry the ball on the front lines, but there has been a good supporting column from the rear."[18]

During his first year, Cubberley had to teach five courses in administration and history of education, though he had never taken a course in either field, and his only work in history had been one undergraduate course in European history. The available literature in the field of education was very thin: books by a few European education theorists, school reports, a few histories, commonsense handbooks by practitioners, and some work in psychology. In a time before rigorous certification standards—requirements that Cubberley strongly advocated—it was unclear to students why they should study education. Faculty members attuned to specialization did not believe that a professor could teach a subject he had not studied and thought that anyone who knew his field could teach it in high school without training in pedagogy.[19]

The determined Cubberley set about to discover what it was he should be teaching. Fired by his vision of public education as an institution necessary for the survival of the state and the welfare of society, he managed to attract good enrollments. He was not impressed with the virtues of specialization by academic disciplines within education; rather, he saw broad teaching obligations as a way of training new professors and insisted that almost all of them take a stint at teaching the history of education. But he did believe in specialization by applied categories such as vocational guidance or secondary-school administration. Jordan was impressed by Cubberley's view of education as "social engineering," his ability to attract students, and his yeoman service in publicizing the university more broadly in the state at a time when it needed to attract students. He judged that the education department won the struggle for survival.

But Cubberley did not succeed in convincing most of the faculty that education was a respectable discipline. For years the old condescension remained, often producing friction in the university committees that set standards for majors and other administrative requirements. Enrollments dropped when only experienced teachers and normal-school graduates could major in education (others were required to major in the subjects they were preparing to teach). Despite the support of some colleagues, Cubberley was never elected to the university's "advisory board" of professors because, as a friend wrote him, " 'Education' was hardly considered to be up to the dignity of a 'Science' or an 'Art', and . . . the head of the Education Department was thereby disqualified from receiving the suffrages of a majority of his associates." Members of the department were not appointed to major committees. Faculty members in other fields objected to Cubberley's successful campaign to raise the educational requirements for certification.[20]

Cubberley's response to the low status of the department was three-fold. First, he tried, not entirely successfully, to persuade his liberal arts colleagues that education was solid because it was scientific. Second, he sought, with zeal and excellent results, to create an esprit de corps among the department faculty and the students in education. Here he employed the history of education much as a Marine commander might teach the history of the Marine Corps, to inspire the troops with the nobility of the enterprise. He invited students to parties at his house. He created an efficient placement network to move graduates ever onward in their careers. He inspired strong personal loyalties, imbuing young men, in particular, with his vision of ambitious service. As faculty he employed mostly young alumni of the department, attaching them by ties of personal loyalty. He also sought to link the department to the educational profession in the state and to make it part of a national movement, tying it into the network of other university scholars who were training administrators, doing surveys, serving as consultants on important commissions, and attempting to professionalize the field. These activities forged a power base outside the university among the leading public-school administrators.

All this status-politics within the university and frenetic activity outside was not without its psychic costs: Cubberley suffered serious ulcers. Some colleagues thought that he was a man free from "inner conflicts," and he did appear so to people dazzled by his habitual appearance of certainty, but such was probably not the case. Compulsory optimism takes its toll, both personally and intellectually. A student who took his class in 1906 recalled that Cubberley assigned John Spargo's angry tract *The Bitter Cry of the Children* and used it not to illustrate "that our government is iniquitous for its shameful neglect of our children," but to point "out how much better our record was becoming year by year."[21]

Cubberley worked assiduously to extend the influence of the department into the state and nation. In his first year he gave 77 lectures, and by retirement he estimated that he had given almost 1,000 addresses. "I am never so miserable as when I have nothing to do," he wrote his cousin, "and work like this gives one a consciousness of being of use in the world and perhaps helping to advance civilization." When he went to Teachers College to obtain his M.A. and Ph.D., he came in touch with other young men who shared his vision of education as a professional field. "It was, in fact, an historical movement that was then being initiated in American education, at Teachers College especially," wrote Sears. Teachers College was the West Point of the educational trust. Cubberley came to know Dean James Russell, another young entrepreneur who became a lifelong friend and ally, took courses with evolutionist historian Paul Monroe, psychologist Edward L. Thorndike and others, and graduated in a class in 1905 which included a striking number of the key figures of modern education. True to form, he wrote his dissertation on school finance in less than three months from start to finish. Thorndike commented after his oral examination that Cubberley was "a good man but not a good scholar."[22]

In addition to his multitude of speeches, Cubberley conducted several city surveys and served as member or consultant on numerous state and federal commissions. He wrote model state education codes and advised extensively on school finance and structural changes. But perhaps his greatest influence outside Stanford came as writer and editor of textbooks in Houghton Mifflin's education series, the largest and most successful set of professional books published to the time of his death. He edited 103 of the 110 books in the series and wrote 10 of them himself. Here Cubberley was able to carry out a longstanding ambition: to demonstrate that education, like other sciences, was developing its own practical specializations. He published works in history, psychology, statistics, administration, methods of teaching, sociology, and many other fields. But equally important, he legitimized by his textbooks the new reforms in schooling: vocational guidance, school hygiene programs, the junior high school, play and recreation, junior colleges, and other favored innovations. By finding young scholars and commissioning their work, he also helped to create scholarly reputations and to establish his position as elder statesman of the field of education. Through the series he gained the power to annoint the new and make it respectable, to define the new science of education. And in the process he built up a fortune which he increased by wise investment in the stock market. In turn, he used his wealth to fund a new education building and other worthy causes at Stanford, an amount which came to the then amazing total of $772,332.03.[23]

In his long career, Cubberley followed the social and educational ideology he had sketched in *Changing Conceptions of Education* in 1909. His prejudices, apparent today, subjected him to little criticism in his lifetime, so much were they shared by his students and readers and by educators generally. He assumed, and in his era did not have to prove, the inherent superiority of white, male, Anglo-Saxon, native-born Americans. About southeastern European immigrants he wrote: "Their coming has served to dilute tremendously our national stock, and to corrupt our civic life." So little criticized was he for such biases that he repeated this statement in a revised edition of his *Public Education in the United States*, published in 1934, after using it already in several works before. He believed that unassimilated immigrants were a menace and thought that the federal government should force all schools to teach in English; he abhorred the Supreme Court decisions that overturned such requirements. Apparently teachers and administrators (mostly native-born and Protestant) found nothing objectionable in his nativism.[24]

He was an elitist who could write that "one bright child may easily be worth more to the National life than thousands of those of low mentality." By and large he thought that genetic endowment explained success and failure in the social order. In an ideal state code for a northern state he advocated the segregation of black students in separate schools, assuming that they were mentally different if not inferior. In his classification scheme for the new Cubberley Library at Stanford he listed Negro education along with education for the blind, retarded, and crippled as part of "education of special classes."[25]

Cubberley's version of educational history was a mixture of selective memory and professional hopes and fears. His interpretation increasingly became an orthodoxy as the twentieth century wore on. He argued that a vast increase in industrial production transformed politics, family life, religion, and education. Concurrent with this economic revolution, and in large part because of it, came rapid urbanization and the influx of southeastern European immigrants. These developments weakened the older village modes of child rearing that had controlled the young and taught them the attitudes and skills they needed to be productive citizens. The school now must take up the slack, while "each year the child is coming to belong more and more to the state and less and less to the parent." Within the school system Cubberley had an intensely hierarchical view of leadership, seeing the superintendency as "the central office in the school system, up to which and down from which authority, direction, and inspiration flow." He praised democracy abstractly but scorned the notion that teachers should participate democratically in determining school policies. To increase "social efficiency" Cubberley argued that the schools should "give up the exceedingly democratic idea that all are equal, and that our society is devoid of classes, as a few critics have in large part done, and to begin a specialization of effort along many new lines in an attempt to adapt the school to the needs of these many classes in the city life." At the same time that it differentiates the curriculum to meet the different destinies of these classes, the school must create loyalty to the existing political economy. The school curriculum is effective only insofar as it is "closely related with the needs and problems of our social, civic, and industrial life."[26]

By present-day standards it would be easy to decry his ideology as atavistic, reactionary, and undemocratic. It is questionable, however, whether either Cubberley or his followers were even aware of their biases, any more than the librarian who accepts bias-laden categories for classifying books. Much of what now appears as garden variety prejudices then seemed confirmed by such "scientific" studies as those conducted by psychologists like Stanford's Kimball Young on groups like "Latin" immigrants. School leaders who believed as ardently as Cubberley in the superiority of business practice—"the boldness and vision, and the demonstration of efficiency in organization, direction, coordination, and control" exhibited in the new corporations—might well see the superintendent as a business executive. And to one who believed in an evolution of society in which the latest stages were the most "progressive" ones, the distribution of status and power in existing institutions, giving white males of native stock the greatest power, seemed to argue that what had evolved was mostly right, though still in need of improvement.[27]

11. THE "EDUCATIONAL TRUST": REFORM FROM THE TOP DOWN

Private Networks and Public Education

A central idea behind the bureaucratization of American public schooling was that of meritocracy, the notion that occupational advancement should be based on ability and achievement. A major complaint about educational employment and preferment had been that it was too often a "political" process. In particular, school reformers at the turn of the century attacked the influence of the "private" and presumably corrupt political machines that constituted a shadow government in many American states and cities and used offices in public administration, including schools, as spoils of office. By contrast, reformers promised that openly stated standards of merit for hiring and advancement could eliminate such covert influence. By creating hierarchically stratified and functionally differentiated school structures and by stating definite qualifications for officeholding, they hoped to design school systems in which expertise and efficiency were the guiding principles for selecting administrators. The universities were the places where able leaders could acquire such expertise.

Americans of many political persuasions had long been suspicious of what they regarded as privileged private associations with access to political power. Such distrust had fueled the anti-Masonic political campaigns of the 1830s. Radicals from Upton Sinclair to William Domhoff have attacked concentrated capitalist power and tried to expose the inner workings of the Black Hand or the power elite. The whole issue of "private power" has often seemed conspiratorial and nefarious.[1]

Yet is is common knowledge both among scholars and everyday citizens that there are private networks that have had much to do with the distribution of influence and advantage in almost every sphere of activity. People who share in such networks often enjoy not only good fellowship, but also special sources of information, influence, trust, and inside tracks to jobs and professional opportunities. Such was the case in public education, and nowhere more so than among the people who sought most vigorously to redesign schools as meritocratic bureaucracies in the early twentieth century. To identify and analyze such networks of influentials and to describe how they change over time is no simple matter. Insiders do not generally want to talk or write in public about their networks, since to do so is to endanger their comparative advantages, create envy, and do violence to the very notions of publicly available meritocratic ladders.

Sociologists of knowledge have called attention to "invisible colleges" of scholars, and political scientists have called attention to the impact of informal elites on legislation and policy formation. Contemporary analysts of school finance reform have identified a relatively small group of influential foundation officers, lawyers, and university social scientists who have spearheaded campaigns in the state legislatures to equalize funding of public education. These approaches suggest a useful way to conceptualize the work of the leading administrative progressives of the period from 1910 to 1930. To speak of a private network is not to imply deviousness or conspiracy, but rather to focus attention on how educators in congruent positions and with similar values and interests worked collectively in different parts of the country under a common leadership. It offers one way to understand how and why reforms nationwide moved in similar directions despite formally decentralized school systems.[2]

Networks resist definition. The word itself is a metaphor for a connecting web with much open space. As we use the term here, we mean an informal association of individuals who occupied influential positions (usually in university education departments or schools, as policy analysts or researchers in foundations, and as key superintendents), who shared common purposes (to solve social and economic problems by educational means through "scientific" diagnosis and prescription), who had common interests in furthering their own careers, and who had come to know one another mostly through face-to-face interactions and through their similar writing and research. They controlled important resources: money, the creation of reputations, the placement of students and friends, the training of subordinates and future leaders, and influence over professional associations and public legislative and administrative bodies. The networks of administrative progressives changed somewhat over time and with shifting practical concerns, but there was considerable coherence in the group.[3]

How did these leaders come to know one another and to discover a common agenda? One way was by attending graduate school together. The Ph.D. class of 1905 at Teachers College, for example, included three preeminent members of the educational trust: George Strayer, Ellwood P. Cubberley, and Edward C. Elliott. Often professors or deans, like Cubberley, Strayer, or Charles Judd of the University of Chicago, made a point of sponsoring their university colleagues and students as members of the emerging network of influentials, thereby augmenting their own status and that of their departments. The school survey movement, as we shall see, offered foundation officials, university professors, and leading superintendents another opportunity to work closely together under circumstances that welded close professional friendships. Similarly, the task of creating intelligence tests for the army during World War I created a cohesive group of psychologists who later worked closely with test publishers and school administrators to introduce tests into the schools. Although professional associations such as the NEA or its Department of Superintendence were too large to qualify as networks in the sense in which we are using the term, within these organizations participation in small governing bodies or commissions did create opportunities to form bonds among elite educators.

An example is the friendship between Frank Spaulding and Cubberley. Spaulding heard Cubberley give a speech in Boston, invited him to see what he was doing as superintendent in Newton, Massachusetts, and was then invited by Cubberley to help conduct a survey of Portland, Oregon, public schools. Cubberley and Spaulding stayed up late in the night at the hotel in Portland discussing what they had been observing and cementing their common professional goals and interests.[4]

The Cleveland Conference, a group formed in 1915, is an instance of a deliberately created network of leading educators. At the conclusion of a massive survey of the Cleveland Public Schools, the survey director Leonard Ayres (of the Russell Sage Foundation) invited several consultants to review his findings. Their discussion had been so stimulating that consultant Charles Judd and two others suggested that a small group of experts be convened "who could more advantageously consider certain educational problems and interests than was possible in the larger groups where educators come together."[5]

Membership in the Cleveland Conference was by invitation only. To the first regular session were invited James R. Angell, Leonard P. Ayres, D.C. Bliss, Charles E. Chadsey, Lotus D. Coffman, Ellwood P. Cubberley, Edward C. Elliott, Abraham Flexner, Paul H. Hanus, Walter A. Jessup, Charles H. Kendall, Paul B. Monroe, Henry C. Morrison, Bruce Payne, David Snedden, Frank E. Spaulding, George D. Strayer, and Edward L. Thorndike. Of the nineteen, eight were graduates of Teachers College and three were professors there. Mostly university professors and superintendents, many were identified with the scientific study of education, and among them they represented a rich background of administrative experience in public schools. By 1920 the membership had grown to sixty-five, in the process not only adding a large number of university professors, but also many large-city superintendents and three officers of foundations that supported educational research and innovation. Over the years, that mix of professionals together with a few lay people from business, the media, and government continued to constitute the conference. In later years other leaders, among them Lyman Bryson of CBS, John Gardner of the Carnegie Corporation, James Bryant Conant of Harvard, Ralph Tyler, and George Stoddard, joined the ranks.

In the early years the guiding spirit of the conference was Charles Judd. He had a vision that both the structure of the schools and the curriculum needed radical revision, but that change would take place "in the haphazard fashion that has characterized our school history unless some group gets together and undertakes in a cooperative way to coordinate reforms." He believed the present pattern of instruction to be "a curious and irrational mixture," wasteful and inefficient. Because of the decentralized control of schools, he observed, "one looks in vain for agencies strong enough to bring about general reforms." The members of the conference should jump into the breach, undertaking "the positive and aggressive task of . . . a detailed reorganization of the materials of instruction in schools of all grades. This proposal involves the stimulation of a much larger group of people than that included in our membership. It is intended that we make the undertaking as broad and democratic as possible by furnishing the energy for organizing a general movement at the same time we stimulate each other to make direct contributions wherever possible." Although using the language of science and social efficiency, Judd (the son of a Methodist minister to India) envisaged an almost evangelical social movement led by the conference members, much as the Yale band of missionaries had earlier spread the Gospel to foreign parts.[6]

There was, of course, some incongruity in the notion of a small, self-appointed group of experts proposing a "democratic" revision of studies from the top down. Judd later would argue during the Great Depression for the abolition of local school boards in an effort to bypass the vagaries of local lay control. In any case, the members of the conference were not convinced that it should undertake Judd's ambitious program. But the annual meeting did offer educational leaders a chance to achieve common understandings and goals in an informal setting—a prelude to more united action in their own domains, whether in a city school system, a foundation, a university, or another position of influence.

Having no constitution, no minutes, no officers save a "factotum," no bylaws, no "public life," the conference was described in 1949 as a club whose "sole object is to make it possible for forty or fifty men to meet once a year and talk about whatever they are interested in for ten or a dozen hours in session and an unpredictable number of hours in lobbies or bedrooms." Members had a chance "to learn about the news behind the news," to get to know leaders in a variety of fields, to share information about new educational programs or jobs or foundation grants or new government programs or regulations. When the Commonwealth Fund decided to give large sums for educational research, for example, its officer Max Farrand outlined the funding program to conference members first.[7]

Not surprisingly, membership in the conference matched the social characteristics of educational leaders more generally: only white males belonged. Not until 1946 did the first black join, and not until the 1960s did women become members. It was indeed an old-boy network.

The private character of the organization was sometimes a source of embarrassment. In 1917 the conference met in the Statler Hotel in Cleveland on the very weekend when the school board was making its final negotiations with its superintendent-elect. Many members of the conference had nominated candidates for the position—a prestigious and highly paid job—and almost half of the members were included in the twenty-two-man short list from which the board selected the winner, Frank Spaulding. Three of the four candidates interviewed were conference members. Eager reporters found that the educational trust was in session at the Statler and badgered Spaulding and his colleagues for inside information. Spaulding later wrote: "As a result of their own close relationship to the matter most members of the Conference felt a keen interest, more than one an intense personal interest in the final settlement—due to the possibility that I might not accept . . . and that with me out of it, the Board would of course try to agree on someone else, who would almost certainly be a member of the Conference." The episode illustrates how small was the inner circle of top "school executives." Judd wrote in his report on the meeting that "the Conference has become a matter of such public concern in Cleveland that it seemed desirable for at least one year to change its seat" to Chicago. Thus the Cleveland Conference shifted its discussions to the windy city.[8]

The networks of the administrative progressives took several overlapping forms, of which discussion groups like the Cleveland Conference were only one. Some networks were especially interested in shaping federal or state legislation. Some were primarily training and placement systems. Some operated through professional associations like the NEA. Some focused on the business profits to be made in education, as in textbooks, tests, school design and construction, and consultations. The career of a leading figure like George Strayer, professor of educational administration at Teachers College, illustrates how such networks interconnected and suggests the linkages among applied research, the training and placement of school superintendents, school surveys, commercial profits in education-related business, and leadership in professional associations. Strayer was a skilled entrepreneur and, like Cubberley, a key member of the educational trust.

Strayer was also one of a small group of influential pioneers in applied research in educational administration. He believed that research should find practical answers to practical problems: how to standardize reports of "child accounting," how to create uniform statistical reporting for school systems, how to equalize state-school finance, how to plan buildings to accommodate anticipated increases in the student population. He worked on numerous federal, state, and NEA commissions to accomplish this agenda. In collaboration with colleagues at Teachers College he developed techniques to estimate future enrollments, to plan standardized buildings, and to rate the quality of the existing school plant. Joined by a small band of fiscal experts, he directed the major 1921–24 school-finance inquiry sponsored by the General Education Board, the Carnegie Corporation, and the Commonwealth Fund. Strayer not only did studies; he also conferred with people who had power to put his recommendations into practice, with bureaus that collected statistics and could change the required forms, with state legislatures and school boards that determined levels and sources of fiscal support, and above all with the city school administrators who guided structural and curricular change. Along the way he also made tidy sums selling his textbooks and his student record cards and scorecards for rating school buildings as well as charging fees for consulting.[9]

Strayer's closest and most important network was probably the group of students he trained. Aspiring superintendents flocked to Teachers College, especially to the "eight-point practicum" Strayer established in the summer session of 1912, a class that aimed at finding solutions to the everday problems school administrators faced. Among the alumni of the 1914 practicum were nine "superintendents of schools in large cities . . . a county superintendent of schools who became one of the most constructive state superintendents in our educational history; three who became deans and directors of important schools of education; Dr. Strayer's colleague Dr. Englehardt; a director of an important experimental school," and others. Even more important than Strayer's influence as a teacher was his role as a placement baron, for he was one of the most powerful sponsors in the nation, especially in recommending educators for city superintendencies and key university positions. At one time sixteen of the eighteen superintendents in the largest American cities were former students of Strayer.[10]

Strayer employed dozens of students in directing his many surveys of state and local school systems. Surveys were systematic studies usually based on a blueprint of what good schools should look like. Living together in hotels far from home, talking at length to reach consensus on recommendations, usually working closely with local educators—such experiences helped to weld together the group of surveyors. The surveys enabled Strayer to give graduate students practical research training, to recruit new students, and to place graduates. Often it was one of his own alumni who invited him to make the survey in the first place. The survey also gave people like Strayer unusual leverage in getting local systems to adopt the changes he advocated.

Finally, Strayer was an influential member of the inner network of leaders in educational associations. President of the NEA in 1918–19, he helped to design and win acceptance for a new governance plan for the organization, a representative assembly. He was a member of the NEA's illustrious Educational Policies Commission and wrote its landmark report on *The Structure and Governance of Education in American Democracy.* President of the American Association of School Administrators, he was a leader in that organization's inner circle. A colleague recalled that at the meetings of that association the Teachers College graduates held "a great reunion." Strayer "held court in the lobby of the leading hotel."[11]

As Strayer's generation of administrative progressives was coming to power, there was an important metamorphosis in the character of educational associations. Like professional and trade groups in many domains, they grew in size, in internal complexity and specialization, and in impact on government. In the process, such private associations became in essence a species of private governments which not only influenced public legislation and administration in their fields of work, but also helped to determine who could enter occupations, what training and licenses practitioners must have, what knowledge or skills were considered legitimate, and what patterns of behavior were considered "professional." In so doing, as Larson has argued, professional associations controlled the marketing of expertise and enhanced their power in a society where legally recognized skills had become an important form of "property." Within such associations small networks of leaders—"hidden hierarchies"—exercised the primary leadership.[12]

In most respects, the development of a major educational association —the NEA—paralleled the history of associations in other fields such as law, medicine, architecture, engineering, library work, and nursing, as well as such academic specialties as economics or history. In the earliest stages the membership was small and elitist. The American Bar Association began with 73 members, the NEA with 43, the American Institute of Architects with 12, and the American Association of Public Accountants with 10. As late as 1900, the membership of the American Bar Association was only 1,540, 1.4 percent of lawyers in the United States; the same year the NEA enrolled only 2,332 members. Typically, says Gilb, the early associations "existed purely for fellowship and the interchange of technical information, or they served as informal clearinghouses for the promotion and organization of work among the 'better' members of the profession." Then, and throughout the history of most associations, the leaders were Caucasian middle-aged males of relatively high standing in their professions and with the free time required for association politics. At first, many professional groups excluded women and minorities either formally or informally, leading to the formation of separate associations for women and blacks. The male-dominated NEA did admit women to membership in 1866, but female teachers mostly joined single-sex local associations in the nineteenth century. The NEA did not become fully integrated racially until the 1960s.[13]

Most of the early national professional associations, like the NEA, had only rudimentary finances and administration. The NEA did not acquire its first full-time secretary until 1898, and in busy times he had to press his whole family into service addressing envelopes and licking stamps. His office was in his home, and he used his own typewriter until the association furnished him one in 1901. The NEA organization was loose; with no permanent headquarters, meeting as a whole once a year in summer conventions (its Department of Superintendence assembled separately in the winter), it relied heavily on a small cadre of leaders who kept in touch with one another through personal correspondence, had no university training in education, and relied little on the authority of "science." Membership and attendance at meetings fluctuated widely. One of its leaders, Charles W. Eliot, noting the casualness of these arrangements and the tendency to appoint committees and make resolutions with little forethought or public debate, observed that "such a body can be easily led, or misled, by designing persons, or persons with fads."[14]

Like many of the other early professional associations, the NEA had some of the characteristics of an elite men's club, at least in its inner governing circle. One leader wrote of his peers that they "were admirable administrators and what is more important they were powerful personalities. . . . They were on terms of great intimacy and friendship." Men were not elected but *tapped,* as in Yale's patrician clubs, to become officers. The president appointed a committee to nominate his successors, and nomination was tantamount to election. Glenn Smith described the process: "Open declaration of candidacy for offices was strictly taboo, but of course if friends and colleagues mentioned one's name prominently, the result might well be election." In his acceptance speech the new president was expected "to express complete surprise at the totally unsought, unexpected, and undeserved honor."[15]

Prominent among the old-guard leaders were Nicholas Murray Butler of Columbia and Charles W. Eliot of Harvard; William T. Harris, the United States commissioner of education, educational philosopher, and former St. Louis superintendent; and superintendents such as William Maxwell of New York, James Greenwood of Kansas City, and Albert Lane of Chicago. "They were the feudal barons of the pedagogical realm, the educational elite of the golden age of rugged individualism," wrote James Russell of Teachers College. "They were the Rockefellers, the Carnegies, the Morgans of our profession, when giants towered over the common herd."[16]

The individual interests of this "old guard" differed. Some were prominent in university circles. Some were self-made city superintendents. Few were formally trained in education or saw themselves as "scientists." Like Harvard's President Charles William Eliot, they were interested in standardizing and improving the quality of the secondary-school curriculum, partly to assure a larger flow of better-prepared students to higher education (throughout the nineteenth century there was a college student shortage). The Committee of Ten report on the high school was Eliot's triumph. There was a close relationship between the NEA and the USOE; educators had lobbied for the office, and commissioners such as Harris relied heavily on the superintendents in the association to help them collect statistics and to disseminate information. For the city superintendents the NEA provided one of the few forums in a decentralized occupation for sharing ideas, for creating national reputations; it was, in Upton Sinclair's phrase, "a dispenser of prominence." The meetings also reassured the small number of men who chose education as a lifelong career that their choice was a wise one and their mission indispensable; so they proclaimed it, frequently.[17]

In the twentieth century several groups challenged the power of this old guard as the NEA changed from a small, elite association to a massive and specialized one in which teachers formed the vast majority of members. One segment of the opposition was militant women teachers, led by organizers such as Margaret Haley. We shall discuss this challenge later. The new group of administrative progressives, the first generation of experts trained specifically in the science of education, was another competing group. These new leaders recognized the value —as did leaders in other occupations—of a large, politically powerful association in exercising influence over state governments and over members of the occupation. They supported increased standards of professional training in education and sought to base their influence on esoteric knowledge. They saw a need to regularize the chaotic politics of the NEA in the first two decades of the twentieth century by reforming its governance into a "representative assembly" in which they, nonetheless, could still exercise the key control through their personal networks of influence.[18]

A refurbished NEA, many administrative progressives thought, might constitute a new organization through which they could put their new conceptions of education into practice, establish their own reputations, make contacts to place the graduates of their own new programs. There was little love lost between the old guard and the new educational experts. Men like Maxwell of New York, for example, were furious at some of the new scientists for attacking as old-fashioned his curriculum and modes of supervision. City superintendents who had come up the hard way through the ranks, without benefit of Teachers College or Stanford, often resented the shortcuts provided by the placement networks which the barons created for their "boys."[19]

The new experts in education and their allies in the schools, especially curriculum specialists, sociologists, and administrators interested in vocationalizing the high school, came to dominate the new curriculum committees of the NEA on secondary education, pushing aside the college professors of academic subjects and university presidents like Eliot who had controlled the Committee of Ten in the 1890s. The usurpers were converts to the doctrines of "social efficiency" that lay at the heart of the educational program of the administrative progressives. Among members-at-large of the committee that wrote the influential report called *The Cardinal Principles of Secondary Education*

The "Educational Trust": Reform From the Top Down

(1918) were three education professors (one a university president who had recently been an education professor), the United States commissioner of education, a normal school principal, a YMCA secretary, and three state and local administrators. Men like Judd were important behind-the-scenes influences on the work of the curriculum committees.[20]

From time to time Judd and some of his peers in the educational trust had doubts about the utility of the politically volatile NEA, seeing it as "moribund" and "threatened with dissolution." He regarded the Department of Superintendence as "infinitely more influential as a gathering genuinely interested in educational reports and hitherto relatively free from the blighting influence of selfish politics." There the educational scientists could speak of their work to men who had the power to put the new designs into effect. An educational journalist observed that educators of substance much preferred to go to the winter meetings of the department rather than to the summer meetings of the association though they might not share Judd's enthusiasm for science.

> They find there the comradeship they seek. These men care vastly more for meeting one another incidentally and personally than they care for the program. . . . The fact that there are always sure to be at least a thousand men in attendance, that this is sure to include nine-tenths of the best known city and state superintendents, half a hundred college men and as many normal men, will lead every aspiring man to go if possible.

By contrast, Judd complained in 1917, the NEA meeting that year in Portland, Oregon, included "practically no one from Teachers College, Columbia; New York University; School of Education of Chicago; Harvard; University of Illinois or any other department of education of the leading universities east of the Rocky Mountains or from Washington, D.C."[21]

The Department of Superintendence, later the American Association of School Administrators, did become the chief forum of the new experts in educational administration. Through it they kept in touch with their former students, held important offices, and reached professional consensus. But astute leaders, like George Strayer and the superintendents and educationists who remained powerful in the NEA, realized that there were dangers in a kind of class and sex warfare in public education in which teachers (three-fourths women) and key administrators (almost all men) went their own ways organizationally—the teachers into unions such as Haley's Chicago Teachers' Federation or the new American Federation of Teachers (AFT) whose chapters were growing rapidly; and the administrators into a separate association. Not only would separate organizations create discord at the local level, but they would also prevent a "united profession" in education from achieving political power at the state and national levels. For a time in the second decade of the twentieth century it seemed to many observers that the de facto separation of management from practice, of supervision from teaching, would split the one *national* educational association apart.[22]

What actually happened, however, was that a key network of influential administrative progressives like Strayer in the universities and their allies in state departments of education and in the local school superintendencies managed to retain effective control of the NEA and its component state associations. Through building hidden hierarchies in such professional associations—in effect, powerful private governments —and in less evident ways in other groups such as the Cleveland Conference and their own placement networks, they gained an awesome power to define their own solutions to educational problems. Their solutions, accepted as standard by a growing number of educators, helped to create a potent professional consensus despite the formal decentralization of power in American public education.

From Patronage to Sponsorship: The Training and Placement of Educational Leaders

One of Cubberley's graduates wrote on assuming his first school superintendency that "the thing which will mean most to me will be Dad Cubberley's estimate of my work. I don't care what other people say— if Dad Cubberley says I've done a good job, I'll consider myself a success." The men who founded the science of school administration and advocated the corporate model of school governance were vitriolic in their condemnation of the older systems of local political patronage that had often determined who would climb the public-school ladders. The notion that "it was not what you knew but whom you knew that counted" violated the most elementary norms of meritocracy. But it is one of the best known secrets in the fraternity of male administrators, a frequent topic of the higher gossip at meetings though hardly ever discussed in print, that there were "placement barons," usually professors of educational administration in universities such as Teachers College, Harvard, University of Chicago, or Stanford who had an inside track in placing their graduates in important positions. One educator commented after spending a weekend with Cubberley in Palo Alto that "Cubberley had an educational Tammany Hall that made the Strayer-Engelhardt Tammany Hall in New York look very weak."[23]

Whatever one actually learned substantively in a graduate program in educational administration, to pay tuition was often to gain the sponsorship of a member of the educational trust, which was as sound an investment as buying a commission in the Czarist army. The new university leaders believed that they were finding able leaders, training them properly, and holding them accountable to high standards.[24]

The influence of university-based sponsors of superintendents and the graduate programs they represented depended, of course, on political configurations in the local school districts. The sponsor was a power broker only if the school board recognized his authority. The corporate model of school governance was predicated on the expertise of the school executive and on reform elites who would select and support him. In Detroit, for example, the local reformers who had fought for a new city charter and abolished the old ward-elected board of education turned for their superintendent to "the new school of professionally trained educators" and elected Charles Chadsey, trained at Teachers College and a protégé of George Strayer. To replace him the board wanted to appoint Randall Condon, another man with a doctorate in education, in lieu of Frank Cody, a local administrator with strong political connections in the Republican machine. The mayor, favoring Cody, quizzed Condon about "his position in the 'Educational Trust,'" but Condon assured him "that he was not connected with any trust which dictates the election of officers and that he had no knowledge of such a trust although he thought such a trust existed." In Minneapolis Frank Spaulding found a school board member "somewhat puzzled over the extent to which the faculty of Columbia Teachers College figured in the recommendations of Superintendents."[25]

The sponsorship system of professors and their alumni was not a matter that insiders wanted to make too public. The situation was not conspiratorial; it simply had to do with preserving advantages in the job market. Numerous scholars have examined the "inner fraternity" of influentials who advanced the careers of younger people in such fields as law, medicine, labor unions, and business. But it was not until Robert Rose's perceptive dissertation in 1969 that sponsorship in the superintendency was documented. According to Rose, in graduate programs of educational administration certain professors identified some of their students as able, ambitious, personable, and loyal future leaders. They taught and counseled them while in the program, often employing them in teaching or consulting. Frequently sponsors were hired as members of screening committees and were asked for recommendations of candidates for superintendencies. In this capacity, professors tended to fall into one of two groups: the *locals* who had a strong sphere of influence in their region (these were normally professors in state universities); and the *nationals,* persons who spoke and consulted across the nation, were active in the councils of AASA, and were frequently consulted about filling superintendencies in the most prestigious and largest districts (these have traditionally been professors in a few major, usually private, universities, of which Teachers College has been the outstanding example). Such professor–sponsors were powerful role models for their protégés, often referring to them as "my boys." They took vicarious pride in the successes of their graduates and kept in close touch with them throughout their careers.[26]

The relation between sponsor and alumnus was one of mutual advantage. In return for assistance in moving ahead on the chessboard of superintendencies, the alumnus helped the professor recruit students, invited the sponsor to consult for or survey his district, notified him of vacancies, helped place graduates, and kept him in touch with the field. The graduate turned to the sponsor for advice and help in getting ahead. His advancement often depended on pleasing his sponsor as well as the local school board (of course, the two were connected).

The system employed by professors at Teachers College illustrated this symbiosis in its fullest development under George Strayer, Paul Mort, and Nicolaus Engelhardt. "All of them," said one of Rose's informants, "had the knack of conveying the feeling that they were definitely aware of you as a person, had an affinity for you, and were concerned with being helpful to you in your future career. . . . They took pride in talking about 'their boys.' " The Columbia "barons" were persons "known to many board chairmen; they were known to practically all superintendents of schools." In the 1939 roster of the AASA, 287 superintendents held Teachers College M.A.'s and 32 had doctorates, a far greater proportion than that represented by any other university.[27]

Other institutions had similar networks of sponsors and students, though none so strong as Teachers College in the 1920s and 1930s. At the University of Chicago, William C. Reavis sponsored students and inspired a Reavis Club. One informant told Rose that Ellwood P. Cubberley of Stanford, "was kind of the sponsor and the mentor for practically all of the administrators in California in the early days." In some institutions—for example, Ohio State University—there were sponsors who knew practically all the superintendents of the state by their first names and had great influence with school boards in their region. It was partially the spread to other universities of professors who had been trained by the Columbia barons that broke the hegemony of Teachers College, for canny graduates emulated their sponsors. One alumnus of Columbia recalled that "once when Strayer and Engelhardt came out to——for a meeting . . . they expressed disappointment that they were not getting some consulting work in this state. I told them I couldn't see why I shouldn't be making that money as well as they." Another reason for the declining influence of the barons from a single university was the increasing use of a panel of consultants from several regions and institutions to screen superintendents.[28]

The fact that the sponsors could help alumni not only to find a first position, but also to move upward into larger and more prestigious districts gave them a powerful leverage. It seems generally to be the case that this relationship was mutually advantageous and normally not coercive. The man who wanted to please Dad Cubberley obviously admired the man and his educational policies; and he could, no doubt, find ways to be useful to his mentor both by emulating him and by more practical means, such as recommending that local staff members attend Stanford or that Stanford faculty members consult in his district. The personal warmth and concern the barons felt toward their boys probably lessened the isolated, anxious character of the superintendent's job.

At the same time, informal norms of the baronial system stressed loyalty. One principal recalled "Strayer's Law" for dealing with disloyal subordinates: "Give 'em the ax." Sensitivity to local values or courage to defend unpopular causes might count less in securing advancement, which usually meant moving to a better location on the administrative chessboard of school districts, than cultivating the approbation of a sponsor. The system did maintain accountability of a sort, for the sponsor wanted his word to count with school boards and expected his alumni to do well. But the network of obligations linked local superintendents more to their sponsors than to their local patrons and clients.[29]

Finally, the sponsorship system placed a premium on similarity of opinions and background characteristics and probably did much unconsciously to insure that the top positions in public education rarely went to women, to minorities, or to others deviating from the male, white, Anglo-Saxon Protestant norm. The ties between sponsors and their boys were forged in informal shared experiences as well as in classrooms or joint professional work. They relied on the kind of trust and quick understanding that often come from homogeneous backgrounds. It was easy to blame George Washington Plunkett of Tammany Hall when he rewarded his Irish-Catholic boys with jobs because he knew their ways and could trust them. The ideology and cultural blinders of the educational trust hid from them the fact that they, like Plunkett, were creating their own systems of patronage.[30]

Of course, there were many school superintendents who made it to the top through the old-fashioned technique of urban politics and who ruled their schools in ways that departed from the rational bureaucratic norms favored by the educational trust. One of these survivors was Frank Cody, superintendent of the Detroit public schools. A consummate politician, trained in the old machine ward days, highly personal in his approaches to leadership, he learned that the new politics of expertise could be profitably merged with the old, that "taking the schools out of politics" was a clever new game that one could play even without the blessing of Dad Cubberley or George Strayer.

The Leader as Political Boss: Frank Cody

Shortly after Frank Cody's election as superintendent of the Detroit Public Schools in 1919, a male board member visited him and said, "Frank, each morning I want you to come over to my office and tell me of your plans for the day before you take any action." "I'll do better than that," said Cody, "I'll come over and kiss you good morning." It was typical of Cody to sidle out of a tight spot with humor. The reformers on the school board were uneasy about their new superintendent, as were the women's clubs and good government groups in the city. If Ella Flagg Young's image in Chicago was that of the inner-directed Scotch pilgrim, Cody's in Detroit was that of the gregarious Irish politician with one wet finger up to gauge the direction of the wind.[31]

Local people knew that he matched in many ways the style of the ward politicians who had worked school politics for decades. He went to a barbershop first thing in the morning for a shave and news of local happenings. He spent much time with school board members in the bar of the Saint Claire Hotel because that was where he could find a quorum. He was active and popular in state and local Republican politics, and a jovial member of numerous lodges, social clubs, and luncheon clubs. His brother Fred was a textbook salesman, well versed (as were most of that breed) in the intricacies of local school politics.

To compound Cody's problems with the reform faction in Detroit, he lacked the educational credentials they wanted. Attending the State Normal School for only one year, he did not even have a B.A., much less a Ph.D. from Teachers College, Columbia. The president of his alma mater thought that was just fine. What education needed, he said, were "more schoolteachers and fewer hot-air artists. Frank Cody is mostly rank and file. Cody is not an educational West Pointer." He was free of such "pedagogical piffle" as "social efficiency" and "objective standards." Cody was hardly a scholar, not even much of a reader.[32]

What the reformers on the school board wanted was precisely a West Pointer, like Charles E. Chadsey, Ph.D., from Teachers College, who had just resigned. Enemies of the university-dominated network might call it an educational trust, but the good government people wanted a certified professional who was above politics. Some members favored Cody, however, and when the prime candidate withdrew, the board voted for Cody four to three, going against the advice of Chadsey, who had said that Cody's political talents were useful in a subordinate but dangerous in a superintendent. The reform group within the board then sought to restrict by resolution Cody's powers in policy and personnel decisions.

The attempt to curb his authority eventually failed, but Cody was a quick student and learned a page from Chadsey's book. Upon his election he had a subordinate release to the papers a paean to public education as a science and business. "Education has attained the position where it may now be called a science. There are many phases of this science . . . each of which requires the full attention of a specialist who has devoted years to a single phase of this subject." He spoke of his "expert advisers" and his "board of directors." And in his report for 1920 he argued that research gave educators a "method which will in time solve every problem, hold a key for every lock. . . . Already the schools are humming with the strength of progress. Already the outlines of a new day may be faintly seen." Whether Cody fully believed in his own millennial rhetoric is questionable. The story is told of him that when one of his psychologists urged the use of more objective examinations, he replied that "what our teachers need is more testicles, not more tests." Seen cynically, the gospel of science was a useful new hustle, a way to sell ideas without appearing partisan. It is clear that Cody's adoption of the educational trust's lingo and program gave him an important defense against his prime critics, the advocates of professional expertise and business efficiency. In any case, he proved to be remarkably long-lived in office, superintendent in Detroit for twenty-three years from 1919 to 1942, through boom and bust, rounding out a career of a half-century in the schools of Detroit and its annexed suburb of Delray.[33]

Actually, Cody never abandoned the political strategies that had linked him successfully to the Detroit community. He remained an active Republican, an energetic clubman, and a man linked closely with business organizations in the city. What he did was to add to this network an alternate network of contacts with the group of cosmopolitan educational leaders whom Chadsey had represented. It was possible to break into this inner circle even without proper educational credentials if one were a successful city superintendent and knew how to play association politics. He became a member of the executive committee of the NEA Department of Superintendence in 1921 and its president in 1929; president of the NEA in 1927; member of the Cleveland Conference; and chairman of Herbert Hoover's White House Conference on Crisis in Education, investigating how schools might deal with retrenchment. Cody was a talented politician in both local and national networks, and each provided a kind of insurance policy against adversity. The web of local people, bound by obligation and friendship, sustained his position in the city and gave him support in hard times like the 1930s. His range of contacts elsewhere, through professional associations, gave him access to expertise valued by his board and knowledge of other job opportunities should he chance to leave Detroit.

Cody learned early that politics counted in getting and holding a teaching job. He gained his first position in Belleville because his father was on the school board; he lost it because a new school board member decided *his* son would make a better teacher. After teaching at the one-room school at Willow Run that Henry Ford later restored in a fit of nostalgia, Cody went on to teach a graded school in Belleville and then went to normal school. There he picked up some tips from the placement director, a kindred spirit, who said it was wise to be in debt to the boss on the school board—good insurance for tenure; and that "if you have a good idea for advancing the schools, get the head school board member to absorb it and to think it is his own." Cody was already learning the indirect style of influence that later became one of his hallmarks. He was also practicing the gamesmanship he later perfected: when he went to get a teacher's certificate, he bet a friend that the examiner had only tests for the second grade. Cody and his crony insisted on being examined for a first grade certificate, and the flustered official gave them a first grade rating for passing a second grade exam.[34]

A man with a dramatic flair, Cody was a master of the art of self-promotion and knew the value of becoming a local legend. His first job after normal school was in Delray, a river town, later annexed by Detroit, where ruffian students had intimidated many teachers before him. He walked down the street past the saloons and scruffy dogs, a pedagogical Matt Dillon, as the boys took his measure. As he entered the schoolhouse, he pulled from his pocket a length of rubber beer hose. A pupil recalled that on

> our first morning with Cody as our teacher . . . he sat behind his desk on the usual mouse-infested dais looking quite stern and dignified. His hair stood up in the uprightest pompadour my young eyes had ever beheld. . . . His red tie covered his bosom so completely that one had to take his shirt for granted. His white-winged collar and white barrel cuffs were to us impressive insignias of his office. Who ever heard in Delray of anyone dressing up so much on a week-day?

Most impressive of all was the blackened, waxed, enormous twirl of his moustache, his "warlike moustache," as Cody later called it. He wanted to get along with all the students, he said, "but if you try to impose on me, w-o-o-oe be unto you!" And with that he slammed his rubber hose with a thwack on the desk. Word got out that he was "a first cousin of Buffalo Bill Cody." The teacher also used the sting of wit; his bons mots at the expense of a boy would go the rounds of the barbershop and the blacksmith shop and the street corners where Delray males gathered. But it was not mainly because of the rubber hose or sharp wit that Cody triumphed, but because of his enthusiasm and friendliness.[35]

His gregariousness served him well as he moved outward into the community and became superintendent. He got to know the local factory foreman and arranged jobs for his pupils; he swapped jokes with bartenders; he had tea with such socialites as the town afforded. But above all he made his way into the all-male preserves of the lodges and businessmen's clubs: the Odd Fellows, the Masons, the Knights of Pythias, and the Delray Club. "There is a free and easy atmosphere in a stag organization which makes for quick friendships and fruitful associations that do not so readily bloom in the relatively sterile soil of a polite drawing room," observed Cody's biographer and colleague. Through such all-male enclaves Cody "developed the friendships which proved invaluable in personal adversity and public council." And here, of course, were sources of support that were blocked to women administrators like Ella Flagg Young.[36]

When the Delray schools were absorbed into the Detroit system in 1906, Cody was reduced in status to a high school principal. In 1913, however, he was promoted to general supervisor in the central office in charge of adult education, community recreation, special education, and summer schools. The next year he became an assistant superintendent. He proved a skillful administrator in these programs of outreach of the schools, greatly expanding their enrollments and rationalizing their operation. His contacts with the Board of Commerce and with local manufacturers focused on "Americanization" of the enormous numbers of immigrants flocking to the factories. Labor unrest and fears of subversive ethnic enclaves prompted employers and the federal government to cooperate with the public schools in attracting immigrants to evening schools where they studied English and American government. An ardent advocate of assimilation, Cody shared businessmen's fears about the "hyphenated class" whose presumed ignorance constituted a danger to the society.

The "West Pointer" Chadsey appointed Cody as assistant superintendent. Although Chadsey distrusted Cody as one tarred with the brush of "politics" and not one of the educationally annointed, he found him very useful as liaison with the ward-dominated school board that had elected him by a fluke. Chadsey despised the board but was forced to gain its approval for all policy decisions, including the appointment of teachers and routine administration. Since Cody was on good terms with board members, Chadsey delegated him to confer with them to secure appointments and to get the work of the schools done—the conference taking place usually, as we have seen, in the bar of the Saint Claire Hotel. Cody was friendly not only with the school politicians, but also with his fellow administrators in Detroit (whom Chadsey saw as ignoramuses and held in contempt because they were "not associated with the educational movement sponsored by the group which he represented"). Caught in the middle, deserted by some of his "friends," Cody seemed a turncoat to both sides, and in 1918 the psychological pressures destroyed his health and forced him to take a six-week leave for treatment and relief.[37]

During this difficult time of ambiguous status between 1913 and his election in 1919, Cody invested much of his energy in cultivating outside allies. He was nominated by the Republicans for the state board of education and was elected in 1913, became active in the Board of Commerce, joined church and social groups, and expanded his memberships in lodges. He entered classier circles, but kept the familiar touch with old cronies. Much like his contemporary, Dale Carnegie, he was convinced that the route to success lay through a crowd of "friends." Underneath the optimism of both men lay considerable insecurity. As superintendent he urged Detroit teachers and administrators to join groups of citizens and befriend all kinds of people. Even on a European trip he tried to obey the Cody rule of making six friends a day. He told graduating high school seniors that "you can get along in this world with very little algebra, but you can't get along without friends. Latin and mathematics are the bunk unless they are complemented with other essentials of a well-grounded education. The greatest knowledge of the world today is the knowledge of getting along with people." Yet underneath the affable surface, Cody was an enigma. Everyone knew Frank —which was what he encouraged his male colleagues to call him—but few knew him intimately. Perhaps no one did.[38]

When Cody took over the superintendency in 1919 he quickly achieved and maintained far more effective control over the large bureaucracy than Chadsey, the certified administrative expert, had ever attained. Despite the jargon of scientific research and business methods, his approach to control remained intensely personal, his system of information and implementation based on networks of loyal subordinates. With his contacts giving him inside information, he was able to anticipate difficulties. When trouble brewed, his standard remedy, as in the much smaller Delray, was to put on his hat and go see the people involved; for lesser matters, a telephone call would do. He knew most of the staff personally or by reputation, could talk with them on a first-name basis, and like a good politician knew their hopes and tastes and weak spots.

An extraordinarily competent man himself, he respected and rewarded ability, but loyalty was the prime virtue. When employees performed badly, he would personally seek to rehabilitate them by transferring them, warning them, or by arbitrating differences—*if* they were loyal. A favorite strategy for dealing with two staff members who were in conflict was to summon them to his office and demand that the accuser repeat charges to the other. If the complainer refused to do so, the case was dismissed, and in other conflicts the confrontation usually resulted in a settlement.

Often Cody relied on humor to sidestep problems. Once he talked with an unmarried woman teacher who was living in the same apartment with her lover. Parents of her students living in the same building had complained. The dialogue:

> "Miss Jones," he inquired, "do you know what?"
> "What?" she asked, logically.
> "There's a *scandal* in your building!"
> "No! There is?"

"Yes!"

"I'll move!" announced Miss Jones, who forthwith did so.[39]

Cody's legendary wit often extricated him from tight corners. Dick Gregory once observed that he learned to be funny as a child because he discovered that bigger boys would not beat him up if he got them laughing. Cody had a way of defeating earnest opponents by making them appear ridiculous. When Congressman Martin Dies of the House Un-American Activities Committee claimed to have discovered ten teachers and administrators who were Communists, reporters asked Cody what he thought about the accusation. Cody replied: "There are eight thousand teachers in our school system, and if ten of them are red and the remainder well read, I would be satisfied." When a member of a school board anxiously asked him what was "the proper length of a teacher's skirt?" Cody replied with his customary male chauvinism that "I cannot tell until I have a look at her." Although he could be pompous in his speeches—especially when his ghost writers inserted the "pedagogical piffle" his normal school president deplored—on his own he was more likely to give such advice to teachers as "be thorough and don't let them throw you out the window." He realized that omni-purpose professional "bafflegab" had its place on solemn occasions when pomposity was expected, but his own lingo was pungent. He used anecdotes and humor as a form of problem solving.[40]

Although Cody knew very well what was happening in his system and although his temper could intimidate his subordinates, his characteristic method of issuing instructions was not giving orders but making hints. This indirection was calculated. A colleague estimated that Cody gave about 90 percent of his orders as suggestions. One of his staff described the process thus:

In a brief two-man conference, Cody let fall a suggestion in which he who willed might read his orders.

The subordinate went to his own office to digest those orders.

He found that the superintendent's ideas conflicted with his own.

He paid Cody a call; in a generalized discussion of the subject, he sought to guide Cody's thinking into his own channel.

If the superintendent saw the point and agreed, he made additional suggestions in which the revised direction was implicit.

If the superintendent disagreed, the disagreement, while not specifically stated, was quickly obvious.

The "Educational Trust": Reform From the Top Down

The approach had benefits and disadvantages. It allowed staff members to insert their own ideas without directly confronting the boss, hence encouraging their inventiveness. But it also placed a premium on ability to read the mind of the superintendent, increasing the personalism and power of his rule.[41]

When subordinates stepped out of line or failed to sense Cody's disapproval, he was a master at stonewalling them with bureaucratic ploys. If a principal, for example, pushed a favorite new idea of which Cody disapproved, he might be referred from one official to another or to a committee that dallied endlessly. "Procrastination, new considerations, variable factors and prolix ramifications would get in their deadly work; the result was usually quite predictable." Cody had his puckish side.[42]

Cody prided himself on having an open door in his office, ever ready to respond to the public, its complaints and suggestions. Newspapermen especially appreciated his willingness and his salty language. Cody was, said one, "the best politician in Detroit, in the best sense of the word." "I always try to find out what the people want done in their schools and the community and then set out to do it," Cody said. "I have always believed that leadership in public life consists of finding out the significant social, economic, political, and educational trends, and then I have used my best administrative judgment in directing those trends in such a manner as to give the people what they want." To a friend he admitted having no conscious philosophy of education: "A school man will always see a lot of things that should be done. He picks out what seems to him to be the most important and does 'em." A colleague observed of him that his "high skill is the art of zig-zagging without allowing himself to be caught in a zig."[43]

Although Cody wore a populist hat and responded to local demands in an opportunistic manner, his actual program resembled the template of reform laid down by the university-based experts like Strayer and Cubberley: carefully planned school buildings, testing and record-keeping systems, departmentalized instruction in the elementary schools, the establishment of junior high schools, elaborate programs of vocational training, the "socialization" of the curriculum with particular attention to Americanization, a research department aimed at "omnipotence in determining the course of instruction," better training of teachers, and a formal hierarchy of supervision. These he sought to install during the 1920s and to defend against retrenchment during the 1930s.[44]

Starting out under the cloud of ward politics, lacking the training and sponsorship of the university barons, Cody rapidly learned how to act like a member of the inner circle when he achieved the superintendency. Despite his talk of finding out what "the people" want, he knew that certain "men were important in the community" and that they and his board "composed of high-type citizens" scorned the old ward game of logrolling and wanted the Detroit schools to adopt the programs of the administrative progressives. In his network of professional peers—as in the Department of Superintendence—he picked up the latest blueprints for school reform. And while modernizing his schools according to these new designs he could easily have persuaded himself as well as his patrons that the new-made education would bring progress. A local and a cosmopolitan, still in touch with his old political supporters and well connected with the city's power elite, he zigged on his new professional course, canny enough to be aware that the old political zag was a thing of the past.

Research That Made a Difference: Numbers Into Norms

The members of the educational trust believed that people could control their own future through the conscious application of "science" to social problems. Better education was the key to social efficiency, a way to bring about a smoothly meshing social order. Research was thus not just a specialized activity of scholars but a means of generating norms of practice.

One apostle of reform through research, David Snedden, was described by a skeptical contemporary as "a knight dressed in the armor of Science driving galloping steeds of Specialization, Mechanization, and Corporate Organization into the millennium of a great culture." The writings and actions of such men expressed a quasi-religious crusade of efficiency against waste, of exact methods of determining educational policies against the older guesswork. Paul Monroe wrote in 1911 that through educational research "truly a decade of the future should show greater results than have generations of the past."[45]

In 1930 George Strayer argued that "significant progress in the administration of city school systems during the past twenty-five years is due primarily to two causes. First, the application of the scientific method to the problems of administration, and, second, the professional training of school executives." According to Strayer, these were the marks of advance:

- development of clear line and staff organization;
- reorganization of traditional uniform elementary and secondary schools into differentiated institutions, including junior high schools, that treated individuals and groups according to abilities and needs;
- creation of special classes for the "backward, delinquent, physically handicapped and the like," vocational tracks, and instruction in subjects like health and physical education;
- professionalization of the occupations of teaching and administration by upgraded standards of education, certification, tenure, specialization of function, and supervision;
- standardization of methods of "pupil accounting" and enforcement of attendance;
- introduction of "sound business administration" in budgeting, plant planning and maintenance, and finance.[46]

What Strayer meant by "research" had an important impact on practice in that quarter century, and most of the changes he cited were implemented. His colleague Carter Alexander gave a useful definition of how entrepreneurs conceived of research in educational administration. It seeks, he wrote, "to discover, in the light of the purposes of education commonly acknowledged, the most efficient procedures in the organization, supervision, finance, and evaluation of the program of educational service." Such an approach he contrasted with one that relies "upon the sanction of tradition or current practice." In theory it was a form of "social engineering," a strategy of identifying practical problems and finding practical solutions empirically tested. It stressed managerial concerns more than those of classroom instruction.[47]

In actuality the administrative progressives tended to have prefabricated solutions to preconceived problems. One reason for this was that they did not inquire in any fundamental or open-minded way into the conflicting goals of education, but tended to take purposes for granted, as "commonly acknowledged" in Alexander's phrase. Jesse Newlon described administrators' ideology as "a confused mixture of the prevailing laissez-faire social and economic philosophy and the philosophy of business efficiency, with a vague democracy and Christian idealism." The administrative progressives often ignored conflicts of class interest or cultural values in society. The engineering analogy is an instructive one. It is as if a group of experts in constructing freeways simply assumed that people wanted them and went about building them through city and countryside without assessing the social costs and alternatives.[48]

There are many reasons why such applied educational research had, as Strayer asserted, considerable impact. One is that professors of edu-

searchers and professors of administration probably saw no incongruity in making money by marketing the reforms they thought to be right and good.[53]

Although social engineers in education were quite clear about their assessment of social and educational needs, they were less clear about the philosophical premises of their values or the political process by which priorities should be set. Somehow the assemblage of facts would speak for itself. Their faith in science as objective measurement, coupled with their contempt for earlier "armchair theorizing" about educational purposes as mere opinion, tended to simplify or even eliminate issues of ethical choice for them.

They wanted to use research for reform in education and society within a framework of privilege and values they rarely questioned. Quantitative studies of the relation between occupations and the distribution of I.Q. scores, for example, seemed to justify the existing social order. If, by and large, the "smart" people had the good jobs and the "dumb" people the poor jobs, then society was as it should be. And not only were the smart people the most prosperous; they were also the most virtuous, statistically speaking. Thorndike concluded that "the correlation between intelligence and morality is approximately .3, a fact to which perhaps a fourth of the world's progress is due." In an increasingly conformist organizational society it was easy to jump from statistical norms to social norms.[54]

Despite, or perhaps because of, these blind spots the scientific movement swept American education. Starting from meager beginnings early in the twentieth century, educational research became institutionalized and won impressive financial support. Educational research bureaus found a secure niche in universities. The number of doctoral theses in education steadily grew from 53 in 1918 to 189 in 1927, while the number of university research bureaus jumped in those years from 7 to 29. In 1922 the NEA founded its Research Department. Several national organizations of educational researchers appeared, including the National Society of College Teachers of Education, the Educational Research Association, and the National Society for the Study of Education.[55]

Foundations began to fund educational research on a large scale in the years following 1910, and two of them—the Russell Sage Foundation and the General Education Board (endowed by John D. Rockefeller)—conducted their own school surveys as well as other research. In 1920 the Commonwealth Fund began a six-year program of awarding about $100,000 per year to educational researchers. In the 1920s the Carnegie

The "Educational Trust": Reform From the Top Down

Corporation sponsored comprehensive studies of curricula in engineering, history, classics, teacher education, intelligence testing, business administration of school systems, and other subjects. In its first three-and-a-half years the Institute of Educational Research of Teachers College received almost $700,000 in funds, mostly from foundations. Walter Monroe estimated that for the late 1920s probably over $5 million a year were spent in educational research, a huge sum considering the novelty of the field and the higher value of the dollar at that time.[56]

Education was, of course, only one of the fields in which applied scientific research was multiplying. David Noble has described the central role of engineers and other researchers and scientific managers in the leading sectors of American business. In agriculture, as well, research and demonstration projects were transforming the nature and scale of farming. The administrative progressives in education were acutely aware of these precedents and models for their own work. They commonly used the increased productivity of scientific farming as an analogy for the scientifically designed educational system they hoped to build.[57]

Some administrative progressives turned to the large business corporation for models of scientific management in education. In particular, they were interested in four aspects of the managerial revolution. First, in city schools they hoped to emulate the corporate model of governance by elite board and expert manager. Second, they believed that efficient management depended on rich and accurate flows of information to the superintendent, much as industrial leaders monitored flows of raw materials through processing to markets (thus educators wanted to know, for example, how many children there were in the district, what new school buildings would be needed, what standardized tests showed about what children were learning, and how regularly children were promoted). Third, educators, like businessmen, wanted to use the budgeting process not only to review past fiscal performance but also to plan ahead, including cost-benefit justification of old and new expenses (Spaulding was a leading exponent of this application of business methods). Finally, they sought to specify in precise ways how teachers in classrooms could turn out pupils with the skills and attitudes the "public" supposedly wanted. People such as Cubberley and Franklin Bobbitt drew elaborate analogies between stockholders and citizens, general managers of factories and superintendents of schools, foremen and principals, and specifications of shop tasks and precisely calibrated lesson plans.[58]

This industrial analogy for schooling put educational research at front stage center. But such an analogy fit better the burgeoning management side of education than it did the work of classroom teachers. The effect of Frederich W. Taylor's work in industrial management was to rationalize and systematize the human factors of production, vesting direction in the experts at the top and deskilling work at the bottom. It went far beyond management practices of information-gathering, planning, budgeting, and public relations that could be easily emulated by "educational executives." To Taylorize the classroom would have meant prescribing and enforcing the specific tasks students performed under the eyes of their teachers. It would have been the last step in separating the management of learning from those who actually taught and studied, in divorcing planning and execution. The ultimate power over education then would have rested in the hands of those researchers who determined the curriculum. Not surprisingly, some educators —like Bobbitt—welcomed such an opportunity to specify classroom learning in minute detail.[59]

Schools never achieved the organizational controls or technological breakthroughs in instruction that would have paralleled mass production increases in industry. The heart of the school—the classroom— proved more resistant to change than did the factory floor. Study after study has shown that the "core technology" of classroom instruction has remained relatively stable, despite periodic cults of efficiency and new reigning philosophies. Indeed, the "cellular" classroom of teacher and students retained well into the twentieth century the institutional imprint of the nineteenth-century graded school. Students were not inert "raw material" to be processed. Behind the classroom door, teachers resisted dictation from above. Even Cubberley, who promoted the industrial analogy, admitted that "education is not working with iron and brass and leather, but with human beings." Cubberley's colleague, Jesse Sears, also an enthusiast for efficiency, wrote after reading works by Taylor that his "analysis of actual performance seemed important to me, yet I realized that the product of educational effort is not as tangible and measurable as is that of business or industrial effort. Education works to achieve values that lie beyond learning to spell or add or read or write, the results of which we can now measure."[60]

Despite the desire of educational researchers and "executives" to emulate business organization, the adaptation of new techniques of management came only piecemeal and in stages. Talk of "business efficiency" in education could not abolish three problems: the "output" of education was far more difficult to measure than the product of a factory; the goals of schooling were more ambiguous than profit and loss in a business; and the connection between the new organizational techniques and either goals or output was by no means clear. Nevertheless, under the corporate model of urban school governance, some rough parallels appeared between the structure of business enterprise and the organization of city schools: a large growth in the staff of the central office (where once only the superintendent and perhaps two or three assistants or clerks held sway); diversification of the structure of the schools into functional divisions such as vocational schools, guidance departments, attendance services, building and maintenance, and special schools for the handicapped; and the creation of research and planning departments to provide evidence on operations and data for forecasting. Forms multiplied and files bulged. New corps of specialists appeared. Indeed, so complex became the subdivisions that large cities sometimes required intermediate layers of supervisors of specialists so that the total number of administrators reporting to the superintendent would not be too great for effective span of control.[61]

Conceptions of research and new organizational forms borrowed from business did influence those who wished to engineer public education into a pedagogical conglomerate parallel to the economic sector. But the borrowing went the other way, too—from education to business. Industrial psychologists learned from school experts how to use ability and aptitude tests. Pioneers in vocational guidance in schools helped to shape personnel departments in business. Schools were often far in advance of industry in the use of cumulative record forms. Social scientists in business employed familiar classroom techniques such as sociometry to detect informal group leaders and role playing to train foremen. Like schools, some industries employed psychological counselors to adapt workers to the organization. Taking all these precedents into account, one psychologist argued that industrial utopia would result if business would make as effective use of applied social science as did educators.

Both educators and businessmen did face some similar problems of "human engineering." With the advent of compulsory schooling, school people found that they had unwilling clients who had to be taught, sorted, co-opted. Employers, too, found that human engineers might help them lessen high rates of turnover, loafing on the job, absenteeism, and strikes among workers who found deskilled work alienating.

As Loren Baritz has shown, employers had waves of enthusiasm for psychological testing and other managerial uses of research, but adult workers often proved recalcitrant, and unions were suspicious of manipulative intent. In public education, where the clients were children and youth, and the tools produced by the new research were presumably for their benefit, less resistance appeared. Willing and usually unwitting servants of the new forms of corporate power, researchers in both schools and industry rarely questioned the premises of the unequal social order they buttressed.[62]

What's the Score? School Surveys and the Politics of Professionalism

"The policy of rating and standardizing has been discovered to be an excellent means of molding public opinion in its constructive attitude toward education," wrote a Johns Hopkins education professor in 1914. The growing movement to survey schools would probably "not have taken form had it not been for the norms, standards, and scales established during the preceding decade," he added. The public and educators wanted to know the score—how did their state or district *rate*? The new experts in education were eager to give the answers as they laid their templates of approved practices on states or localities and measured their approximation to the new professional models. The survey enabled them to compare one system with others.[63]

From one point of view the school survey movement was but a late episode in a long romance between educators and facts, especially facts that could be used to inspire reform. Early school crusaders like Horace Mann and Henry Barnard, filling pages with reams of statistics, had used their annual reports to publicize meager training and pay of teachers, run-down schoolhouses, and chaotic curriculum. In 1845 Mann's friends on the Boston School Board had created the first large-scale written testing program to find out what pupils were learning, in large part to justify the need for change and to support Mann in his battle with the schoolmasters. Faith in the benefits of the diffusion of knowledge—that characteristic hope of the enlightenment mind—undergirded the formation of the United States Bureau of Education and the information-gathering and information-dispensing functions of state departments of education. In 1885 John Philbrick published a classic study of city school systems in the conviction that comparison of defects and virtues of urban education would produce a beneficial standardization.[64]

In 1897, on the eve of the scientific study of education, muckraker-scholar Joseph Meyer Rice presented his survey of instruction in spelling to the Department of Superintendence of the NEA. The moguls were not amused, for they liked their own facts better. "The educators who discussed his findings and those who reviewed them in the educational press united in denouncing as foolish, reprehensible, and from every point of view indefensible, the effort to discover anything about the value of the teaching of spelling by finding out whether or not the children could spell," wrote Leonard Ayres later. But soon the scientific, comparative survey would sweep the nation as a kind of crusade, leading one observer to call one such survey "An Educational Revival."[65]

George Strayer defined a survey as

> an inquiry concerning public education which seeks to acquaint the public with all of the educational agencies supported in whole, or in part, by public moneys, with respect to their organization, administration, supervision, cost, physical equipment, courses of study, teaching staff, methods of teaching, student body, and results as measured by the achievements of those who are being trained or have been trained therein.

In theory, the survey informed the public about existing conditions, educated it about proper standards, and inspired citizens to improve the schools. The survey fit in beautifully with the notion of expert leadership becoming prominent in university programs of research and training in education and with elite approaches to urban reform in the Progressive era. It helped muckrakers to expose evils, foundation officials to gain leverage to change society, and federal or state educational bureaucrats to enlarge governmental power to regulate or standardize.[66]

At first, local superintendents generally resented school surveys and saw them as investigations by outsiders made with invidious intent. Rapidly, however, the technique became accepted and used both by school people and by outside experts to create the kind of professionalization that both the surveyors and the local educators desired. By the late 1920s, specialized institutes for field studies located in universities became the chief agency for surveying; the largest and most famous was the one headed by George Strayer at Teachers College. In 1928, eleven of the twelve major city surveys that year were directed either by Strayer or by one of the men he had trained.

Some of the early-twentieth-century studies of school systems were classic examples of muckraking, often initiated by a few local people who invited outside experts to expose defects and propose remedies. An instance of this occurred in Greenwich, Connecticut, in 1911, when citizens asked Ayres to investigate their schools. He found that there was a nonsystem of education, "a school conglomeration," that the town had been pinchpenny, and that the only statistic of the school system that was above average was the number of vermin. For the second richest town in the United States such conditions were appalling. What was needed, said Ayres, was "a permanent school policy and an intelligent public sentiment that shall demand, as the inalienable right of each child, pure air, sufficient warmth for comfort, uncontaminated water, lighting that does not ruin eyesight, protection from the perils of fire, school locations not dangerous to health, and decent toilets." Ayres addressed his report to the public in a twenty-four-page pamphlet that used pictures and comparative statistics to shame the people of the town into remedying the situation.[67]

Members of the privately financed New York Bureau of Municipal Research specialized in exposing inefficiency in education, and its reports were critical of any departure from a priori standards. In St. Paul, for example, the surveyors deplored that the superintendent of schools worked in a "noisy and public office," a choice deliberately made by the superintendent so that "he might be accessible to the citizens" of the city. One member of the Bureau of Municipal Research, William H. Allen, helped to initiate a massive inquiry into the New York schools led by Harvard professor Paul Hanus. Hanus later concluded that Allen wanted a hatchet job to discredit the schools since Allen disliked Superintendent William H. Maxwell and wanted a position for himself in the system. The survey of the Portland public schools in Oregon in 1913 was also close to the muckraking genre, revealing inefficient administration and extreme rigidity in instruction under Superintendent Frank Rigler.[68]

Not surprisingly, the earlier generation of city school superintendents, who had dominated the NEA during the 1890s and had been the most prestigious public educators at the turn of the century, reacted negatively to the scientific whippersnappers who now tried to tell them how to run their schools. Like Henry Adams, who had been told that the way to make a name as historian was to "break glass," the younger educational scientists, often based in universities or foundations and private research bureaus, sought to build their own reputations by attacking the achievements of the old guard. Maxwell, a giant of the earlier generation, was scornful of "time-wasting, energy-destroying statistical research." Why was it that college professors themselves did not apply such tests to their own work, grading "English compositions of Seniors on a scale graduated from the style of William H. Allen, of New York, up to the style of Charles W. Eliot, of Harvard?" The new quantifiers were panaceamongers, he said, inebriated with their own infallibility. A number of other superintendents joined Maxwell in regarding the new investigators as yet another species of pesty outsiders.[69]

After the first shock of the muckraking style of reports and the gradual replacement of the old-guard superintendents by people trained to appreciate quantitative approaches to reform, local educators began to soften their attitudes toward surveys. Instead of conflict between outside experts and district officials, the relationships became increasingly amicable. Strayer argued in 1914 that a survey should not be an investigation of incompetence, a thinly disguised trial of incumbents, but, rather, constructive in intent, cooperative with district leaders, and designed to produce public support for changes which backward fellow educators or a sleepy public may not have recognized.[70]

The superintendent of schools in Boise admitted that educators sometimes feared a survey because it might "stimulate that spirit of unrest which is always present whether or not it be justified" but argued that when Strayer, Judd, and Elliot came to study his system, it had the opposite effect. Take hold of the survey, he said to fellow superintendents, and use it to prove that you are doing a good job and to educate the public "to bear the burden of further constructive effort." People attacked superintendents for too much industrial training or too little, for not enough grammar or too much, and "we are damned if we do and we are damned if we don't." An outside group of experts, he said, could strengthen the position of the superintendent by approving what was efficient and endorsing needed changes, above all by expressing a consensus of professional judgment on what a good school system should be. Although some surveys showed extravagant expenditures of public funds, he pointed out, by far the larger number demonstrated the need to spend more to achieve equitable and effective schooling. A prominent surveyor, Calvin Kendall, state superintendent in New Jersey, argued that surveys had produced useful inventories of conditions, taught school people how to use new tools and scales of measurement of instruction, showed citizens the complexity of social engineering done by superintendents, exposed the need for new funds and buildings, instructed boards about how to delegate decisions to the superintendent, and suggested more effective modes of teaching.[71]

Foundations such as John D. Rockefeller's General Education Board (GEB), the Russell Sage Foundation, and the Carnegie Corporation became interested in upgrading poor school systems through the use of statistical comparisons and surveys. We have already shown how the GEB underwrote research used as publicity in the educational crusade in the southern states in the early twentieth century. Both Sage and the GEB had their own research departments that conducted surveys of states and local districts, led by such distinguished scholars as Ayres and Abraham Flexner. Flexner's famous 1910 survey of American medical schools had convinced foundations of the value of such studies in standardizing and rating educational institutions. In 1912 Ayres published an index for Sage that assessed the comparative efficiency of educational systems in the forty-eight states, ranking each according to composite performance on a series of ten variables, including average daily attendance, per-pupil costs, length of school terms, and teacher salaries.[72]

The foundations also sponsored and sometimes conducted state surveys in which an important focus was inequity in educational opportunities in different districts of the state. The emphasis in most of these comparative surveys was on the supply side of the educational equation, on such matters as buildings, per-pupil expenditures, and training of teachers. Hence the studies could be—and were—used to increase and equalize funding for education. Reformers exhorted citizens in states or localities low in the ratings to raise their standing; state departments of education developed scorecards that patrons could use to rank their local schools as "standard" or "superior."[73]

One important type of school survey, often sponsored by foundations or coordinated by the United States Bureau of Education, was designed to help state legislatures to revise school laws. Here the impact was greatest when legislators were predisposed to reform, as was the case in many parts of the country. Between 1905 and 1910, twenty-eight states appointed educational commissions to investigate educational problems; some of these employed experts to help in the work. In 1914 the Carnegie Foundation for the Advancement of Teaching conducted the first truly comprehensive survey of a state educational system. Invited by the Vermont legislature, the Carnegie group under its president, Henry Pritchett, presented lawmakers with specific suggestions for new legislation to reorganize the schools. Many other states from Virginia to California employed survey techniques, ranging from a fullfledged investigation of the results of instruction in the former state to Cubberley's personal writing of the legislative committee's report on reorganization of schools in the latter. The aim of most foundation officials and most surveyors was not muckraking or reform so much as it was to arouse public interest in improvement that would be "not too far removed from present conditions" to be impractical.[74]

The Oklahoma study authorized by the legislature in 1921 and conducted by the United States Office of Education was an example of a

The "Educational Trust": Reform From the Top Down

survey that discovered gross inequalities in schooling of whites, Negroes, and Indians, both in finance and in educational achievement. While most state surveys ended with recommendations for state laws, some argued that rallying the people to action in their local communities was equally important. In New York State, for example, the Commonwealth Fund supported a rural school study in which farm groups, such as the Grange and the Dairymen's League, joined forces with the state department of education to publicize hearings on education and the findings of the survey. The committee of representatives from these organizations concluded after hundreds of local meetings that, "regardless of legislation such as it hopes eventually to see enacted, the reawakening that has come among our rural school patrons and the stimulation of interest and broadening of vision on the part of those engaged in the teaching profession have been much more to the State than all time and money expended."[75]

The social psychology of surveys illustrated how new norms of leadership spread through private networks of experts and their colleagues in the schools. As early as 1912 the surveyors were so closely linked as a group that when a member of the Portland Chamber of Commerce wrote to seven educators across the nation for nominations of people to do a survey of city schools, they nominated each other with astonishing regularity. When surveyors gathered in cities such as Butte or Cleveland, they cemented professional friendships and ideological consensus in long discussions of what they had seen in the schools. They were able to create and retail their own reputations and those of the superintendents they studied. Above all, surveyors could exercise power by defining what was normal and desirable by adapting national standards to local conditions. The fact that the Cleveland Conference grew out of the Cleveland survey was no accident; it revealed how local collaboration grew into national networks and in turn reinforced the experts' desire to extend their influence.[76]

The practical results of surveys depended, of course, not only on the political and professional savvy of the outside experts, but also on local willingness to make changes. Several surveys in Chicago were opposed or ignored by school people, in part because they were initiated by outsiders. In Baltimore, three early surveys produced minimal results until a change in the school board and the superintendency in 1919–20 made the system responsive to an investigation by George Strayer and a staff of 110 members. Before taking the Baltimore superintendency, Henry West, a Ph.D. from Johns Hopkins University, insisted that the school board have outsiders thoroughly study the district system. Cooperating with Strayer, he reported the findings of the survey at monthly luncheons attended by the mayor, city financial officials, the school board, civic leaders, and newspaper reporters. Even before the survey was completed, some recommendations were implemented, including a $22 million building program, a reorganization of schools and creation of kindergartens, the addition of many new administrators, the adoption of new courses of study, and the founding of a research department serving the schools.[77]

Leonard Ayres had also used a similar plan of informational lunches with city influentials during his Cleveland survey. "As the weekly lunches have increased in popularity," Ayres wrote in 1915, "the newspapers of the city have given increasing amounts of space to the consideration of educational problems and the discussion of the weekly reports. On more than one occasion, the report of the weekly educational luncheon has backed everything else off the front page except the date and the weather." In Ayres's view, the main purpose of the survey was "to educate the public . . . to tell them in simple terms all the salient facts about their public schools and then to rely upon the common sense, the common insight, and the common purpose of the people as the first great resource in working out their problem." His techniques of publicity did help win assent; eight years later, after Spaulding's superintendency, Raymond Moley found that 74 percent of the survey recommendations had been carried out.[78]

One study of implementation of surveys underscored the importance of support by newspapers and by "leading citizens" as the two most important variables, next to realistic reform plans. Doing the survey was only the beginning; equally important was getting the report into the hands of leaders in legislatures and cities, lining up women's groups and professional organizations to push reform, and creating legislative lobbies. Successful implementation required overcoming fiscal and educational conservatism—especially in the rural-dominated state legislatures—a concerted campaign of publicity, and the organization of interest groups sympathetic to the surveys.[79]

In 1929 Hollis Caswell published a study of the impact of some of the more important of the hundreds of city school surveys during the previous generation, examining changes in organization and administration, school finance, personnel, school program, plant, and health and physical education. His list of questions about recommended reforms was the standard template of changes desired by the administrative progressives. The results he reported were impressive on the whole. Over half the school systems replied that after the school survey they had made changes in finances, in diversification of the school program, and in personnel practices, about half of those as a direct or indirect result of the surveys themselves. That the surveys promoted standardization was clear. That they benefited professionals is even more obvious. In 74 percent of the systems, for example, the salaries of teachers were raised; in 64 percent school building programs were adopted; and in 50 percent bond issues were approved.[80]

The impact of the survey movement on life in classrooms and on individual pupils is harder to assess than fiscal or organizational changes. To Judd the survey was an instrument of human accountability and taught the lesson that "the time has long since past when the community can look with any complacence on the failure of a child." To Strayer the key to instruction was individualization, for science now made it possible, he thought, to adapt school organizations and curricula to human differences. Ayres took pride in statistics showing that the number of children graduating from elementary school doubled between 1908 and 1915, a period when studies called attention to the multitude of overaged children held back in the grades. "The only great organized industry in America that has increased the output of its finished product as rapidly as the public schools during the past seven years," he asserted, "is the automobile industry."[81]

12. LOCAL SUPERINTENDENTS: SOCIAL ENGINEERS AND CURATORS OF THE MUSEUM OF VIRTUE

While some educators gained national reputations, university experts trained leaders for top positions, and researchers developed plans and procedures for the transformation of schooling, the formal governance of public education remained highly decentralized in the local districts. The superintendents in these local districts often served as transmitters of new professional outlooks and programs but also had to satisfy their school boards. Some of them, especially in the urban and larger suburban systems, were mobile cosmopolitans, trained in the new university programs in educational administration, and well integrated into the national networks of the administrative progressives. But the vast majority of American superintendents were heads of small school districts, comparatively local in their orientation, and limited in their experience and connections. In 1930, for example, about half of the district school superintendents worked in cities of under 5,000 in population.[1]

While advocates of the new science of education sought to reform public schools from the top down and influenced the definition of what was normal and desirable in education, the local superintendents in small communities had to be concerned with making the schools conform to local expectations. They may have been more worried about muddy playgrounds or the length of teachers' skirts than about introducing intelligence tests. The older conception of the educational leader as exemplar of approved virtues, as curator of the museum of virtue, did not die in the twentieth century but was alive and well in the small towns and countryside. But even there, educators ambitious to make administration into a lifelong career tried to keep in touch with their peers and to gain a sense of being part of an emerging profession by earning graduate degrees and attending professional meetings.[2]

Much of what linked superintendents as a group and gave them ties to the members of the educational trust was a common set of background characteristics. They were far from a random sample of the population. Differences of sex, religion, ethnicity, education, and age had much to do with rising to the top of local school systems. Another common bond was similar occupational socialization. Their shared backgrounds and work experience helped to determine who would lead in American public education and how they would lead.[3]

Social Characteristics as Sorting Mechanisms, 1899–1960

For more than fifty years students of educational administration have conducted extensive surveys of the social background, education, and career lines of school superintendents. Despite numerous and significant defects—of sampling, rate of return of questionnaires, temptations to exaggerate in self-reports (as in numbers of books read), and interpretations long on exhortation and short on analysis—the surveys are an invaluable source of data on the historical development of the occupation. While these data are approximate at best, one fact stands out: the remarkable consistency in the portrait of superintendents since 1899. While the governance and goals and structure of American schools have changed substantially in this century, the social attributes of superintendents have apparently remained relatively constant.[4]

Local Superintendents

Superintendents in the twentieth century have almost all been married white males, characteristically middle-aged, Protestant, upwardly mobile, from favored ethnic groups, native-born, and of rural origins. Typically, superintendents have had long experience in education, beginning their careers as young teachers, going on to principalships, and then becoming superintendents (in larger communities they often became assistant superintendents along the way). In disproportionate percentages they have been older sons in larger than average families. Mostly they remained in the same state for their entire careers as superintendents. They have been joiners, participating actively in civic and professional groups. Most of them picked up their advanced education while they practiced their profession, with long gaps of time between their academic degrees. They have been disproportionately Republican and have generally been moderate to conservative in their social philosophies.[5]

Hardly any superintendents were members of racial minorities until the 1960s, and then precious few. Before then some blacks had reached high administrative posts, though not the superintendency, in dual school systems in the segregated South and in border cities, but in the North few blacks had even become principals. Perhaps the most striking version of powerlessness is found in the Bureau of Indian Affairs (BIA). BIA schools scattered in reservations across the nation have been far more responsive to white bureaucrats in Washington than to the communities they served. Likewise Mexican-Americans and Puerto Ricans have typically constituted an infinitesimal percentage of school leaders even in communities where their children constituted a majority of pupils.[6]

Religion provided an important informal criterion for selection to the superintendency. Being Protestant and an active church member was an important requirement for selection as superintendent, especially in small- or medium-sized communities. Among 796 superintendents who reported their religion in Frederick Bair's study in 1934, only 6 were Roman Catholic, none Jewish, and none agnostic; 93 percent reported that they attended church. Neal Gross found in the mid-1950s that not only did superintendents and school boards in culturally pluralistic Massachusetts overwhelmingly prefer hiring white males, but also that some admitted to favoring Protestants over Catholics or Jews. (Twenty-eight percent of superintendents, for example, thought their successor should be Protestant; 35 percent thought he should not be Jewish; 20 percent did not approve of the selection of a Catholic.)[7]

Gender, too, was critical. As we shall discuss later, practically all superintendents were men, even though women predominated in teaching.

The portrait of the typical superintendent suggests interesting anomalies. Superintendents were almost all married males, whereas teachers were 85 percent female in 1920 and typically single at that time; almost all native-born, and mostly Anglo-Saxon, when the United States was a nation of immigrants from dozens of lands (in 1910, 40 percent of Americans were first or second generation immigrants); overwhelmingly Protestant in a religiously pluralistic nation and in a public service in which the separation of church and state made religious distinctions constitutionally irrelevant; raised in rural areas, when the nation was undergoing rapid urbanization; and middle-aged in a sea of schoolchildren and mostly young teachers.[8]

Probably none of these characteristics is surprising. Surely they are not accidental. If such characteristics as sex, age, and race did not count in a systematic way, one would have found a more random distribution. In most respects superintendents matched leaders in comparable occupations (though they were more upwardly mobile than most leaders in other fields and more rural in origin). Superintendents also tended to match the characteristics of the school board members that hired them —again not accidentally. Numerous studies of school boards, beginning early in the century, have shown that school board members also were white, middle-aged, predominantly male Protestants who came disproportionately from the upper reaches of the occupational and social structures of their communities. Of course communities differed markedly in their social composition, and both school board members and superintendents probably varied accordingly, for schools were more locally controlled and locally oriented than most other complex organizations.[9]

The very ambiguity and diffuseness of the goals of schooling, and the consequent difficulty of measuring "success" or "failure," probably reinforced the significance of maleness, mature age, "proper" ethnicity, acceptable church membership, and appearance (not surprisingly, superintendents were taller than the average, giving people someone to look up to). These characteristics gave the schools a higher social credit rating. For a superintendent to be a member of a respectable church and to have a stable marriage gave moral certification, a comforting sign of reputability. Like the banker's conservative dress, such social characteristics were an outward sign of safe leadership in an ambiguous enterprise.[10]

Local Superintendents

Rural Backgrounds

Superintendents grew up predominantly in rural areas and small communities. The AASA study of superintendents in 1933 reported that 69 percent went to high school where the population was under 5,000. Bair reported an even larger percentage that came from rural backgrounds in his study (about half of his superintendents' fathers were farmers). Almost two-thirds of his sample worked on farms as children. Superintendents who wrote autobiographies often commented about their distaste for hoeing and harvesting but were proud of their lifelong habits of early rising and hard work. Commonly their homes offered little intellectual stimulation; 25 percent of superintendents told Bair that there were *no* books in the home that were important to them as children. Richard Carlson has shown by a reanalysis of 1958 data on superintendents that they differed from the general population in that they grew up far less frequently in large cities and much more than average in places with populations of between 2,500 and 10,000. In this respect they also contrasted with leaders in government, business, and the military, who came more frequently from large cities.[11]

Thus the public schools have for a long time drawn administrators heavily from rural areas and small communities. Perhaps one reason is that the school employees in the nation's isolated rural communities were among very few role models of white-collar workers for young persons who wished to escape the plow and the farm kitchen. As Carlson observed, big cities offered more diverse and visible opportunities for ambitious youth. Cubberley wrote that to become a small-town principal was to gain "at once a special standing. . . . The people naturally look up to him as a man of more than ordinary training and importance."[12]

Although superintendents often sought to escape the drab routine of farm lives they knew as children, many tended to glorify boyhood in the countryside. They often saw the city as a source and center of social problems, although professionally it offered far greater opportunity and autonomy in personal life. It is likely that the rural-raised superintendent would have gained little firsthand knowledge of the out-of-school life of the city child and would have seen the role of the urban school, as did many trainers of administrators, as compensatory. Ironically, the further his ambition propelled him—to the big city—the further he traveled from the source of virtue, small-town America. In 1933, 37 percent of superintendents in cities over 10,000 attended high schools in places whose population was under 2,500; another 23 percent came from communities of 2,500–5,000, and only 12 percent from cities of 100,000+. Overwhelmingly native-born, Anglo-Saxon, Protestant, raised in the provincialism of the homogeneous small town, the school superintendent was likely to regard his own values and patterns of belief as self-evidently "American" and thus correct (and so he was assured when he met in convention with his peers or took courses with administration professors, most of whom were of similar backgrounds). After all, those values had worked for him in his upward ascent.[13]

Because of their relatively humble origins superintendents appear to have been somewhat more upwardly mobile than leaders in other occupations. In Bair's sample, for example, two-thirds of their parents had gone no further than grade school; half were farmers; and, except for a liberal sprinkling of ministers and teachers, few of the rest were executives or professionals. Carlson discovered similar evidence in a later period. Superintendents generally had to enter their work through the relatively low-status occupation of teacher. In comparison with lawyers, doctors, most executives in business and government, and typical military officers, they started lower in the ranks and remained there longer. In some respects their career pattern was similar to that of a Catholic bishop, who normally had to serve a long stint as curate (or assistant to a pastor), then as pastor, and then, finally, win his episcopacy. Another parallel might have been the career of a police chief, who began as a patrolman, worked up as sergeant and lieutenant, and finally moved to the top office. For superintendent, bishop, or police chief, long experience counted heavily in advancement. It is the effects of this long work experience in schools—as student, teacher, and administrator—on the superintendent's role conception and performance that we now explore.[14]

Occupational Socialization and Advancement

"Teaching makes the teacher," Willard Waller wrote in 1932 in his insightful book *The Sociology of Teaching*. Whatever teaching does for students "teaching does something to those who teach." In a similar way, one might say that school work makes the superintendent. The typical superintendent in the twentieth century was a career educator for over twenty years. He almost always started as teacher, then worked as principal, and, in city schools, frequently worked as assistant superintendent (in 1960 in cities from 100,000 to 500,000 in population, 48 percent of superintendents had been assistant superintendents, while the percentage increased to 71 in cities over 500,000). Thus the career ladder differed somewhat according to the size of the school system, but in both small and large districts the school chiefs had almost all been teachers and principals.[15]

Most occupational groups have norms to which the worker is expected to conform. "When the teacher has internalized the rules which bind him," Waller observes, "he has become truly a teacher. . . . A person is not free in any occupation until he has made conformity a part of himself. When conformity is the most natural thing for him, and he conforms without thought, the teacher is free, for freedom is only an optical illusion that results from our inability to see the restrictions that surround us." Even if one dissents from Waller's bleak sociological determinism, his point nonetheless contains much truth.[16]

Comparison of occupational groups sometimes highlights the socialization process. The occupational development of bishops offers some useful analogies to that of superintendents. Both groups have tended to come from pious, middle-class families whose fathers have less than a high school education. Both spend the greater proportion of their lives under the aegis of a single institution, the church or the public schools. Both churchmen and superintendents are much in the public eye both at work and abroad in their communities and are expected to display conspicuous virtue rather than to take risks. Both move up through subordinate positions in regular sequence starting at the bottom of the organization. In each case seniority and persistence in the organization count heavily in advancement, in part because of the difficulty of measuring "success." Conformity to rules and loyalty to superiors are typical and valued qualities in both institutions. Access to informal networks of sponsors, such as that gained by advanced training at favored institutions (Teachers College or the North American College at Rome, Italy), often hastens advancement.

An importai.t difference between the two groups, however, is that the priesthood normally requires early vocational commitment, whereas superintendents, in the past at least, often drifted into administration over a long period of time. Another significant difference is that advancement to the top position in the church depends on clerical superiors in a complex bureaucracy; superintendents are elected by local lay boards.[17]

The superintendent normally begins his career in public education as a student in kindergarten or first grade. Thus its standard operating procedures become familiar at age five or six and are reinforced by almost unbroken familiarity until retirement, as Larry Cuban has pointed out. It is often hardest to question that which is most obvious. While educators, like most Americans, tend to place an exaggerated value on "innovation"—admen even invent the NEW Old Dutch Cleanser—basic strategies and structures of schooling usually show great continuity over time, in part, perhaps, because of the self-evidence of these routines to school people who have known them since childhood. Although educators ordinarily change their perspectives on schooling as they shift their roles from student to teacher, or from teacher to administrator, they normally do not need to undergo the powerful resocialization through training that transforms, for example, civilian recruits into army lieutenants.[18]

Willard Waller has given us a vivid sociological portrait of teachers who served in small districts. It was in such communities that most superintendents started their careers as teachers. In the towns studied by Waller in the early 1930s the beginning teacher was expected to meet the converging expectations of students, peers, principals, and parents about conservative dress, firm demeanor, and other forms of behavior thought proper for teachers. Evaluation forms used by principals and superintendents commonly rated the loyalty (or "cooperation") of the teacher, punctuality, efficient processing of forms, tact, and, above all, effectiveness in discipline. Almost never did they inquire about the teacher's sense of humor. Evaluating the results of instruction might be difficult, but anyone could determine whether the classroom window shades were drawn at half-mast or if the room were quiet. "One suspects," wrote Waller, "that 'professional ethics,' a creation of executives for the guidance of subordinates, is really loyalty under another name." Loyalty and tact, the preeminent virtues of the domestic servant, were also prized in educators as public servants. Toward the pupils, however, the teacher was encouraged to develop social distance. And the peer culture of teachers, like that of police, reinforced the norm of "not making waves."[19]

Was it paradoxical that the educator in a small community was expected to conform to the proper morals and mores of the town, but was often regarded as something of an outsider, not quite integrated into the social life of the community? Evidence abounds that townspeople kept a vigilant eye on the out-of-class behavior of educators, and that moral "lapses" resulted in firings far more often than did incompetence in teaching. Many communities assumed that teachers would become ex-officio Sunday School instructors. Yet teachers often complained that they were kept at arm's length socially, that women teachers were

America's vestal virgins, and that men teachers were treated by other men rather as ministers and other quasi townsmen.

The paradox begins to dissolve when one realizes that often the public school served as a place where children learned that honesty is always the best policy, that the United States had statesmen of stainless steel, that proper diction and upright character go hand-in-hand. "Among these ideals are those moral principles which the majority of adults more or less frankly disavow for themselves but want others to practice," wrote Waller; "They are ideals for the helpless, ideals for the children and for teachers." As "a paid agent of cultural diffusion" of these ideals the teacher must be shielded from the untoward realities of saloons and cigars, seduction and salacious talk. "It is part of the American credo that school teachers reproduce by budding." Over time most teachers who remained in the profession probably internalized the community's stereotyped expectations; one teacher who resisted such stereotypes called her poignant book of poetry *Teachers Are People.*[20]

Generalized moral expectations of the community shaped the behavior of teachers and administrators both in and outside the classroom, but so did the need to maintain order in the school—what Waller called a "despotism in a state of perilous equilibrium." Carlson has observed that the public school, like the prison and the state mental hospital, occupies a special niche in the ecology of institutions: it has involuntary clients and cannot select among them. Some students want to be in school and are rewarding to teach; others resist, actively or passively, and pose special problems of control. It was the beginning teacher who often had to contend with the latter category of student, since a common perquisite of seniority was to teach the willing student. Even experienced teachers had nightmares of class disruption or disastrous visits from supervisors. The task of getting and keeping order, and of imparting instruction to unwilling pupils, shaped the structure of both classroom and school.[21]

Entering the white-collar occupation of teaching from lower-middle-class backgrounds, most teachers did not hold notably liberal attitudes (although studies of teachers' attitudes were somewhat inconsistent). Even if their pedagogical training stressed progressive methods—on which there is again mixed evidence—the "reality shock" of initial teaching probably did most to determine their behavior. Veteran police told rookies to forget the police academy and to learn from peers about the real world of the beat. Similarly, the most important socialization to teaching came from the craft wisdom of the teachers' subculture and the social character of the classroom. Like the veteran policeman advising the recruit to be firm, the older teacher sometimes told the younger, "Don't smile 'till Christmas." One study of attitudes of novices before and after the initial teaching experience concluded, for example, that experienced "teachers became less concerned with pupil freedom and more concerned with establishing a stable, orderly classroom, in which academic standards received a prominent position. The change was accompanied by a decline in the tendency to attribute pupil misbehavior or academic difficulty to the teacher or to the school."[22]

Learning to adapt to the moral and educational demands of the community and to preserve the tenuous authority of the classroom, then, were important parts of the socialization of the teacher and left their mark on the administrator moving up the ladder to a superintendency. The majority of teachers—both male and female—left the classroom after a brief stint. Of those who remained in education, the women teachers found that their mobility was mostly horizontal; they tended to move to larger communities or to choicer spots in the same system. Only a few women applied for and gained administrative jobs, normally the lower-status ones. For the men who wanted more pay, authority, and scope for altruistic hopes, the ladder of ambition within education led through the principalship to the superintendency. On the way they learned how to win the favor of community influentials and to run an orderly school.[23]

In a small community the jumps from the classroom to the principal's office to the superintendency were often not very large. In 1929 Fred Ayer published a study of what principals and superintendents actually did. His sample included mostly small districts. Ayer's findings are revealing: superintendents and principals performed many of the same tasks with about the same frequency: both commonly taught classes (71 percent of his superintendents taught in the high school of their district); the work of both superintendents and principals was very heterogeneous and often quasi-clerical or janitorial; and community liaison was a vital and time-consuming part of the job. Superintendents interacted frequently with parents, ministers, medical workers, salesmen, lay board members, and leaders from local associations. The job required a good deal of social energy.

Ayer did not simply list dignified "professional" categories of duties —such as supervision, financial management, curriculum, or pupil services—but rather specified tasks, the percentages of superintendents who performed them, and their frequency (daily or weekly). Thus it is possible to construct a picture of how they spent their time. For example: 86 percent went to the post office daily to get school mail; 93 percent inspected toilets weekly; large percentages typed their own work, operated the mimeograph machines, checked to see if teachers arrived on time, inspected the janitor's work, and personally saw to building maintenance and construction; and smaller percentages wound the clocks and wrote memory gems on the blackboards daily. Although they typically taught classes, and almost all had risen to the superintendency through the ranks, their relationship with other teachers (mostly female) tended to be paternalistic. It was common for them to meet teachers at the railroad station, find them places to board in town, and advise them "on social and moral conduct," including "appropriate and sanitary dress."[24]

It is clear that these superintendents saw themselves—and were seen by the communities they served—as guardians of decorum and morality. Indeed, as John Meyer and Brian Rowan have observed, it was in part these community understandings that gave symbolic structure and organizational coherence to schooling. Because the actual outcomes of public education were hard to measure, it was all the more important to preserve ritual and decorum. Community contacts and ceremonies such as assemblies took up much of the superintendent's day. Typically, superintendents attended church regularly, and many taught Sunday School as well. As we mentioned earlier, 73 percent said that they read religious literature weekly to improve themselves professionally.[25]

"Is the small town superintendency a glorified janitorship?" asked a writer in *School Executives Magazine* in 1931. The answer, not surprisingly, was yes. He must be "official chaperone for all teachers," quick to censure the woman who puts her feet on the landlady's davenport or attends a dance on a school night. He teaches a class; visits all classrooms regularly; monitors pupils at recess; "is the final court of appeal in all disciplinary matters; handles all business from the hiring of teachers to the purchase of stamps; keeps office hours for parents who are frank to question the soundness of his educational principles; arranges extracurricular activities, out-of-town contests, and ad infinitum." He is expected to show "the wisdom of Solomon with the humility of Uriah Heep and the tact of an ambassador." On duty at all times, he may be called "at midnight to shoo amorous couples from the schoolhouse steps," buttonholed at a social meeting to discuss "school drain pipes" or "the sheerness of the seventh grade teacher's hose." All his traits were open to public scrutiny, his opinions dissected, his family a favorite topic of conversation. The superintendent's wife suffered all kinds of constraints on her actions. In other articles, disenchanted superintendents spoke out sometimes anonymously about the trials of local politics, local pride, and religious prejudice that made the superintendent an anxious servant of a fickle public.[26]

Given the fishbowl character of the job in small communities, it is not surprising that some administrators protested their lot. What is perhaps most significant is that so few did so. Indeed, in two studies of outside interest-group pressures on superintendents, over half the school chiefs replied that they had experienced none. It is likely that through long and continuous socialization as student, teacher, and principal most superintendents came to internalize the values of the communities they served and that they accepted role prescriptions not as restrictions but as normal expectations—in short that they were "free" (in Waller's sense) through unconscious conformity. A large proportion of superintendents never left their own states during their entire careers; a study of midwestern administrators showed that only 13 percent of administrative moves were out-of-state. It was possible for many superintendents to find communities in which their values matched those of most of the patrons so that dissonance was minimized. Such administrators might feel it no more unreasonable to expect schools to be museums of virtue than for their churches to set high ethical standards. The high goals of an educational "celestial city" might give resonance even to menial tasks. They were "locals," attuned to the ethos of particular places and times, not "cosmopolitans" like their more mobile brethren, many of whom fled the small town for the city.[27]

Superintendents in small towns typically grew up in the communities they served or in ones much like them. As they passed from student to teacher to principal to superintendent they experienced a broader perspective and growing authority until ultimately they became the most important link between community and school system. Some of them acquired new ideas about education in their training and in their professional associations and became carriers of an adopted cosmopolitanism. Some, also, came in conflict with community factions or influentials. But their general socialization probably inclined them to reinforce the traditional values of the community and to perpetuate the structures and styles of pedagogy that they had known and their patrons preferred.[28]

There were important differences, as well as similarities, in the experience of educators in large cities as compared with small communities. Career ladders contained the same initial rungs—teacher and principal —but there were additional rungs before the top on the differentiated and multi-tiered urban systems. Partly as a result of these intermediate steps, the median age of superintendents in large cities was about seven to ten years higher than that of small-city school chiefs in the years from 1923 to 1960. Increasingly the doctorate became required for the job in large cities (over 50 percent of those in cities of over 100,000 had doctor's degrees in 1952 as compared with only 6 percent in cities of from 2,500 to 10,000). Big-city superintendents tended to move from their small communities of origin into the city rather than remain in familiar surroundings; as late as 1960, only 13 percent of superintendents in cities of from 100,000 to 500,000 in population, for example, had attended high schools in cities of over 100,000.[29]

Big-city school systems of the twentieth century were structurally far more complex than those of small districts, and their managers operated in a quite different manner. If the small-city school system was, in effect, a quasi-church (pan-Protestant) in which it was appropriate for the superintendent to say that he improved himself professionally by reading religious literature, the large urban district resembled in some respects a business corporation. Under the meritocratic theory, promotion within the system depended on rational criteria: specialized educational training and credentials, favorably evaluated performance, and orderly progression up the hierarchical ladder or appointment from a similar background in another system. Numerous cities developed examination and promotion systems; New York's Board of Examiners was one of the most elaborate.[30]

In practice, the system often did not work as the elites intended. Ethnic or religious criteria played no formal role in selection by merit, but informally they were significant in many cities, as different ethnic groups succeeded in moving up the hierarchies of school districts. In Boston, for example, Peter Schrag found that in the 1960s all members of the central administration "are graduates of Boston College, all have risen through the ranks and have been in the system for more than three decades, all are well over 50 years old, all are Catholics, and all, excepting only Superintendent William H. Ohrenberger with his German background, are Irishmen." In Chicago and elsewhere top administrators sometimes gave expensive cram courses designed to prepare aspiring educators for the "merit" examinations. "Getting the attention of superiors" became an art form to many teachers ambitious to rise in the system. Knowing the right people could sometimes turn a bureaucratic stone wall into a triumphal arch. In cities the "right people" might be one's superiors within the system—especially for those moving up the middle rungs on the ladder—or they might be school board members or other community influentials.[31]

Small districts and vast city systems provided rather different contexts, then, for occupational socialization and advancement. The big city offered educators escape in their private lives from the vigilant eye of public opinion in the small town and thus served as a refuge for cosmopolitans who did not share small-town values. To a large degree centralization detached schools from neighborhoods. The sheer size and diversity of the urban systems offered different routes upward for persons of different talents. The model of meritocracy shaped the *formal* screening process for advancement, yet *informally* such influences as ethnicity, religion, friendship, as well as old-fashioned graft did not disappear as factors in promotion.

It was not only superintendents but their patrons as well (the parents and the public) who felt they knew what a "school" was and how to judge the newfangled against the traditional standards. Both superintendents and their communities filtered ideas for change through their own firsthand experience, and this provided an important element of continuity amid change. The social backgrounds of the local superintendents, like those of the members of the educational trust, linked them to the pietist past of small-town America. They were a fraternity bonded by common personal histories quite as much as by shared ideals of scientific management.

13. DEMOCRACY, BUREAUCRACY, AND GENDER

In 1909 Ella Flagg Young, superintendent of schools in Chicago and soon to become the first woman president of the NEA, made a confident prediction. "Women are destined to rule the schools of every city," she said. "I look for a majority of big cities to follow the lead of Chicago in choosing a woman for superintendent. In the near future we shall have more women than men in executive charge of the vast educational system. It is woman's natural field and she is no longer satisfied to do the larger part of the work and yet be denied the leadership." A brilliant scholar and cautious observer and commentator, Young was not given to grandiloquent gestures. Why was she so hopeful?[1]

As Young spoke, powerful movements were gaining momentum among women teachers in New York, Chicago, and other cities. They were protesting the domination of top administration and professional associations by males, higher pay for male teachers, and the way in which scientific management was turning teachers into operatives who had to do the bidding of their superiors. A leading theorist of democratic planning among teachers and an advocate of Dewey's philosophy, Young observed:

> There has been a tendency toward factory-evolution and factory-management, and the teachers, like children who stand at machines, are told just what to do. The teachers, instead of being the great moving force, educating and developing the powers of the human mind in such a way that they shall contribute to the power and efficiency of this democracy, tend to become mere workers at the treadmill, but they are doing all thru this country that which shows that it is difficult to crush the human mind and the love of freedom in the hearts and lives of people who are qualified to teach school. As a result they are organizing federations to get together and discuss those questions which are vital in the life of the children and in the life of the teachers—you cannot separate the life of the children and the life of the teacher if you know what you are about.[2]

From the beginning of the graded urban school, the feminization of teaching had been closely linked with the bureaucratization of education. Male managers controlled their subordinates in part through the greater status and power accorded men in the larger society. Educational organizations thus reflected the inequitable social relationships of gender. But early in the twentieth century women were organizing to bring about changes. Why should not women share in directing the system when they do most of the work? Why should not women teachers be able to have greater autonomy to shape classroom instruction? Why should not women have greater say in forming the agenda and taking the leadership in professional associations? The militance of women teachers, shared by a handful of women administrators like Young, was transforming the debate on such issues from *why?* to *why not?* This was a major shift in consciousness and, potentially, in relative power.

The conflict between women teachers and·male managers that was erupting during the first two decades of the twentieth century lay behind Young's prediction, as did other developments we shall discuss. What actually happened, however, sadly belied her optimism. Despite some early gains, women lost even their tenuous toehold on good jobs. In the NEA the challenge of women was deflected as new governance arrangements secured continuing power for male administrators while it gave women certain symbolic concessions. And although women teachers continued to experience some freedom of action in the privacy of their classrooms, reforms largely proceeded from the top down and administration remained hierarchical as well as male dominated.

When Young spoke in 1909, the fact of unequal opportunity for female administrators in public schools was apparent. Young herself was an anomaly; almost all city superintendents were men, and she was the first woman to head a big-city school system. Although women predominated as teachers—the pool from which administrators were drawn—they held nowhere near a proportionate number of leadership positions. Several decades later the situation was even worse for women. Table 13.1 compares the figures for 1905 in cities of over 8,000 in population with nationwide statistics for 1972–73 (the two sets of statistics are roughly comparable because of the massive consolidation of districts that had taken place by the latter date, when only about 13 percent of pupils attended schools with fewer than 1,800 pupils). In public schools as in many other complex white-collar organizations there continued to be a sexual structuring of opportunity that discriminated against women. The inequalities might be summarized by a few rules of thumb:

- Men were most likely to be found in administrative positions conferring the greatest power, pay, and prestige;
- Men predominated in positions where the job required supervising other males, while women were often found in administrative positions where they dealt mostly with other women and with children;
- Men were sought for positions such as superintendent or high school principal that linked the educational system with its external environment, where maleness gave the school a higher social credit rating because of the higher status of men in the community. Women were more likely to be in administrative positions that looked inward toward the system.

It was not outlandish for Ella Flagg Young to claim early in the twentieth century that women would become the key leaders in public education. One reason was that women had seen real progress in recent years. Another was that they saw themselves as part of a social and political movement that sought greater equality for women, not only for themselves but also for the betterment of society. And finally, women in the early twentieth century seemed to be capturing an increasing percentage of supervisory positions; the number of women administrators was rapidly rising.

Young saw her election to the Chicago superintendency as evidence

TABLE 13.1

Percentage of Female Professional Public-School
Employees, 1905 and 1972–73

	1905	1972–73
Elementary School Teachers	97.9	84.0
Elementary School Principals	61.7	19.6
High School Teachers	64.2	46.0
High School Principals (Senior High)	5.7	1.4
District Superintendents	—	0.1

SOURCES: 1905: National Education Association, *Report of the Committee on Salaries, Tenure, and Pensions of Public School Teachers in the United States to the National Council of Education, July, 1905* (Winona, Minn.: NEA, 1905), p. 52; 1972–73: Andrew Fishel and Janice Pottker, "Women in Educational Governance: A Statistical Portrait," *Educational Researcher* 3 (July/August, 1974): 5–6.

of epochal changes that had taken place during her own lifetime. "Why, when I began teaching here in Chicago, back in 1862, it would have been absolutely impossible for a woman to have been given even a principalship," she said. "I received then $25 a month. This week I began at $10,000 a year." She claimed that when she earned a position as principal, "I was one of the first five or six women principals in the country." As the 1905 NEA survey showed (see table 13.1), over three-fifths of elementary principals in cities of over 8,000 were female, and large numbers of women were being appointed as supervisors in such fields as music, drawing, vocational subjects, and physical training. They were also winning a few district superintendencies and positions as assistant superintendents and directors.[3]

Decision-makers seemed slowly to be shifting from assuming that leaders should be men to admitting that women should be considered as potential administrators. This was a change from the nineteenth-century concept of women as ideal subordinates. When women first replaced males as teachers in urban public schools, they were valued not only because they were cheaper and supposedly more nurturing and skillful instructors of young children, but also because they were presumed to be more compliant with the direction of male superintendents than were the old schoolmasters. Growing numbers of women in the teaching force and bureaucratization went hand in hand, with male superintendents in firm control of the system. Men praised female teachers because they were willing to work according to the dictates of their superiors and would require little direct supervision because they bowed to male authority. Their dependent situation in parental families and schools made them more content with their lot in the classroom "less intent on scheming for future honors or emoluments" than men.

In turn, the presence of a man as boss calmed public fears that women could not handle discipline problems or manage the business side of the system. A male leader of approved character gave the enterprise of public schooling a secure standing in the community, for, running things was man's sphere.[4]

And so it went, for some time, but capable and ambitious women like Young began to seek "future honors or emoluments," and the old assumption that men were destined to command began to erode. In 1919 Louise Connolly described one episode in this process of change in her perceptive article, "Is There Room At the Top for Women Educators?"

> Twenty years ago there walked into the office of a school superintendent, who was a big-headed, great-hearted man, an irate lady.
> "I took the train as soon as I heard it," said she. "You may refuse to answer if you want to. Why did you nominate a stupid, uncouth fellow like Smith to the new office of assistant superintendent?"
> "Yes," said the superintendent, "I know. But he is an honest man, and will not play politics."
> "I can count at least fifteen honest women in your corps," said the irate lady, "who are also cultured and clever."
> He of the big head and great heart rumpled his hair and acknowledged, "As the Lord lives, *I never thought of a woman.*"
> That could not happen today. In such cases the superintendent and all the male candidates think busily of women—and of how to fend them off.[5]

Competition for the good jobs was not easy for women, but at least they were entering the race. One reason for this was that many women leaders in education—principals, activists in teacher organizations, progressive educators, suffragists—saw themselves as part of a women's movement that was gaining political momentum and enlisting important allies among militant feminists and moderate but influential members of women's clubs and similar organizations. As Margaret Gribskov has observed, this kind of feminism in educational administration went well beyond individual ambition or seeking single goals such as the vote. In Chicago, Young was only one of a band of sophisticated and articulate women who sought to analyze social problems, to devise solutions and take action, and to work themselves into positions of power. One thinks, for example, of the pathbreaking reformist social-science studies of women and children by professors such as Edith and Grace Abbott and Sophonisba Breckinridge, Florence Kelley's attacks on child labor, or Jane Addams's combination of intellectual and practical leadership in a variety of social reforms.[6]

Some of these activists saw the entry of women into school administration as yet another enlargement of women's sphere, comparable to Catharine Beecher's earlier assertion that teaching belonged to women because of their feminine qualities. Reformers like Young had reason to believe that in certain sectors of public administration that were regarded as "woman's natural field"—not only in education but in other agencies dealing with women and children—women might assume leadership. A common argument made by suffragists was that if given the vote and certain offices, women could perform civic house cleaning. Many associations of both white and black women—college alumnae groups, temperance societies, women's clubs—actively promoted such reforms and supported female candidates such as Young for high office. Female educational administrators, in turn, ranked high among career women in their support for suffrage (fifth in a list of twenty occupations in a sample analyzed by Richard Jensen).[7]

An important element in the reform movement of activist women was the new militant leadership appearing among teachers. In New York and Chicago, large all-female teacher organizations pressed for equal pay for equal work and better salaries and working conditions. In New York the 14,000-member Interborough Association of Women Teachers successfully challenged higher pay for men teachers and promoted the career aspirations of its militant president, Grace Strachan. In Chicago Margaret Haley and Catherine Goggin were astute strategists for the Chicago Teachers Federation (CTF)—composed of women elementary teachers—and supported Young in her quest for the superintendency and for the NEA presidency. It seemed to many observers that in time most urban teachers would belong to such organizations and that they would be a powerful lobby for the appointment of women as school administrators. Organizationally, women educators seemed to be gaining power in education rapidly during the first two decades of the twentieth century.[8]

Margaret Haley was the main leader among those female militants who challenged the male old guard in the NEA and sought to force them to attend to the concerns of the women teachers who made up the vast majority of the profession. A brilliant and tough teacher union organizer, Haley was first noticed by the old guard in 1901 when she rose to challenge a complacent set of speeches by William T. Harris and his admirers at the Detroit convention. Harris had listed statistics showing how public education was flourishing, and one of his respondents had argued that it would be well if wealthy philanthropists would give money to public schools. In response Haley attacked the idea of big business support, saying that it would stifle the autonomy of teachers and pointing out that teachers were grossly underpaid. Harris, crochety, told the convention: "Pay no attention to what that teacher down there has said, for I take it she is a grade teacher, just out of her school room at the end of school year, worn out, tired, and hysterical. . . . It was a mistake to hold NEA meetings at this time of year . . . and if there are any more hysterical outbursts, after this I shall insist that these meetings be held at some other time of the year." Capitalists were the great benefactors of society, he reassured the audience. Nonsense, replied Haley, who had been bringing railroads and utility companies to court for not paying their school taxes: "I know the facts. Mr. Harris, either you do not know or have not stated the facts." After the exchange, an eyewitness declared of the aging Harris: "In the educational system we don't bury the dead. We let them walk around to save funeral expenses."[9]

Haley had a vision of an NEA as an organization "within the control, and to be administered in the interest, of the thousands of teachers who contribute to its income. The aim of our opponents is to turn the association over in perpetuity to a small, self-perpetuating, independent, and self-governing organization, within the National Education Association, and yet not subordinate to it." The attempts to centralize control of the NEA, she believed, were part of a larger "conspiracy to make a despotism of our entire school system . . . a 'mine' to be 'worked for all it is worth.' " She hoped to remodel a new NEA on the Chicago Teachers Federation that she had built. It is not surprising that Nicholas Murray Butler and his friends regarded her as "a fiend in petticoats" and the organized teachers of Chicago, Milwaukee, and New York as Bolshevists. Nor is it surprising that a solid phalanx of old-guard members sitting in a front row at the Los Angeles meeting in 1907 stood up when they heard a woman speak from a back row, looked back in alarm and then sat down with relief when they found out that it was not Margaret Haley.[10]

The assertiveness of the teachers disrupted the genteel old guard, who had little conception of why women like Haley were pressing their cause. Charles W. Eliot had a simple answer: they were morally obtuse. "It is an extraordinary and very discouraging fact," he wrote, "that, whenever a large number of women get excited in a cause which seems to them in general good and praiseworthy, some of them become indifferent to the moral quality of the particular efforts by which it seems possible to promote that cause." Haley's successful campaign to elect Young in Boston illustrated, thought Eliot, "a general moral ignorance or incapacity which is apt to be in evidence whenever women get stirred in political, social, or educational contests."[11]

Democracy, Bureaucracy, and Gender

As we shall see, however, the previously almost all-male hierarchy of the NEA reacted to the challenge of women's unions by subverting them, giving them symbolic gains, such as a woman president every other year, and promoting an ideology of professionalism that blurred actual lines of cleavage between men and women, administrators and teachers. In statistical reports the NEA and most other agencies stopped breaking down tables by sex at the end of the second decade of the twentieth century. Amid the proliferation of other kinds of statistical reporting in an age enamored of numbers—reports so detailed that one could give the precise salary of staff in every community across the country and exact information on all sorts of other variables—data by sex became strangely inaccessible. This silence could hardly have been unintentional. As a result of this failure to record by gender, those who took an interest in what was happening to women in school administration and to comparative male and female salaries had to compile figures laboriously from scattered sources.[12]

In the early twentieth century, however, women did seem to be winning an increased share of leadership positions in public education, especially in states where women had the vote in school elections and where they could compete for state and county superintendencies. Edith Lathrop, specialist in rural education in the United States Office of Education, wrote an article in 1922 urging college-educated women to enter careers in public education. She observed that nine states—all west of the Mississippi—had elected women as state superintendents by that year, the largest number since North Dakota began the trend in 1893. She also pointed out that the number of female county superintendents had increased from 276 in 1900 to 857 in 1922, mostly concentrated in the West and in places where county superintendents were elected rather than appointed. "The college girl who is ambitious for educational leadership, won by way of political competition," she added, "may well take Horace Greeley's advice to young men anxious for opportunity and a career: 'Go West, young man, go West!' " She mentioned as well that women held many administrative positions in city school systems. The barriers seemed to be coming down.[13]

The number of positions held by women and the amount of political activism and social reform did seem to be climbing upward to justify the hopes of Young and her peers. But a closer analysis of the jobs actually occupied by women, the long-term trends, and the blunting of feminist militance in educational associations reveal a more depressing prospect.

To say that the fate of women in educational administration in the twentieth century is depressing is not to deny that there were many impressive individual leaders. There clearly were state and county women superintendents who gave inspiring leadership, and many women were leaders in educational reform. But by and large, women had to fight hard even for modest positions, and they fell further and further behind as time went on. As Connolly put it in 1919: "Woman has arrived in numbers only in the lower strata of the upper crust. She has been invited considerably to care for the blind and deaf, and very largely to train the deficient and feebleminded." Important though these jobs may have been, they kept women tending the powerless, an extension of child-care roles. Statistics on employment of female administrators in local districts amply document Connolly's statement that they were in the lower strata. In 1922 there were only thirty-one female city superintendents in the United States. A decade later the number had increased, but there were still twenty-five states in which no woman served as a district superintendent. The few women chief administrators were concentrated in the poorest paid and least prestigious positions in small communities in rural states like Vermont, New Mexico, Alabama, and Idaho.[14]

Women working as central-office administrators in city school systems were mostly clustered in sex-segregated positions in which they interacted primarily with female elementary teachers (and sometimes also taught children). In Pittsburgh, for example, the sixty-two women supervisors were distributed in art, household economy, hygiene, child welfare, kindergartens, music, and commercial studies. Typically, they occupied staff positions rather than holding line responsibilities in the central administration, and their work was usually not of the kind that offered visibility and power leading to advancement in the hierarchy.[15]

Connolly pointed out that in bureaucratized twentieth-century school systems "there is an inclined plane which is also a graduated screen, and the men govern the grade and the scale." Because they may feel that " 'the women voters (or the women's clubs) will make a fuss' or that 'the suffragists will get after us,' or that 'women ought to be represented,' a place—usually in the supervisorship of primary work, or domestic work, or welfare work—is set apart for some women, *and the woman is selected by a board of men.*" Male judgment in such matters was less than ideal:

A male board of examiners has been known to select for a position of grave responsibility a girl two years out of college, with a B.A. and a high color, turning down a sallow lady of 35, with three degrees, ten years of fruitful experience, and a notable capacity for gentle leadership. Doubtless a board of women would make equally egregious mistakes in rating young men.

However casual might be their standards for apprising female supervisors of women, male administrators believed firmly that the masculinity of their male colleagues should be protected from female bosses. "Don't worry," a state superintendent told some local superintendents when he was pressured to hire a woman as assistant superintendent, "I'm not going to send a person in petticoats to inspect your work."[16]

Of all the administrative positions held by large numbers of women, perhaps the elementary principalship offered the greatest opportunity for autonomy and instructional leadership. The fear of men being supervised by "a person in petticoats" did not apply to most primary schools after the almost complete takeover of elementary education by female teachers. In 1905 women held a strong edge over men as elementary principals in cities. Subsequent surveys showed that the percentage of women dropped from 55 in 1928, to 41 in 1948, to 38 in 1958, and to 22 in 1968.[17]

As school administrators women often fared better when they were elected by their fellow citizens—male and female—than when they were appointed by a male board or superior. In western states a number of capable women worked their way via the ballot box up the ladder from classroom teacher to county superintendency to state superintendency. The actual work they did and the rewards they received suggest, however, that the county and state superintendencies were not prizes to be compared with the best jobs in cities.[18]

The county superintendencies did not pay well; the salary was typically below that paid to high school principals and well below that of superintendents in small cities. The job was rigorous, requiring officials to travel long distances over dusty or muddy roads to visit dozens of small schools. In a decentralized system, the authority of county superintendents depended more on their personal talents than on the office. Nationally, the median years of training beyond the elementary school were only 7.8, while over half of the superintendents did not hold a B.A. While such a job was a step up from the classroom, it was hardly a position of much pay, prestige, or power.[19]

Much the same could be said of the state superintendency. Women fared best in winning state superintendencies when the office was elective rather than appointive, especially in the mountain and far western states where women had early gained the vote. Their salaries were lower than the national average and staffs were smaller than the median. In most places the state superintendent exercised little power. Educational reformers complained for over a hundred years that state executives were figureheads who collected statistics, disbursed funds, and relayed messages from the legislature and state board, with little opportunity for initiative or leadership. They usually earned less than city superintendents. But when the pay and prestige of the office increased—usually with its becoming an appointive office—the number of women dropped.[20]

The hopes of women leaders at the beginning of this century were not realized, and their temporary gains were reversed. By and large, they filled the posts that men did not want, and when their jobs became attractive to men, they were displaced. How did males maintain and then increase their hold on the top jobs in education?

In the first place, the school boards that overwhelmingly appointed men to positions as city superintendent, state superintendent, and similar jobs were themselves composed largely of men. Women, of course, vastly outnumbered men in the initial pool of teachers from which aspiring administrators were drawn. When the performance of female and male administrators has been compared—as in much research on elementary principals, for example—the work of the two sexes has been judged comparable. From such work one might assume a meritocratic system to be neutral as to gender. Yet study after study has shown that male boards have believed males to be superior candidates for the top positions. Thus the attitudes of the lay decision makers have obviously been a major reason for the scarcity of women at the top.[21]

Was this a herd instinct of men to favor their own, a bias without a sound rationale in organizational or societal realities? Probably not. Men did enjoy—and do enjoy—important advantages both within the system and in linking it with the surrounding community.

Within the district males had access to the men at the top of the district hierarchy and could get to know them with an intimacy normally inaccessible to women. In 1936 Helen Davis described the problem women faced:

> However fair and democratic the management tries to be, it is and probably always will be true that thinking is matured, plans are weighed in the balance, implications and alternatives worked out—in other words, decisions really made—on the golf course and around the luncheon table rather than at staff meetings. Moreover it is by this same process that individual growth is stimulated and that administrators get to know and to estimate properly the capacities of their staff members.

Democracy, Bureaucracy, and Gender

It was, and is, much more common for male superiors in school systems to serve as sponsors for other men; what Davis called "rigid social customs" made friendships between men and women highly suspect. Men also had unusual opportunities to get the attention of superiors and to curry public favor through activities like coaching successful teams, a notable and visible exercise of leadership.[22]

Men have had similar advantages in the community, ways of tying the schools to the power structure of the larger social environment. They could join all-male organizations like the Rotary Clubs and chambers of commerce and there gain important information, friendships, and political support. One western superintendent told of his hunting and fishing with men in the Chamber of Commerce, thereby winning firm friends who supported him in his reform plans "not because they were advocates of the educational principle upon which the experiment was based, but because they wanted their friend to win." In a society that was deeply biased in its distribution of power, in which informal networks and voluntary organizations of the influential were often single-sex, being male was a strong asset.[23]

In the cultural beliefs of that larger society, marriage operated with an opposite valence for men and women. For men, marriage was normally an asset if not a tacit requirement in upward mobility, whereas for women it was often a liability if not an actual barrier. Surveys of male school superintendents, as we have seen, have shown consistently that they were almost all married. There were numerous articles and books of advice telling "Mrs. Administrator" how to help her husband in his two-person career.[24]

By contrast, women who wished to persist in education up the normal ladder to become top administrators faced both external and internal barriers. The early advocates of employing women as teachers assumed that they would, of course, leave their work when married and that marriage was the goal of all proper women. In fact, until recently, most women in public schools have been young and single; in 1900 only 10 percent were married and in 1940 only 22 percent. Not only did most women internalize these cultural norms, but official policies also barred married women from educational employment. In 1928 the NEA found that about three-fifths of urban districts prohibited the hiring of married teachers and half forbade married teachers from continuing in their jobs. The situation grew worse during the Depression, as thousands of districts passed new bans.[25]

In 1936 Helen Davis wrote that education, like other professions, "will be occupied on the whole by two kinds of women, those who refuse marriage except on their own terms and those who have not been able to find husbands, while the general run of able and so-called 'normal' women will be excluded because they prefer marriage." Women were thus presented with a dilemma that men did not face: the forced choice, in most cases, between a public career and the intimacy of marriage. And single women who continued in education met negative stereotypes about spinsters.[26]

Men enjoyed another special advantage in their careers: in graduate work in educational administration the professors were almost all men and they recruited and sponsored chiefly males. The sponsor system was not called an "old-boy" network by accident. Connolly commented that the new university experts professed liberal attitudes toward women but shunted them to "positions demanding drudgery." The result was that "with no more formulated or explicit organization than the capitalists have employed toward the proletariat, [they] have closed ranks and have, like the amiable Quaker in *Uncle Tom's Cabin*, intimated, 'Friend, thee isn't wanted here,' and, as the old adage has it, 'set her down without it.'" Not that this impulse to protect privilege was openly acknowledged: "You may search the educational literature of the past two decades for this tendency and you will search in vain! The journals which they edit, the conventions which they run, and associations which they form, say nothing about it. . . . They just say nothing, and keep Alice out—if they can. There are Ella Flagg Young episodes ever and anon, but they are [lonely] Monadnocks, not mountain chains in the educational landscape."[27]

Young, who had come up through the ranks, resented the shortcuts to power for men provided by the placement networks which the barons created for their "boys." She came back from the 1913 meeting of the NEA with a warning reported in the *Chicago Tribune:*

> It was perfectly evident that the departments of education in the universities of Columbia, Harvard, Chicago, Yale, Michigan, Illinois, and Wisconsin were more in evidence than ever before in any meeting of the National Education Association. Those departments in the universities seem to be trying to gain control not only of the department of superintendence but of the National Education Association generally, so they might place graduates in desirable positions throughout the country, regardless of the fact that they have had a very limited experience.[28]

In professional associations like the NEA—in which reputations were made and norms established—men continued to dominate decision making even after concessions were made to co-opt the women through devices such as a supposedly representative assembly adopted in 1920. At the first convention under the new charter in 1921, out of 553 delegates there were only 81 elementary teachers, compared with 33 state superintendents, 104 city superintendents, and 88 principals; in all, an estimated 297 delegates were administrators, and those were overwhelmingly male. Leadership on the NEA boards and committees and in the state associations was also predominantly male. The key NEA power wielders, the executive secretaries, continued to be men. The presidents of the rival American Federation of Teachers were also almost all male, despite the early leadership of women in the union movement. All but 8 of the 40 presidents of the major black teachers' association were men.[29]

Despite a few educators—mostly women—who sought to highlight sexual inequities, most leaders in the NEA supported the ideology of a united profession that officially knew no boundaries between teachers and administrators, men and women. All "professionals" shared similar purposes and interests. The belief system that undergirded this official ideology of professionalism was meritocratic and universalistic: if males were running things, it was because they were more committed and competent professionals. No one saw more clearly than Connolly the ironies in the male-formulated version of hierarchical idealism:

> To see one of these crusaders haranguing a hall full of elementary school teachers about "the ideals of our profession," willingly carrying the load of their docility up the Hill of Difficulty, and to see this host of privates, conscientiously striving to amalgamate the impulses to independent action, scientific observation, and freedom . . . with the meticulous obedience and close formation which tomorrow's routine is going to require of them, is a humorously pathetic spectacle. But the lads are in earnest.[30]

The rituals of the associations and the ideals of professionalism served an important purpose in obscuring the facts of top-down management by males. They were all the more effective because not only were the lads in earnest but the women (who made up four-fifths of the "profession") generally accepted the rhetoric of professionalism as well. It was not until the last generation that male hegemony came to be seriously questioned again in educational associations, in the profession as a whole, and in the larger society. But Ella Flagg Young had already raised many of the key questions of bureaucracy, democracy, and gender.

The Leader as Democrat: Ella Flagg Young

"A person, whether leader or follower, girded with moral purpose is a tiny principality of power." Ella Flagg Young illustrated James Mac-Gregor Burns's aphorism. As a shy, severe young woman of seventeen she began her career in Chicago in 1862 as a teacher of roughneck students called "the cowboys," young men who herded cattle on the outskirts of the city and many of whom towered over their five-foot instructor. Over the years she went on to become a demonstration teacher in a normal school, high school teacher, elementary-school principal, assistant superintendent, professor at the University of Chicago, principal of a normal school, and finally superintendent of the Chicago School District from 1909 to 1915. Largely self-educated until she earned a Ph.D. after the age of fifty, she was a brilliant scholar who helped John Dewey to translate his philosophical ideas into educational practice. A woman of great courage, she not only fired a school engineer (janitor) against the wishes of a school board member (a political bombshell at the time), but also resigned her position three times in protest against policies she abhorred.[31]

Although she disdained the spoils system and the power of business lobbies in school politics, she was an astute politician in the alternative politics of women's groups and professional associations and a fifty-year survivor in the tumultous tangle of bureaucratic succession within the Chicago system. Initially trained in the pattern of rigid subordination common to women teachers and eventually presiding over the hierarchy of the second largest bureaucracy in American education, herself compulsively strict in personality, she nonetheless articulated and sought to practice democratic participation in school administration. Far more than her mentor Dewey, she was aware of the challenge of putting his ideal of democracy into action in large and complex organizations. Raised as a Scotch Presbyterian who had committed the Westminster catechism and parts of the Gospels to memory, she became a convert to evolutionary thinking and an advocate of scientific method in education but never lost her pietist sense of duty.[32]

As her own millennial vision of the function of education developed over time, Young maintained her conviction that the schools should focus on character. Her conception of the ethical person changed, however, from the individualistic view of the virtuous citizen common in the nineteenth-century school ideology to the Deweyan concept of democracy as social activity based on understanding of purposes arrived at through group deliberation. It was a long journey from the Westminster catechism to the joyous panorama of public education she sketched as she retired from the superintendency:

> In order that teachers may delight in awakening the spirits of children, they must themselves be awake. We have tried to free the teachers. Some day the system will be such that the child and teacher will go to school with ecstatic joy. At home in the evening the child will talk about the things done during the day and will talk with pride. I want to make the schools the great instrument of democracy.[33]

She was the first woman to become superintendent of schools in a large city. How did she become that anomaly, a female big-city superintendent? At least part of the answer seems to lie in Young's family, her ways of coping with social expectations of women's domestic roles, her abilities and attitudes, her network of woman supporters and male mentors, and the conditions existing in Chicago at the turn of the century.[34]

Young's parents took her seriously and sought to develop not only her intellect but also her independence of spirit. Her mother was a tolerant, skeptical, extremely competent person. "There is nothing strange in the fact that I have taken so readily to practical affairs, and have the ability to manage," said Young. "My mother was manager of our household, and we always looked to her for guidance. She attended to household finances and directed practical matters. Her mind was practical and forceful in business details, and from her I learned to face situations squarely." Her father was a skilled sheet-metal worker who had attended school only until age ten, but who read widely. Relentlessly, but in a kindly way, he insisted that his daughter Ella understand what she was learning both from books and from experience. She watched him day after day working at his forge and thus "got an early training in handiwork and industrial processes. I had manual training before such things were thought of, especially for girls." Because she was a sickly child, she was kept out of primary school. She taught herself to read when she was about eight. A shy, intellectual child, she enjoyed the company of adults more than that of peers. When she went to grammar school, the teacher recognized her ability and made her a monitor in the arithmetic class, seating her in a desk next to the principal. Upset by Ella's growing priggishness, her father demanded that she be seated with the other children.

Young never completed grammar school or attended high school but still was able to pass the teachers examination at the age of fifteen. She then entered the normal school, which sought to standardize instruction in Chicago by teaching rigid methods of drill, posture, and deportment to fledgling teachers. Young's father questioned these rote methods, telling Ella that she should use her intellect to develop her own style. Her mother advised her to drop out of the normal school, suggesting that Ella could not become a good teacher since she did not understand young children, having never associated with them. In her mother's judgment, she was apt to be too severe with herself for faults and hence intolerant toward others' lapses. Taking the caution seriously, Young visited classrooms until she found a warm and skillful teacher upon whose style she could model her own behavior. When she began teaching the class of "cowboys" herself, she was an intense person dressed in black with jet hair parted in the middle, with "eyes that looked you through and through," but she found ways to teach them directly and without affectation, managing to control a difficult class without the harsh discipline then common.[35]

Her parents had not taught her a narrow conception of sex roles, but rather encouraged her to develop a forceful mind and personality. Her lack of conventional schooling and peer modeling also encouraged her independence. Her marital history in a curious way liberated her for a fulfilling career. In 1868 she married an older man, William Young, who was sickly and died shortly afterward. As a widow, Young faced no barriers to continuing her career yet avoided the stigma attached to single women. The two other women who headed big-city school systems had similar husband-free careers. Superintendent Susan Dorsey of Los Angeles was abandoned by her husband, a Methodist minister; Superintendent Ira Jarrell of Atlanta rejected a marriage proposal and chose to remain single.[36]

Throughout her adult life Young found support, as did Catharine Beecher and Emma Willard, from female networks of friends, colleagues, and political and social allies. Beginning with her principalship she formed a study group of teachers who met at her home to discuss literature and to read aloud plays by Shakespeare and the Greek dramatists. And in a much smaller group of close friends she gained the intimacy that sustained her in her arduous public life.[37]

In Chicago, as in many other cities, organizations of teachers and administrators were customarily divided by level (for example, elementary and secondary), by function (for example, principal), and, most important, by sex. Since all but a fraction of the teachers and about half of the administrators were women, this gave Young a valuable base of organizational support. The Chicago Teachers Federation gave her political support both in the state capitol (Young was appointed to the state board of education) and in the city, where Haley carried weight with local labor leaders. The bond of gender also helped elect Young president of the NEA in 1910.[38]

Finally, Young received political support from women's clubs and networks of women reformers like Jane Addams. These groups and teacher associations persuaded thousands of women to sign petitions and to demonstrate support on two occasions—first when Young resigned in 1899 over the autocratic policies of the new superintendent and then in 1913 when members of the school board harassed her. In Chicago, women's clubs were an important source of pressure for educational reform and served as significant allies to Young in her work: she was herself an active clubwoman and an advocate of suffrage and women's rights.[39]

Although these networks supported Young, she climbed the ladder by meeting uniform meritocratic standards of performance. When she wanted to become a principal, she insisted on taking the qualifying examination and was marked first on the list. Until that time women had been excused from taking the test, but after her success the board required all aspirants to pass it. When she became chair of a large committee of principals, a male colleague offered to lead group discussions for her. She refused, learned parliamentary procedure, and became an expert leader.

Throughout her career, she also had male mentors in high positions who recognized her talents, stimulated her growth, and sponsored her mobility. From Superintendent W. H. Wells she learned much about curriculum; Superintendent Josiah Pickard advanced her career and taught her about new methods of gradation and classification; Superintendent George Howland prompted her enthusiasm for scholarship and literature and appointed her as assistant superintendent; and most important, her fruitful association with John Dewey deepened her understanding of how children learn and how democracy worked at the same time that she taught him the everyday meaning of his theories.

When she was fifty years old, Young decided to apply to take a seminar with Dewey. As she went to get his signature, she recalled, "I looked up the long flight of stairs of Cobb Hall and watched the eager faces of the young people and decided that it was a place for young people and that I should not take up the work." But as she was about to leave, a young man offered to get Dewey's permission. Once in his seminars on logic, metaphysics, and ethics, Young flourished; here was a mind that could challenge her own. In Dewey's exploration of how evolutionary thought helped explain human learning, in his version of naturalistic ethics laced with millennial Christian and democratic values, in his vision of the social role of education as described in *School and Society* (1899), she found philosophical doctrines that resonated with her own experience and reflection. Impressed with her open-mindedness and intelligence, Dewey in turn found that "she gave me credit for seeing all the bearings and implications [of my theories] which *she* with her experience and outlook got out of what I said." Dewey reflected that Theodore "Roosevelt's knowledge of politics is the only analogue of Mrs. Young's knowledge of educational matters with which I am acquainted."[40]

Young's thesis, which she later published as *Isolation in the School,* was the distillation of her views on how teachers might participate in decision making in education and her treatise on democracy in school administration. Whereas Dewey generally thought in more abstract terms about educational organization, hers was a firsthand knowledge informed by the same ethical passion for participation. Her *Isolation,* said Margaret Haley, became "the Bible of the teachers of the United States on the question of academic freedom."[41]

For Young to put democratic theories of school administration into practice was no simple matter. She was an intense person who set extraordinary high standards of performance for herself and others. One of her admirers wrote of her efforts as assistant superintendent that "she was called hard, cold, severe, mannish, without sympathy, and in general, very critical." Personal qualities of distance and severity that might have been perceived as desirable in a male supervisor in the patriarchal culture of the late Victorian period were regarded as harsh and unfeminine in a woman.

Even more important than the issue of her personality was the rigidly hierarchical character of the Chicago schools in that period. To a degree Young at first accepted this bureaucratic discipline as natural and inevitable. When she attended normal school, for example, she attempted to emulate the cast-iron methods of discipline she learned there. Even as late as 1899, when she resigned as assistant superintendent because of disagreement with the superintendent about his autocratic ways of dealing with teachers, she resisted attempts to persuade her to reconsider her withdrawal, saying that once she had criticized her superior, she should no longer stay as his subordinate. "As you well know," she wrote sympathetic heads of teacher groups, "I hold positive views regarding official courtesy and official discipline. . . . Under the circumstances it would not be in accord with my theories of discipline for me to continue as district superintendent."[42]

Democracy, Bureaucracy, and Gender

Through her work with Dewey and her own developing understanding of democratic processes in organization, however, she came to question her concepts of "official discipline." As principal of the Skinner grammar school she had encouraged teachers to develop their own ways of teaching and had taken pride in their diverse methods. "No one can work in another's harness" she told teachers, and in the faculty meetings she encouraged free discussion. As assistant superintendent she sought to give principals and teachers greater autonomy. After her work at the University of Chicago had helped to give theoretical underpinnings for her practice, she announced in 1901 her conviction that "no more un-American or dangerous solution of the difficulties involved in maintaining a high degree of efficiency in the teaching corps of a large school system can be attempted than that which is effected by what is termed 'close supervision.' " In her teaching at the university she never lectured or imposed her views on students, but rather guided their discussion by pointed questions. "Often persons in the class expressed dissatisfaction that she did not express definitely the ends she expected them to arrive at," said one of her students, "but she always kept in the background so that one was never quite sure of her deepest thoughts on the matter."[43]

She followed the same pattern of encouraging others to think when she became principal of Cook County Normal School in 1905. She succeeded Colonel Francis Parker and Arnold Tompkins, two strong-minded and charismatic men who had sought to place their stamp on the school. Young, by contrast, rejected their idealized view of the child and the cult of personality in leadership and complained that what the faculty wanted "me to do is give them some stock phrases which they can use on all occasions instead of doing their own thinking." Requiring teachers and students to do independent thinking was, of course, in itself a form of imposition of a particular value perspective. She insisted not only that the faculty express their disagreements openly, but also that they give breathing space to student teachers and not treat them as "girls" but as responsible teachers. Her encouragement of free discussion did not mean a lack of conviction, however. She had a program of changes she promoted to link the normal school more closely to the city schools for student teachers in immigrant districts.

In 1909, when Young became superintendent, there had been a decade of struggle between the teacher organizations, especially the Chicago Teachers Federation, and the superintendent and board. At one point in her career she had had doubts about the collective power of teachers, as in their pressing for larger salaries, although she had endorsed their collaboration in planning instruction. But as assistant superintendent she had seen groups of women come in to present their case for more pay to an emotionless board, and then, when the teachers left, smirks appear on the lips of the men as they chose to ignore the powerless women. Young concluded from this experience that in a society in which business interests combined in massive organizations and power blocks, the teachers, too, needed to combine to accomplish their purposes. For the most part, she and the CTF leaders cooperated. Haley and the teachers were pleased when Young instituted teachers' councils, a plan she had sketched in *Isolation in the Schools,* as a means of enlisting the advice of teachers in policy making and curriculum change. For the superintendent and principals to determine policy was "the reasoning of a member of the ruling class," she believed. "We are now face to face with the fact that a democracy whose school system lacks confidence in the ability of the teachers to be active participants in planning its aims and methods is a logical contradiction in itself."[44]

Young's conception of loyalty was that of hardworking dedication to broad common purposes, to the welfare of the children. She did not conceive of loyalty in the personal terms of a political machine—a group of friends dependent on her goodwill, an official clique. She appointed administration subordinates with whom she disagreed and some who, in hard times, opposed her. She did not even provide herself with a secretary until 1915, and had no cabinet of aides personally tied to her success. One result was that she was grievously overworked, and another was that she was exposed to almost constant sabotage of her efforts both within and without the system. Male high school teachers and principals formed one such opposition group. Textbook salesmen and real-estate operators eager to make excessive profits on school sites connived with board members against her. Business groups opposed to the unionized women teachers attacked her for her links to Haley. Religious bigots entered the campaign, too, accusing her—probably because of her ties to the heavily Catholic CTF—of being a Catholic. Amid the political turmoil surrounding her administration, she found steadfast support, however, from newly enfranchised women liberals led by friends such as Jane Addams.[45]

During her superintendency Young recommended changes in the educational program that resembled the progressive reforms introduced in other urban systems at the time: creation of new specialists such as deans for girls, speech teachers, assistant principals, women physical education teachers, and vocational guidance counselors; revision of the curriculum; and creation of vocational classes and specialized high schools.

Young was a prominent member of the group of liberal professional people in Chicago, including such people as Dewey and George Herbert Mead, who fought against a narrow conception of class-based vocational training to be administered largely by and for businessmen. She believed in Dewey's vision of vocational *education* (as opposed to training) which would link manual work with the broadest mental development, would teach students the meaning of interdependent roles in industrial society, and would provide them with the skills needed for cooperation in the planning of work. Just as she wanted teachers to share decision making about what and how they should teach, so she believed that alienation and isolation could result from separating the planning of work from its execution. She called on teachers to go beyond the school to try to "influence conditions so positively that those children they teach and whose characters they aim to help shall not be trained for labor that blights the powers." She pointed out further that the great mass of women must do some industrial work, but that they were denied the best jóbs even in the fields traditionally reserved to their sex: Do women "go out into the world and manage the great restaurants, the kitchens of the great hotels? Certainly not. Men cook in the large establishments. . . . If you or I want a tailor-made dress, we look around for a man to make it."[46]

Born in the year when Mann was waging his battle with the Boston schoolmasters, and living until World War I, Young bridged in her lifetime the older religious conceptions of character and the newer form of evolutionary optimism and faith in democracy she shared with Dewey. Of his *Democracy and Education* she wrote:

Sometimes teachers, philanthropic workers, and generous givers speak of education of the children of the laborer and the immigrant as something that will make society safer for the upper classes. In this book the philosophy seeks and points the way that would make education the great instrumentality helping children and youths to grow into citizenship in a government intended to be of, by, and for all.[47]

14. DISSENT AND ACQUIESCENCE

The educational trust, with its aims of scientific management and reform from the top down, did not sweep the field of educational leadership uncontested. As we have shown, Ella Flagg Young and her allies among militant women teachers had a contrasting vision of democracy in education, one that owed much to John Dewey's philosophy. Educators advanced theories that competed with those of the administrative progressives. Some dissenters protested the use of intelligence tests. Some called for greater sensitivity to ethnic differences in curriculum and instruction. A few criticized the business-oriented corprate model of governance. Many worried about the effects of vocational tracking. Some called for a libertarian and child-centered pedagogy that followed the pupil's free trajectory of growth and curiosity. The social reconstructionists had a radical vision of using public schooling to transform society into a planned cooperative commonwealth. Academic traditionalists continued to stress basic disciplines and perennial moral verities rather than the utilitarian goals of social efficiency. While dissent played an important part in keeping alternative conceptions of schooling alive, the administrative progressives largely succeeded in winning public acquiescence in their program of reform and their goal of depoliticizing public education.[1]

None of the critics was more cogent or influential than John Dewey. He warned in 1902 that "it is easy to fall into the habit of regarding the mechanics of school organization and administration as something comparatively external and indifferent to educational ideals." The opposite was true, he believed: one could not have a democratic educational system if planning was divorced from execution, management from practice. Democratic ends could not be divorced from pedagogical means. He criticized the ideology and program of the administrative progressives in two fundamental ways. He maintained that teachers and students could engage in true education only if the purposes, content, and methods of learning emerged from shared social activity. And he attacked the shallow scientism and conservative social values of the proponents of scientific management.[2]

Dewey believed that every school should become "an embryonic community" which would train children to a "spirit of service" and "effective self-direction," thereby providing "the deepest and the best guarantee of a larger society which is worthy, lovely, and harmonious." The loving and wise family, not the factory, was his social model. The school could reconstruct a harsh and competitive society only if it were a miniature example of a more just and effective polity. Democracy, he argued, "is more than a form of government; it is primarily a mode of associated living, of conjoint communicated experience." Since democracy rejected external authority and relied on "voluntary disposition and interest," the classroom would have to create conditions under which a variety of individuals, profiting from their diverse perspectives, could discover and act on common purposes.[3]

Thus top-down management of a "democratic" school system was a contradiction in terms. The processes of schooling should be congruent with the character of the cooperative society Dewey sought to achieve. His political values were explicit, but he thought that the administrative progressives were covertly embedding conservative premises in their version of objective educational science. "If we are satisfied upon the whole with the aims and processes of existing society," he wrote, then "the attempt to determine objectives and select subject-matter of studies by wide collection and accurate management of data" would suffice, for it would perpetuate the status quo. "But if one conceives that a social order different in quality and direction from the present is desirable . . . quite a different method and content is indicated for educational science." Dewey also attacked the shallow and atheoretical quality and promotional bias of much educational research. Merely counting things did not make an investigation scientific, nor did statistics produce "a magical guarantee of a scientific product." Researchers on the make were too eager to "convert scientific conclusions into rules and standards of classroom practice" in the hope of proving their work useful. Few of the administrative progressives heeded his warnings about the conservative bias of their "science" or halted their rush to convert numbers into norms.[4]

Some educators, however, shared Dewey's concerns about applied research and called for a training of administrators which would give them a broader and more liberal perspective on social issues. The most articulate critic of administrative training was Jesse Newlon, professor at Teachers College and a colleague of Dewey's. While superintendent of the Denver public schools Newlon had pioneered in an early form of "democratic administration" and had actively enlisted teachers in reshaping the curriculum. His book *Educational Administration as Social Policy* was a sustained attack on the drab scientism and implicitly conservative bias endemic in the training of administrators. Through analysis of the contents of textbooks and courses in educational administration Newlon concluded that most graduate instruction focused on administrivia and virtually ignored the "critical examination of educational and social implications of the structures and procedures discussed." If superintendents were to become educational and community leaders, he argued, they needed to study educational philosophy, curriculum theory, social sciences, and educational policy.[5]

Newlon and Dewey were members of a group of scholars at Teachers College in the 1930s who envisaged a radical role for educational leaders. The crisis in capitalism induced by the Great Depression led them to believe that education could help to create a planned economy. A leader in that group of social reconstructionists, George Counts, had already made a series of path breaking studies in the 1920s that showed the class and racial bias of secondary education, the dominance of school boards by elites, and the fancifulness of believing that schools could really be "above politics." In 1932 he asked in a forthright address "Dare the School Build a New Social Order?" Other scholars, like the historian Merle Curti, analyzed the elitist character of school leadership in the past and present and called for educators to bring about fundamental social change. Although this group of educational radicals promoted a searching discussion of the links between education and the political economy in their journal *The Social Frontier,* it reached only a small segment of the profession and expressed aspirations that little matched those of the great majority of leaders. It was not until the 1960s that similarly radical voices could be heard again in education.[6]

If the hope that educators could use the schools to build a new social order now seems utopian—especially in the light of the elite character of school boards and the traditional values of school administrators— another assumption of the liberals and radicals of the 1930s is reminiscent of Strayer and Cubberley: almost all believed in granting greater power and autonomy to professional educators. Whatever their political persuasion, educational theorists generally lacked a comprehensive vision of a lay polity of education or an appreciation for the uses of controversy and conflict. Coupled with their belief in autonomy for the professional was a fear of "pressure groups," for they tended to see "outside" groups as intruders and not as legitimate forces for change. Liberal educators worried that groups like the National Association of Manufacturers or the American Legion might demand probusiness or ultrapatriotic propaganda; conservatives had their doubts about advocacy groups pressing for sex education or socialist indoctrination; and most leaders feared the influence of "politicians" or religious factions. Indeed, in the professional literature on school governance, most lay forms of political expression—beyond a sanitized version of school boards or supportive PTA's—were suspect. One consequence, as we suggest in Part III, is that even liberal educators generally failed to see broad social movements such as civil rights as a positive impetus for educational change.[7]

It may be argued, then, that the administrative progressives suc-

ceeded in convincing a whole range of fellow professionals that education should be depoliticized, if by that one means not that educators
should always agree, but that lay people should be kept at arm's length.
This might be called the politics of lay acquiescence. Indeed, after the
series of campaigns to centralize control of urban schools, the politics
of public education did become relatively quiescent. To be sure, open
public protest did appear in some places: rural people resisted consolidation of one-room schools; labor-union officials in Chicago argued that
intelligence testing and junior high schools were undemocratic; thousands of Jews in New York City protested in the streets against the
introduction of a kind of vocational training that might condemn their
children to menial jobs; fundamentalists passed laws to ban Darwinism;
and many local controversies arose over the financial side of education,
tax rates, teachers' salaries, contracts for buildings and supplies, or disputes over the cost of "fads and frills." But the older ethnocultural
politics, which had mobilized large numbers of citizens, largely died
down, and no pervasive new set of issues emerged to unite voters in
opposition to the programs of the administrative progressives.[8]

It is difficult to determine the significance of this relative calm in
school politics. The administrative progressives themselves thought
they knew its meaning: the public was well pleased with the new-
style schooling, for did not the greatly increased public expenditures
and enrollments demonstrate support? There is some evidence, however, for a contrary view that education was a reform imposed upon
a reluctant working class by elites. Study after study of school dropouts has demonstrated that workers' children did not relish school. In
one experiment in Milwaukee, for example, 8,000 youth in part-time
continuation schools were asked if they would return full-time to
school if they were paid about the same wages as they earned at work;
only 16 said that they would. But a distaste for school among young
workers was not the same thing as organized opposition or a compelling alternative vision. To the degree that labor was organized, as in
the American Federation of Labor, it consistently supported compulsory schooling and also advocated the form of vocational schooling
that ultimately triumphed—one under the control of public-school
officials. Public challenges to the program of the administrative
progressives generally attacked marginal features of the system, not
its basic assumptions or impact. In short, the administrative progressives managed to make the system, and their own powers within it,
seem inevitable and legitimate. Above politics, not seeming to serve
any one faction exclusively, public education deserved public confi-

dence, they believed, and within the schools they claimed a right to say what was normal and desirable.[9]

In public education the members of the educational trust played a role similar to that of entrepreneurs in the leading sectors of the American economy. While there were lagging sectors both in public schools and in business, ultimately even these backwaters felt the surge of change. One reason that the administrative progressives exercised such influence was that they acted in concert politically, ideologically, and programmatically with the most powerful forces in America, the economic and professional elites that were transforming the ways in which the society conducted its business both private and public. The hegemony of business ideology made uplift through scientific management seem self-evidently virtuous. The ideology of depoliticized expertise splintered opposition and defused the effectiveness of protest.

So pervasive was the ideology of scientific efficiency and the influence of business and professional elites that urban schools all over the nation converged in their institutional evolution, especially after centralization of control. In 1909 Cubberley wrote that previous "advances in organization and in the enrichment of curriculum have nearly all been forced upon the school by practical men from without." By "practical men" he meant businessmen, and part of the strategy of the administrative progressives was precisely to align themselves with such elites in the process of proposing educational reforms. Thus the new professional consensus in the educational trust typically had behind it the prestige and political impetus of the "practical men" who sat on school boards.[10]

Even superintendents who differed in their backgrounds, values, and styles of leadership as much as Young, Cody, and Spaulding presided over schools that developed in similar directions. Chicago, Detroit, and Cleveland all grew in complexity of program and administrative structure, adding vocational education, guidance programs, junior high schools, testing and research bureaus, and highly differentiated curricula for different groups of students. Young, Cody, and Spaulding all cited such increments to the system in listing their achievements.

The huge scale and complexity of urban school systems constrained the ways in which superintendents could exert leadership. Sheer size made personal impact difficult and the task of coordination herculean. Young recalled in 1916 that:

> When I began teaching in the city of Chicago, the teaching force was so small that the superintendent, who had his institutes once a month, had in one schoolroom the teachers of the high school, the principal of the high school

—there was then only one—the principal of the elementary schools, and all the grade teachers. There we met and discussed, on the same level, the subjects which were presented to us, or which were raised by persons present. But today it is simply impossible for the teachers in a great city or for even the principals in a city like New York, to meet and discuss freely the questions—a few do the talking, and they talk to the galleries.[11]

Cody might create a personal legend by his colorful personality, and Young might foster an ethos among teachers by the democratic ideals she personified, but both ended up by creating ever more complicated bureaucracies in which the symbolic impact of their leadership became obscured by layers of hierarchy.

As schools grew bigger, leaders controlled their systems increasingly by rules and delegation rather than by personal knowledge and presence. They created regulations to coordinate the parts. They assigned responsibility for specific tasks to specialized subordinates. Authority was no longer personal and diffuse, as in a small system in which a leader could know particular teachers and children and parents. Now authority depended on position and flowed from the top down. Viewed from above such a system seemed a rational model of scientific management; viewed from the teachers' perspective it often seemed hermetic and autocratic; viewed from outside, it often seemed so complex and opaque as to be hard to influence.[12]

Within the systems, informal networks of communication and influence developed alongside the formal organizational chart. Through such informal groupings school staff could combine to sabotage or advance the purposes of the top officials. Aspiring young administrators found it essential to learn such intrabureaucratic politics in order to advance, while superintendents who neglected to gain the support of informal networks discovered the power of the dragged foot.

There were some educators who perceived the pathologies of bureaucracies engineered by the administrative progressives and tried to reform them from within. In their careers one can discover prefigurations of the changes to come after 1954 when new social movements would transform American education once more. Of these dissenters, none was more perceptive or inventive than Leonard Covello, teacher and principal in New York's East Harlem.

The Leader as Community Organizer: Leonard Covello

Covello saw that the attempt to standardize education from above meant that schooling was often mismatched with the diverse cultures of the students' families. He realized that the hierarchical and autocratic nature of school administration lowered morale among teachers and blocked their initiative. He knew that the complexity of the system made it seem opaque and alien to parents. He rejected much that the administrative progressives had sought to install: intelligence tests that labeled children stupid and unteachable; vocational tracks that relegated them to humble jobs; an ethnocentric curriculum that taught them to be ashamed of their ethnic background.

Covello was a teacher and principal in the largest and perhaps the most complex school system in the United States. He learned, even within that huge organization, to use informal networks to create a sense of shared purpose and morale that made his school a community rather than an outpost of a distant headquarters at 110 Livingston Street. The school itself became a center of its neighborhood because Covello knew how to tap the community's natural groupings, the existing bonds of partial community, to build a greater sense of common purpose in East Harlem. Such an approach to leadership enabled him to surmount the barriers that bureaucratic structures created within the school system and between the school and its neighborhood. His skill in understanding informal organization, his ability to mobilize people to accomplish joint purposes, represented one way in which older direct and personal styles of leadership could survive even in a large bureaucracy.

To the boys of Benjamin Franklin High School he was "Pop Covello," to teachers, a friend who inspired a common dedication. Victim of a thoughtless cultural chauvinism himself as a child, he created a school that honored and reflected the cultural diversity of its community. He refused to use the school to adjust students to an unjust society: he insisted that together he and the community mobilize to change it.

Leonard Covello was a pioneer in creating bilingual, bicultural education; storefront schools; community advisory committees for schools; multicultural education; programs to prevent school dropouts; school-based community-service and political-action programs; methods of troubleshooting in race riots; and much else. He was also an early critic of the misuse of I.Q. tests with culturally different populations. He did all this in the 1920s and 1930s in the largest school bureaucracy in the nation. He began as a high school teacher in New York City before World War I and served as principal of Benjamin Franklin High School for twenty-two years from 1934 to 1956. What is most significant about him is that as he put his ideas into practice they formed a coherent whole. His ideal was a school that was community-centered rather than subject-centered or child-centered. And he used the school, its students and staff, as an agency for organizing the people of East Harlem to improve their lives.[13]

Covello came to this country from his hometown of Aviliano in southern Italy at the age of ten. Both in Italy and in East Harlem where his father settled, he knew poverty and harsh daily labor. But perhaps more important for his later career, he learned firsthand the pain of the clash of cultures between the American school and that of his family and townspeople, the shock of a forced assimilation that taught him to be ashamed of his name, his language, and the lowly standing of his people. "I remember in those days how we used all our resources to keep our parents away from school—particularly our mothers," Covello recalled later, "because they did not speak English and still dressed in the European way with the inevitable shawl. We didn't want these embarrassing 'differences' paraded before our teachers. . . . In trying to make a good impression on our teachers, it was always at the expense of our family and what was Italian in us." Under pressure from his father to go to work, Covello quit high school. But friends persuaded him to return, to attend Columbia, and then to become a teacher.[14]

By the time he went to Dewitt Clinton High School as a foreign language teacher, Covello had become proud of the Italian language and culture. He joined or helped to found a half-dozen Italian-American voluntary associations inside and outside the schools and became the first person, probably, to teach Italian in an American high school. His purpose was not only to acquaint his Italian students with their own high culture, but also to use the language as a bridge between the home and the school. Seeing how effectively Covello related to Italian boys other teachers regarded as roughnecks, the principal invited him into his office and said: "These boys are not easy to handle. . . . To put it bluntly, it will be your job to look after these boys. . . . I want you to become the father-confessor of these East Side boys."[15]

Known to the people of East Harlem as "Pop," Covello became more like an older brother or father to the boys than another member of the bureaucracy. Firm but affectionate with them, he could share their trials at home, their sense of rejection and conflict at school. Even three decades later they were still Joe and Lupino and Vito to him, not long-gone and nameless ex-students. One of his students of that period later recalled: "He filled a hero void for most of us, not a cowboy hero, not a blood and thunder hero, but a true hero. His dedication could show in his own quiet way . . . he was a real big brother and a real father." He spent much of his time after school visiting their homes, directing Italian plays, teaching Italian adults. Loyal both to Garibaldi and Lincoln, he was helping to invent bilingual, bicultural education.[16]

As time went on, his conception of service through education broadened and deepened, reaching beyond the Italian community. His notion of multicultural education came to include all ethnic groups. He began to see that the school could become a center to organize broad change. He believed that New York school administrators and planners thought too much "in *mass* terms," on a bureaucratic citywide basis of standard units rather than in terms of the actual distinct individuals, cultures, and neighborhoods that made up the city.

Covello went through several stages in his thinking and action; these were also seen in later forms of ethnic education. The first stage was one of saying *"include me, understand me,* my group *belongs* in the curriculum."* Hence Covello argued for instruction in Italian. The next stage was to connect the school more closely with the home and community life of Italian immigrants. Both of these stages helped administrators and teachers to work more effectively with youth who might otherwise have been alienated and difficult. But Covello's vision of a community-based school went beyond adapting the school to ethnic cultures so that students would in turn adapt to the school. In particular, his vision went far beyond co-optation of unruly students. He believed that the school itself should mobilize neighborhood people to bring about social justice.[17]

Covello showed what he meant when he became principal of the new Benjamin Franklin High School in East Harlem, his home, in 1934. This school was the product of a political movement of which Covello was a leader. East Harlem previously had had no high school, despite its dense population of over 200,000 people. Covello joined forces with city politicians, among them Vito Marcantonio and Mayor LaGuardia, to create Franklin High School, and later he lobbied for a magnificent new building on the East River. Not afraid of political action, he was a master of orchestrating groups to press for change. This was a skill he wanted his students and their families to learn: how to analyze social and economic problems and how to gain the power to correct them.

The community became the heart of the curriculum in many ways. In art the students painted murals of their neighborhood; in social studies they studied land values and housing conditions; in literature they read authors of the various nationalities and races represented in the school. Students joined with teachers, parents, and other adults to pressure governments for new public housing; they worked together to create playgrounds in vacant lots; they led "block beautiful" and sanitation campaigns; and they produced a community newspaper.[18]

Covello wanted the high school to be a center for collective action, for learning, for recreation for all groups and ages. His storefront center became a meeting place for many different groups from little children to adult music clubs. He started community advisory councils in which hundreds of local citizens, students, and teachers participated. The school was open in the evenings. Covello described what a typical night might be like:

> I could sit in my office [during parent conferences] and listen happily to the hum of knowledge. Young men and adults . . . were now completing their high school education at night. In other rooms immigrants of varying ages and nationalities struggled with the complexities of the English language, sometimes taught by their own sons, while others prepared for citizenship tests. In the gymnasium a basketball game was in progress, as often as not involving two Jews, two Italians, three Negroes, two Puerto Ricans, and a fellow named O'Reilly. In the library, the Parent-Teacher Association was holding a meeting while from the auditorium might come the shrill sounds of an argument that meant that the Community Advisory Committee was in session.[19]

Covello had no aversion to arguments and disputes. Nor did he interpret the absence of conflict as a sign of progress. East Harlem was a violent place—the open violence of the youth gangs and the Cosa Nostra, the more hidden psychological violence of hunger and dark crowded tenements, the anger of incomprehension between parents and children. Covello wanted to channel this energy of conflict into collective political and social actions that would improve the lives of people, that would give them voices and power. What hurt him most was the occasional outburst of conflict between the powerless, as when poor whites fought poor blacks. After one such incident, blown out of proportion by the press into race riot, he invited several hundred parents into the school auditorium and told them: "People who struggle for bread can't hate each other."[20]

PART III

Dreams Deferred, 1954-?

Public goods are defined as goods which are consumed by all those who are members of a given community, country, or geographical area in such a manner that consumption or use by one member does not detract from consumption or use by another. . . . The distinguishing characteristic of these goods is not only that they *can* be consumed by everyone, but that there is *no escape* from consuming them unless one were to leave the community by which they are provided. . . . Actually, of course, a private citizen can "get out" from public education by sending his children to private school, but at the same time he *cannot* get out, in the sense that his children's life will be affected by the quality of public education.

Albert O. Hirschman
*Exit, Voice, and Loyalty: Responses to
Decline in Firms, Organizations,
and States*

15 OLD IDEALS AND NEW CLAIMANTS

"I have a dream," Martin Luther King, Jr., told a gathering of 200,000 citizens at the Lincoln Memorial on 28 August 1963. "I have a dream that my four little children will one day live in a nation where they will not be judged by the color of their skin but by the content of their character." One day, he dreamed, "this nation will rise up and live out the true meaning of its creed."[1] "What happens to a dream deferred?" asks black poet Langston Hughes:

Does it dry up
like a raisin in the sun?
Or fester like a sore—
And then run?
Does it stink like rotten meat?
Or crust and sugar over—
like a syrupy sweet?
Maybe it just sags
like a heavy load.
Or does it explode?[2]

King's call for a new America based on an old dream deferred, like Rosa Parks's courageous decision in Montgomery in 1955 not to give up her seat on the bus to a white, was part of a crusade to realize social justice. An important part of that civil-rights movement was a desire to use public education to resolve the contradiction between racism and those democratic and egalitarian values which Gunnar Myrdal called an "American Creed." In its historic decision on school desegregation in the *Brown* case in 1954 the United States Supreme Court sought to align educational policy with that creed and thereby gave impetus to a campaign that mobilized citizens, both black and white, to recreate American education.[3]

The civil rights and other protest movements stimulated a third great period of reform of the common school. Again, as in Horace Mann's era, powerful visions of a brighter future animated reformers in education, but this time people demanded social justice for those who had been pushed to the bottom of society and largely ignored. Again, as in the mid-nineteenth century, leaders of social movements pressed for change, but this time they sought not so much to build new institutions as to gain equity and voice in existing but unresponsive school systems. Again, as in the early twentieth century, reformers from foundations, universities, and government sought to redesign public education, but now they regarded themselves more as advocates for the dispossessed than as neutral experts. School reform became a highly politicized domain.[4]

Public education in the 1960s became front-page news as a battleground in the War on Poverty and the quest for racial equality. Across the land in the generation following *Brown* appeared major changes in public education: desegregation, federal aid to schools serving poor children, dozens of state and federal categorical programs aimed at neglected populations, legislation guaranteeing racial and sexual equity, new entitlements for handicapped pupils, state laws demanding accountability and minimum standards for promotion and graduation, bilingual-bicultural programs, career education, and a host of other reforms large and small. The courts took an increasingly active role in school governance and finance. Teachers became more militant and well organized and won collective bargaining rights that preempted many traditional powers of school boards and superintendents. Although there was much talk about "community control" and some actual attempts to decentralize school governance in large cities, in fact much decision making migrated upward from the local district to the state and federal legislatures and other agencies. Such centralization challenged and fragmented the authority of local administrators. Indeed, reformers justified such intervention into local districts by arguing that local educators had neglected the needs of the poor and minorities.

The generation following *Brown* produced not only a headlong rush of educational reforms, but also sharply different assessments of the meaning and value of the changes. For liberals the early years of the War on Poverty and the campaign for civil rights were a heady time. It seemed as if American faith in schooling had never been stronger. People talked of educational moon-shots—the contemporary equivalent of earlier millennial rhetoric. Long awaited reforms such as federal aid to education and civil-rights laws promised real solutions to old problems. Statistics seemed to demonstrate progress. Between 1960 and 1970 expenditures per pupil (in constant 1970 dollars) increased from $665 to $955. In the same decade the percentage of students completing high school jumped from 62 to 75, while by 1975 the educational attainment of young adult blacks and Hispanics nearly equaled that of whites of the same age. By the end of the 1960s desegregation proceeded at a rapid pace in the South (though northern cities lagged behind). New laws and court decisions secured the rights and broadened the opportunities of blacks, females, the handicapped, and linguistic minorities.[5]

But was the cup half-full or half-empty? Minorities protested that reforms were too slow and too parsimonious. And scholarly studies raised questions about the effectiveness of programs that had initially caught the liberal imagination. Research by James Coleman and his associates published in 1966 showed that disparities between the resources of schools attended by whites and minorities were far smaller than had been expected, casting doubt on the liberal belief that educational resources largely accounted for divergent educational performance of pupils. Early evaluation of expensive federal programs seemed to show minimal results (though later studies made when programs were more carefully designed and monitored did show gains). In another major study Christopher Jencks argued that schooling did not do much to equalize adult incomes.[6]

The conclusions of such scholarly studies proved to be deflationary, we believe, largely because of the way in which they asked their initial questions. Basically, such research has translated the question "Do schools make a difference?" into two subquestions: (1) Do fairly small additions of resources to the basic educational system substantially narrow differences of test performance among different social groups? (2) Can schools produce substantial equality of condition in American society—that is, can they equalize income and status?

The answer to both questions is probably no. But the questions were peculiar. For decades scholars had already demonstrated that poor children did not do well on standardized tests even when they had been given similar opportunities in school; achievement in school had never been randomly distributed across class and ethnicity. And whoever claimed—before the 1960s at any rate— that schools *could* create equality of adult income? It is odd to criticize educators for not accomplishing what they never tried to do and could not do under the most favorable conditions.

Liberal reformers have faced criticism from both radicals and neo-conservatives in recent years. Radicals have claimed that schools reflect and perpetuate the racism and class bias of the capitalist political economy and argue that the educational reforms of the 1960s and 1970s detracted attention from the underlying problems. Neo-conservative commentators have questioned whether spending more money on schools really improves education; they worry that "forced busing" creates white flight while not improving academic achievement; they attack the premises and processes of affirmative action; and some of them have begun to advocate free-market approaches to educational reform, including vouchers or income tax credits that would allow parents to send their children to private schools.[7]

Even though liberal reformers, radicals, and neoconservatives have differed in their analyses and prescriptions, they tend to agree on one thing: they have little good to say about the "educational establishment"—the existing managers of the educational system. Liberals complain that educators are rigid and resistant to needed changes. Neo-conservatives portray the managers as ineffectual and self-serving. Radicals see educators as agents—and sometimes apologists—for a destructive and hierarchical political economy. Similarly negative images appear in popular books about education: Charles Silberman speaks about the "mindlessness" of educators; Jonathan Kozol of their racism; and radical utopians, such as Ivan Illich, call for the abolition of formal schooling.[8]

Neither saviors nor villains, school leaders have felt themselves scapegoats in an era of conflict, exaggerated expectations, and angry rhetoric. They have seen themselves as targets of attack for problems over which they have had little control, people of goodwill caught in a vortex of social change.

Our own view is that the conflicts of the 1960s and 1970s resulted from dreams deferred, from contradictions between an ideology of equality and democracy and basic cleavages of race, sex, and class too long papered over by a consensus that ignored the powerless. The liberals of the 1960s responded positively to the real problems highlighted by protest movements, but by overpromising to win political support they contributed to later disillusionment with schooling. Neo-conservatives accurately criticized the hodgepodge quality of many reforms, but we do not find their faith in private sector solutions to social problems convincing. (Indeed, in another decade, observers may consider conservatives' trust in market solutions to issues of social justice as utopian as the liberals' faith in bigger government.) Radicals were of course right in asserting that schools cannot by themselves erase economic inequalities, but they generally left unsettled the question of what schools *can* do to promote a more just society.

Despite the roller coaster of hope, disillusionment, and retrenchment —both fiscal and ideological—we believe that the protest movements and reforms of the last generation have produced real gains for people who were previously neglected and underserved. Many of the problems that have become apparent in recent years in public schools can be understood, in fact, as the sign of a heightened consciousness of unfinished business in public education. We would not wish to turn back the clock to the days of business-as-usual of the 1950s, but the political and ideological disarray of the 1980s suggest that a major task today is to secure a new common ground for the common school.

16. BUSINESS AS USUAL

In a sketch of the work of local school administrators prior to the civil-rights movement, Keith Goldhammer comments that

> older superintendents will recall [those] days . . . and nostalgically ruminate about what it was like when they didn't have to be concerned about so many uncontrolled variables; when their major job was "education," and no one in the community expected, or possibly would even tolerate, policies that intro-

duced school operations into the arena of social action and social policy. The schools were seen as isolated enclaves within the mainstream of American society.

Goldhammer adds that many parents saw schools as the dispensers of valued credentials and hence as the gateway to opportunity in a society that increasingly demanded expertise. Conformity to school demands was the price favored students paid for advancement up the ladder.[1]

Cubberley and his peers would have been quite at home among the educational leaders of the early 1950s, many of whom—then in their late forties and fifties—had been their students. By then many of the changes in governance and in the structures of public education sought by the administrative progressives had become well established. The levels of academic and professional training of administrators had risen rapidly, stimulated in part by more rigorous state requirements for certification. According to the progressives' plan, urban schools had become multilayered, functionally differentiated systems headed mostly by superintendents trained in university programs. Secondary education had become so universal that educators were now concerned about attracting the remnants of nonattenders labeled "dropouts." The campaign to consolidate rural schools was accelerating so fast that the number of school districts was cut in half between 1950 and 1960. On the eve of its centennial in 1957, the NEA had become a complex holding company of departments that totaled almost 700,000 members. The NEA claimed to speak for a united profession, but it was still dominated by administrators as it had been in the 1920s.[2]

Local superintendents and school boards enjoyed considerable autonomy and faced few constraints from federal or state governments or even from community pressure groups. School board elections were rarely arenas of conflict; high-status members tended to recruit successors like themselves, portraying their task as disinterested attention to the welfare of the whole community. Such boards gave superintendents much room for professional discretion. Most of the literature on school boards and administrators "dealt with the problems of avoiding conflict," writes Goldhammer, "rather than the containment or use of conflict as an administrative device." There were few places where teachers were militant or where they practiced collective bargaining. Charles E. Lindblom's characterization of politics as "the science of muddling through" well describes the early 1950s, when incrementalism in reform left unchallenged the larger educational framework while concentrating on improving the parts.[3]

Business as Usual

In the tumultuous year 1969 political scientist Stephen Bailey wrote that "reviewing traditional—even recent—literature about American school boards is a strange and unsettling experience." The reason for his reaction was that "the described value systems and life styles of school boards, and the perceptions of reality of the authors who have written about them, seem romantically archaic and irrelevant." Reading the standard studies, he continued, "is a little like studying modern geography with a pre-World War II textbook, and a pre-World War I atlas." At center stage in the 1950s were the school board and the superintendent. Local "interest groups" occasionally entered into dialogues. In the wings, giving faint signals, was the state department of education. The school lawyer was the man who defended the school board when a student slipped on the icy steps of the high school and her parents sued the district. Now and then people debated abstractly about the dangers of federal control *if and when* (and it seemed unlikely) the Congress should decide to give federal aid. Yearly the board decided how much of a raise it could afford to give the teachers. Ethnic issues—if perceived at all—were generally treated as problems in "intergroup relations" to be solved by experts in intercultural education.[4]

The superintendents of the early 1950s guided public education in an era when familiar goals, systems of governance, programs, and professional norms seemed to work. Their code of ethics stressed principles that Cubberley would have applauded: keeping schools out of politics, especially resisting pressure groups; impartially administering the rules; preserving the integrity and dignity of the profession; and keeping the faith that "what happens in and to the public schools of America happens to America." Public schools had successfully weathered great challenges: the Depression and World War II. During the 1930s educators had pruned budgets but expanded secondary enrollments and wrote eloquent justifications of public education in a series of books and pamphlets issued by the Educational Policies Commission. During the war they struggled to find enough teachers to staff the schools but knew that public education was essential to a triumph of democracy over totalitarianism. In the postwar years they scrambled to build enough classrooms to house the children of the baby boom, buttressed by the belief that they were working within a sound and continuous professional tradition. The school administrators' yearbook expressed this sense of confidence in 1952 in sentences that might have been written by Cubberley himself: "It is the superintendent of great heart and courageous spirit, possessed of sound judgment and deep understanding, who will carry the profession and the schools forward. . . . His world will be immeasurably enriched by his service and leadership."[5]

This is not to say that leaders in public education faced no opponents. They did, but the opposition tended to galvanize them into unity. The same yearbook of 1952 warned that "today's mid-century attacks upon the schools are not more powerful nor more vicious than those of 100 years ago. The Horace Manns and Henry Barnards had to win support by sheer missionary zeal and convincing logic." Who were these attackers, and what did they want? There were some McCarthyites who worried that the schools were soft on communism. That was easy enough for anxious school leaders to disprove; and in case anyone had doubts left, the AASA passed a resolution barring Communists from teaching in public classrooms. But the other major concern of critics in the early and mid 1950s—especially academic conservatives—was intellectual flabbiness, associated in their minds with something they called "progressive education."[6]

The two kinds of criticism became easily merged in the cold war ethos of the time. America was falling behind the Russians—as shown in Sputnik's ascent into space in 1957 while our rockets fizzled and tumbled onto their pads—because our schools weren't teaching the basics and instructing the gifted as well as the Russians trained Ivan. Glossy popular magazines were full of laments. *Life* published an "urgent" series on the "Crisis in Education" in which it charged that students wasted their time on frivolous elective courses, people were graduating from high school who could only read at the fifth-grade level, teachers were incompetent, and discipline was poor. Such notables as Admiral Hyman Rickover, historian Arthur Bestor, and businessman Albert Lynd pressed their case against frills and for fundamentals in widely read books and popular media. Bestor declared flatly on the cover of *U.S. News and World Report* that "we are less educated than 50 years ago."[7]

Bestor had an explanation for this disaster, one that flattered the power if not the wisdom of people he called "educationists." The decline of standards was the result of a deliberate watering down of the curriculum and perversion of purpose by an "interlocking directorate" of university professors of education, school administrators, and state departments of education. Some "educationists" retaliated by calling their critics "congenital reactionaries" and "dogma peddlers." It was an age fond of scapegoats.[8]

The deeper causes of malaise, then as now, arose from fundamental shifts in the society and economy as well as transformations in the educational system. High schools were then enrolling students who formerly would not have been in school but at work; much of the "life adjustment" (the new version of "progressive") curriculum was aimed at adapting secondary education to such pupils. A specialized, hierarchical workplace demanded more credentials and new forms of expertise. A cold war psychology justified a survival-of-the-fittest mentality by pitting the United States against communism.[9]

Into the ruckus walked an unelected national school superintendent, scientist, and former Harvard president, James Bryant Conant, who became a Moses leading troubled citizens and educators to a promised land of consensus. A committed anticommunist and advocate of meritocracy, Conant was also a friend of public education who saw it as a means of inculcating common beliefs and providing an avenue of social mobility for talented youth who might otherwise find the channels of advancement clogged. He believed in tracking students by academic ability except in social studies classes, where they were to learn principles of citizenship together. In his writings on the high school and junior high school he provided a pragmatic checklist of reforms to meet the objections of critics. His mode of reform was incremental, strengthening schooling for the gifted while preserving the basic structure of public education.[10]

While the national debate over the purposes and content of schooling helped to shape the agenda of educational decision making, the key locus of control in the 1950s remained largely at the local level. There, occasional flash floods of public concern—over the three Rs, or sex education, or training the gifted, or subversive teaching—swept the usually dry arroyos of school politics, but the basic power alignments we have described did not shift substantially nor did the basically conservative consensus of the period change in any fundamental way.[11]

A generation of careful studies of school boards prior to 1950 had demonstrated that members came largely from those at or near the apex of power in their local communities. James Coleman describes the way elites dominated business-as-usual in public education:

> In local communities, the political structure is most often dominated by the property-owning classes, including the social and business elite of the community . . . communities, both suburban and independent, and small or medium-sized cities, are not governed through a strong competition by political parties, but are governed by an oligarchy among whose members there is more consensus than conflict.

Such lay leaders, he adds, "have three interests which together lead in the direction of a system of preferential or differentiated education." They want an excellent education for their own children; they want to keep property taxes low; and they wish to preserve the existing social order "without the disruption caused by high social mobility." Instead of creating schools explicitly divided by class, as formerly in England, such local oligarchies prefer to concentrate "children in schools according to background (whether through concentration of residence or through selection)" with "greater educational effort expended on children from better backgrounds." Coleman found, for example, that "close linkages of the school administrators and staff with the structure of power in the community helped create greater opportunity for children from 'better' families" in high schools he investigated in Illinois in the 1950s. Academic and vocational tracks largely segregated social groups in the larger schools, and, even in the smaller schools with ungrouped classes, "teachers and students knew who 'should' be good students, and who should not." Despite possibilities for advancement for especially talented pupils—Conant's ideal of contest mobility—the schools as a whole reflected the inequalities found in the larger local community. The most striking examples of such transmission of inequality were to be found in southern communities which buttressed the caste system by sharply different treatment of the two races.[12]

How is one to understand the role of school administrators in local communities in which elites controlled school boards? One traditional approach was to see them essentially as captives of the powerful. The school superintendent, according to W. Lloyd Warner, "comes into a pre-existing sociocultural complex with all its local values, beliefs, prejudices, and ground rules. . . . He is compelled by the pressures around him to organize his thoughts and activities in accordance with the demands made upon him by the people who wield the power in the community." Recently, a number of scholars have favored a contrasting interpretation. They have stressed that school administrators have their own distinct professional cultures, values, and interests and have demonstrated considerable ingenuity in co-opting the lay boards that supposedly decided public policy. By controlling the flow of information to school board members, by claiming impartial expertise, and by obfuscation when necessary, they have turned school boards into rubber stamps for their policies. This has been particularly true, political scientists assert, in large and heterogeneous urban districts where bureaucracies seem opaque to public scrutiny and so multilayered that even the officials at the top could not penetrate the maze. With its apolitical ideology, public education has become a textbook case of a closed system.[13]

Captive or commander—was the local superintendent of the 1950s either? We think not. Rather, as we suggested in Part II, we believe that district decision making reflected a symbiosis of lay elites and professional leaders who shared basic values and served each others' interests. Business and professional elites—Coleman's "oligarchies"—respected the principle of managerial expertise; school superintendents admired successful people and needed their support. In such informal settings as the Rotary Club school leaders could become friends with power wielders. There is little evidence that busy school board members had the time or inclination to try to influence the everyday decisions required in running a school system. Conversely, superintendents appear to have been well aware of the "zone of consent" within which they might maneuver with impunity, as William Boyd points out. In some cases, especially as pillars of the community in smaller districts, they may have been so much at one with local values that they were not even aware that limits existed. The result of such a common set of understandings could well have appeared to be a "closed system" run by professionals or a cave-in by school administrators to the powerful, yet to these participants it was neither—at least in those long periods when the arroyos of school politics were dry. From time to time, when community dissent increased, boards and superintendents might have been at odds and either might have been unseated by elections. But the norm for both boards and administrators was to contain or ignore conflict, to keep outsiders at arm's length—or, when necessary, to co-opt them.[14]

The power of elites consisted, then, in setting the agenda for the schools, and the superintendent's professional freedom existed within those boundaries. The agenda and the boundaries differed according to the size and heterogeneity of the community and the values and interests of the board members and educators. But what was often not noticed in the 1950s, with its urge for business-as-usual, was what was *not* on the agenda. This "other face of power" was becoming apparent, however, to the leaders of new protest movements, who were stymied in community after community when they tried to force local elites to face up to the inequities protesters sought to correct. To bring about real social change they would have to build new coalitions, use new methods, and reach to higher levels of government for leverage.[15]

17. PROTEST MOVEMENTS AND SOCIAL JUSTICE

In the years following *Brown* the schools increasingly became a battle-ground of contending forces. Much of the leadership came from people outside the traditional domain of educational policy makers, from protest groups that no longer accepted business as usual. Groups that had been denied equal rights and equal dignity no longer regarded their status as fixed in the order of things. The 1960s, in particular, was an era of massive social movements on the left: among them, the civil-rights movements of the blacks, feminists, and Hispanics. Typically, leaders and followers in such movements were protesting conditions and attitudes they encountered in their everyday experience: the indignity of Mississippi blacks walking on a red clay road to a one-room segregated shack while whites rode past in a yellow bus to their school; tenements with leaking gas and leaking roofs; textbooks that ignored Mexican-Americans or presented them only in demeaning stereotypes; capable women training novice males to be their bosses. Subordination no longer seemed immutable but instead a challenge.[1]

Protesters often centered demands on schools not because public education was uniquely oppressive but because it seemed the nearest portal to greater opportunity. "Education," Myrdal observed, "has always been the great hope for both individual and society. In the American Creed it has been the main ground upon which 'equality of opportunity for the individual' and 'free outlet for ability' could be based." Protest groups sought not simply opportunity for individuals but collective advance for their race or sex or ethnic group, however. While initially drawing on the universal and liberal doctrine of equal rights—that is, no discrimination according to race or sex or other social distinction—protest movements also produced a strong group consciousness that led to separatist ideologies.[2]

At first most protest groups sought equal access and status in schools and other mainstream institutions, using a traditional ideology of unfettered opportunity. Martin Luther King eloquently expressed this aspiration. The quest for racial desegregation and for equal pay for men and women represented this side of the drive for equality. But other protest leaders came to pose goals other than sameness of treatment. Like nineteenth-century immigrant groups, they wanted the public schools to legitimize cultural differences, to teach their own history, use their languages in the classroom, and honor a diversity not encompassed by Anglo conformity. And some protest leaders, despairing of achieving equity within a system controlled by existing power-holders, decided that only community control by their own group could achieve justice. Coveting novelty and vivid scenes for the nightly television news, the media often played up the extremist side of dissent, featuring militants: black college students with guns and bandoliers of bullets, or "bra-burners," typical neither of the black nor feminist movements.[3]

Protest groups on the left engendered protest groups on the right. In the South the Ku Klux Klan and White Citizens Councils organized to fight desegregation, followed later in the North by opponents of busing, both violent and genteel. Antifeminist associations countered women's rights groups. Fundamentalists banded together to restore traditional religion and patriotism, to replace evolution with Genesis, and to restore the Bible and prayer to classrooms. Tax limitation groups rapidly gained clout in the 1970s.[4]

Activists in protest groups started with strategies that Horace Mann would have recognized. They sought to appeal to a sense of guilt and responsibility by showing how social evils conflicted with American articles of faith. The road to redemption lay through renewed commitment to realizing those values through a revitalized public education. They sought to mobilize their own people and arouse the conscience of those who had the power to bring about change. Unlike Mann and his fellow common-school crusaders, however, they were outsiders who had been denied voice and influence. Often stymied when persuasion, confrontation, boycotts, and other tactics of change failed to bring results in the entrenched power structures of local communities, they took their case to cosmopolitan allies in the churches, the courts, the foundations, and state and national governments. The law—both in the form of legislative acts and court decisions—provided essential support from the highest levels of government.[5]

Established educational leaders, like superintendents in urban districts, had been unaccustomed to confrontations, mass protests, and legal challenges. They were ill-prepared to deal either with protesters —whom they tended to regard as outside pressure groups—or with mandates from above to change their behavior. Reactive more than initiatory, they generally failed to discern ways in which the social energy generated by protest movements could be harnessed to improve public education for those who needed it most. As Larry Cuban observes, they knew how to respond to established interest groups and school boards that operated in familiar, orderly ways, but they had little practice in coping with the mobilized protest of groups of outsiders.[6]

The ideology of professionalism and the professionalization of ideology contributed to this defensive response. The ideology of professionalism had taught school administrators that they, and not outside "pressure groups," were the proper arbiters of policy. The professionalization of ideology had narrowed their older broad-based rationale for public schooling into a justification for the status quo and restricted administrators' ability to hear or persuade a pluralistic public. Taught to regard conflict as pathology, they mostly failed to perceive its potential for renewal.

Public educators had always regarded the schools as an agency for improving the society and for providing greater equality to individuals. That indeed had been the claim of the crusaders in the mid-nineteenth-century movement that built the common school. The administrative progressives believed that they had the blueprint for engineering a harmonious, smoothly functioning society through education. But when presented with demands for justice by groups that had been excluded from full participation in that society, many leaders of the 1960s complained that they were in the business of "education, not social engineering." Educators had not created social problems—indeed had mitigated them, they thought—and could not exceed the community's speed limit in righting social wrongs.

In research on controversies over desegregation in eight large cities in 1965, Robert L. Crain and David Street found such attitudes common among the ten superintendents they studied. Seven rejected the demands of civil-rights groups for integration, while three counseled their boards to adopt a liberal response. When interviewed about the reasons for their actions, the superintendents stressed three points. The first was that schools should be color-blind—that no group should receive special treatment. The second was that the purpose of the schools was " 'educational' rather than 'social.' " And last, education should be left to the professionals: "Lay persons are dismissed as unqualified to make recommendations, and their criticisms are frequently answered with flat disagreement or with vague, overly detailed, and off-the-point replies." One of the superintendents, Benjamin C. Willis of Chicago, temporarily resigned when his judgment about racial issues was questioned. Heirs of a tradition that abhorred interference with administrators' prerogatives, unaccustomed to bargaining with dissenting groups, the traditional leaders of public education were white males who were not disposed by conviction or experience to respond creatively to demands that they share their policy-making power. Caught between local confrontations and laws and court degrees from above, however, they discovered that change was unavoidable.[7]

The ferment in public education produced by the social movements of the last generation—particularly those on the left—is unprecedented in the history of American public education. A closer look at the most important of these—the civil-rights protest—suggests the dynamics of such campaigns: their origins, the twists and turns which the movement took, and their linkage with the courts and other government agencies to challenge and transform public schools.

Throughout history people have suffered discrimination, disruption of their daily lives, and severe deprivation without open protest. "For a protest movement to arise out of these traumas of daily life," write Frances Fox Piven and Richard Cloward, "people have to perceive the deprivation and disorganization they experience as both wrong and subject to redress." Pressed to the bottom of society, blacks in the South knew that the caste system was cruel and unjust, but the whole weight of white power—the economic system, the political and legal system, the official beliefs taught in the schools—sustained racism. The system was unjust, but was it mutable? When a long string of cases against educational segregation culminated in *Brown*, southern blacks took hope that the caste system could be changed. Black historian Vincent Harding writes that "we believed, for a time, that our essential struggle was against the injustices lodged in the deep South, and in this struggle we now had the resources and the moral power of the nation's highest tribunal and all the corrective institutions. It was a heady idea, a profoundly inspiring one, and it provided a tremendous additional impetus and audacity to the earlier stages of the post-1954 struggle."[8]

The Supreme Court's decree represented reform from the top down, accomplished after courageous and astute work by National Association for the Advancement of Colored People (NAACP) lawyers and their grass-roots clients. The white establishment now seemed to have declared for racial equality in education. But for nearly a decade the burden of realizing desegregation in practice fell on southern blacks. Southern white resistance sometimes took savage forms of bombing, killing, and beating of protesters, both black and white. Sometimes it was more subtle, though equally daunting, as when employers threatened the livelihood of their black workers. Starting with the Montgomery bus boycott in 1955, protest against segregation was a mass movement of ordinary but courageous people guided by leaders such as King and aided by outside allies. Black leaders in the South had come mostly from a small middle-class cadre of educators, doctors, ministers, and civil-service employees. Educated blacks suffered more economically than the less educated Negroes in comparison with whites of equivalent attainment and were often forced to take an accommodationist stance by the white power structure. Thus the middle class had a particular stake in securing civil rights and in destroying the Jim Crow system. Many of them—teachers, for example—were especially vulnerable to punishment by the White Citizens Councils. But one group that was dependent chiefly upon other blacks for their prestige and salaries was the ministers in the black churches, especially in the cities, and from this sector of the middle class came a high proportion of the early civil-rights activists. The churches provided face-to-face communities, a common set of beliefs about oppression, and a sense of morale for collective effort.[9]

Harding describes how "transformative black power" gathered force in such communities of belief that claimed providential redemption for the downtrodden:

> At the bedrock of our people's believing was a profound conviction that God was real and actively moving on our side. For most of us still in the South, this God was still the God of the mainline black religious experience in America, a terrifying, tender, loving, present God, constantly intervening in history, determined that justice should prevail for his downtrodden people. Though we are tempted to deny such things now, that belief in an active, Divine cooperation in our cause, helped give men and women courage to live and sometimes to die for what they believed to be right (and righteous).

Here were combined "many of the prerequisites of protracted movements for freedom, liberation, independence" and "a sense of participation in the movement of a universal force for good; a people's belief in themselves, their intrinsic worthiness; and their belief in the presence of allies, within or without the immediate struggle situation." They had their own millennial vision and believed that not only the eyes of the North but of the whole world were witness to their struggle.[10]

No one symbolized the moral force and universal aspirations of the early stages of the civil-rights movement better than King. Urging blacks and their white allies to take history into their own hands, he expressed the goals of social transformation in terms that resonated with traditional Christian and democratic values at the same time that he and others led blacks in boycotts and sit-ins, organized confrontations with segregated school systems, planned stragegy in black churches, and marched on Washington to demand that white domination be broken once and for all.

Black college students hastened the process of desegregation by courageous direct action techniques of sit-ins, voter registration drives, and protest demonstrations. Like the black ministers, the students were less vulnerable than many other middle-class blacks to direct economic sanctions, and they were sustained by the common ideals of their fellow students. Beginning in 1960, the student sit-ins involved 75,000 demonstrators, 3,600 of whom were arrested in a year-and-a-half.[11]

Outside resources aided southern blacks in their struggle. White liberals poured in funds to support the NAACP Legal Defense Fund, the Southern Christian Leadership Council (SCLC) headed by King, and the campaigns of organizations like the Congress of Racial Equality (CORE) and the Student Non-Violent Coordinating Committee (SNCC). Many whites also went to the deep South to participate in the voter registration drives and demonstrations. The media vividly portrayed the struggles against the caste system. Gradually the federal government saw that force would be required to back up the court's decision.[12]

The goals of the southern civil-rights movement were clear and could be denied by citizens only by disavowing basic American moral and political principles. To abolish caste, to destroy discrimination based on race—these purposes could and did unite the mass of people who marched on Washington in 1963 and the Congress when it passed the Civil Rights Act in 1964. Because of the massive resistance of the South and the paltry help offered by the federal government up to that time, however, the pace of desegregation of schools had been glacial. In ten years only 2.32 percent of southern schools had mixed the races. Only coordinated unambiguous pressure from the top down could realize the promise of *Brown* and justify the sacrifices of the southern blacks and supporters. The Civil Rights Act enabled the Department of Justice to take segregated districts to court.[13]

The Office of Education also drew up desegregation deadlines to comply with the act, and the passage of the Elementary and Secondary Education Act of 1965 provided the office with the possibility of withholding substantial funds from noncomplying districts. The United States Commissioner of Education, Harold H. Howe II, announced in 1966 that the time for gradualism had passed, for a revolution was stirring, and it depended on "the schools to determine whether the energies of that revolution can be converted into a new and vigorous source of American progress, or whether their explosion will rip this nation into two societies." As J. Harvie Wilkinson III argues, the threat of cutting off federal funds for noncompliance with the Department of

Health, Education, and Welfare (HEW) guidelines proved less potent than the use of the guidelines by increasingly activist federal district courts. Indeed, after the Supreme Court announced in *Green* v. *County School Board* in 1968 that it was the "affirmative duty" of school boards to eliminate dual systems, the judges forced the South to desegregate at a rapid pace. By 1971 an estimated 44 percent of southern black students attended schools where whites were in a majority, compared with only 28 percent of blacks in the North.[14]

The combination of a mass social movement of blacks together with the assistance of white liberals in and out of government—a linking of the dispossessed with the powerful, aided by the sanction and ultimately the muscle of the courts—finally brought down the caste system in southern schools. The situation of blacks in the North was different, and in some ways even harder to ameliorate. Harding notes that "by 1964, the wedge of black movement had taken on very different manifestations in cities of the North" from its program in the South. The symbolic and tangible victories of southern blacks were a source of pride to their northern brethren, but the crusade for civil rights did not respond to their own most nagging problems: unemployment and underemployment, poor housing, unresponsive and inadequate education, and police harassment. Pushed off the fields of southern farms by mechanization and attracted by the lure of the metropolis, millions of poor black farmers had migrated to northern cities in the 1940s and 1950s. There they encountered depression-level poverty, institutional racism, and a sense of powerlessness. In the early 1960s, a time of prosperity for the nation as a whole, their incomes dropped; in Watts, for example, median family income declined by 8 percent during that decade, and 42 percent were classified as poor. The high unemployment rates of teenagers—between 20 and 30 percent in 1967—suggested that a permanent underclass was in the making. The middle-class leaders of black organizations like the NAACP and the SCLC were not particularly successful in reaching the people of these urban ghettos.[15]

Between 1964 and 1968 waves of riots and rebellions swept northern cities where blacks were concentrated. Both frustration and desire—"locked-in passions, angers, fantasies, fears and hopes," Harding writes—fueled the outbursts. No clear-cut leadership guided the rebellions, but the targets were clear enough: the symbols of white control, the police and local merchants. Violence drew attention to the grievances of ghetto blacks and prompted many white leaders to support an invigorated War on Poverty and reforms in police, welfare, and school departments. But along with the rebellions came a splintering of ideology and leadership in the black protest movement itself. Some militants argued that only self-determination and control over schools and other institutions in their own communities could counter the pervasive racism of the larger society. Such calls for black power fractured the liberal black-white alliances characteristic of the southern civil-rights campaign. White activists, spurned by black militants and drawn to other causes, turned from civil-rights work to attack the Vietnam War. Rhetoric of militants escalated as rivals competed for leadership and control over antipoverty funds. Rarely more than token, the efforts of the War on Poverty and the Office of Economic Opportunity did little to allay the deep unrest that had led to the riots, described accurately by Bayard Rustin in 1965 as "outbursts of class oppression in a society where class and color definitions are converging disastrously."[16]

Middle-class blacks did make substantial gains in educational attainment and in income in the generation following *Brown*. Blacks gained the vote in the South and dismantled the most obvious features of the Jim Crow system. But overall, the income of blacks declined relative to whites, and the problem of an underclass of poor blacks in city slums and in the southern countryside persisted. The black protest movement in its many forms revealed the contradictions between professed American values and the structural realities of American society. It "thrust a wedge deep into the old America," Harding writes, "splitting it, along age lines, along class lines, along ideological lines, opening faults within institutions."[17]

Similar social movements followed the civil-rights movement in rapid succession, each with separate factions but basically seeking equality of power and dignity. Feminists, Hispanics, and Native Americans, for example, adopted strategies comparable to those used by blacks and gained a new awareness of injustice and sense of group identity. Each, in turn, made new demands on the public schools, both by confronting local power-holders and by seeking new federal legislation and court decisions. While the injustices faced by each group reflected basic structural inequalities, often the media and legislatures paid attention for but a short span of time, creating what Anthony Downs calls an "issue-attention-cycle" of alarmed concern, a quick search for remedies, disillusionment with results, and then a return to neglect. America has been faddish about its problems. But federal laws and court decisions, once on the books, did provide continuing support for expanded rights and entitlements. The Civil Rights Act of 1964 and Title IX of the Educational Amendments of 1972, for example, gave leverage to women in gaining equal access to higher education, in removing sex labeling from jobs and in challenging occupational discrimination, and in fighting sex bias in public schools. Hispanics won federal and state support for bilingual education. Indians gained a somewhat greater degree of control over their schools.[18]

By the late 1960s local school administrators found themselves in an environment both inside the schools and in their communities that was often far different from what they had known in the early 1950s. With important and notable exceptions, local superintendents had not taken the lead in desegregation (indeed, their major organization, the AASA, had fudged on the issue in the early years after *Brown*). Growing up in a different ethos of professionalism, many had trouble sharing decision making with new and often angry groups that had only recently found a collective voice and preferred confrontation to genteel lobbying. Many educators wanted to redefine the demands of lay protesters in such a way that they could retain the initiative as professionals who defined what was best for others. Thus they accepted the challenge of teaching minority children more effectively, but they wanted to diagnose the pedagogical issue as one of "deficits" in the "target population" for which standard compensatory remedies (like ones the progressives used for immigrants) would suffice.[19]

Established leaders in education also failed to recruit substantial numbers of minorities and women to the higher administrative echelons. Indeed, when desegregation finally came to the dual systems of the South, many hundreds of black principals in the formerly segregated schools were fired or demoted. Hispanic and black principals were increasingly being hired in schools elsewhere where protest groups and militant students demanded affirmative action and where minority administrators helped to cool hot spots, but such jobs often placed the principals in an awkward position of having to respond to cross-cutting expectations from employers and minority students. Black superintendents were most often hired to preside over districts that were in serious fiscal straits and disciplinary turmoil. As blacks have more recently been gaining greater political control over cities where they form a majority of the voters, however, there may be more opportunities for black superintendents like Alonzo Crim of Atlanta to create what he calls a "community of believers" in education, both inside and outside the system, to renew troubled school districts.[20]

Like blacks, women are trying to enter positions of educational leadership not on a flood tide of expansion but during an ebb tide of retrenchment. Turnover in administrative jobs may be greatest in school districts that have the toughest instructional and budget problems. Ruth Love's appointment to the troubled Chicago superintendency (the first woman superintendent there since Young) may be a harbinger of a broader trend for both blacks and women—and for black women like Love. One woman administrator has joked that it is best to go "where things are in so much trouble that nobody will notice that you are a woman." It is possible but by no means certain that the militance of feminists will in time increase the number of women at the top of school systems, as it did early in this century. The women's movement has illuminated institutional sexism in public schools and spurred the ambition of many female educators. The conspiracy of silence in professional associations over unequal opportunity for women has ended as groups like the NEA have mounted attacks on sexism. But early surveys of the actual gains of women in administration have been discouraging. In the relatively liberal state of Wisconsin, for example, when the women's movement was gathering momentum from 1970 to 1975, the number of female administrators dropped. No female superintendents were appointed and, where vacancies occurred in other positions, men were more often chosen to fill them, even where the previous incumbent had been a woman.[21]

Looking at the general impact of protest movements on social justice in education and on changing forms of leadership in public schools, however, we believe that there has been a net gain (which may now be endangered by federal policies and budget-cutting in the Reagan administration). School administrators at every level have learned new negotiating skills and have often discovered that behind the activism of social movements was a vitality that could be used to renew education. They have discovered that sharing decision making with community groups—whether at the district-wide level or in local school-community councils—can improve public support and parental participation. New programs, like Title I, and funds for bilingual programs have brought needed resources to the task of educating children at the bottom of the social system. Recent studies of well focused Title I programs have shown that they can and do improve schooling for students most in need of effective education. Leaders and staffs have become far more sensitive to cultural differences, and curricula and textbooks now far more accurately reflect the cultural pluralism of the larger society than in the 1950s. Educators have also become more conscious of the ways in which schools transmit sexual stereotypes, and under pressure from the federal government and feminists in the profession some have sought to eliminate sexual bias in sports, vocational education, and the curriculum. Categorical programs have redistributed resources to help precisely those groups most active in social protest movements and in the process have created constituencies in support of the poor and minorities.[22]

It was a new world that administrators were facing in the 1960s, one in which the older concepts of authority were eroding and new groups were demanding to be heard. Many tried to retreat to business as usual. But a few educators who shared King's vision wanted to use the new social movements to remake education for the dispossessed. One such person was the black leader Marcus Foster, an administrator first in the Philadelphia public schools and later superintendent of schools (before his tragic assassination) in Oakland, California.[23]

The Leader as Mobilizer: Marcus Foster

When Marcus Foster arrived in the midst of a controversy in 1970 among factions of the black and white communities in Oakland, a newspaper reporter asked him, "How do you feel about coming into this kind of an activist situation?" He replied that he "would rather face a militant group and take my chances than have to deal with community apathy."[24]

The son of educators, Foster attended the Philadelphia public schools and returned to teach there after college. Like a number of other middle-class black teachers, he knew the system and how to work within it. But he also realized, especially when he moved into his first principalship in an elementary school, that the system was systematically failing to serve the poor, especially black children. He learned one reason when he went into the room of a woman touted as one of the best teachers in his new school. There on the bulletin board was a blue sea with little boats, each marked with a child's name. One row of them bore the message "we are sailing," the next "we are drifting," and the last "we are sinking." That symbolized to him the lack of warmth, of confidence, of skill that was producing more and more shipwrecks in the school. Once serving a white middle-class clientele, teachers had lost faith both in their own ability to teach and the children's ability to learn. Foster began then to formulate the concepts of leadership he would use in the rest of his career. In *Making Urban Schools Work* he listed some of these principles:

> People are always more important than the system.
> Success is important to the integrity of any group.
> People tend to rise and fall to the level of their expectations.[25]

How did he translate these into practice in his elementary school? His first step was to convince teachers that the children could make dramatic progress if they concentrated on a useful manual skill: handwriting. When that campaign worked, he moved to another relatively easy task: memorizing number facts. He gave awards to pupils who earned entry into the "440 Club" by doing forty numerical operations in four minutes. And so he moved the pupils and teachers through a series of campaigns in spelling, in enriching oral language, and finally to the real goal: learning to read. Each success showed them that they *could* learn. He built morale that reached beyond the schoolhouse doors into the families.[26]

Apathy had been the chief problem in the first schools where Foster served as principal. When he took on his biggest challenge—reforming Gratz High School—he found deeply ingrained self-deprecation that led to apathy and rising anger that led to conflict. Foster had found that giving students and teachers a steady progression of opportunities to become successful, building a sense of esprit de corps, had proved effective in fighting apathy. But he also learned not only how to "manage" crises in the confrontation years of the mid-1960s, but also how to channel the energy released by conflict into reform of the system. He put his leadership principles this way: "The energy that is found in interpersonal conflict should be channeled toward solution of the underlying problems." He added: "In a conflict situation, all sides usually have legitimate concerns."[27]

As troubleshooter for Superintendent Mark Shedd, Foster often found himself in the position of mediator and teacher, helping administrators to understand why student and community activists wanted change and instructing the activists on how to accomplish their aims within the system. At stake was a new way to legitimize authority in urban education, to replace the top-down familiar bureaucratic authority with a new legitimacy based on responsiveness to people who had been traditionally powerless.

When Foster went to Gratz High School as principal, black activists inside and outside the school were demanding dramatic change. The leading black newspaper had published an exposé declaring that the school was racked with violence and gang warfare, had unsanitary and miserable facilities, and was failing to teach the students. The white principal came under attack as a scapegoat. Foster received a call: "There's a dangerous situation at Gratz. We feel that you're the one we need." Recognizing that he was entering a battleground in which many of the staff were hostile to him and to black militants, Foster told the faculty at his first meeting: "I realize that if one's friend is moved out rather unceremoniously, one must be upset. Or else I question his loyalty. Clearly you have loyalty to your former principal. You should have. But there is the possibility that your loyalty can be transferred. So make no apologies for feeling kindly toward your old friend."[28]

Even if feelings had not been so polarized, the objective problems Foster faced were staggering. The school, built for 2,600, had an enrollment of 3,800; its dropout rate was 78 percent; only 3 percent of its graduates went to college. Foster found that "Gratz had no band, no debating team, no gym team, no swimming team, no honor society, no dances. Gratz students often viewed themselves as victims, having no control over their future, no place to go— not even down because, being at Gratz, they were already at the bottom." In one class he discovered that a girl was writing a theme entitled "Gratz is for rats."[29]

Believing that "massive problems are solved little by little," Foster began by attacking high truancy, bringing back dropouts, and personally trying to attract high ability students by going to their homes and promising them honors courses and college scholarships. But simply getting students in class was only the beginning; it was also necessary to improve the curriculum. He greatly expanded the vocational courses and tied them directly to job experiences and employment. Working with militants, he introduced African themes in regular courses and sponsored the first high school course in Philadelphia in Afro-American history. In two years he so strengthened the college preparatory courses, tutoring, and guidance that the number of students going on to higher education jumped from 18 to 168. As an essential part of his campaign to raise morale, he helped organize extracurricular activities, built a new educational and recreational center in the ghetto, and reinvigorated the sports program. He sought and gained help from local advisory committees, businessmen, foundations, and alumni of the school. Henry Resnik has given a portrait of the man at work:

> Foster could address a large audience and give the impression that he was talking to every member of it individually. For him, a walk through the halls of his school was an uninterrupted series of greetings, warm smiles, handshakes, and words of praise—signs that he knew exactly who each one of the students was and cared about them all. . . . But Marcus Foster was no teddy bear. He was an imposing man—six-foot-five, on the portly side—and in his usual business suits . . . and thick round glasses, he projected firm authority.[30]

Like Covello's Franklin High, Foster's Gratz became not only a place to educate students, but also a center for mobilizing the community and teaching it how to gain power. This became clear when the Gratz community won a bitter fight with City Hall over extending the school by adding new buildings and playing fields. On judgment day—the key school board vote going against the mayor's wishes—organizers in the school hired ten buses to take neighborhood people to the meeting, and the black community spoke with one voice, "with whites in supporting rather than leading roles." Foster observed that "the notion of strength through unity, of organizing to take responsible stands . . . woke up a lot of people. The lesson was: if it could be done at Gratz, it can be done whenever we have just causes."[31]

That was just one battle won. The mayor of Oakland recalled another such controversy shortly before Foster's assassination. They had worked together at a community meeting all day and late into the evening. When the group had found a solution, the mayor and Foster left together, got in their cars, and drove off. The mayor pulled up beside Foster at a stoplight, his presence unknown to the superintendent. "I looked over and there he was with a smile upon his face, singing at the top of his voice. I can't begin to tell you the impression made upon me, because to me it typified the ebullience, the magnificent joy of life—the joy he took in working with the community."[32]

Like Leonard Covello, who was also a genius at using group conflict to energize schooling, Foster had qualities of leadership under stress that have been scarce in every age and place. To adapt so firmly established and routinized an institution as the public schools to new social needs and conflicting protest groups requires enormous resilience, social energy, empathy, and a pragmatic attitude toward organizational conventions. When the older closed system of school governance based on expertise and controlled access to decision making began to decay —especially in the conflict-ridden cities—the tasks and challenges of leadership changed radically. Multiple actors, raised expectations, declining trust, and growing conflict among groups with different agendas were producing fragmentation and ferment that resulted from too many dreams too long deferred. Marcus Foster offers one example of an educational leader with the vision and compassion to put it all back together.

18. WHO'S IN CHARGE HERE?

Who's in charge here? If one asked a local superintendent that question at the end of a hectic Tuesday in 1974, the answer might have been *"no one."* Or perhaps, "Where are you now when we need you, Rube Goldberg?" An article that year in the *New York Times* reported that "the American school superintendent, long the benevolent ruler whose word was law, has become a harried, embattled figure of waning authority." Battered by confrontations with community groups, "browbeaten by once subservient boards of education," hemmed in by teacher union contracts, constrained by the courts, confined by endless federal and state regulations, local superintendents complained that they were losing control of their organizations. On the West Coast a professor of educational administration observed sadly:

> It used to be that a school superintendent, if he was at all successful, would have the feeling that he had the ability to mount a program and carry it through successfully. I think at the present time very few superintendents would be able to say honestly that they have this feeling. They are at the beck and call of every pressure that is brought to them. They have lost initiative. They don't control their own time. . . . Mid-administration is very much floundering. They don't know whether they are teachers or administrators. . . . There has been a change in the role of administrators from one who plans and carries through to one who works with groups of people in joint planning and ultimate realization of something the group can agree on.[1]

Urban high school principals, once barons with great power in their large buildings, made similar laments. "At one time," said one, "we considered ourselves educators. I think the problem is much too complicated, the organization is much too vast, the ramifications are too great, the partners in the enterprise are too many for us to serve any longer as educators." Arthur J. Vidich and Charles McReynolds studied twenty-three principals in New York in the tumultuous school year 1967–68. They found the schoolmen

> on the defensive, confronting an educational world they neither made nor anticipated; it is not surprising that their model for the future as well as their defence against the present is their vision of the past. . . . They thus become defenders of the status quo at the very time that the maintenance of their claims to professional expertise and educational leadership requires them to respond creatively to the crisis that continually confronts them.

Having made it up through the system through competitive examinations and professional performance, they "resent the intrusion of 'politics' into their professional domain. They do not think of themselves as political men and they are not prepared by experience or ideology to engage in the hurly-burly of the political arena; their own 'politicking' is more of the nature of bureaucratic intrigue." Their image of the high school principal was that of

> a dignified, erudite, and slightly distant figure, autonomous in authority, and respected both inside and outside the school. In both respects the principals of today feel cheated. Within the school their freedom of action has been narrowed by the teachers' unions and the increasing bureaucratization of the school system. Outside the school they feel subject to continuing attacks from many critics including disrespectful and sometimes openly hostile attacks from members of the "community."[2]

New York, with its baroque bureaucracy of 110 Livingston Street and its bitter and violent conflicts over community control was an exaggerated version of the disintegration of earlier forms of governance and the demolition of consensus on education. A number of studies of other cities showed that superintendents did retain much of their earlier initiative in policy making. But in most school districts throughout the nation, in the two decades following 1960, major changes took place in structures and processes of decision making. Collective bargaining with teachers' associations produced thick contracts specifying not only salaries but many details of everyday work. Decisions by federal and state courts set limits on religious ceremony and instruction, prescribed how students could be suspended and assigned to special classes, required help for limited-English-speaking pupils, guaranteed freedom of expression for teachers and students, revised school finance, proscribed sexual inequities, and ordered desegregation. State governments demanded new forms of "accountability," including tests of minimum competence for promotion and graduation. Federal and state governments created dozens of new categorical programs, each with complex guidelines and reporting requirements. Pressures from local protest groups and mandates from higher governments increased citizen participation in decision making, especially in the form of school advisory councils. And many important decisions were made by private organizations quite outside any formal public control: textbook publishers, for example, determined much of the basic content of the curriculum, while agencies like the Educational Testing Service had a crucial role in deciding which students would be admitted to colleges and graduate schools.[3]

Local school leaders have always been responsive to outside influences as well as to community constituencies. The common-school crusaders often emulated what their peers were doing elsewhere, as when George Atkinson copied the graded schools of Boston when building public education in Oregon City. Superintendents in the twentieth century welcomed new ideas emanating from the university experts and gained status in their own communities by associating themselves with a new science of education and ideology of business efficiency. For the most part, local leaders had taken the initiative in such encounters with outside reformers, however, and the result was to enhance their own careers and authority. By contrast, many of the changes of the 1960s and 1970s resulted from adversarial relationships: protestors seeking equality of treatment; courts requiring changes in administrators' behavior; and teachers demanding more money. Often protesters and their supporters—popular writers, social scientists, foundation and government officers—portrayed local educators as unjust or ineffectual foot-draggers. On educational leaders, it seemed, rested the burden of remaking society, and the inevitable failure to do so undermined their authority. This seemed unfair and onerous to superintendents who were, by their own lights, doing their best.[4]

Conflict did not come only from outsiders hostile to the ideal of a stable "closed system" run by professional managers and their experts. It also broke out within the hierarchy of school employees, especially among militant teachers. In the period from 1910 to the 1950s professional educators had disagreed about matters of philosophy and curriculum— about vocational training, for example—but by and large they agreed about the value of expanding the educational system and the desirability of buffering school politics from local lay influences. Indeed Myron Lieberman expressed a common sentiment of educators when he wrote in 1960 that local control of schools was the chief reason for "the dull parochialism and attenuated totalitarianism" of American public education. Much of the ideology behind the consolidation of rural schools stressed the need to free children from the provincialism of their parents, and educators from prying local communities. The very idea of a common professionalism among teachers, administrators, and various kinds of specialists, buttressed by state-enforced certification and by the professional ethos of educational associations, had implied that school employees shared similar interests and should present a united front to the public.[5]

In the 1960s, however, fragmentation developed within the profession. Teachers, in particular, came to believe that their interests were distinct from those of administrators, and they banded together to seek teacher power. The once weak teachers' unions now grew rapidly in number and influence, especially in the large cities, while state and local teacher associations affiliated with the NEA became more militant in pressing for higher salaries, better working conditions, and control over the educational process, including curriculum. Especially in the cities, the NEA began to use tactics similar to those of the AFT when it negotiated with local boards. Once anathema even to the AFT, strikes by teachers multiplied, while collective negotiations became mandated by law in most of the populous states. As teachers worked collectively to press their economic and political demands, they split away from administrators; conflict shattered the once-unified NEA. Principals and other middle managers were caught in the power squeeze and sometimes formed bargaining units of their own. Adversarial relationships became common place in a profession that once had prided itself on consensus.[6]

This new militance of teachers arose from many sources, as Marshall Donley, Jr., has argued. An obvious motivation was the desire to earn more money. In the expanding economy of the 1960s teachers felt a strong sense of relative economic deprivation when they compared themselves with other workers of comparable education. In the increasingly large and bureaucratized school systems of the postwar period they also tended to feel alienated from the managers and felt they could only influence policies by banding together in power blocs. Much of the militant leadership both in the AFT and the NEA came from young male teachers in large cities, people who had committed themselves to careers in public education and in many cases worked in the toughest ghetto classrooms. Well educated and self-confident, they refused to be reconciled to the genteel poverty and bureaucratic subordination that had too often characterized teaching as an occupation. Finally, the example of the upswelling protest movements of the 1960s demonstrated to alienated teachers that assertiveness and organization paid dividends. Eager to expand unionism to white-collar workers, organized labor provided funds and skilled staff to recruit teachers into the AFT and to conduct collective bargaining.[7]

Once a negligible factor in local school board politics and in state and national political arenas, teacher organizations have used the collective-bargaining process to gain substantial influence not only over pay and working conditions, but also over the educational program in many communities. At the federal level and in many states organized teachers have become an effective political interest group, not only giving political donations to favored candidates, but also enlisting teachers as campaign workers and as lobbyists. As a result of this new political militance of teachers, educational governance has shifted substantially. Indeed, some observers now believe that teachers have garnered too much influence and have called for collective negotiations to be held in open sessions, perhaps with restrictions on what could be bargained, and with lay citizens (other than school board representatives) on the negotiating committee.[8]

Another important new actor in the politics of education has been the federal government. In 1950 the United States Office of Education (USOE) was a minor bureaucracy with a staff of 300 and a budget of $40 million; its duties, as in the nineteenth century, were largely those of collecting and providing educational information. Beginning on a small scale in the National Defense Education Act (NDEA) of 1958 and culminating with the massive Elementary and Secondary Education Act (ESEA) of 1965, the Congress under pressure from protest groups and President Lyndon Johnson's prodding broke the century-long legislative logjam that had blocked large-scale federal aid to public schools. Federal expenditures jumped tenfold from 1958 to 1968, in the latter year constituting about 10 percent of the public costs of schooling. The largest sums were targeted under Title I for improving the education of low-achieving students in low-income neighborhoods, while other funds were available for a large number of categorical programs.[9]

The USOE became for the first time a significant part of the governance and finance of American education, though its powers were still circumscribed. It was primarily a channel for funds and an interpreter of the intent of Congress through guidelines. Now officials at the state level and in local districts studied federal regulations and accounting procedures, and sent back reports to Washington in ever-growing streams. Local and state administrators who were appointed as accountants of the new categorical programs became linked to their counterparts in Washington by common line items in the federal budget. The new regulations, funding, programs, monitors, and accounting systems created a whole new network of governance proliferating within the older state and local structures.[10]

The new categorical programs represented a host of reforms: environmental education, bilingual instruction, compensatory teaching for low-achieving pupils, arts in schools, prevention of drug and alcohol abuse, ethnic studies courses, head-start and follow-through programs, programs for the handicapped, creation of alternative schools, assistance in desegregation, and many more. There was nothing new about creating programs by accretion. It had long been a quintessentially American habit to postpone reforms by educating the next generation to be better than their parents. The process was familiar: discover a social problem, give it a name, and teach a course designed to remedy it. Alcoholism? Teach about temperance in every school. Venereal disease? Develop courses in social hygiene. Youth unemployment? Improve vocational training. Carnage on the highways? Give driver education classes to youth. Too many rejects in the World War I draft? Set up programs in health and physical education. Although the impetus for such reforms had generally come from outside the schools, the faith in education was flattering and provided jobs for hosts of new experts.[11]

What *was* different now was centralization of funding for the new federal programs. With the exception of vocational schooling—which had been partially funded and closely supervised from Washington since the Smith-Hughes Act in 1917—most of the other reforms had either been incorporated voluntarily by local districts or required by state governments and only loosely monitored. The architects of federal educational policy in the mid-1960s, especially those aimed at the poor and minorities, devised *categorical* programs rather than general aid because reformers believed that local districts were not adequately serving children at the bottom of society. The federal government's explicit role in education continued to be limited: it could not directly influence selection of teachers, class size, purchase of textbooks, or length of school day or year. Indeed, in the language governing federal programs it was stated that no laws "should be construed to authorize any department, agency, office, or employee of the United States to exercise any direct supervision or control over the curriculum, program of instruction, administration or personnel of any education institution, school, or school system." That was not interpreted to mean, however, that the Congress could not provide funds for special purposes. It also did not mean that USOE could not issue guidelines interpreting the meaning of broad statutes like the Civil Rights Act or Supreme Court decisions (which were binding as the law of the land, as in the case of desegregation or education of children whose parents did not speak English).[12]

Because of centralized funding of a patchwork of categorical programs without an overall centralized control of schooling, then, the federal government established regulations to ensure at least minimum compliance with the purposes of the separate acts. Individually, the new categorical programs served laudable purposes; indeed, the attention to low-income students and issues of cultural diversity was long overdue. In addition, the Congress and the American people had the right to know that their money was being spent for the purposes intended, especially after investigators had uncovered some gross misappropriations of Title I funds. But the new way of regulating federal programs through the states and in local districts produced unintended consequences in governance more serious than the annoyance a new paperwork empire created for busy school officials. It produced a fragmentation of allegiance and effort.

The net result of what John Meyer calls "fragmented centralization" in federal programs "is an organizational theorist's nightmare, and something of a bad dream for administrative practitioners, who must send and receive a blizzard of reports to and from distinct reporting agencies." Under most categorical funding, local schools have been required to create distinct programs for labeled populations with separate accounting systems for each. Sometimes laws or court decrees have mandated that districts provide services for particular groups—for example, providing for the handicapped the "least restrictive environment"—at the same time that they forbid the use of certain federal funds to accomplish those purposes. Thus the ban on "commingling" grants from Title I of ESEA, which has resulted in "pull-out" programs for the disadvantaged, conflicts with the mainstreaming philosophy underlying the law on the education of the handicapped. Similarly, regulations that bilingual programs be kept separate from monolingual classrooms have led to a concern that children are kept in bilingual classes beyond the point of need and that federal requirements may be promoting "tracking, segregation, and limited communication between special and regular teachers."[13]

Thus the need to label children in specified ways in order to receive federal or state funds may inhibit local administrators and teachers from combining funds to meet the needs of pupils in a flexible and individualized manner. The result has been *the artificial separation of similar services* across federal programs," argue Brenda Turnbull, Marshall Smith, and Alan Ginsburg. It is the children who suffer.[14]

Organizational theorists have argued that schools are prime examples of "loose coupling," of disconnecting "policies from outcomes, means from ends, and structures or rules from actual activity." This complicates management and means that schools sometimes react to demands from society by symbolic compliance and new rituals rather than by changing the educational process itself. The legitimacy of schools may thus result more from maintaining agreed-upon institutional forms—such as certification of teachers, accreditation, and grade levels—rather than from meeting standards of performance. One result of the proliferation of new categorical programs, therefore, has been a great increase in accounting, additional bureaucratization in which designated administrators seek to demonstrate that their schools are in compliance with often inconsistent or even conflicting requirements. As Meyer observes, the solution for top administrators under such circumstances is to have each categorical program officer operate as if in an institutional tunnel, reporting to specialists above in the state or federal bureaucracy in accordance with accounting requirements but ignoring the rest of the programs in the same school district. It was best for superintendents, Meyer comments, "to remain in ignorance of the exact content of the various programs, reports, and budgets (so as to maintain a posture of incompetence, rather than one of dishonesty)."[15]

When administrators of categorical programs are paid by federal or state funds, it is only natural that they have divided loyalties: to the special program officers above them in the state or federal programs and to the district and its pupils. Such difficulties with categorical programs are the products not of malevolence but of the structural features of the programs themselves. Often the accounting systems have little to do with what actually takes place in classrooms because of the "loose coupling" found in educational organizations and the ambiguity of measuring what happens in schools. "Regulations" in education are different from those in fields where the technology is more precise. It is one thing for a clean-air inspector to see if a filter has been installed in a smokestack and determine whether it is effective; it is quite another to determine what are the processes and effects of "environmental education." The federal government may *regulate* education, but it hardly *controls* it.[16]

Such pathologies are clearly unintended, and we do not mean to imply that programs aimed at underserved groups should be abandoned in favor of general aid—or no federal assistance at all. There is convincing evidence that a decade of Title I programs has improved the schooling of poor children. The categorical programs have created political constituencies that favor more funds for educating poor and minority children, and that is desirable, for the poor rarely have enough advocates in the halls of power. The programs also have hired large numbers of minority professionals and paraprofessionals who provide minority pupils with examples of their own people who have secured middle-class jobs. But what is needed now, we believe, is a refashioning of federal aid so that it provides funds earmarked for upgrading the education of underserved students while granting more autonomy to local educators—especially in individual schools—to decide with their advisory committees how best to use the additional resources in their particular communities. We shall return to this theme later, for we hold that improving leadership in individual schools is a key to improving public education generally. We are not impressed with the results of *instructional* leadership imposed from the top down.

Like the federal government, many state governments have also created categorical programs, some of which suffer from the same defects of patchwork reform by accretion and regulation. Such reforms rarely fade away, especially if they are structural additions and enlist a consituency of supporters (like driver education). The states have been the major arena for reformers pressing for equalization of school finance and for laws establishing collective bargaining for teachers; largely as a result of lobbying by teacher associations, twenty-eight states in 1978 had mandated collective bargaining.[17]

But state legislatures were not simply responding to the political clout of teacher associations. Lawmakers also reflected public disenchantment with the results of the new funds poured into schools and responded by passing laws demanding accountability. The most important of these were mandates for minimum competency testing, passed in thirty-three states by 1978. What was certain was that legislators wanted teachers and pupils to get "back to basics"; what was less clear was how educators could achieve such results, for education had an uncertain technology at best, and the implication that teachers had not all along been trying to teach "basics" was questionable. How to scale the tests, and what to do with pupils who failed, raised new and troubling problems for educational leaders.[18]

Listing the reforms and attempted reforms in only one state—admittedly a hyperactive one, California—suggests why educators in the late 1970s felt (in Michael Kirst's phrase) in "a state of shock and overload." In one decade they faced challenge after challenge, mostly from outside the system. The federal and state governments kept adding new programs for them to put into operation, totaling at least fifty and including such reforms as minimum competency tests for graduation, school-community advisory councils, and new and elaborate individualized plans and remediation for the handicapped. Enrollments started dropping after sharp surges in the 1950s and 1960s, while the percentage of Hispanic students almost doubled during the 1970s to 23 percent. School finance was in such flux as a result of the *Serrano* decision, which required equalization, and Proposition 13, which put a cap on local taxes, that the legislature created four distinct systems of paying for public education. "Public school employees," says Kirst, "now find themselves living in an uncertain world of year-to-year bailout financing." As if that were not enough, in 1980 an initiative to limit spending appeared on the ballot (and lost), while voucher advocates tried hard (and lost) to put on the ballot a proposal for parental choice of schools. It was little wonder that morale of school people was low as they were being asked to do far more with less public support, both fiscal and psychological.[19]

In addition to the rise of teacher power and federal and state regulation, another source of diminished autonomy for local educators during the last generation has been increased use of the courts to resolve educational disputes. Both social-movement organizers and professional reformers have turned to the courts to mandate reforms in a variety of fields ranging from the classification of pupils to civil rights for minority groups, women, and students. As a result, judges have become major agents in shaping educational policy. Much of this work has corrected serious social injustice and ensured constitutional rights of minorities and women. Litigation has also made strategic sense for a highly placed group of liberal activists who lacked a broad political base and wanted rapid change. Legal actions have appealed to cosmopolitan professional reformers—social scientists, lawyers, foundation officials, and others—discouraged with the tedious and difficult task of developing public sentiment and support for new educational policies. A network of such reformers, for example, spearheaded the campaign in the courts to equalize state funding of education. In addition to using the courts to achieve major policy changes in the schools, lawyers have also represented the interests of aggrieved individuals, thereby adding to the volume of legal decisions in education.[20]

Much of this increased use of the courts can be traced to a failure of traditional centers of decision making in education to achieve a new political or ethical consensus about education. While the increased use of law in settling educational disputes has led to important victories for justly aggrieved groups and individuals, it has not come without costs. It has increased the fragmentation and factionalism that recently have come to characterize the politics of education. It has placed a responsibility in the hands of judges—not always wisely exercised in view of the limited range of legal remedies—to decide complex educational questions. Because the adversarial method characteristic of legal debate and decisions lacks the element of compromise that is common in other modes of political action, it has often worked to polarize opinions and exacerbate differences. Thus recourse to the courts has signaled a breakdown of other forms of persuasion and a loss of trust that competing groups can bridge their differences or blunt the sharp edges of discord.[21]

Amid controversies in the courts and arguments over the proper functions of federal, state, and local educational agencies, another form of fragmented governance has received scant attention. As David Cohen argues, the debate over reforming school politics has generally ignored a potent form of influence in public education: centers of private power. These private agencies include textbook companies, profit or nonprofit corporations that produce tests (such as The Educational Testing Service), professional associations and unions, accreditation agencies, and many other groups that are not accountable through formal political channels. As a result of the increased influence of such private groups, Cohen claims, "the reality of power in education is becoming incongruent with the formal structure; increasingly the political forces that determine local school decisions are neither locally nor democratically controlled."[22]

The power of private groups to define what is normal and desirable is hardly new. The administrative reformers of the Progressive era not only exemplified such influence in their own careers but also justified such politically unaccountable groups of experts as the intelligence testers and the professional standard-setters in accreditation agencies. But amid the recent fragmentation of educational governance and the multiplicity of specialized organizations with narrowed visions of their purpose, the power of such private groups within their own domains has increased. As in the Progressive period, the recent growth of private power has been closely linked with an increased social and economic division of labor and a greater stress on technical expertise. Government officials, like ordinary citizens, have become dependent on the advice and services of private individuals and organizations in their specialized domains. This dependency has given private groups a kind of power that is not conspiratorial or necessarily self-serving in its effects on public policy, but not openly accountable through normal political processes either.[23]

Rube Goldberg himself could not make an organization chart of the official—not to mention the private and informal—lines of authority, regulation, and accounting that now exist in American public education. An organizational theorist's nightmare indeed! It would take a political scientist's lifelong work to disentangle even the local story. The system goes on, and behind the classroom doors hundreds of thousands of teachers probably do more or less what their predecessors did in the 1950s before people began to worry about who's in charge. But in a time of retrenchment, both ideological and fiscal, relying merely on institutional momentum for coherence can be a chancy affair. To make hard choices it is important to develop a deliberate coherence that can enlist the loyalty of citizens.

19. ARE A NEW COHERENCE AND COMMUNITY OF COMMITMENT POSSIBLE?

Are a new coherence and community of commitment possible to achieve in public education? We believe so, but it will be no easy task to recreate coherence in governance and program in a fragmented system. It will be even more difficult to recreate—on new terms—a new social contract between the people and their public schools, for there has been a subtle but powerful erosion of the traditional American faith in public education.

The public-school system is probably the closest Americans have come toward creating an established church. Challenges to that system by dissenters in the last generation have amounted to a new reformation, undermining the authority of established leaders, demystifying beliefs, and splintering allegiances. Both the older providential interpretation of the common school and the Cubberleyan tale of progress through professionalism no longer seem credible. The dissenters were deeply committed to improving schooling as a way to realize long deferred dreams of equality and democratic participation. In the process of struggle they revealed the flaws and contradictions in actual public schools. Revisionist scholars documented what dispossessed groups had known all along, that such failings of public schools were not incidental blind spots, but were embedded in inequalities in the larger society. Protesters in this reformation became agnostics: Could schools make a difference? Was the American faith in schooling a delusion?

It is easy to imagine a future in which community of commitment to public education atrophies, competition for scarce resources increases, and public schools endure a slow death, especially in those communities where the poor and minorities predominate. In most parts of the nation the number of students is declining, and schools face retrenchment and tax revolts. In the 1980s the resurgence of privatism, the newborn faith in the market system, the ambivalence of nervous liberals about their own prospects, and the desire to cut back on public services and redistributive social programs are ominous signs that even the modest commitment to equality of the last generation is waning. Many politicians now seem convinced that Americans need MX missiles more than school lunches and Title I. Advocates of vouchers and tuition tax credits for private schooling suggest that family choice should reign supreme and that education is more a consumer good than a public good. And if people who have a choice believe that public education is a mess— as the media insistently say—why should sensible people send their children to public schools at all?

Retrenchment in public schools may well bring conflict, decay, and exodus of the middle class. Morale is low in many districts as staff debate who is to walk the plank next. Decisions to cut back or eliminate existing programs inflame conflicting goals and interests. Constituencies collide. It is much easier to be tolerant of differences when new functions are added than when they are swept away. It is one thing to disagree about where to place a new elementary school and quite another to decide which one to close. Reform by accretion brings good feelings; retrenchment tends to produce accusations and hand-wringing. It may well be that the earlier millennial optimism and relative comity that characterized public education depended in large part on the fact that public education was traditionally an expanding enterprise. In the past, educators regarded expansion of the functions of the school as progress and tended to consider growth as a sign of managerial ability. Now leaders accustomed to managing growth face slowdown.[1]

While administrators and teachers ride a fiscal roller coaster, students suffer in countless districts. In studies of high schools in San José, California, and New York City Daniel Duke and his colleagues document the human costs of retrenchment. They find that at San José High School —where 65 percent of the students are Mexican-Americans and 15 percent black, Portuguese, or Asian—fourteen teachers have been dropped, along with twenty paraprofessionals and other staff in 1979 after the passage of Proposition 13. In the process the school has cut half the existing programs in athletics, the band, and other extracurricular activities, and many of the special courses in reading, English as a second language, and electives in industrial arts, music, and physical education. The school day has been shortened by one period, while class sizes have swelled. Teachers have almost no free time to tutor or counsel individuals; many decide to concentrate their efforts on the minority of students who are motivated and capable. The very activities that have made school more palatable to reluctant students—hands-on work in shops, special help in English, sports, and other extracurricular activities—have been hardest hit. Not surprisingly, absenteeism, violence, drug and alcohol use, and gang conflict increase when the staff assigned to handle these problems find themselves overwhelmed with work they cannot find time to do.[2]

In three New York high schools, hit still worse by cutbacks in 1975, Duke and his associates find even more depressing conditions: bigger classes, lowered expectations, missing or worn-out instructional equipment, sparse electives and extracurricular activities, heavy backlogs in disciplinary cases and administrative tasks, and decaying facilities. One school had 3 counselors for 4,500 students. Not surprisingly, scarcity provokes competition, conflict, and teacher and administrator burnout. Under New York's open enrollment system, the high schools compete for two kinds of students in particular: whites and the handicapped (because extra funds are available in special education). "It is the disadvantaged youngster—the one already most likely to be undermotivated to attend school and a low achiever—who will suffer the most from retrenchment," the researchers argue. The system of competition has led sometimes to "fraud and hucksterism." "We heard of non-existent programs fabricated expressly to lure students to high schools and of schools that obtained handicapped students but were unable or unwilling to offer them adequate instruction."[3]

The result of all this is that "when students come to be regarded as objects—either obstacles or desired commodities—the schools are no longer in the business of helping youth—youth are valued because of what they can do to help schools!" Competition has also increased within schools: between teacher and teacher to gain better class sizes or motivated students or scarce textbooks and equipment; between teachers and administrators over assignments and discipline; and between students, as teachers decide which of the multitude are worth paying attention to. "Questions—seemingly out-of-place in U.S. public schools—are raised about which students most 'deserve' an education."[4]

These may be extreme cases of downward spiral as a result of retrenchment, but if the public and educators do not take action to reverse the trend, such schools may become harbingers of the future, especially in urban education. The great irony is that the present could potentially be a favorable time in American history to concentrate on improving the quality of schooling, for after a century of struggling to find enough teachers and build enough classrooms to keep up with the rapidly expanding number of new students, now most communities have surplus space and plenty of trained teachers. In 1970 Paul Woodring wrote in the *Saturday Review* that "the present oversupply of teachers will make it possible to establish higher standards . . . and the slower rate of growth, resulting from the declining birth rate of the Sixties, will enable schools to give more attention to educational quality." There is no intrinsic reason why declining enrollments need produce a declining industry called public education. But in an era of stagflation in the economy and conservative reaction against social services, those who are determined to preserve and improve public education must be able to state a coherent case.[5]

Coherence is not exactly the strong suit of contemporary public education. Public-school leaders in the past have mostly been able to absorb demands for change by accretion without changing much the central core of instruction. As a result, American education has been both faddish in particulars and resistant to change in its basic mode of operation. Reformers of the 1960s—cheerfully ignoring history—promised quick pedagogical fixes to old and intractable problems. Much of the public skepticism about schools and desire for a return to the three Rs result from overpromising in the last generation. In governance the changes in recent years have created an incoherent patchwork. And as special-interest groups have each pushed separate goals, the larger purposes that once gave resonance and integration to the complex enterprise of public education have atrophied.

One could predict a dismal future for the public schools. Retrenchment could repeat the haphazard process of incrementalism, only in reverse: educators could set in motion a process of decrementalism, of peeling away parts of the system, with little sense of unified purpose. The economics of scarcity could stimulate factionalism and bitter competition among educational interest groups. As loyalty to public schooling as a common good erodes, parents who have the opportunity could choose exit to private schools rather than work to improve the public system. Public education could become a place of last resort.

Such a future is neither necessary nor desirable. It should be possible to consolidate the real gains achieved for neglected groups in the last generation while creating greater coherence in education where it counts the most—in the actual classrooms where children learn. Americans can develop a greater sense of common purpose in public education without losing the energy and variety generated by pluralistic politics. But to do so will require an educational leadership politically adept at building proschool coalitions, willing to abandon a narrow professional ideology, and skillful in creating coordinated programs in individual schools. To ask for such leadership is not to demand implausible heroes; both in past and present there have been many people who have demonstrated these qualities.

There is no one template for effective leadership, for it varies, as we have argued, by time and place and by location in the educational system. To achieve coherence and effectiveness in governance and program requires rethinking what decisions should best be made at different levels of the system and how to create a productive balance —always in tension in our federalized polity—between local and centralized influence. And building a community of commitment to public education requires a tough-minded idealism that seeks a public good while recognizing the pluralistic values and interests of Americans.

The history of governance in education shows swings, both rhetorically and actually, between centralization and decentralization. We have argued that the common school was originally created and governed by a broad base of local lay participants, that during the Progressive era it became increasingly insulated from control by lay people, and that during the last generation there have been conflicting pressures toward both centralization and decentralization. It is tempting to oversimplify the normative issue of who should govern. In the twentieth century many observers have argued that decision making should move upward and away from local lay boards. The administrative progressives, as we have shown, favored government by experts. Liberals and activists in protest movements, aware of how decentralization fostered inequities among districts and how local boards could and did discriminate against groups that had little power, have typically wanted state and federal governments to intervene in the interests of social justice. More recently, in response to conservatives wanting "the government off our backs," many leaders have called for less federal and state regulation.[6]

In a society so diverse as America's and with governmental structures so complex, educational leaders face the never-ending task of balancing parochial and universal values, local political demands and mandates from central agencies. Simply arguing that the "community" should "control" its schools ignores the many ways in which local decision makers have been able to use schools to perpetuate racial, class, religious, and sexual discrimination. To claim that "experts" know best or that state or federal governments have the wisdom to decree a "one best system" is not only arrogant—it also disregards the checkered recent history of instructional "reforms" imposed from without. As Arthur Wise and others have argued, there is no sufficiently solid technology of teaching to warrant the imposition of one uniform system. Similarly, the search for "teacher-proof" curricula has proved to be vapid.[7]

School leaders face the challenge of weighing professional knowledge and skill together with the need to involve community members in decisions. Here again there have been sharp swings of the pendulum among policy advocates from those who argue that educators are experts needing to be shielded from outside meddling to those who declare that professional wisdom is a sham. Sensible policy, we believe, recognizes the tension of the claims. Educators know their work better than anyone else and need not shuffle, but effective discharge of their duties requires them to work in partnership with parents and patrons. In no other way can they secure the community of interest that public education demands.

What kind of division of labor in school governance makes sense? Constitutional questions such as those concerning separation of church and state, racial and sexual equity, and rights of expression have entered the purview of the Supreme Court after a hundred years of struggle. Because local school districts have often violated such rights—and continue to do so—they cannot be final arbiters of basic rights. Likewise, local districts do not have the power to correct financial inequalities among communities; only state and federal legislatures can do that. Federal and state governments have also sought to induce or compel local schools to equalize opportunities for poor children and minorities. We see such activities of the courts and higher governments as legitimate concerns in a coherent system of school governance: guaranteeing rights and seeking greater equity.

But how should leaders at the federal and state levels go about influencing what happens in local districts? Typically they have used a variety of techniques: regulation, funding special programs, supporting and disseminating curricula, providing specialized services, and focusing attention on particular issues such as instruction in reading or special education. Recent categorical programs have spotlighted special unmet needs and combined funding with elaborate regulations. Even people sympathetic to the goals have worried about the fragmentation of governance and increase in paperwork that ensued. States have also passed laws requiring "accountability" of teachers and testing of minimum competency of pupils.

We are not persuaded that centralized control of categorical programs actually accomplishes the generally laudable purposes that inspired the legislation. We believe that a better approach is to continue to target funds and attention to underserved groups of students while giving local educators greater discretion about how to achieve results. Now a number of federal programs are required by law to be isolated from regular school studies. This strategy has splintered attention and multiplied red tape for school people rather than encouraging them to develop a coherent educational program for children who need one most. There are some good examples of centrally funded but locally shaped programs of the sort we have in mind. One is California Superintendent Wilson Riles's School Improvement Program designed to give state money to local schools to implement reforms of their own devising, developed in conjunction with parents and patrons. Such plans are not panaceas, either, but they move in the right direction.[8]

In recent years scholars have discovered some home truths forgotten by eager reformers who wished to impose curricular changes, new teaching strategies, and modes of accountability from the top down. They have found that schools are not computer consoles replete with buttons for top administrators to push. Increasingly, researchers like Michael Rutter, John Goodlad, and Ronald Edmonds have gone beyond asking why programs fail. They have investigated why some schools, even in tough neighborhoods, work well. From such studies of success, not pathology, it has become apparent that what counts most in the academic and social learning of children is what happens in their classrooms and in their particular schools. The principal, the students, the teachers, and parents and others must share the sense of being a community of instructors and learners working toward definite goals, with clear but cooperative leadership and high expectations.[9]

Analyses of schools that work well, that teach children effectively, that have high morale, and that respond to cultural diversity typically show that they have the kind of positive ethos that Philip Selznick in another context has called an institutional "success myth." Such a "socially integrating" sense of purpose allows people in these institutions to complete a sentence that begins: "What we are proud of around here is. . . ." "For creative leadership," Selznick writes, "it is not the communication of a myth that counts; rather, creativity depends on having the will and the insight to see the necessity of the myth, to discover a successful formulation, and above all to create the organizational conditions that will sustain the ideals thus expressed." There is nothing mysterious or superhuman about this kind of esprit and coherence of ideals and program: Foster, Covello, and countless educators, priests, coaches, and musicians have developed such an ethos. Many thousands of principals, parents, and teachers today are creating an ethos in their schools that says to students that adults care about what young people are making of their lives.[10]

The building principal in such schools is less an in-house bureaucrat or accountant than a *principal teacher* (the origin of the title, now long forgotten) and a mobilizer, departing from the tradition in American public education of separating management from practice and administration from teaching. This kind of leader must have expertise in curriculum development and teaching and must also be able to generate a sense of common purpose. Such leadership also requires substantial changes in the traditional relation between principals and central bureaucracies in large cities. Norman Drachler, former superintendent of the Detroit public schools, writes:

> When in England recently, I was very much impressed with the power of the English counterpart to our principal, the headmaster. Funds were allocated to the headmaster in low economic areas for him or her to do what they thought was best without even a preliminary report to the local headquarters. In this nation we entrust to a principal the educational future of some 3 to 4 thousand students, a building often amounting to 10 or 15 million dollars, a payroll of half a million dollars—but we do not trust him or her with ten dollars worth of petty cash.[11]

If there is any educational leader at the school district level charged with the task of inspiring and coordinating such renewal it is the local superintendent. Since the pattern of business-as-usual of the 1950s was challenged, local school chiefs have faced a multitude of new actors in school politics and a bewildering array of new regulations and programs. Lightning rod for protest, negotiator for contending groups both within and outside the schools, mediator among different levels of government, the superintendent is still responsible for the effectiveness of instruction.

Now as in the past, the challenges facing superintendents differ in various kinds of communities. There are still many small towns where superintendents and schools closely mirror the values of their communities and where public education has been little touched by the tumultuous events and increasing skepticism of recent years. In such districts leaders continue to encounter the tension between professional and local norms. Simply giving community influentials the kind of schooling they want for local children may perpetuate old forms of discrimination and fail to prepare pupils adequately for lives they may face if they leave their small towns. The local superintendent, standing

A New Coherence and Community of Commitment

at the juncture of outside forces—court mandates, federal and state governments, new professional outlooks—and the local community, can be a critical mediator between the small town and the broader society.

In prosperous suburbs, educational leaders may face less tension than rural educators between their own values as professionals and the expectations of community people, since both are more likely to share in a cosmopolitan ethos. But upper-middle-class suburban parents are precisely the citizens most capable of exercising the choice of public or private education; rural and inner-city parents have fewer alternatives. Thus educational leaders in affluent communities must not only convince parents that public schools are best for their children, but must also persuade taxpayers without children of school age that public schools deserve their support and concern.

The leadership of big-city school systems may well be among the most demanding jobs in the United States today. Urban educators must reach concentrations of students who are poor, who are discriminated against because of race or ethnicity, whose parents speak many different languages, and who live in neighborhoods where violence and abysmal rates of unemployment are everyday facts of life. To repair the effects of generations of injustice urban educators are now asked to do more with less as revenues decline. No sector of the system of public education stands more in need of public support, yet none has been so battered by criticism.[12]

Today, retrenchment in finances and declining enrollments face superintendents in all communities. Contraction forces hard choices not so necessary in times of expansion and accretion. In the last two decades of conflict and growth, changes have hit superintendents in such rapid succession that it has been easy for them to lose that larger sense of coherence that makes sense of the parts and gives criteria for choices. Amid the competition of constituencies for attention, it has been difficult to remember that public schools exist to serve all children, not simply those with the loudest or most recent advocates.

Superintendents facing those hard choices can define declining enrollments and cutbacks as a nightmare of contending forces and vested interests. In making budget cuts it will be tempting to find targets of least resistance rather than to make decisions based on collaborative reappraisal of what makes a coherent and effective system of instruction. But defined in another way, the need to decide what is essential —and to enlist colleagues and community in that debate—can remedy the incoherence produced by easy money and rapid growth. We do not mean to slight the pain and real human costs of retrenchment or the problems created by declining enrollments, but cutbacks need not signal decline of the public school as an institution.

During the 1930s public schools survived under far more stringent budgets—and many improved substantially—but that demanded astute leadership, not a Maginot line psychology. During the Great Depression the friends of public education faced an emergency in many ways worse than the present. The elementary-school population was declining, schools were closing, taxes were drying up, teachers were being fired, programs were being abolished, and Americans were questioning not only the value of education but the whole fabric of traditional beliefs. Faced with these challenges, school people responded in various ways. Some timidly hunkered down and tried to avoid offending anyone. But many leaders saw the Depression as a time for reformulation of the basic meanings of public education. One agent of this effort was the Educational Policies Commission, which sought to unify the educational profession, to find a common ground for commitment to public education, and to present this case to the public, together with more specific arguments for reforms—such as greater equity in school finance. Public schools made some important gains. The percentage of seventeen-year-olds graduating from high school grew more rapidly during the 1930s than ever before or since. Many school systems, relieved of the pressure of numbers of young children, entered an age of educational experimentation.[13]

Times of trial and contraction, like eras of expansion, can be occasions for leadership. We believe that one of the most important needs in public education today is to clarify and strengthen the grounds of commitment to public schooling. In the optimistic mood of the early twentieth century, Michael Sadler could say—as we quoted him at the start of this book—that "the American school is radiant with a belief in its mission, and it works among people who believe in the reality of its influence, in the necessity of its labors, and in the grandeur of its task." Today no one talks that way about public education; it would sound corny and unconvincing. But such a faith has been a powerful force in shaping American schools in the past. Ideas do count in history, and those who effectively use them can exert great influence over the course of events, as the careers of Horace Mann and Martin Luther King, Jr., illustrate.

A public philosophy of education as Thomas Jefferson or Mann or Dewey or Covello might have understood the phrase has declined in recent years, a casualty of the same phenomenon of fragmentation that has splintered governance and program in public schooling. When we urge the reformulation of a community of commitment to public education we are not simply advocating that old ideas be warmed over and served up as a new consensus. When we talk of coherence of purpose, we are not denying the worth of pluralism or the necessity of conflict of values and interests. When we ask leaders to help to generate a new public philosophy of education, we are not looking for authoritative philosopher-kings. Quite the opposite: we believe that the new debate over purpose must recognize new conditions, diversity of interests and cultures, and the need for broad participation. But without the creation of a stronger community of commitment we fear the atrophy of a critical institution through which Americans have continuously debated and shaped their future.

Public-opinion polls about education present a confusing picture. It is easy to interpret them to mean that Americans have already abandoned an earlier faith. Year after year citizens have complained about poor discipline and drug abuse in schools, insufficient attention to the "basics," and many other problems. From 1974 to 1979 people gave ever-lower ratings to the quality of their schools; in the latter years, only 35 percent gave an A or B grade to public education. But it is essential to compare confidence in public schools with belief in other institutions. What was happening was a growing skepticism and concern about almost every kind of institution, including that most sacrosanct one, the family. In 1981 respondents in the Gallup Poll gave public schools higher grades in their domain than they did parents for raising their children to be "self-disciplined and responsible young people."[14]

Between 1966 and 1974, in the era of Vietnam and Watergate, confidence in leaders dropped sharply in almost every domain. Here is a list of social institutions in descending order of public confidence in 1966: medicine, the military, education, major business companies, the U.S. Supreme Court, Congress, organized religion, the federal executive branch, the press, television, and organized labor. In 1980 the Gallup Poll asked its sample the question: "How much confidence do you, yourself, have in these American institutions to serve the public's needs?" In this survey the public schools came in second, after the church, but ahead (in descending order) of the courts, local government, state government, national government, labor unions, and big business. Another sign that citizens ranked public education relatively high in value is that after referenda cutting taxes, voters typically said that their target was not the public schools.[15]

The point is not that Americans are satisfied with their public schools

—they are not. Rather, in an era when they are generally disenchanted with leaders and institutions, there is still an important residue of the traditional faith that public schools serve important public purposes. The average citizen profoundly disagrees with some scholars who argue that schooling does not much influence one's chances in life (of course many scholars disagree with that argument, too). When asked "How important are schools to one's future success?," 82 percent of the respondents in the 1980 Gallup Poll answered "extremely important" (up six points since 1973).

Rebuilding public confidence in and commitment to public education is a complex and difficult task, but as the polls show, it does not start from zero. One place to begin in creating a community of commitment is with parents of school-aged children, but they are not likely to be impressed with the hype and hucksterism that have afflicted incremental educational reform in recent years. They believe that good schooling is essential for their sons and daughters. An obvious way to gain the loyalty of citizens is to convince them that educators are attentive to the changes they think necessary. This will be most difficult to achieve in big cities. Only powerful coalitions of people with a stake in these cities can reverse the downward spiral. Atlanta's superintendent Alonzo Crim, for example, has done much to mobilize such support through appealing to parents, businessmen, church leaders, college and university people, and other groups to build a community of commitment. And inside the schools Crim has sought to inspire principals, teachers, and pupils with a sense of common purpose reminiscent of Marcus Foster's goal-setting in Gratz High School in Philadelphia.[16]

One cannot build a constituency for public education solely on a coalition of parents and educators. As the population as a whole ages and the proportion of children decreases, the percentage of voters who are parents of school-aged children will drop sharply. In 1960 one in two voters in California, for example, had children in school. In 1980 the proportion was about one in four. A coherent philosophy of public education cannot rest simply on the self-interest of parents and students, and indeed it never has. The best case for public education has always been that it is a common good: that everyone, ultimately, has a stake in education.

What might be some common grounds of agreement on such a public philosophy of education? A commitment to a common school starts with values that are not subject to empirical demonstration—in short, they are beliefs about what sort of a society America should become. That is really what most discourse on purpose is about in education: a preferred future expressed as a particular kind of training for the young.

And that is precisely one of the arguments of *public* education: discourse and action concerning public schools provide an opportunity for citizens to become concerned not simply about what is good for themselves or their own children but also what is necessary to bring about a more just and effective society. This is an old and valid argument, much ignored of late. Such arenas for public debate and action are hard to find, especially ones that so intimately involve the immediate community. Much decision making about major economic concerns takes place behind the closed doors of vast corporations or multinational consortia like OPEC. Matters of great political moment are often decided in legislative committees far from the ken of citizens, while administrative agencies promulgate regulations as law with minimal public debate. But public schools are everywhere, are more open to citizen participation than most other institutions, and directly influence the lives of the almost one in four Americans who are students and teachers or school administrators.

The public school represents the only commitment by which American society guarantees to look after the needs and interests of all citizens, at least when they are young. In general the United States has been very backward in providing public services, particularly of a redistributive nature such as health care, child care, housing, and decent support services for the aged. But in the case of public education, Americans have provided free elementary and secondary schooling for all the younger generation and more widely available and diverse higher education for adults than is available anywhere else in the world.[17]

At the present time, public services, including education, are under attack from many quarters. We believe that many public services do help in the needed task of redistributing benefits in a society marked by sharp inequalities and that this is hardly the time to cut back on what is already a sorry national record of concern for those who need help. In particular, the universality of elementary schooling helps to identify and assist children who start out life with handicaps—poor health, malnutrition, poor eyesight or hearing, or emotional or learning difficulties. The public commitment to educate every child is the beginning of a broader trusteeship and sense of commonwealth. Obviously, class, race, sex, and ethnicity restrict an individual's participation in public education at all levels and the benefits he or she is able to derive from it. The fact of discrimination does not justify cutting back on the only commitment America has made to serve all future citizens; rather, it should be a spur to reform.

The difficulties we face today are large, but no more so than those confronted by people at the turn of the century, who coped with masses of immigrants in overcrowded urban classrooms and grossly underfinanced rural schools. But then Americans had a vivid sense of the potentiality of public education. "The community's duty to education," wrote a philosopher of that time, "is . . . its paramount moral duty. . . . Through education society can formulate its own purposes, can organize its own means and resources, and thus shape itself with definiteness and economy in the direction in which it wishes to move." Once aroused, he believed, the community would provide public schools with the commitment and support they needed. The writer was John Dewey, who realized more than any other American of the past century how fully democracy and social justice need to be recreated in each generation.[18]

Afterword

After reading historical works we often find ourselves wanting to know more about how the book came to be: How did an author become interested in a topic, who or what influenced her or him, what interpretations were considered but rejected, what questions remained? A finished book is a bit like a completed structure: the excavations are filled, the scaffolding taken down, the debris swept up. The actual messiness of building is hidden from view. An architect may learn most about a house in the process of construction. In this afterword—aimed at fellow scholars—we talk briefly about the origins and construction of our book and acknowledge some of our many intellectual debts.

A word first about our collaboration. Hansot, trained as a political theorist, has for many years been interested in the relationship between belief systems and social change. Her research on utopian blueprints for society explored the coerciveness resulting when an individual or single group defined a common future for others. Through working in the United States Congress and federal agencies she sought to understand alternative modes of determining public goods and a more incremental kind of policy making. In postdoctoral work in organizational studies at Stanford University she became interested in the historical development of organizations and, in particular, was attracted to the study of leadership in public education because it combined utopian visions with successful institution-building.

At the time we began our collaboration, Tyack was seeking ways of combining two intellectual pursuits. The first was a series of social histories of educational occupations—superintendents, teachers, and truant officers—in which he sought to explain who was recruited to such jobs, how they became socialized at work, and how they developed ideologies to give meaning to their lives. The other study began as a historical analysis of compulsory schooling. In the process of writing on that subject he discovered that he was investigating an institutional bayou rather than a mainstream. Instead of asking why state legislatures passed laws to compel a small minority of parents to send their children to school, it was far more heuristic to ask why and how a multitude of Americans created the system of public schools in communities across the nation and voluntarily sent their children to them. He was also seeking ways of combining intellectual and social history.

Our conversations convinced us that our common research interests could be combined by focusing on leadership in public education and that in such a study one could explore the interaction of belief systems and behavior. In addition, we discovered a common commitment to the renewal of public education—partly as a result of teaching in different elementary schools in 1978—and hoped that such a book might enlighten contemporary policy. Thus we decided to analyze the origins and fate of the traditional American faith in public education and its institutional embodiment in schools together with the loss of coherence in ideology and program in recent years.

Historians like labels such as "revisionism." Our book may be hard to classify. We concentrate on public schooling rather than using the broader "cultural revisionist" definition of education so ably represented by Lawrence Cremin.* We do not apologize for focusing on public schools, for we believe that so central an institution gives ample scope for understanding continuity and change in the broader society and also provides a needed structural coherence for research. But we share Cremin's interest in the importance of broadly held ideas and in a mode of exposition that moves from individual to organization to the larger society. From the "radical revisionists" we learned much about the importance of class, power, and conflict, though we often rephrased the questions they asked, and we arrived, at times, at rather different evaluations of the common school.

Our approach departs from some of the more common ways of thinking about leadership. One of the oldest conventions is to portray leaders as great men (or, rarely, great women) who achieve because of their intrinsic qualities; a related modern mode of analysis is to identify the psychological traits of leaders. While we do find some common characteristics in most of the leaders we describe in this work—they tend to have high social energy, for example, and clear conceptions of their work—we dispute that leaders need be extraordinary people and are uncomfortable with the implications of looking for larger-than-life

---

*Tyack indicates his points of agreement and disagreement with Cremin in a review of Cremin's, *American Education: The National Experience,* in *American Journal of Education,* in press.

heroes to extricate schools from difficulties today. Ordinary people in modest everyday ways have made important differences in the lives of people around them; it is not only in times of crisis that leaders emerge. There are many contexts for leadership, many styles of bringing about change. Indeed, leadership is so dependent on context that it cannot be understood apart from time and place.

We also find problems in the way most scholars have studied leadership in organizations. The majority of studies focus on leadership in small groups and have been undertaken, for the most part, by social psychologists in military and industrial settings typically preoccupied with managerial concerns about productivity and morale. Other studies generalize from the behavior of college students (usually prosperous white males) in highly controlled settings. Such small-group studies have typically been *framed*, treated in isolation from the history, purposes, and structure of the larger organization and its place in American society.

Similarly, when social scientists examine the work of administrators at the top of complex organizations, they tend to apply highly normative concepts of leadership. This results in denigration of everyday management as system maintenance and restricts the occasions when administrators may be said really to "lead." An opposite tendency, found especially in fulsome rhetoric about educational leadership, is to demand prodigies of imagination, force, and sensitivity from bureaucratic heads. It is often difficult to see, under the padding of presuppositions, how administrators went about their ordinary business, how normal problems got solved, conflicting claims adjusted, procedures made more effective—or the reverse. The administrator is portrayed either as a routinized bureaucrat or as an institutional Moses who parts the Red Sea. We believe that the everyday work of creating and running schools is important and undervalued.

Above all, we think it useful to question the search for universal and eternal generalizations and instead to pay attention to the changing context of ideas, interests, and political and economic structures within which educational leaders have operated. We made a conscious decision not to employ a single, encompassing theory to interpret diverse developments over the century-and-a-half that we discuss in this book. We employ explanations from social science not as time-free and objective generalizations but rather as time-bound and partial ways of seeing —essentially as elegantly simplified ways of highlighting key features of the historical landscape, much as different maps can be used for different purposes.

The puzzles posed by that landscape are the starting points for our work. Our major concern throughout has been *how* things happened, and this has led us to a middle rather than a comprehensive level of generalization when we discuss *why* things happened. In Parts I and III we draw heavily on the social science literature on social movements, for example, and in Part II on theories about interlocking networks of elites, recognizing in each case the importance of countervailing forces and alternative modes of explanation. Our overall interpretation presupposes diversity of motives, interests, and organizational and societal contexts in different periods.

We have seen the challenge as one of integrating partial modes of explanation and diverse evidence into a plausible narrative, not of subordinating the diverse evidence to a single and schematic theory. We are aware of the difficulty of that task. Scholars who have different ideas about *why* things happened or what was their *worth* may distill different meanings from this book. Since we regard the generation of new questions and controversy as the heart of inquiry, we hope that our study will prompt continuing reformulations rather than simply revive old skirmishes.

We turn now to the shaping of some of the ideas in this book. In the midst of writing a study of compulsory schooling, Tyack concluded that he was looking through the wrong end of the telescope. By focusing on state power and bureaucratization he was ignoring the mainstream of mid-nineteenth-century public education, the spread of a decentralized system of rural and small-town common schools created largely by local initiative, though systematically connected with a broader leadership interested in using the state to standardize schooling. Joint work on a quantitative study of school enrollments with John Meyer, Joane Nagel, and Audri Gordon led Tyack back to his earlier interest in the work of Protestant ministers in the common-school movement on successive frontiers. Fifteen years ago, in research parallel to that of Timothy Smith, he had suggested that public schools were part of a "Protestant *paideia*" (a phrase suggested to him by Richard Storr). Meyer indicated that the sociological literature on social movements might provide a useful theoretical framework for understanding the links between religion, political ideology, and economic interests, while John Higham's discussion of a broad-based "Protestant-republican" ideology provided a way to link belief systems with institution-building. Some other recent studies have also been models to us in the difficult task of blending social and intellectual history. In particular, Daniel Rodgers's analysis of the work ethic

Afterword

and Paul Johnson's illumination of the links between evangelical religion and economic change showed how pervasive belief systems could help to shape—and were shaped by—economic and social institutions. In the notes to Part I we indicate our debts to these and other scholars.

In Part II we move to leadership in the kind of complex organizations Tyack had earlier discussed in *The One Best System*. Our concern here, however, was with questions only briefly discussed there: How did educational elites emerge, how did they exercise their influence, and to what end? Here, we sought to connect changes in educational leadership with the transformation of the economy and the supposed depoliticization of the school. In an era when large corporate organizations increasingly came to dominate, decision making changed in many sectors of society. In interpreting these developments we found especially helpful the studies of professional elites by Magali Sarfatti Larson and Corinne Gilb, of managerial and technical elites by Alfred Chandler and David Noble, and of changed modes of political decision making by Walter Dean Burnham, Robert Wiebe, and Samuel Hays. We also learned from recent radical educational historians and from the pathbreaking early study of the cult of efficiency by Raymond Callahan (though our interpretation departs in a number of ways from the work of these colleagues). In doing our research on the new generation of school managers and experts we became aware that there are few detailed studies of political responses of the working class to the changes engineered by the elite—or indeed, of any large-scale organized resistance to their program—and we look forward to the forthcoming study of working-class educational politics by Paul Peterson and Ira Katznelson for clues to this important puzzle.

Our notes to Part III reveal our indebtedness to a group of social scientists in education and related fields who have sought patterns of meaning in what often seemed a formless kaleidoscope of change. We are grateful for the many conversations we had with colleagues in the Stanford School of Education and the stimulation generated by the Institute for Research on Educational Finance and Governance (IFG) under the leadership of Henry Levin; in particular, we benefited from talking with John Meyer, James March, Michael Kirst, and Paul Peterson. That section of the book also reflects the influence of Albert Hirschman's study of decline in organizations. Through conversations about educational reform—and by her own example—Dee Tyack has reminded us that classroom instruction remains the key to the renewal of public education. We appreciate her criticism and encouragement.

We are deeply indebted to various organizations for financial support of different phases of this study: to the National Institute of Education, through its grants to IFG; to the Center for Advanced Study in the Behavioral Sciences, for providing a year of challenging nondistraction to Tyack; to the Organizational Research Training Program at Stanford, where Hansot held a postdoctoral fellowship; and to the Ford Foundation; and to the Carnegie Corporation that sponsored related earlier studies.

While writing this book we presented provisional parts of its argument at several universities—University of Chicago, Harvard University, University of Illinois at Champaign-Urbana, University of Rochester, University of Wisconsin at Madison, and the University of California at Los Angeles—and at a number of professional meetings and in journal articles. We received much useful criticism from colleagues in the process, and we wish especially to thank scholars who criticized Tyack's lecture in honor of R. Freeman Butts at the convention of the American Educational Studies Association in 1979 and colleagues who met to discuss the articles (including our own) that appeared in Daedalus (Summer, 1981). The school administrators Tyack taught in two successive summer seminars sponsored by the National Endowment for the Humanities gave us much practical criticism and encouragement.

A number of scholars commented on part or all of earlier drafts: J. Myron Atkin, Eric Bredo, Edwin Bridges, Daniel Calhoun, Hollis Caswell, Larry Cuban, Joseph Featherstone, David Hogan, Carl Kaestle, Michael B. Katz, Susan Lloyd, and Daniel Rodgers. Whatever improvement has appeared in successive drafts owes a great deal to their prodding, their challenges, and their encouragement.

We have been fortunate to work with an outstanding group of research assistants on different parts of this study: Robert Cummings, Karen Harbeck, Michael Imber, Harvey Kantor, and Theodore Mitchell. They and other student colleagues working on some related projects have not only aided us immensely with the everyday tasks of research, but also helped us to make sense of the evidence. To Thomas James we owe a special debt for his superb skills as editor of an earlier draft: wise in his criticisms of substance, meticulous about details, he saved us from many mistakes.

It is conventional to absolve colleagues from the faults of a book. This we do, of course. But more problematic to us is the other side of the

Afterword

coin: what about ideas that come so smoothly into the flow of scholarly talk that they unconsciously become incorporated as part of one's own mentality? We have no doubt that colleagues will find notions imbedded here that they implanted in conversations, perhaps years ago. We thank them.

Reno, Nevada
Stanford, California
September, 1981

Notes

Lest this book double in size from bibliographical elephantiasis, we tried to keep citations modest, indicating the secondary works we have found most useful and thought-provoking and only a sampling of the primary sources we have consulted. Notes give full citations for the first use of a source within each numbered section of the book, then abbreviations.

PROLOGUE

1. Michael Sadler, "Impressions of American Education," *Educational Review* 25 (1903): 219; Sol Cohen, "Sir Michael Sadler and the Sociopolitical Analysis of Education," *History of Education Quarterly* 7 (1967): 281–94; A.D. Mayo, "The Reconstruction of the American Common School," *Proceedings of the Ohio Teachers Association,* 23 (1871): 8.

2. John Dewey, *My Pedagogic Creed* (1897; reprint ed., Washington, D.C.: Progressive Education Association, 1929), p. 17; Ellwood P. Cubberley, *Changing Conceptions of Education* (Boston: Houghton Mifflin, 1909); Samuel Bowles and Herbert Gintis, *Schooling in Capitalist America: Education and the Contradictions of Economic Life* (New York: Basic Books, 1976); Godfrey Hodgson, "Do Schools Make a Difference?" *Atlantic Monthly,* 231 (1973): 35–47; Michael W. Kirst and Walter I. Garms, "The Demographic, Fiscal, and Political Environment of Public School Finance in the 1980s," (Stanford, Calif.: Institute for Research on Educational Finance and Governance, 1980).

3. Alfred Chandler, Jr., *The Visible Hand: The Managerial Revolution in American Business* (Cambridge,: Harvard University Press, 1977); Harry Braverman, *Labor and Monopoly Capital: The Degradation of Work in the Twentieth Century* (New York: Monthly Review Press, 1974).

4. NEA, Department of Superintendence, *Educational Leadership: Programs and Possibilities* (Washington, D.C.: NEA, 1933), pp. 159, 278, 325–30, 334–35.

5. Merle Curti, *The Social Ideas of American Educators* (Paterson, N.J.: Littlefield, Adams, 1935); George Counts, *The Selective Character of American Secondary Education* (Chicago: University of Chicago Press, 1922); Counts, *School and Society in Chicago* (New York: Harcourt, Brace, 1938); the pioneer work of recent revisionism, and in many respects still the best, is Michael B. Katz, *The Irony of Early School Reform: Educational Innovation in Mid-Nineteenth Century Massachusetts* (Cambridge: Harvard University Press, 1968).

6. David K. Cohen and Bella H. Rosenberg, "Functions and Fantasies: Understanding Schools in Capitalist America," *History of Education Quarterly* 17 (1977): 132.

7. Michael Walzer, *Radical Principles: Reflections of an Unreconstructed Democrat* (New York: Basic Books, 1980), p. 298.

8. Karl Marx, *Eighteenth Brumaire of Louis Bonaparte* (New York: International Publishers, 1963), p. 15.

9. John Higham, "Hanging Together: Divergent Unities in American History," *Journal of American History* 61 (1974): 10; Clifford Geertz, "Ideology as a Cultural System," in *Ideology and Discontent,* ed., David Apter (New York: Free Press, 1964), pp. 47–76.

PART I

Section 1

1. U.S., Congress, Senate, *Congressional Record,* 47th Cong., 1st sess. 13 June 1882, vol. 13, pp. 4822–23; this undated theme and other records of the Ashland, Oregon, school are deposited in the O. C. Applegate Papers, University of Oregon, Eugene, Oregon.

2. Aaron Gove, "Trail of the City Superintendent," *Addresses and Proceedings of the NEA, 1900,* p. 215; Frederick Hugh Bair, *The Social Understandings of the Superintendent of Schools* (New York: Teachers College Press,* 1934), pp. 156–69; John Bunyan, *The Pilgrim's Progress* (Harmondworth: Penguin, 1965). The following biographies and autobiographies of administrators are samples of a large literature: Samuel P. Abelow, *Dr. William H. Maxwell, the First Superintendent of Schools of the City of New York* (Brooklyn: Schebor, 1934); Selma Berrol, "William Henry Maxwell and a New Educational New York," *History of Education Quarterly* 8 (Summer 1968): 215–28; Frank K. Burrin, *Edward Charles Elliott, Educator* (Lafayette, Ind.: Purdue University, 1970); Detroit Public School Staff, *Frank Cody: A Realist in Education* (New York: Macmillan, 1943); Willard B. Gatewood, Jr., *Eugene Clyde Brooks: Educator and Public Servant* (Durham, N.C.: Duke University Press, 1960); Solomon P. Jaeckel, "Edward Hyatt, 1858–1919: California Educator," *Southern California Quarterly* 52 (1970): 33–50, 122–54, 248–74; Francis Wayland Parker, "An Autobiographical Sketch," in William M. Giffin, *School Days in the Fifties* (Chicago: A. Flanagan Company, n.d.), pp. 110–37; Jesse B. Sears and Adin D. Henderson, *Cubberley of Stanford and His Contribution to American Education* (Stanford, Calif.: Stanford University Press, 1957); Edward Austin Sheldon, *Autobiography,* ed. Mary Sheldon Barnes (New York: Ives-Butler, 1911); David Snedden, *Recollections of Over Half a Century Spent in Educational Work* (Palo Alto, Calif.: The Author, 1949); Frank E. Spaulding, *School Superintendent in Action in Five Cities* (Rindge, N.H.: Richard Smith, 1955); John Swett, *Public Education in California: Its Origin and Development, with Personal Reminiscenses of Half a Century* (New York: American Book Company, 1911); Lester L. Tracy, Jr., *Life and Educational Contributions of Joseph D. Elliff* (n.p. Gamma Chapter, Phi Delta Kappa, 1953); Frank P. Whitney, *School and I: The Autobiography of an Ohio Schoolmaster* (Yellow Springs, Ohio: Antioch Press, 1957); also see bibliography by Warren Button in *A Bibliography of American Educational History,* ed. Francesco Cordasco and William W. Brickman (New York: AMS Press, 1975), pp. 228–48.

3. For a sampling of "necrologies," see *Addresses and Proceedings of the NEA,* 1885, pp. 13–18; *1886,* pp. 246–58; *1887,* pp. 664–66; *1888,* pp. 677–84; *1889,* pp. 44–51; *1890,* pp. 42–46; *1892,* pp. 598–605; *1894,* pp. 222–51; *1896,* pp. 218–29; *1898,* pp. 282–93; *1899,* pp. 232–49; *1900,* pp. 712–15; *1901,* pp. 387–90; *1903,* pp. 369–74; *1904,* pp. 361–65; *1905,* pp. 329–35; *1907,* pp. 297–326; *1908,* pp. 492–98.

4. U. S. Bureau of the Census, *Historical Statistics of the United States: Colonial Times to 1970* (Washington, D.C.: GPO, 1975), 2: 1103, 1141; NEA, *Studies in State Educational Administration,* mimeographed, no. 9, (Washington, D.C.: Research Division, NEA, 1931), pp. 5–6; Donald Warren, *To Enforce Education: A History of the Founding Years of the United States Office of Education* (Detroit: Wayne State University Press, 1974).

5. U. S. Bureau of the Census, *Historical Statistics,* 1: 11–12; James Blodgett, *Report on Education in the U. S. at the Eleventh Census* (Washington, D.C.: GPO, 1893), p. 45; Lewis Solmon, "Estimates of the Costs of Schooling in 1880 and 1890," *Explorations in Economic History,* supp. 7 (1970): 575, 531–81.

6. Maris Vinovskis and John Bernard, "Beyond Catharine Beecher: Female Education in the Antebellum Period," *Signs* 3 (1978): 856–59; Willard Ellsbree, *The American Teacher: Evolution of a Profession in a Democracy* (New York: American Book Company,

*We use the shortened form, Teachers College Press, for Columbia University Contributions in Education, the published series of theses.

1939); Carl Kaestle and Maris Vinovskis, *Education and Social Change in Nineteenth Century Massachusetts* (Cambridge: Cambridge University Press, 1980), pp. 200–6; Edgar Wesley, *NEA, The First Hundred Years* (New York: Harper & Row, 1957), p. 397.

7. Warren, *To Enforce Education* pp. 4–5; NEA, *State Educational Administration*, pp. 5–6.

8. Michael Katz, "From Voluntarism to Bureaucracy in American Education," *Sociology of Education* 44 (1971): 297–332; Carl Kaestle, *The Evolution of an Urban School System: New York City, 1750–1850* (Cambridge: Harvard University Press, 1973); Michael B. Katz, *The Irony of Early School Reform: Educational Innovation in Mid-Nineteenth Century Massachusetts* (Cambridge: Harvard University Press, 1968); Selwyn Troen, *The Public and the Schools: Shaping the St. Louis System, 1838–1920* (Columbia, Mo.: University of Missouri Press, 1975); Samuel Bowles and Herbert Gintis, *Schooling in Capitalist America: Education and the Contradictions of Economic Life* (New York: Basic Books, 1976); David Tyack, *The One Best System: A History of American Urban Education* (Cambridge: Harvard University Press, 1974).

9. John Meyer, et al., "Public Education as Nation-Building in America: Enrollments and Bureaucratization in the American States, 1870–1930," *American Journal of Sociology* 85 (1979): 591–613; Sydney Ahlstrom, *A Religious History of the American People* (New Haven: Yale University Press, 1972); H. Richard Niebuhr, *The Kingdom of God in America* (New York: Harper & Bros., 1937); Robert Baird, *Religion in America* (New York: Harper & Bros., 1844).

10. Schurz as quoted in George Fredrickson, *The Inner Civil War: Northern Intellectuals and the Crisis of the Union* (New York: Harper & Row, 1965), p. 8; Per Siljestrom, *The Educational Institutions of the United States: Their Character and Organization*, trans. Frederica Rowan (London: John Chapman, 1853), pp. 11, 39–42, 47; Francis Adams, *The Free School System of the United States* (London: Chapman and Hall, 1875), chap. 1.

11. Timothy Smith, "Protestant Schooling and American Nationality, 1800–1850," *Journal of American History* 53 (1967): 679–95; David Tyack, "The Kingdom of God and the Common School: Protestant Ministers and the Educational Awakening in the West," *Harvard Educational Review* 36 (1966): 447–69; Ernest Tuveson, *Redeemer Nation: The Idea of America's Millennial Role* (Chicago: University of Chicago Press, 1968).

12. Robert Wiebe, "The Social Functions of Schooling," *American Quarterly* 21 (1969): 147–50; compare the founding of churches in H. Richard Niebuhr, *The Social Sources of Denominationalism* (New York: Living Age Books, 1957).

13. John Higham, "Hanging Together: Divergent Unities in American History," *Journal of American History* 61 (1974): 13–14; James Bryce, *The American Commonwealth*, 2 vols. (New York: Macmillan, 1910), 2: 770.

14. In *American Education: The National Experience, 1783–1876* (New York: Harper & Row, 1980), Lawrence Cremin gives a rich portrait of a whole variety of educational institutions that converged with public schools to produce a national and Christian *paideia*, see esp. chap. 14.

15. Robert McCloskey, ed., *The Bible in The Public Schools: Arguments Before the Superior Court of Cincinnati in Case of Minor v. Board of Education* (New York: Da Capo Press, 1967), p. 213; David Tyack and Elisabeth Hansot, "Conflict and Consensus in American Public Education," *Daedalus* 110 (1981): 1–25.

16. Joshua Fishman, *Language Loyalty in the United States* (The Hague: Mouton, 1966).

17. Troen, *St. Louis System*, chap. 1.

18. Eric Foner, *Free Soil, Free Labor, Free Men: The Ideology of the Republican Party before the Civil War* (New York: Oxford University Press, 1970); William T. Harris, et al., *A Statement of the Theory of Education in the United States as Approved by Many Leading Educators* (Washington, D.C.: GPO, 1874); Carl Kaestle, "Social Change, Discipline, and the Common School in Early Nineteenth Century America," *Journal of Interdisciplinary History* 9 (1978): 1–17.

19. As late as 1880, 72 percent of Americans still lived in rural areas—U.S. Bureau of the Census, *Historical Statistics*, 1: 12; Daniel Nelson, *Managers and Workers: Origins of the New Factory System in the United States, 1880–1920* (Madison: University of Wisconsin Press, 1975), chap. 1; Stanley W. Lindberg, ed., *The Annotated McGuffey: Selections from the McGuffey Eclectic Readers, 1836–1920* (New York: Van Nostrand, 1976); on inequalities of wealth, see Edward Pessen, "The Egalitarian Myth and the American Social Reality:

Wealth, Mobility, and Equality in the 'Era of the Common Man,' " *American Historical Review* 76 (1971): 989–1034; for examples of attitudes of employers and workers toward education and economic opportunity, see U.S. Senate Committee upon the Relations between Labor and Capital, *Report*, 5 vols. (Washington, D.C.: GPO, 1885), esp. 1: 1129, 680, 599, 582; 2: 710, 731, 733, 734; 789, 791–92; 4: 728–31.

20. O. C. Applegate Papers; I am here citing the themes and other records from an article in which I quoted extensively from them: David Tyack, "The Tribe and the Common School: The District School in Ashland, Oregon, in the 1860's," *The Call Number* 27 (1966): 13–23.

21. Tyack, "Ashland," p. 19.

22. M. R. Orne, *The Country School: An Entertainment in Two Scenes* (Boston: Walter H. Baker, 1890), pp. 2, 14–15; for a discussion of "culture as a percolation down from the top," see Oscar Handlin, *John Dewey's Challenge to Education* (New York: Harper & Row, 1959), 27–39.

23. Tyack, "Ashland," pp. 20–21.

24. Ibid., pp. 21–22. For the troubled history of one part of this folklore, see Daniel Rodgers, *The Work Ethic in Industrial America 1850–1920* (Chicago: University of Chicago Press, 1978); Joanna Bowen Gillespie, "An Almost Irresistible Engineery: Five Decades of Nineteenth Century Methodist Sunday School Library Books," *Phaedrus*, in press; E. P. Thompson, *The Making of the English Working Class* (New York: Vintage Books, 1963), chap. 11; in *Rockdale: The Growth of an American Village in the Early Industrial Revolution* (New York: Alfred A. Knopf, 1978), Anthony Wallace discusses the importance of evangelical and millennial thinking in Pennsylvania manufacturing towns; Paul Johnson, *A Shopkeeper's Millennium: Society and Revivals in Rochester, New York, 1815–1837* (New York: Hill and Wang, 1978); Ahlstrom, *Religious History of the American People*, pp. 789, 847.

Section 2

1. Lee Soltow and Edward Stevens, "Economic Aspects of School Participation in Mid-Nineteenth-Century United States," *Journal of Interdisciplinary History* 8 (1977): 221–43.

2. Ibid.; for a discussion of variance in school attendance, see Michael Katz, "Who Went to School?" *History of Education Quarterly* 12 (1972): 432–54.

3. Michael Katz, "From Voluntarism to Bureaucracy in American Education," *Sociology of Education* 44 (1971); Carl Kaestle, *The Evolution of an Urban School System: New York City, 1750–1850* (Cambridge: Harvard University Press, 1973), chap. 1.

4. David Potts has demonstrated the power of local boosterism in higher education in "American Colleges in the Nineteenth Century: From Localism to Denominationalism," *History of Education Quarterly* 11 (1971): 363–80; and in " 'College Enthusiasm' " as Public Response, 1800–1860," *Harvard Educational Review* 47 (1977): 28–42.

5. Albert Fishlow, "Levels of Nineteenth-Century Investment in Education," *Journal of Economic History* 26 (1966): 418–36; Fishlow, "The American Common School Revival: Fact or Fancy?" in *Industrialization in Two Systems: Essays in Honor of Alexander Gerschenkron*, ed., Henry Rosovsky (New York: John Wiley 1966), pp. 40–67; Lawrence Cremin, *The American Common School: An Historic Conception* (New York: Teachers College Press, 1951).

6. Mary Gordon, "Patriots and Christians: A Reassessment of Nineteenth Century School Reformers," *Journal of Social History* 11 (1978): 554–73; Alison Prentice, *The School Promoters: Education and Social Class in Mid-Nineteenth Century Upper Canada* (Toronto: McClelland and Stewart, 1977), chaps. 1, 2; Winthrop Hudson, *American Protestantism* (Chicago: University of Chicago Press, 1961), chap. 2; Louis Wright, *Culture on the Moving Frontier* (New York: Harper & Bros., 1955), chap. 5.

7. Carl Kaestle and Maris Vinovskis, *Education and Social Change in Nineteenth Century Massachusetts* (Cambridge: Cambridge University Press, 1980), chaps. 2–4; Gordon, "Patriots and Christians," p. 561.

8. Kaestle and Vinovskis, *Education and Social Change*, chap. 8; Charles Bidwell, "The Moral Significance of the Common School: A Sociological Study of Local Patterns of

School Control and Moral Education in Massachusetts and New York, 1837–1840," *History of Education Quarterly* 6 (1966): 50–91.

9. Fishlow, "Investment in Education."

10. John Folger and Charles Nam, *Education of the American Population* (Washington, D.C.: GPO, 1967), chaps. 1, 4; W. Vance Grant and C. George Lind, *Digest of Educational Statistics,* 1974 ed. (Washington, D.C.: GPO, 1975), p. 34.

11. David Tyack, "The Tribe and the Common School: Community Control in Rural Education," *American Quarterly* 24 (1972): 3–19.

12. Jonathan Sher, ed., *Education in Rural America: A Reassessment of Conventional Wisdom* (Boulder, Colo.: Westview Press, 1977); Lewis Solmon, "Estimates of the Costs of Schooling in 1880 and 1890," *Explorations in Economic History,* Suppl. vol. 7 (4): 574–76.

13. Kaestle and Vinovskis, *Education and Social Change,* chaps. 5–6.

14. Solmon, "Costs of Schooling," pp. 539, 557; there were, of course, many families and children who resisted public schooling—one response, that of working-class truancy, is discussed in David Tyack and Michael Berkowitz, "The Man Nobody Liked: Toward a Social History of the Truant Officer, 1840–1940," *American Quarterly* 29 (1977): 31–54 (the records on truancy give rich evidence of alienation of many working-class families and children).

Section 3

1. John Higham, "Hanging Together: Divergent Unities in American History," Journal of American History 61 (1974): 13, 14; William McLaughlin, *Revivals, Awakening, and Reform: An Essay on Religion and Social Change in America, 1607–1977* (Chicago: University of Chicago Press, 1978); John R. Bodo, *The Protestant Clergy and Public Issues, 1812–1848* (Princeton, N.J.: Princeton University Press, 1954); William Clebsch, "America's 'Mythique' as Redeemer Nation," *Prospects: An Annual of American Cultural Studies* 4 (1979): 79–94.

2. Charles Foster, *An Errand of Mercy: The Evangelical United Front, 1790–1837* (Chapel Hill: University of North Carolina Press, 1960), pp. 55, 121; Clifford Griffin, *Their Brothers' Keepers: Moral Stewardship in the United States, 1800–1865* (New Brunswick, N.J.: Rutgers University Press, 1960); Lois Banner "Religious Benevolence as Social Control: A Critique of an Interpretation," *Journal of American History* 60 (1973–74): 23–41; James Maclear, " 'The True American Union' of Church and State: The Reconstruction of the Theocratic Tradition," *Church History* 28 (1959): 41–62; the urban side of the story is treated in Paul Boyer, *Urban Masses and Moral Order in America, 1820–1920* (Cambridge: Harvard University Press, 1978); and Timothy Smith, *Revivalism and Social Reform in Mid-Nineteenth Century America* (New York: Abingdon Press, 1957).

3. Edwin Rice, *The Sunday-School Movement 1780–1917 and the American Sunday-School Union 1817–1917* (Philadelphia: American Sunday School Union, 1917), p. 63, chaps. 3–6; this account, rich in documentation from the ASSU archives, is more a primary source than a secondary account, informed by the conviction of an insider that the ASSU was an agency of Providence.

4. Ibid., p. 94, chaps. 3, 6.

5. Foster, *Errand of Mercy,* pp. 139–40.

6. Robert Lynn and Elliott Wright, *The Big Little School: Sunday Child of American Protestantism* (New York: Harper & Row, 1971), p. 71.

7. Rice, *Sunday-School Movement,* chap. 7; Lynn and Wright, *Big Little School,* chap. 2.

8. Foster, *Errand of Mercy,* pp. 193, 196, 224; Lynn and Wright, *Big Little School,* pp. 30–31.

9. Alexis de Tocqueville, *Democracy in America,* 2 vols., ed., Phillips Bradley (New York: Vintage Books, 1945), 1:46.

10. Nancy Atkinson, ed., *Biography of Rev. G. H. Atkinson, D.D.* (Portland, Ore.: F. W. Bates and Co., 1893), chap. 7, pp. 111–12; George Atkinson to Josiah and Sophronia Little, 7 June 1858, Atkinson Papers HM 4480, The Huntington Library, San Marino, Calif. These items are reproduced by permission of The Huntington Library and will hereafter be cited as HM (followed by the manuscript number).

11. Nancy Atkinson, *Atkinson*, chap. 7, pp. 111–12; Atkinson to Milton Badger, 14, Sept. 1848, American Home Missionary Society Papers, Chicago Theological School, Chicago, Ill. (hereafter cited as AHMS); George Atkinson, "Early History of the Public School System in Oregon," in *Biennial Report of the Superintendent of Public Instruction of Oregon, 1876*, pp. 7–11; George Himes, *Memorial Church in Memory of Rev. George Atkinson* (Portland, Ore.: n.p., n.d.) pp. 2–3.

12. Atkinson to Milton Badger, 2 March 1853, AHMS; O. Dickinson to Milton Badger, 15 Sept. 1853, AHMS; Ezra Fisher, *Correspondence* (Portland, Ore.: Oregon Historical Society, 1919), pp. 208, 213, 225, 312; Atkinson to Josiah Little, 31 Dec. 1849, HM 4445.

13. Atkinson to Milton Badger, 25 June 1850, AHMS; Horace Lyman to Milton Badger, 13 April 1850, AHMS; Atkinson to Milton Badger, 7 Jan. 1850, AHMS; Atkinson wrote (Josiah and Sophronia Little 10 March 1854, HM 4473) that he was concerned about his own children: "We fear for them and daily feel more the responsibility and difficulty of training them." Rev. David Blaine to parents, 21 June 1854, from typescript volume of letters owned by Mrs. Friend S. Dickinson and Mrs. Ralph C. Angell of Portland, Ore. Even the churchgoers had their faults. Mrs. Blaine wrote her parents in despair on 19 May 1855, saying that after she had spent hours scrubbing the church the "people came in and with all the mud on their shoes, and stuck them upon the seat before them. Mothers let their children stand on the seats, the nasty tobacco chewers squirted their juice around, and the umbrellas were all set running with water right in the seats, so that by night it looked much worse than before I cleaned it."

14. Atkinson to Milton Badger, 25 June 1850, AHMS; Horace Lyman to Milton Badger, 13 April 1850, AHMS; Atkinson to Milton Badger 14 Oct. 1850, AHMS; Atkinson to Josiah Little, 22 April 1859, HM 4483; Atkinson to Milton Badger, 17 April 1851, AHMS.

15. George Campbell, *A Sermon at the Ordination of the Rev. George Atkinson* (Newbury, Vt.: L.J. McIndoe, 1847), pp. 20–21; Ray Allen Billington, *The Protestant Crusade* (New York: Macmillan, 1938), chap. 5, 6; Atkinson, MS Diary of 1847–48 Voyage, p. 129; Atkinson, typescript Diary, 18 and 26 March, 2 and 23 April, 22 May 1849, Oregon Historical Society, Portland, Oregon (hereafter cited as OHS); Fisher, *Correspondence*, p. 290; Atkinson to Josiah Little, ca. March 1855, HM 4475.

16. Trustees of Portland church to Milton Badger, 3 April 1852, AHMS; Atkinson wrote to Milton Badger on 24 Nov. 1849, that Lyman's teaching would "be most favorable introduction" to Portlanders: Atkinson, Diary, 21 July 1853, OHS.

17. Alfred Powers and Howard Corning, eds., "History of Education in Portland," mimeographed (Portland, Ore.: W. P. A. Project., 1937), pp. 306–8, chaps. 1–3; *Report of the Proceedings of the State Teachers Association* (Salem, Ore.: W. H. Byars, 1884); William Fenton, "Father Wilbur and His Work," *Oregon Historical Quarterly* 10 (June 1904): 16–30; Erwin Lange, "Oregon City Private Schools, 1843–59," *Oregon Historical Quarterly* 37 (December, 1936): 308–28; Ida Stauffer, "A History of Educational Activities of the Congregational Church in the Pacific Northwest" (Master's thesis, University of Oregon, 1927); Read Bain, "Educational Plans and Efforts by Methodists in Oregon to 1860," *Oregon Historical Quarterly* 21 (March, 1920): 63–94. Based on data supplied in Clifford Constance's useful *Chronology of Oregon Schools, 1834–1958* (Eugene: University of Oregon Books, 1960), I have compiled the following list of the founding of private schools, 1847–1900, by religious denominations (the figures in parentheses indicate schools that were incorporated but never opened): Roman Catholic, 33; Episcopal, 11; Methodist, 10 (6); Baptist, 6 (2); Presbyterian, 6 (2); Adventist, 6; Christian, 5 (1); United Brethren, 4; Lutheran 3; Jewish 3; Congregational, Evangelical, and Friends, 2 each; and unaffiliated or undesignated, 28 (19). The period of most active school-founding was 1880–1900 when the majority of Catholic schools were started. The early schools had a very high rate of mortality, many of them lasting less than five years (and thirty incorporated schools never opened).

18. Lange, "Oregon City Private Schools," p. 49, reported that a resident of Oregon City offered to board a teacher and provide a free room for the "public" school; in a letter to Josiah Hale, 23 March 1874, HM 4512, Atkinson told of his efforts as general missionary to build churches, establish reading rooms, distribute tracts, and encourage the workers in the field.

19. Atkinson, "Public School System," p. 12; Thomas Eliot, "History of Schools of Multnomah County," *Oregonian* 7 March 1876; Atkinson's newspaper articles began appearing

in the *Oregonian* in 1866; Eliot, his successor as county superintendent, was a Unitarian minister; Nancy Atkinson, *Atkinson*, pp. 25–26; Powers and Corning, "Portland," chaps. 1–4.

20. George Atkinson, "The Culture Most Valuable to Prepare Law-Abiding and Law Respecting Citizens," *Addresses and Proceedings of the NEA, 1888*, pp. 114–17, 119–20; the exclamation "The Bible our text book!" is not included in the NEA version but appears in the transcript included in Nancy Atkinson, *Atkinson*, pp. 120, 239; see also the collection of articles on "The School Question" culled from periodicals and reprinted in *The Christian World* 21 (Feb. 1870): 40–63; W. C. Anderson and F. M. Haight, *Review of Dr. Scott's Bible and Politics in the Light of Religion and the Law* (San Francisco: Towne & Bacon, 1859); and J. E. Rankin, *The Claims of the Bible to a Place in the Schools* (St. Albans, Vt.: E. B. Whiting, 1860).

21. John Eaton, "George Atkinson," *Pacific University Bulletin* 40 (1944): 12.

Section 4

1. Joseph Gusfield, ed., *Protest, Reform, and Revolt: A Reader in Social Movements* (New York: John Wiley, 1974), p. 2; Gusfield also has a perceptive discussion of social movements in *International Encyclopedia of the Social Sciences* (n.p.: Macmillan and the Free Press, 1968), 16: 445–52; Roberta Ash gives a brief history of social movement in *Social Movements in America* (Chicago: Markham, 1972); for a brief survey of recent scholarship on social movements, with particular attention to changes within organizations, see Mayer Zald and Michael Berger, "Social Movements in Organizations: Coup d'Etat, Insurgency, and Mass Movements," *American Journal of Sociology* 83 (1978): 11, 39–42, 47.

2. Robert Wiebe, "The Social Functions of Schooling," *American Quarterly* 21 (1969): 147, 148, 147–150; Daniel Walker Howe, ed., *Victorian America* (Philadelphia: University of Pennsylvania Press, 1976), pp. 22, 23–35.

3. Information on these men compiled from Dumas Malone, ed., *The Dictionary of American Biography*, 20 vols. (New York: Scribner's, 1928–36).

4. John Ohles, ed., *Biographical Dictionary of American Educators* (Westport, Conn.: Greenwood Press, 1978); Imber's study is included as app. A of our final report to The National Institute of Education, Washington, D.C., on our leadership project, Grant No. OB-NIE-G-80-0111; he is currently revising it for publication.

5. Vincent Lannie, ed., *Henry Barnard: American Educator* (New York: Teachers College Press, 1974), p. 15.

6. Obituaries of Parsons and Baldwin in *Addresses and Proceedings of the NEA, 1889*, pp. 48–49; *1899*, pp. 234–35; Stephan Thernstrom, *The Other Bostonians: Poverty and Progress in the American Metropolis, 1880–1970* (Cambridge: Harvard University Press, 1973), pp. 221–27.

7. "Necrologies" cited in n. 3, section 1, above.

8. Newton Dougherty, "Newton Bateman," *Addresses and Proceedings of the NEA, 1905*, pp. 331, 329–31.

9. Lannie, *Barnard*, pp. 56, 51.

10. Ibid., p. 75; for another model of rousing interest in education, see the Lyceum movement: Carl Bode, *The American Lyceum: Town Meeting of the Mind* (New York: Oxford University Press, 1956).

11. Paul Mattingly, *The Classless Profession: American Schoolmen in the Twentieth Century* (New York: New York University Press, 1975), pp. 67–68; Lloyd Jorgenson, *The Founding of Public Education in Wisconsin* (Madison: State Historical Society of Wisconsin, 1956), 123.

12. Mattingly, *Classless Profession*, pp. 34–38; Mary Gordon, "Patriots and Christians: A Reassessment of Nineteenth Century School Reformers," *Journal of Social History* II (1978): 557–8.

13. Allen O. Hansen, *Early Educational Leadership in the Ohio Valley* (Bloomington, Ill.: Public School Publishing Co., 1923).

14. Sheldon Davis, *Educational Periodicals during the Nineteenth Century* (Washington, D.C.: GPO, 1919), p. 16, chap. 6; Richard Thursfield, *Henry Barnard's American Journal of Education* (Baltimore: The Johns Hopkins University Press, 1945).

15. Lannie, *Barnard*, p. 23; Rice's account (Edwin Rice, *The Sunday School-Movement 1780–1917 and the American Sunday-School Union 1817–1917* (Philadelphia: American Sunday School Union, 1917) of the ASSU gives evidence of more effective central organization than have most of the reports by early state superintendents that we have read.

16. William Carr, *John Swett: The Biography of an Educational Pioneer* (Santa Monica, Calif.: Fine Arts Press, 1933), pp. 77–80; the best way to savor the job of school superintendent is not to focus only on the famous reports of the highly literate leaders like Mann, but to sample the reports of average state and county superintendents, whose concerns were often less global than Mann's (how to get school trustees to build a separate privy for boys and for girls, for example).

17. Jorgenson, *Public Education in Wisconsin*, pp. 37, 148, 121–29; Merle Curti, *The Making of an American Community: A Case Study of Democracy in a Frontier County* (Stanford, Calif.: Stanford University Press, 1959), chap. 16.

18. Jorgenson, *Public Education in Wisconsin*, p. 66; Ohles, *Biographical Dictionary* pp. 477–78.

19. Edward Stevens, "The Role of the Newspaper in Promoting Education and the Common School, 1800–1840," (Unpublished manuscript, College of Education, Ohio University, Athens, Ohio); Michigan Superintendent quoted in Adams, *Free School*, p. 30.

20. Stanley Elkins and Eric McKitrick, "A Meaning for Turner's Frontier," *Political Science Quarterly* 69 (1954): 325, 330–39.

21. Curti, *American Community*, chap. 15; Patricia Albjerg Graham, *Community and Class in American Education* (New York: John Wiley, 1974), p. 138; conversation with Prof. Frederick Wirt of the University of Illinois about his current project; Elvin Hatch, *Biography of a Small Town* (New York: Columbia University Press, 1979), chaps. 4, 10; George Counts, *The Social Composition of Boards of Education* (Chicago: University of Chicago Press, 1927); W. W. Charters, Jr., "Social Class Analysis and the Control of Public Education," *Harvard Educational Review* 23 (1953): 268–83.

22. Curti, *American Community*, pp. 428–38.

23. Wiebe, "Social Functions," p. 149.

24. Calvin Stowe, "Americanization of the Immigrant," *Transactions of the Fifth Annual Meeting of the Western Literary Institute and College of Professional Teachers* (Cincinnati: Executive Committee, 1836), p. 71; editorial on "immigration," *The Massachusetts Teacher* 4 (1851): 289–91.

25. Ferdinand Buisson, "Report of the French Commission on American Education," as printed in U. S. Bureau of Education, *Circular of Information*, no. 5 (Washington, D.C.: GPO, 1879), p. 12.

26. *Addresses and Proceedings of the NEA, 1877*, p. 6; Daniel Webster, *Works*, 6 vols. (Boston: Little, Brown, 1854), 1: 41–42; Edward Everett, *Orations and Speeches on Various Occasions* 4 vols., (Boston: Little, Brown, 1878), 2:316–21, 323.

27. Horace Mann, "Fifth Report" (1841), in Horace Mann, *Annual Reports of the Secretary of the Board of Education* (Boston, Lee and Shepard, 1891), 3:92–128; Buisson, "French Commission," p. 13.

28. John Eaton, "George Atkinson," *Pacific University Bulletin* 40 (1944): 12; Alexis de Tocqueville, *Democracy in America*, 2 vols., ed. Phillips Bradley (New York: Vintage Books, 1945), 1: 320; for a variety of ways to interpret motivation and interest in educational reform, see David Tyack, "Ways of Seeing: An Essay on the History of Compulsory Schooling," *Harvard Educational Review* 46 (1976): 355–89.

29. Jonathan Messerli, *Horace Mann: A Biography* (New York: Knopf, 1972), is the most comprehensive biography; in his chapter on Mann in *The Social Ideas of American Educators* (New York: Scribner's, 1935), Merle Curti raises important questions about Mann's relation to reform in a capitalist society; Burke Hinsdale's biography of Mann, *Horace Mann and the Common School Revival in the United States* (New York: Scribner's, 1898), is still useful in linking him to the broader common-school movement; Mary Mann's biography, *Life of Horace Mann* (Boston: Walker, Fuller, 1865), contains many long extracts from his letters, diary, and other writings.

30. Mary Mann, *Mann*, p. 11; Messerli, *Mann*, p. 14.

31. Mary Mann, *Mann*, pp. 13–14.

32. Ibid., pp. 17–18.

33. Ibid., chaps. 2–3; Messerli, *Mann*, chap. 12, pp. 240–43.

34. Messerli, *Mann,* chap. 11.

35. Horace Mann, *Annual Reports,* p. 1; Mary Mann, *Mann,* chaps. 3, 4.

36. Mary Mann, *Mann,* pp. 10, 70, 80; Lawrence Cremin, ed., *The Republic and the School: Horace Mann on the Education of Free Men* (New York: Teachers College Press, 1957), pp. 1–15; Mattingly, *Classless Profession,* pp. 50–60; A. D. Mayo, *Horace Mann and the American Common School* (Washington, D.C.: GPO, 1898).

37. Carl Kaestle and Maris Vinovskis, *Education and Social Change in Nineteenth Century Massachusetts* (Cambridge: Cambridge University Press, 1980), pp. 215, 216, 217, chap. 8.

38. Ibid., 214, 75–77.

39. Michael Katz, "From Voluntarism to Bureaucracy in American Education," *Sociology of Education* 44 (1971); U. S. Commissioner of Education, "Compulsory Attendance Laws in the United States," *Report for 1888–89* (Washington, D.C.: GPO, 1889), 1: chap. 18, pp. 470–531.

40. Horace Mann, *Annual Reports,* pp. 6–7.

41. Messerli, *Mann,* p. 340.

42. Ruth Elson, *Guardians of Tradition: American Schoolbooks of the Nineteenth Century* (Lincoln: University of Nebraska Press, 1964); Curti, *Social Ideas,* pp. 130–31.

43. Mary Mann, *Mann,* p. 80; Curti, *Social Ideas,* chap. 4.

44. Raymond Culver, *Horace Mann and Religion in the Massachusetts Public Schools* (New Haven: Yale University Press, 1929); Messerli, *Mann,* chap. 16, pp. 412–23; the sheer volume of the pamphlets generated in the fight between Mann and the Boston schoolmasters is awe inspiring.

Section 5

1. Nancy Cott, *The Bonds of Womanhood: 'Women's Sphere' in New England, 1780–1835* (New Haven: Yale University Press, 1977); Kathryn Sklar, *Catharine Beecher: A Study in Domesticity* (New Haven: Yale University Press, 1973).

2. Myra Strober and David Tyack, "Why Do Women Teach and Men Manage? A Report on Schools," *Signs* 5 (1980): 494–503.

3. John T. McManus, *Ella Flagg Young and a Half-Century of the Chicago Public Schools* (Chicago: A. C. McClurg, 1916), p. 144; Carroll G. Pearse, "Some Reminiscences of the Association Meeting of 1884," *Addresses and Proceedings of the NEA, 1934,* pp. 241, 246.

4. E. C. Stanton, S. B. Anthony, and M. J. Gage, *The History of Woman's Suffrage,* 6 vols. (New York: Fowler and Wells, 1881–1922), 1: 514.

5. Thomas Woody, *A History of Women's Education in the United States,* 2 vols., (1929; reprint ed., New York: Octagon Books, 1966), 1: 460–518; Keith Melder, "Women's High Calling: The Teaching Profession in America, 1830–1960," *American Studies* 13 (1972): 19–32; Melder, "Training Women Teachers: Private Experiments," (Paper delivered at American Educational Research Association, San Francisco, April, 1978); Melder, "Mask of Oppression: The Female Seminary Movement in the United States," *New York History* 55 (1974): 261–79.

6. Anne Firor Scott, "The Ever Widening Circle: The Diffusion of Feminist Values from the Troy Female Seminary, 1822–1872," *History of Education Quarterly* 19 (1979): 12; Scott, "What, Then, Is the American: This New Woman?" *Journal of American History* 65 (1978): 700–1.

7. Cott, *Bonds of Womanhood;* Willystine Goodsell, ed., *Pioneers of Women's Education in the United States* (New York: McGraw-Hill, 1931).

8. Scott, "New Woman," pp. 698–99; Scott, "Feminist Values"; on meanings of "sisterhood," see Carroll Smith-Rosenberg, "The Female World of Love and Ritual: Relations between Women in Nineteenth Century America," *Signs* 1 (1975): 1–29.

9. Sklar, *Beecher;* Mae Elizabeth Harveson, *Catharine Esther Beecher: Pioneer Educator* (Philadelphia: University of Pennsylvania Press, 1932).

10. Sklar, *Beecher,*

11. Woody, *Women's Education,* 1: 322, 323; Catharine Beecher, *The Duty of American Women to Their Country* (New York: Harper & Bros., 1845), pp. 322–323.

12. Sklar, *Beecher*, pt. 1; Marion Caskey, *Chariot of Fire: Religion and the Beecher Family* (New Haven: Yale University Press, 1978), chap. 3.

13. Sklar, *Beecher*, p. 34.

14. Ibid., p. 28; Catharine Beecher, *Educational Reminiscences and Suggestions* (New York: J. B. Ford & Co., 1874).

15. Sklar, *Beecher*, pp. 96–97; Catharine Beecher, *Suggestions Respecting Improvements in Education, Presented to the Trustees* (Hartford: Packard & Butler, 1829), p. 46.

16. Beecher, *Improvements in Education*, p. 45; Woody, *Women's Education*, 1:321.

17. Joan Burstyn, "Catharine Beecher and the Education of American Women," *New England Quarterly* 47 (1974): 386–403.

18. Catharine Beecher, *An Essay on the Education of Female Teachers* (New York: Van Nostrand & Dwight, 1835), pp. 15, 17, 14, 14–18.

19. Sklar, *Beecher*, pp. 177–83.

20. Ibid., pp. 178–80.

21. Per Siljestrom, *The Educational Institutions of the United States: Their Character and Organization*, trans. Fredrica Rowan (London: John Chapman, 1853), p. 197; Maris Vinovskis and John Bernard, "Beyond Catharine Beecher: Female Education in the Antebellum Period," *Signs* 3 (1978): 865–69.

22. Sklar, *Beecher*, pt. 5: for a perceptive study of the internal life of a girls' school, see Susan Lloyd, *A Singular School: Abbott Academy, 1828–1973* (Hanover, N.H.: University Press of New England, 1979); for a comparison of Beecher with other women educators, see Barbara Cross, ed., *The Educated Woman in America: Selected Writings of Catharine Beecher, Margaret Fuller, and M. Carey Thomas* (New York: Teachers College Press, 1965).

Section 6

1. David Montgomery, "The Shuttle and the Cross: Weavers and Artisans in the Kensington Riots," *Journal of Social History* 5 (1972): 411, 412, 439.

2. Paul Johnson, *A Shopkeeper's Millennium: Society and Revivals in Rochester, New York, 1815–1837* (New York: Hill and Wang, 1978), 141, 40–45, 140, 138.

3. Paul Kleppner, *The Third Electoral System, 1853–1892* (Chapel Hill: University of North Carolina Press, 1979), pp. 183, 185; Richard Jensen, *The Winning of the Midwest: Social and Political Conflict, 1888–1896* (Chicago: University of Chicago Press, 1971), pp. 63–66.

4. *Addresses and Proceedings of the NEA, 1869*, pp. 23, 19.

5. A. D. Mayo, "Object Lessons in Moral Instruction in the Common School," *Addresses and Proceedings of the NEA, 1880*, pp. 7, 9.

6. John Jay, "Public and Parochial Schools," *Addresses and Proceedings of the NEA, 1889*, p. 172; Archbishop John Ireland, "State Schools and Parish Schools—Is Union between Them Possible?" *Addresses and Proceedings of the NEA, 1890*, pp. 179–85; for a fascinating letter from Ireland defending his speech, see John T. Ellis, ed., *Documents of American Catholic History* (Milwaukee: Bruce, 1956), pp. 489–95; George Atkinson, "The Culture Most Valuable to Prepare Law-Abiding and Law-Respecting Citizens," *Addresses and Proceedings of the NEA, 1888*, pp. 115, 117, 120–21; Mayo, "Object Lessons," pp. 6–7; Daniel Dorchester, *Romanism versus the Public School System* (New York: Phillips and Hunt, 1888), pt. 1.

7. For transcripts of the Cincinnati case of *Minor* v. *Board of Education*, see *The Bible in the Public Schools* (Cincinnati: Robert Clarke, 1870); for a nuanced study of religious conflict in Cincinnati see Francis Michael Perko, "A Time to Favor Zion: A Case Study of Religion as a Force in American Educational Development, 1830–1870," (Ph.D. diss. Stanford University, 1981); Alvan Roe, in *Addresses and Proceedings of the NEA, 1875*, p. 123; Bible reading, however, seems to have been less common in the West—as early as 1859, the Reverend W. C. Anderson and Fletcher Haight bewailed the neglect of the Bible in California schools in *Review of Dr. Scott's Bible and Politics*; Clarence Darrow, *Farmington* (New York: Scribner's, 1932), p. 72; Superintendent of Public Schools, *Fourth Annual Report* (Portland, Ore.: David Steel, 1877), p. 57.

8. R. W. Clark, "Different Aspects of the Conscience Question," *Christian World* 21 (February 1870): 62; Josiah Strong, *Our Country* (Cambridge: Harvard University Press, 1963), p. 55 and passim; T. P. Stevenson, *Religion and Schools: Notes of Hearings before the Committee on Education and Labor, United States Senate, Friday, February 15, 1889, and Friday, February 22, 1889* (Washington, D.C.: GPO, 1889), p. 4.

9. James Carper, "A Common Faith for the Common School? Religion and Education in Kansas, 1861–1900," *Mid-America: An Historical Review* 60 (1978): 149, 150, 147–61.

10. James Clarkson, "General Grant's Des Moines Speech," *Century Magazine* 55 (March 1898): 788.

11. *Congressional Record,* 44th Cong., 1st sess., (vol. 4, Aug. 4, 1876): pp. 5189–92, 5587–91; Herman Ames, *The Proposed Amendments to the Constitution of the United States during the First Century of Its History* (Washington, D.C.: GPO, 1897), pp. 277–78; Sister Marie Carolyn Klinkhamer, "The Blaine Amendment of 1875: Private Motives for Political Action," *Catholic Historical Review* 42 (April 1956): 15–49; David Tyack, "Onward Christian Soldiers: Religion in the Common School," in *History and Education: The Educational Uses of the Past,* ed. Paul Nash (New York: Random House, 1970), pp. 212–55.

12. *Congressional Record,* 50th Cong., 1st Sess., (vol. 4, Feb. 4, 1888): p. 1218; Charles Kinney, Jr., *Church & State: The Struggle for Separation in New Hampshire, 1630–1900* (New York: Bureau of Publications, Teachers College, 1955), pp. 123–24; for comments on Blair's paranoic outburst, see John Shea, "Federal Schemes to aid Common Schools in the Southern States," *American Catholic Quarterly Review* 13 (1888): 346–59; John W. Evans, "Catholics and the Blair Education Bill," *Catholic Historical Review* 46 (1960): 273–98; *Congressional Record,* 50th Cong., 1st sess., (vol. 19, May 25, 1888): pp. 4615, 433–34, 2nd Sess., Vol. 20, Dec. 21, 1888): p. 1218.

13. Isaac Hecker, "Unification and Education," *The Catholic World* 13 (1871): 6, 1–14.

14. Ibid., p. 13.

15. Robert D. Cross, "The Origins of the Catholic Parochial Schools in America," *American Benedictine Review* 16 (1965): 194–209; Vincent Lannie, *Public Money and Parochial Education: Bishop Hughes, Governor Seward, and the New York School Controversy* (Cleveland: The Press of Case Western Reserve University, 1968).

16. Lloyd Jorgenson, *The Founding of Public Education in Wisconsin* (Madison: State Historical Society of Wisconsin, 1956), p. 145.

17. Ibid., p. 147, 146–48; Kleppner, *Third Electoral System,* 230–31.

18. Selwyn Troen, *The Public and the Schools: Shaping the St. Louis System, 1838–1920* (Columbia, Mo.: University of Missouri Press, 1975), chap. 3; Tyack, *One Best System,* pp. 104–8.

19. *The Hearing at the State House, Boston, Mass., before the Joint Committee on Education, March 20th to April 25th, 1889* (Boston: Committee of One Hundred, 1889), p. 2; Kleppner, *Third Electoral System,* p. 349.

20. *Hearing at the State House,* pp. 2–3, 5, 8; Kleppner, *Third Electoral System,* pp. 351–52.

21. Paul Kleppner, *The Cross of Culture: A Social Analysis of Midwestern Politics, 1850–1900* (New York: Free Press, 1970), pp. 71–74; Robert Ulrich, "The Bennett Law of 1889: Education and Politics in Wisconsin," (Ph.D. diss. University of Wisconsin, 1965).

22. Roger Wyman, "Wisconsin Ethnic Groups and the Election of 1890," *Wisconsin Magazine of History* 51 (1968): 271, 269–93.

23. Jensen, *Winning of the Midwest,* p. 129; Wyman, "Wisconsin Ethnic Groups," p. 271; Newton Daugherty, "Recent Legislation upon Compulsory Education in Illinois and Wisconsin," *Addresses and Proceedings of the NEA, 1891,* pp. 393–403.

24. *Addresses and Proceedings of the NEA, 1891,* pp. 294–97.

25. Ibid., pp. 295, 298, 393–403.

Section 7

1. Horace Mann Bond, *The Education of the Negro in the American Social Order* (New York: Prentice-Hall, 1934), p. 179, chap. 8; Albert Fishlow, "Levels of Nineteenth-Century Investment in Education," *Journal of Economic History* 26 (1966); Albert Fishlow, "The

American Common School Revival: Fact or Fancy?" in *Industrialization in Two Systems: Essays in Honor of Alexander Gerschenkron*, ed., Henry Rosovsky (New York: John Wiley 1966); Edgar Knight, ed., *A Documentary History of Education in the South before 1860*, 5 vols. (Chapel Hill: University of North Carolina Press, 1949–53); Roy Honeywell, *The Educational Work of Thomas Jefferson* (Cambridge: Harvard University Press, 1931).

2. Charles Dabney, *Universal Education in the South*, 2 vols. (Chapel Hill: University of North Carolina Press, 1936), 1: chaps. 1–6; Dabney's account is in some ways a primary source since he was an insider in the educational awakening of the early twentieth century; for a contrary account, and still the best history of education in a single southern state, see Horace Mann Bond, *Negro Education in Alabama* (Washington, D.C.: Associated Publishers, 1939).

3. John Ezell, "A Southern Education for Southrons," *Journal of Southern History* 17 (1951): 302–27; Edgar Knight, *Documentary History*, 5: 317–81; William Taylor, "Toward a Definition of Orthodoxy: The Patrician South and the Common Schools," *Harvard Educational Review* 36 (1966): 425, 412–26.

4. Taylor, "Orthodoxy," 413; Knight, *Documentary History*, 5: 317–81.

5. *New Orleans Black Republican*, 29 April 1865, as quoted in James Anderson, "Ex-Slaves and the Rise of Universal Education in the New South, 1860–1880," in Ronald Goodenow, ed., *The Rise of Public Education in the New South* (Boston: G. K. Hall, 1981); Herbert Gutman, "Observations on Selected Trends in American Working-Class History Together with Some New Data that Might Affect Some of the Questions Asked by Historians of American Education Interested in the Relationship between Education and Work" (Paper delivered at the Conference on the Historiography of Education and Work, Stanford University, 17–18 August 1979); Carter Woodson, *The Education of the Negro Prior to 1861: A History of the Colored People of the United States from the Beginning of Slavery to the Civil War* (Washington, D.C.: The Associated Publishers, 1919).

6. Booker T. Washington, *Up From Slavery* (Garden City: Doubleday, 1901), pp. 23, 28–29; John Alvord quoted in Anderson, "Ex-Slaves," p. 8, from U.S. Bureau of Refugees, Freedom, and Abandoned Lands, *Fifth Semi-Annual Report, January 1, 1868* (Washington, D.C.: GPO, 1868), p. 12.

7. W. E. B. DuBois, *Black Reconstruction in America* (1935; reprinted., New York: Russel and Russell, 1962).

8. Henry Swint, *The Northern Teachers in the South, 1862–1870* (Nashville: Vanderbilt University Press, 1941), p. 89; Cremin, *American Education: The National Experience, 1783–1876* (New York: Harper & Row, 1980), pp. 518–19.

9. Bond, *Education of the Negro*, p. 178, chap. 11; Doxey Wilkerson, "A Determination of the Peculiar Problems of Negroes in Contemporary American Society," *Journal of Negro Education* 5 (1936): 324–50.

10. Thomas Jones, *Negro Education: A Study of the Private and Higher Schools for Colored People in the United States*, 2 vols. (Washington, D.C.: GPO, 1917); DuBois quoted in James McPherson, "White Liberals and Black Power in Negro Education, 1865–1915," *American Historical Review* 75 (1970): 1385, 1369–71; Andrew Billingsley, *Black Families in White America* (Englewood Cliffs, N.J.: Prentice-Hall, 1968), pp. 120–21.

11. C. Vann Woodward, *Origins of the New South, 1877–1913* (Baton Rouge: Louisiana State University Press, 1951), pp. 20, 60–64; U. S. Commissioner of Education, *Report for 1887–88*, (Washington, D.C.: GPO, 1888), pp. 86–87; Theodore Mitchell, "Tobacco, Whiskey, and Schools: School Reform and School Reformers in the Post-Reconstruction Period," (Seminar paper, Stanford University, Palo Alto, Calif., 1979).

12. The statistics were compiled from U.S. Commissioner of Education, *Reports* for the years indicated and adapted from table 1 in Meyer et al., "Public Education as Nation-Building," pp. 594, 597; Folger and Nam, *Education*, app.; Dabney, *Universal Education*, 2: chap. 5; Wycliffe Rose, *School Funds in Ten Southern States* (Nashville, Tenn.: The Peabody Education Fund, 1909).

13. Jabez Curry, *A Brief Sketch of George Peabody (1795–1869) and A History of the Peabody Education Fund through Thirty Years* (Cambridge, Mass.: John Wilson and Son, 1898).

14. Dabney, *Universal Education*, 1: 128, 207–8, chap. 7.; Woodward, *Origins of the New South*, pp. 60–62.

15. Dabney, *Universal Education*, 2:93, chap. 22; Woodward, *Origins of the New South*, pp. 396–406.

16. Dabney, *Universal Education*, 2: chaps. 9, 28; Bond, *Education of the Negro*, chap. 7.

17. Henry Bullock, *A History of Negro Education in the South from 1619 to the Present* (Cambridge: Harvard University Press, 1967), pp. 77, 93; Bond, *Education of the Negro*, pp. 144, 349–51; James Anderson, "Education as a Vehicle for the Manipulation of Black Workers," in Walter Feinberg and Henry Rosemont, eds., *Work, Technology and Education* (Urbana: University of Illinois Press, 1975), pp. 21–26.

18. Dabney, *Universal Education*, 2: 74, 80, chap. 5.

19. Ibid., 2: 107, 543, chap. 7.

20. Ibid., 2:11; Louis Harlan, *Separate and Unequal: Public School Campaigns and Racism in the Southern Seaboard States, 1901–1915* (1958; reprint ed., New York: Atheneum, 1968); Bond, *Education of the Negro*, 153.

21. Harlan, *Separate and Unequal*, p. 254; Richard Wright, *12,000,000 Black Voices* (New York: Viking Press, 1941), p. 64; Charles Johnson, *The Shadow of the Plantation* (Chicago: University of Chicago Press, 1934), chap. 4.

Section 8

1. Herbert Gutman, *Work, Culture, and Society in Industrializing America* (New York: Alfred A. Knopf, 1976).

2. Ernest Tuveson, *Redeemer Nation: The Idea of America's Millennial Role* (Chicago: University of Chicago Press, 1968).

3. John Higham, "Hanging Together: Divergent Unities in American History," *Journal of American History* 61 (1974): 18–19.

4. John D. Philbrick, *City School Systems in the United States* (Washington, D.C.: GPO, 1885).

5. Michael Katz, *Class, Bureaucracy, and Schools: The Illusion of Educational Change in America* (New York: Praeger, 1971); Stanley Schultz, *The Culture Factory: Boston Public Schools, 1789–1860* (New York: Oxford University Press, 1973); Carl Kaestle, *The Evolution of an Urban School System: New York City, 1750–1850* (Cambridge: Harvard University Press, 1973).

6. M. C. Bettinger, "Twenty-Five Years in the Schools of Los Angeles," *Publications of the Historical Society of California* 8 (1910): 68–69. David Tyack, *The One Best System: A History of American Urban Education* (Cambridge: Harvard University Press, 1974), pts. 2, 3.

7. Michael Katz, *Class, Bureaucracy, and Schools*, pp. 82–85.

8. Charles Francis Adams, "Scientific Common School Education," *Harper's New Monthly Magazine* 61 (1889): 934–42; for a perceptive study of Adams's ideology, see George Fredrickson, *The Inner Civil War: Northern Intellectuals and the Crisis of the Union* (New York: Harper & Row, 1965), pp. 205–9.

9. Charles Francis Adams, "The Development of the Superintendency," *Addresses and Proceedings of the NEA, 1880*, p. 64.

10. Ibid., pp. 63, 65, 61–76.

11. Ibid., pp. 71, 75.

12. G. W. A. Luckey, *The Professional Training of Secondary Teachers in the United States* (New York, 1903), p. 157.

13. Wesley, *NEA*, p. 397; *Addresses and Proceedings of the NEA, 1894*, p. 300.

14. *Addresses and Proceedings of the NEA, 1882*, pp. 77, 82.

15. Ibid., pp. 82, 85.

16. *Addresses and Proceedings of the NEA, 1880*, pp. 16–17.

17. Wesley, *NEA*, p. 265.

18. David Tyack, ed., *Turning Points in American Educational History* (Waltham, Mass.: Blaisdell Publishing Company, 1967), pp. 358, 352–63.

19. Henry Wilson, "New Departure of the Republican Party," *Atlantic Monthly* 27 (1871): 109, 120.

20. Donald Warren, *To Enforce Education: A History of the Founding Years of the United States Office of Education* (Detroit: Wayne State University Press, 1974), chaps. 2–4; Gordon Lee, *The Struggle for Federal Aid, First Phase: A History of the Attempts to Obtain Federal Aid for the Common Schools, 1870–1890* (New York: Teachers College Press, 1949), pp. 72, 71–74, 78–79.

21. Lee, *Federal Aid*, pp. 42–55; Isaac Hecker, "Unification and Education," *The Catholic World* 13 (1871):4.

22. Lee, *Federal Aid*, pp. 158, 159, 73, 141–43.

23. In his article "The Changing Shape of the American Political Universe," *American Political Science Review* 59 (1965): 7–28, Walter Dean Burnham describes his data base on "Partisan Division of American State Governments, 1834–1974," from which we compiled our figures (computer tapes available from the Inter-University Consortium for Political and Social Research, Ann Arbor, Mich. order no. ICPSR 0016); Michael Berkowitz, "An Act to Enforce the Educational Rights of Children," (Seminar paper, Stanford University, 1972).

24. Ellwood Cubberley, *Changing Conceptions of Education* (Boston: Houghton Mifflin, 1909), p. 63.

25. Singleton, "Protestant Voluntary Associations and the Shaping of Victorian America," in Daniel Walker Howe, ed., *Victorian America*, (Philadelphia: University of Pennsylvania Press, 1976) p. 56.

26. A. E. Winship, "What the Superintendent Is Not," *Addresses and Proceedings of the NEA, 1899*, pp. 308–9.

Section 9

1. Frank Whitney, *School and I: The Autobiography of an Ohio Schoolmaster* (Yellow Springs, Ohio: Antioch Press, 1957), pp. 28, 30–31.

2. Selma Berrol, "William Henry Maxwell and a New Educational New York," *History of Education Quarterly* 8 (1968): 215–28; Samuel Abelow, *Dr. William H. Maxwell: The First Superintendent of Schools of the City of New York* (Brooklyn: Scheba, 1934), pp. 77–88, 97–99, 103–14, 124–25, 142–43, 152–53; William Maxwell, *A Quarter Century of Public School Development* (New York: American Book Company, 1912), pp. 396–417.

3. Michael Sadler, "Impressions of American Education," *Educational Review* 25 (1903): 217–31; Sol Cohen, "Sir Michael E. Sadler and the Socio-Political Analysis of Education," *History of Education Quarterly* 7 (1967): 287, 281–94; Edward Krug, *The Shaping of the American High School* (New York: Harper & Row, 1964).

4. Joseph Cronin, *The Control of Urban Schools: Perspectives on the Power of Educational Reformers* (New York: The Free Press, 1973); on utopian avoidance of conflict, see Elisabeth Hansot, *Perfection and Progress: Two Modes of Utopian Thought* (Cambridge, Mass.: M.I.T. Press, 1974).

5. Walter Dean Burnham, "The Changing Shape of the American Political Universe," *American Political Science Review* 59 (1965): 25, 23.

6. Samuel Hays, "Political Parties and the Community-Society Continuum," in Walter Dean Burnham and William Chambers, eds. *The American Party Systems* (New York: Oxford University Press, 1967), pp. 165, 152–81; David Tyack and Elisabeth Hansot, "From Social Movement to Professional Management: An Inquiry into the Changing Character of Leadership in Public Education," *American Journal of Education* 88 (1980): 291–319.

7. Corinne Gilb, *Hidden Hierarchies: The Professions and Government* (New York: Harper & Row, 1966).

8. Ellwood P. Cubberley, *Changing Conceptions of Education* (Boston: Houghton Mifflin, 1909), 50–51; Lawrence Cremin, *The Wonderful World of Ellwood Patterson Cubberley* (New York: Teachers College Press, 1965), pp. 1–5, 42–52; James Gilbert, *Work Without Salvation* (Baltimore: The Johns Hopkins University Press, 1977), pp. 110–11.

9. Alfred Chandler, *The Visible Hand: The Managerial Revolution in American Business* (Cambridge: Harvard University Press, 1977); Daniel Nelson, *Managers and Workers* (Madison: University of Wisconsin Press, 1975); Daniel Rodgers, *The Work Ethic in Indus-*

trial America (Chicago: University of Chicago Press, 1975); Harry Braverman, *Labor and Monopoly Capital* (New York: Monthly Review Press, 1974); Samuel Haber, *Efficiency and Uplift: Scientific Management in the Progressive Era, 1890–1920* (Chicago: University of Chicago Press, 1964).

10. U.S. Bureau of the Census, *Historical Statistics of the United States From Colonial Times to 1970* (Washington, D.C.: GPO, 1975), 2:915; Gabriel Kolko, *Wealth and Power in America* (New York: Praeger, 1962), p. 14 (the data refer to national personal income before taxes).

11. Thomas Cochran, *Business in American Life: A History* (New York: McGraw-Hill, 1972), p. 304, chap. 18; for an account of the impact of businessmen on one school of education, see Arthur Powell, *The Uncertain Profession: Harvard and the Search for Educational Authority* (Cambridge: Harvard University Press, 1980), chaps. 5, 6; David F. Noble, *America by Design: Science, Technology, and the Rise of Corporate Capitalism* (New York: Alfred A. Knopf, 1979); Stephen London, "Business and the Chicago Public School System, 1890–1966," (Ph.D. diss., University of Chicago, 1969); Peter Shane, "The Origins of Educational Control: Class, Ethnicity, and School Reform in Boston, 1875–1920," (B.A. Honors thesis, Harvard University, 1974).

12. Charles E. Lindblom, *Politics and Markets: The World's Political-Economic Systems* (New York: Basic Books, 1977), chaps. 13, 14; for a sample of the congruence in thinking about administration in the spheres of business, universities, and the public schools, see the speeches in *Public Schools and Their Administration: Address Delivered at the Fifty-Ninth Meeting of the Merchants' Club of Chicago, Saturday, December 8, 1906* (Chicago: The Merchants' Club, 1906); for a discussion of "corporatism" as a theme in business and political history, see Ellis Hawley, "The Discovery and Study of 'Corporate Liberalism,'" *Business History Review* 52 (1978): 309–20; and Louis Galambos, "The Emerging Organizational Synthesis in Modern American History," *Business History Review* 44 (1970): 279–90.

13. W. B. Pillsbury, "Selection—An Unnoticed Function of Education," *Scientific Monthly* 12 (1921): 62–74.

14. Norton Grubb and Marvin Lazerson, *Education and Industrialism: Documents in Vocational Education, 1870–1970* (New York: Teachers College Press, 1974).

15. Harvey Kantor and David Tyack, eds., *Work, Youth, and Schooling: The Vocationalizing of American Education* (Stanford, Calif.: Stanford University Press, forthcoming 1982); Michael Imber, Unpublished essay on continuation schools (University of Kansas, Lawrence, Kans.).

16. Cubberley, *Changing Conceptions,* pp. 55, 65–66, 59.

17. Jesse Newlon, "George Strayer: An Appreciation," *School Executives Magazine* 49 (1930): 451.

Section 10

1. Ellwood Cubberley to Adinoram Gray, 27 February 1896, Cubberley Papers, Stanford University Archives, Palo Alto, Calif.

2. Robert Havighurst, ed., *Leaders in American Education* (Chicago: University of Chicago Press, 1971), pp. 21, 157, 324, 271, 401–2; and biographies of the educational leaders in Dumas Malone, ed., *Dictionary of American Biography* 20 vols. (New York: Scribner's, 1928–36); *Leaders in Education, A Biographical Directory,* 3rd ed. (Lancaster, Pa.: Science Press, 1948); and *National Cyclopedia of American Biography* (New York: James T. White, 1930).

3. James Russell, *Founding Teachers College: Reminiscences of the Dean Emeritus* (New York: Teachers College Press, 1937), pp. 12, 69.

4. See the autobiography by Judd, for example, in Carl Murchison, ed., *A History of Psychology in Autobiography,* 7 vols. (Worcester, Mass.: Clark University Press, 1932), 2: 207–35.

5. Jean Quandt, "Religion and Social Thought: The Secularization of Post-Millennialism," *American Quarterly* 25 (1973): 391, 390–409.

6. Cubberley, *Changing Conceptions,* 15; Clyde Griffen, "The Progressive Ethos," in

Stanley Coben and Lorman Ratner, eds., *The Development of an American Culture* (Englewood Cliffs, N.J.: Prentice-Hall, 1970), p. 130.

7. G. Stanley Hall, *Life and Confessions of a Psychologist* (Boston: Appleton, 1923), p. 177; Frank Spaulding, *One School Administrator's Philosophy: Its Development* (New York: Exposition Press, 1952), p. 166, chaps. 1, 2, 4, 6.

8. William Bullough, " 'It is Better to be a Country Boy': The Lure of the Country in Urban Education in the Gilded Age," *The Historian* 35 (1973): 185, 190, 183–95.

9. On the notion of career, see Burton Bledstein, *The Culture of Professionalism: The Middle Class and the Development of Higher Education in America* (New York: W.W. Norton, 1976), chap. 5.

10. Jesse Sears and Adin Henderson, *Cubberley of Stanford and His Contribution to American Education* (Stanford, Calif.: Stanford University Press, 1957), pp. 57, 59.

11. Magali Sarfatti Larson, *The Rise of Professionalism: A Sociological Analysis* (Berkeley: University of California Press, 1977), p. 137.

12. Dorothy Ross, "The Development of the Social Sciences," in Alexandra Oleson and John Voss, eds., *The Organization of Knowledge in Modern America, 1860–1920* (Baltimore: The Johns Hopkins University Press, 1979), p. 128; on the history of the social sciences, also see Mary Furner, *Advocacy and Objectivity: A Crisis in the Professionalization of American Social Science, 1865–1905* (Lexington: University Press of Kentucky, 1975); and Thomas Haskell, *The Emergence of Professional Social Science: The American Social Science Association and the Nineteenth Century Crisis of Authority* (Urbana: University of Illinois Press, 1977); as Harold Silver notes in his essay review of these works, Furner and Haskell do not pay much attention to the educational goals of the early social scientists or the scientific aspirations of educators: Silver, "In Search of Social Science," *History of Education Quarterly* 19 (1979): 277–81.

13. George Frazier, "Cubberley As His Friends Knew Him," *School Executives Magazine* 51 (1932): 339, 339–42, 380; Sears and Henderson, *Cubberley*, p. 106.

14. Harold Benjamin, "Ellwood Patterson Cubberley—A Biographical Sketch," in John Almack, ed., *Modern School Administration* (Boston: Houghton Mifflin 1933), pp. 349–77; Sears and Henderson, *Cubberley*, chap. 2.

15. Ellwood P. Cubberley, "The School Situation in San Francisco," *Educational Review* 21 (1901): 364–81; Sears and Henderson, *Cubberley*, p. 50.

16. Ellwood P. Cubberley, *Public School Administration: A Statement of the Fundamental Principles Underlying the Organization and Administration of Public Education* (Boston: Houghton Mifflin, 1916), chap. 10, pp. 135, 131, 136–37.

17. Sears and Henderson, *Cubberley*, pp. 57–59; this biography is richly detailed and practically a primary source on the Stanford years, since Professor Sears was a colleague and friend of Cubberley's for many years.

18. Sears and Henderson, *Cubberley*, p. 63.

19. Ellwood P. Cubberley, "Certification of Teachers," *Fifth Yearbook of the National Society for the Study of Education* (Chicago: University of Chicago Press, 1906), pt. 2, 73–77; Cremin, *Cubberley*; Sears and Henderson, *Cubberley*, chap. 6.

20. Sears and Henderson, *Cubberley*, pp. 70–71; Powell describes similar condescension at Harvard in *Uncertain Profession*.

21. Frazier, "Cubberley," shows the great esprit he generated among alumni; Sears and Henderson, *Cubberley*, pp. 82, 279, 101.

22. Sears and Henderson, *Cubberley*, pp. 72, 101; Cremin, *Cubberley*, p. 4; Raymond Callahan, *Education and the Cult of Efficiency* (Chicago: University of Chicago Press, 1962), chap. 8.

23. Sears and Henderson, *Cubberley*, chaps. 10, 12.

24. Cubberley, *Changing Conceptions*, pp. 14–15; Cubberley, "The American School Program from the Standpoint of the Nation," *Addresses and Proceedings of the NEA, 1923*, pp. 180–88; in "Cubberley: The Wizard of Stanford," *History of Education Journal* 5 (1954): 73–81, George Arnstein gives a muted criticism of Cubberley for his ethnic biases, the first such criticism we have discovered.

25. Cubberley, "American School Program," pp. 183–84; Cubberley, *State and County Educational Reorganization* (New York: Macmillan, 1914), p. 4.

26. Cubberley, *Public School Administration*, p. 222; Cubberley, *Changing Conceptions*, pp. 63, 56–57.

27. Kimball Young, *Mental Differences in Certain Immigrant Groups* (Eugene: University of Oregon Press, 1923); David Tyack, *The One Best System: A History of American Urban Education* (Cambridge: Harvard University Press, 1974), pp. 198–216.

Section 11

1. Lucy Salmon, *Patronage in the Public Schools* (Boston: Women's Auxiliary of the Massachusetts Civil Service Reform Association, 1908); on anti-Masons, see Paul Johnson, *A Shopkeeper's Millennium: Society and Revivals in Rochester, New York, 1815–1837* (New York: Hill and Wang, 1978), pp. 62–63, 66–71, 73–77, 89–92.

2. Michael Kirst, "A Tale of Two Networks: The School Finance Reform versus the Spending and Tax Limitation Lobby," *Taxing & Spending* 3 (1980): 43–49; James Kelly, *Looking Back, Moving Ahead: A Decade of School-Finance Reform* (New York: Ford Foundation, 1980).

3. We have profited from talking with Michael Kirst and Paul Peterson about how networks operate.

4. Jesse Sears and Adin Henderson, *Cubberley of Stanford and His Contribution to American Education* (Stanford, Calif.: Stanford University Press, 1957), pp. 172–74, 194, 223; for the network of psychologists, see Paul Chapman, "Schools as Sorters: Lewis M. Terman and the Intelligence Testing Movement, 1890–1930," (Ph.D. diss., Stanford University, 1979).

5. Manuscript one-page history of the Cleveland Conference, Cleveland Conference Papers, The Spencer Foundation, Chicago, Ill. (hereafter cited as CC Papers). We are grateful to H. Thomas James for giving us access to these records, which consist primarily of discussion agendas for yearly meetings, together with a few letters and lists of members. The agendas are a fascinating index of the issues educational leaders felt to be most interesting or problematic.

6. Charles Judd to D.C. Bliss, 26 January 1915, and membership lists and card files; Charles Judd to Members of CC, 14 January 1918; Charles Judd to Members of CC, 21 January 1918, pp. 1–2, CC Papers.

7. W. W. Charters, "The Cleveland Conference, 1915–1949", CC Papers; Farrand was a member of the conference in the 1920s, CC Papers.

8. Charles Judd to Members, 25 January 1917, CC Papers; Frank Spaulding, *School Superintendent in Action in Five Cities* (Rindge, N.H.: Richard Smith, 1955), pp. 525–26.

9. Jesse Newlon, "George Strayer: An Appreciation," *School Executives Magazine* 49 (1930): 451; see also biographies of Strayer in *National Cyclopedia of American Biography*, current vol. A, pp. 337–38 and in *Leaders in Education, A Biographical Directory*, 3rd ed., pp. 1033–34; George Strayer, "Progress in City School Administration during the Past Twenty-Five Years," *School and Society* 32 (1930): 375–78.

10. Newlon, "Strayer," p. 452; Hollis Caswell to David Tyack, 8 September 1980; Dr. Caswell writes that Strayer was a demanding teacher who "encouraged students to develop independently. . . . But when you deviated you had to . . . be able to stand up and support your position. . . . He advanced those he thought were able to take a bigger job."

11. Caswell to Tyack, 8 September 1980; George Strayer, "The Education of the Superintendent of Schools," *Teachers College Record* 46 (1944): 169–76; Strayer, "Building the Profession of School Administration," *The School Executive* 56 (1937): 248–50, 270; Strayer, "Job Analysis and the Problem Attack in the Training of Superintendents of Schools," in *Fifteenth Yearbook of the National Society of College Teachers of Education*, ed. Stuart Courtis (Chicago: University of Chicago Press, 1927), pp. 146–54.

12. Magali Sarfatti Larson, *The Rise of Professionalism: A Sociological Analysis* (Berkeley: University of California Press, 1977), chap. 9; Corinne Gilb, *Hidden Hierarchies: The Professions and Government* (New York: Harper & Row, 1966), pp. 131, 129.

13. Gilb, *Hidden Hierarchies*, pp. 128–29; Michael Schultz, Jr., *The National Education Association and the Black Teacher: The Integration of a Professional Organization* (Coral Gables, Fla.: University of Miami Press, 1970).

14. Mildred Fenner, *NEA History* (Washington, D.C.: NEA, 1945), pp. 25–26; Gilb, *Hidden Hierarchies*, pp. 121–24; Edgar B. Wesley, *NEA, The First Hundred Years* (New

York: Harper & Bros, 1957), p. 397; Charles Eliot to Thomas Bicknell, 9 January 1913, quoted in Gordon Seely, Jr., "Investigatory Committees of the National Education Association: A History of the Years 1892–1918," (Ph.D. diss., Stanford University, 1963).

15. Nicholas Murray Butler, *Across the Busy Years*, 2 vols. (New York: Scribner's, 1939–40), 1: 200–1; Glenn Smith, "The Changing of the Guard: William Torrey Harris and the Passing of the Old Order in the NEA," AERA Paper, 1978, ERIC ED152668.

16. Russell, *Founding Teachers College: Reminiscences of the Dean Emeritus* (New York: Teachers College Press, 1937), p. 31.

17. Upton Sinclair, *The Goslings: A Study of the American Schools* (Pasadena, Calif.: The Author, 1924) p. 234; Seely, "Investigatory Committees," chaps. 1–3.

18. Smith, "Harris," pp. 19–20; Ralph Schmid, "A Study of the Organizational Structure of the National Education Association, 1884–1921," (Ph.D. diss., Washington University, 1963).

19. William Maxwell, "Good and Bad in New York Schools," *Educational Review* 47 (1914): 67–68; A. E. Winship, "Is There an NEA 'Ring'?" *Journal of Education* 51 (1900): 376—Winship's answer was *yes*, but they were mostly city superintendents, all male, and only loosely connected with "scientific" training in education, which was in its infancy in 1900.

20. Seely, "Investigatory Committees," chaps. 6–8; Krug, *High School*.

21. Charles Judd, "The National Education Association in 1919," *School Review* 47 (1919): 546–47; A. E. Winship, "Why Do Men Prefer the Winter Meeting?" *Journal of Education* 74 (1911): 157–58; and Winship, "The Portland Meeting," *Journal of Education* 86 (1917): 117–19.

22. Fenner, *NEA*, pp. 49–50; on real and potential confrontation by sex in the NEA, see section 13 below.

23. George Frazier, "Cubberley As His Friends Knew Him," *School Executives Magazine* 51 (1932): 341; Salmon, *Patronage;* Robert Rose, "Career Sponsorship in the School Superintendency," (Ph.D. diss., University of Oregon, 1969), pp. 82–83, 43–44, 85, 87–88.

24. Caswell to Tyack, 8 September 1980, stresses the high expectations and standards of judgment of men like Strayer.

25. Detroit Public School Staff, *Frank Cody: A Realist in Education* (New York: Macmillan, 1943), pp. 204, 221–22; Spaulding, *School Superintendent*, p. 418.

26. Robert Rose, "Career Sponsorship in the School Superintendency," (Ph. D. diss., University of Oregon, 1969) chaps. 2–3.

27. Ibid., pp. 71–73, 75–76, 81; statistics compiled by Robert Cummings from roster of members in AASA *Yearbook* for 1939.

28. Rose, "Career Sponsorship," pp. 82–83, 43–44, 85, 87–88.

29. William Patterson, *Letters to Principal Patterson* (Washington, D.C.: Daylion Co., 1934), p. 104.

30. The sponsor system was one response to the sort of vulnerability to local pressures described by an anonymous author, "A Veteran Fighter in the Field of American Education," in the article "Why Superintendents Lose Their Jobs," *School Board Journal* 52 (1916): 18–19; and the changing fads in education noted by George Henry, "Alas, the Poor School Superintendent," *Harpers* 193 (1946): 434–41; on similarity of social backgrounds, see section 12 below.

31. Detroit Public School Staff, *Cody*, p. 227; this biography is also in effect a primary source since it was compiled mostly by members of his staff and reveals how the Cody myth was pictured in its institutional memory.

32. Ibid., pp. 536, 60–100.

33. Ibid., pp. 245, 262, 172–98; conversation with Norman Drachler, former superintendent of the Detroit Public Schools, April, 1979.

34. Detroit Public School Staff, *Cody*, pp. 47, 500–1, 38–59, 33–35; Charles Spain, "Frank Cody—An Appreciation," *School Executive Magazine* 50 (1930): 216–18.

35. Detroit Public School Staff, *Cody*, pp. 34–35, 63, 64, chap. 4; William McAndrew, "Picturing Frank Cody," *School and Society* 30 (1929): 473–81.

36. Detroit Public School Staff, *Cody*, pp. 74, 493.

37. Ibid., pp. 206, 174–75, 204.

38. Ibid., pp. 157, 159, 161, 205–6, 209, 493, 530, 545–46; Arthur Moehlman, *Public Education in Detroit* (Bloomington, Ill.: Public School Publishing Company, 1925), chaps. 13–14; for an account of board politics, see Spaulding, *School Superintendent*, pp. 412–16.

39. Detroit Public School Staff, *Cody,* pp. 401–2, 395–401.

40. Ibid., pp. 404, 426, 306.

41. Ibid., pp. 410–11; for a more bureaucratic (and probably ghost-written) account of his stewardship, see Frank Cody, "The Superintendent: His Administrative and Supervisory Staff," *School Executives Magazine* 50 (1930): 259–61.

42. Detroit Public Schools, *Cody,* p. 397.

43. Ibid., p. 6, 85, 234; McAndrew, "Cody," p. 477.

44. Detroit Public School Staff, *Cody,* pp. 261, 236, 436–89; for a sample of his Depression-years reports, see Detroit Public Schools, *The Superintendents' Annual Report, 1938–39,* mimeographed (Detroit: Detroit Board of Education, 1939).

45. Norman Woelfel, *Molders of the American Mind* (New York: Columbia University Press, 1933), p. 183; Walter Drost, *David Snedden and Education for Social Efficiency* (Madison: University of Wisconsin Press, 1967); Paul Monroe, "Quantitative Investigations in Education," *School Review Monographs,* no. 1 (Chicago: University of Chicago Press, 1911), p. 32; for a brief history of educational research see Lee J. Cronbach and Patrick Suppes, eds., *Research for Tomorrow's Schools: Disciplined Inquiry for Education* (New York: Macmillan, 1969), chap. 2, pp. 74–76.

46. Strayer, "Progress," pp. 376, 378.

47. Carter Alexander, *Educational Research: Suggestions and Sources of Data with Specific Reference to Administration* (New York: Teachers College Press, 1927), p. 1.

48. Jesse Newlon, *Educational Administration as Social Policy* (New York: Scribner's, 1934), p. 94; Raymond Callahan, *Education and the Cult of Efficiency* (Chicago: University of Chicago Press, 1962).

49. Walter Monroe et al., *Ten Years of Educational Research, 1918–1927* College of Education, University of Illinois, Bureau of Educational Research, Bulletin no. 42 (Urbana, Ill., 1928), pp. 182–83, 189; for different definitions of "research," together with studies of investigations that made a difference in practice, see Patrick Suppes, ed., *Impact of Research on Education: Some Case Studies* (Washington, D.C.: National Academy of Education, 1978).

50. Newlon, *Educational Administration,* p. 260, appendix.

51. Monroe et al., *Educational Research,* p. 21; Cubberley, *Public School Administration,* 325–26.

52. Arthur Powell, *The Uncertain Profession: Harvard and the Search for Educational Authority* (Cambridge: Harvard University Press, 1980), chaps. 4–6; Lawrence Cremin, David Shannon, and Mary Townsend, *A History of Teachers College, Columbia University* (New York: Columbia University Press, 1954).

53. Chapman, "Schools as Sorters"; Murray Nelson, "Building a Science of Society: The Social Studies and Harold O. Rugg," (Ph.D. diss., Stanford University, 1975).

54. Thorndike as quoted in Merle Curti, *The Social Ideas of American Educators* (New York: Scribner's, 1935), pp. 482, 459–498; Clarence Karier, ed., *Shaping the Educational State, 1900 to the Present* (New York: The Free Press, 1975), chaps. 5–6.

55. Monroe et al., *Educational Research,* p. 47, chaps. 2–3.

56. Ibid., pp. 62–65, 50.

57. David F. Noble, *America by Design: Science, Technology, and the Rise of Corporate Capitalism* (New York: Alfred A. Knopf, 1979); Franklin Bobbitt, "Some General Principles of Management Applied to the Problems of City-School Systems," in *Twelfth Yearbook of the National Society for the Study of Education* (Chicago: University of Chicago Press, 1913), pp. 7–96; Cubberley, *Public School Administration.*

58. Bobbitt, "Principles of Management"; Spaulding, *School Superintendent;* William Theissen, *The City Superintendent and the Board of Education* (New York: Teachers College Press, 1917).

59. On Taylorism, see Samuel Haber, *Efficiency and Uplift: Scientific Management in the Progressive Era, 1890–1920* (Chicago: University of Chicago Press, 1964).

60. Ellwood P. Cubberley, *Public School Administration: A Statement of the Fundamental Principles Underlying the Organization and Administration of Public Education* (Boston: Houghton Mifflin, 1916), p. 338; Jesse Sears, *An Autobiography* (Palo Alto, Calif.: The Author, 1959), p. 102; Callahan, *Cult;* Upton Sinclair attacked this Taylorizing of teaching in *The Goslings.*

61. Tyack, *One Best System,* pp. 184–85.

62. Loren Baritz, *The Servants of Power* (Middletown, Conn.: Wesleyan University

Press, 1960), p. 193; Chapman, "Schools as Sorters"; Paul Violas, *The Training of the Urban Working Class* (Chicago: Rand McNally, 1978); Joel Spring, *Education and the Rise of the Corporate State* (Boston: Beacon Press, 1972).

63. Edward Buchner, "School Surveys," in U.S. Commissioner of Education, *Report for 1914* (Washington, D.C.: GPO, 1915), 1: 515; Jesse Sears, *The School Survey* (Boston: Houghton Mifflin, 1925); Gail Shea, "The Influence of the Academic Community on Urban School Reform: A Case Study of the Chicago Educational Commission of 1898," (Master's thesis, University of Chicago, 1979)—Shea shows the great impact of university scholars, businessmen, and city superintendents on the Harper survey and the minimal input of teachers and average citizens.

64. Otis Caldwell and Stuart Courtis, *Then and Now In Education: 1845, 1923* (Yonkers-on-Hudson, N.Y.: World Book, 1925); John Philbrick, *City School Systems in the United States* (Washington, D.C.: GPO, 1885).

65. Leonard Ayres, "History and Present Status of Educational Measurements," *Seventeenth Yearbook of the National Society for the Study of Education* (Bloomington, Ill.: Public School Publishing Company, 1918), 2: 11; Monroe, et al., *Educational Research*, chap. 2.

66. Strayer, "Report of the Committee on Tests and Standards of Efficiency in Schools and School Systems," *Addresses and Proceedings of the NEA, 1914*, p. 302; Hollis Caswell, *City School Surveys: An Interpretation and Appraisal* (New York: Teachers College Press, 1927), p. 39 and passim; a useful guide to the survey literature is a "Topical Analysis of 234 School Surveys," School of Education, Indiana University, Bureau of Cooperative Research Bulletin no. 4, (Bloomington, Ind., 1926), p. 3; Monroe et al., *Educational Research*, pp. 38–39.

67. Ayres report quoted in Edward Buchner, "School Surveys," 1: 528–29; Buchner also wrote reports on school surveys in the U.S. Commissioner of Education, *Reports* for 1915, 1916 and 1917, and wrote separate studies of school surveys as U.S. Bureau of Education Bulletin no. 45 in 1918 and Bulletin no. 17 in 1923 (Washington, D.C.: GPO); Charles Judd, "Summary of Typical School Surveys," *Thirteenth Yearbook of the National Society for the Study of Education* (Chicago: University of Chicago Press), 2: 72.

68. Judd, "School Surveys," p. 78; Paul Hanus, *Adventuring in Education* (Cambridge: Harvard University Press, 1937), p. 186, chap. 12; Ellwood Cubberley, *The Portland Survey* (Yonkers-on-Hudson, N.Y.: World Book, 1916).

69. William Maxwell, "Comment," *Addresses and Proceedings of the NEA, 1915*, pp. 398, 401; Russell, *Teachers College*, p. 31.

70. Strayer, "Tests and Standards," pp. 303–4.

71. C.S. Meek, "The Public School Survey," *Addresses and Proceedings of the NEA, 1914*, pp. 311–13; Calvin Kendall, "Comment," *Addresses and Proceedings of the NEA, 1915*, p. 389; James Van Sickle, "The Investigation of the Efficiency of Schools and School Systems," *Addresses and Proceedings of the NEA, 1915*, pp. 379–84; also see comments on Van Sickle's speech by Leonard Ayres, ibid., pp. 384–89.

72. Henry Pritchett, "Educational Surveys," in Carnegie Foundation for the Advancement of Teaching, *Ninth Annual Report of the President and Treasurer* (New York: Merrymount Press, 1914), pp. 118–23; Judd, "School Surveys," p. 76; Leonard Ayres, *A Comparative Study of the Public School Systems in the Forty-Eight States* (New York: Russell Sage, 1912).

73. Buchner, "School Surveys," 1: 515; for similar interest in surveys in higher education, see Noble, *America by Design*, chap. 7.

74. Edward Buchner, "Educational Surveys," in U.S. Commissioner of Education *Report for 1914*, 1: 556, and *Report for 1915*, 1: 491; Pritchett, "Educational Surveys."

75. Edward Buchner, "Educational Surveys," in U.S. Bureau of Education Bulletin no. 17 (Washington, D.C.: GPO, 1923), pp. 19, 3–19.

76. Tyack, *One Best System*, p. 137; Caswell, *City School Surveys*, p. 39.

77. George Strayer, "A Comprehensive School Survey and Its Consequences," *Addresses and Proceedings of the NEA, 1923*, pp. 1016–17; Rick Ginsberg, "School Surveys: An Historical Perspective, Chicago, 1897–1964," AERA paper, April, 1980.

78. Leonard Ayres, "Significant Developments in Educational Surveying," *Addresses and Proceedings of the NEA, 1915*, pp. 996, 994; Raymond Moley, "The Cleveland Surveys —Net," *The Survey* 50 (1923): 229–31; Leonard Ayres, *The Cleveland School Survey*, Summary vol. (Cleveland: Survey Committee of the Cleveland Foundation, 1917).

79. R. E. Garlin, "Factors Conditioning the Success of School Surveys," *School and Society* 28 (1928): 337–40; and Garlin, "Giving Publicity to City School Surveys," *School and Society* 26 (1927): 277–80.

80. Caswell, *City School Surveys,* pp. 56–57, 67, 69, 73; Leonard Koos, "The Fruits of School Surveys," *School and Society* 5 (1917): 35–41; Lawrence Averill, "A Plea for the Educational Survey," *School and Society* 7 (1918): 187–91.

81. Judd quoted by Edward Buchner, "Surveys," in U.S. Commissioner of Education, *Report for 1916,* 1: 354; Strayer, "Progress"; Leonard Ayres, "Comment," *Addresses and Proceedings of the NEA, 1915,* pp. 388, 385.

Section 12

1. NEA, Department of Superintendence, *Educational Leadership: Progress and Possibilities,* Eleventh Yearbook (Washington, D.C.: NEA, 1933), p. 104 and passim.

2. Willard Waller's *The Sociology of Teaching* (1932; reprint ed., New York: John Wiley, 1965) is also a brilliant sociology of administration; we draw heavily on his ideas, including his belief that schools (especially in the small towns he studied) were "museums of virtue."

3. We recognize the dangers of jumping from description of social background to explanations of attitudes or political or managerial behavior (there have been numerous criticisms of the "status anxiety" interpretation of progressivism, for example, and Alexander George has cautioned about the tendency to reductionism in social background analysis). What we attempt here is simply an analysis of personal characteristics—e.g., age, sex, religion, ethnicity—that served as informal requirements for selection and that shaped the outlook of school administrators.

4. These data are summarized in app. 1 and 2 (compiled by Robert Cummings) in David Tyack, "Pilgrim's Progress: Toward a Social History of the School Superintendency, 1860–1960," *History of Education Quarterly* 16 (1976): 295–300.

5. Ibid. 295–300; Lotus D. Coffman, "The American School Superintendent," *Educational Administration and Supervision* 1 (1915): 17.

6. Horace Mann Bond, *The Education of the Negro in the American Social Order* (New York: McGraw-Hill, 1934), chap. 19; David Tyack, *The One Best System: A History of American Urban Education* (Cambridge: Harvard University Press, 1974), pp. 109–25, 217–29; Margaret Szasz, *Education and the American Indian: The Road to Self-Determination, 1928–1973* (Albuquerque: University of New Mexico Press, 1974).

7. Frederick Bair, *The Social Understandings of the Superintendent of Schools* (New York: Teachers College, 1934), pp. 89, 161; Neal Gross et al., *Explorations in Role Analysis: Studies of the School Superintendency Role* (New York: John Wiley, 1958), pp. 336, 338; Richard O. Carlson, *School Superintendents: Careers and Performance* (Columbus, Ohio: Charles Merrill, 1972), pp. 29–34; E. P. Hutchinson, *Immigrants and Their Children* (New York: John Wiley, 1956), p. 3; Myra Strober and David Tyack, "Why Do Women Teach and Men Manage? A Report on Schools," *Signs* 5 (1980): 494–503.

8. Tyack, "Pilgrim's Progress," and Strober and Tyack, "Why Do Women Teach."

9. W. W. Charters, Jr., "Social Class Analysis and the Control of Public Education," *Harvard Educational Review* 24 (1953).

10. On the importance of ambiguity in educational goals, see Michael Cohen and James March, *Leadership and Ambiguity: The American College President* (New York: McGraw-Hill, 1974).

11. NEA, Department of Superintendence, *Educational Leadership,* p. 346; Bair, *Social Understandings,* pp. 85–88; Carlson, *School Superintendents,* pp. 18–19.

12. Ellwood P. Cubberley, *Public School Administration: A Statement of the Fundamental Principles Underlying the Organization and Administration of Public Education* (Boston: Houghton Mifflin, 1916), pp. 136–37; Carlson, *School Superintendents,* pp. 18–19.

13. NEA, Department of Superintendence, *Educational Leadership,* p. 346; Albert P. Marble, "City School Administration," *Educational Review* 8 (1894): 165–66; William A. Mowry, *Recollections of a New England Educator, 1838–1908* (New York: Silver, Burdett, 1908), p. 9; Marvin Lazerson, *Origins of the Public School: Public Education in Massachusetts, 1870–1915* (Cambridge: Harvard University Press, 1971), chap. 1; R. Richard Wohl, "The 'Country Boy' Myth and Its Place in American Urban Culture: The Nineteenth

Century Contribution," *Perspectives in American History* 3 (1969): 77–156; Dana F. White, "Education in the Turn-of-the-Century School," *Urban Education* 1 (1969): 169–82.

14. Bair, *Social Understandings*, 148–53; Carlson, *School Superintendents*, p. 21; Douglas T. Hall and Benjamin Schneider, *Organizational Climates and Careers: The Work Lives of Priests* (New York: Seminar Press, 1973), chap. 2; John D. Donovan, "The American Catholic Hierarchy: A Social Profile," *American Catholic Sociological Review* 19 (1958): 98–112; James Q. Wilson, *Varieties of Police Behavior: The Management of Law And Order in Eight Communities* (Cambridge: Harvard University Press, 1968), chap. 3.

15. Waller, *Sociology of Teaching*, p. 375; AASA and NEA Research Division, *Profile of the School Superintendent* (Washington, D.C.: NEA, 1960), p. 107.

16. Waller, *Sociology of Teaching*, p. 420.

17. Hall and Schneider, *Organizational Climates;* John Tracy Ellis, "On Selecting Catholic Bishops for the United States," *Critic* 27 (1969): 47; John Tracy Ellis, "On Selecting American Bishops," *Commonweal* 85 (1967): 643–49; Henry J. Browne, "Father, Statesman, Administrator," *Continuum* 2 (1965): 605–11; Robert Dwyer, "Conformism and the American Hierarchy," *Continuum* 2 (1965): 611–18; Jay P. Dolan, "A Critical Period in American Catholicism," *Review of Politics* 35 (1973): 523–36; Donna Merwick, *Boston Priests, 1848–1910: A Study of Social and Intellectual Change* (Cambridge: Harvard University Press, 1973); Joseph H. Fichter, S.J., *Religion as an Occupation: A Study in the Sociology of Professions* (South Bend, Ind.: University of Notre Dame Press, 1961), pp. 34–128, 134–37, 153–71, 176–84; W. W. Charters, Jr., "The Social Background of Teaching," in N. L. Gage, ed., *Handbook of Research on Teaching* (Chicago: Rand McNally, 1963), pp. 741–44.

18. Larry Cuban, *Urban School Chiefs under Fire* (Chicago: University of Chicago Press, 1976), chap. 5; John Van Maanen, "Observations on the Making of Policemen," *Human Organization* 32 (1973): 407–17.

19. Waller, *Sociology of Teaching*, pp. 424–25; Marian A. Dogherty, *'Scusa Me Teacher* (Francestown, N.H.: Marshall Jones, 1943); Henry W. Button, "A History of Supervision in the Public Schools, 1870–1950," (Ph.D. diss., Washington University, 1961), chap. 7; Van Maanen, "Making of Policemen"; my authority on the proper traits of servants is Mr. Hudson in the television production, "Upstairs, Downstairs," on PBS.

20. Waller, *Sociology of Teaching*, pp. 34, 40, 45, chap. 4; Agatha Brown [pseud.], *Teachers Are People*, 3rd ed. (Hollywood, Calif.: David Graham Fischer Corp., 1925); on invasions of teachers' civil liberties, see Howard K. Beale, *Are American Teachers Free? An Analysis of Restraints upon the Freedom of Teaching in American Schools* (New York: Scribner's, 1936).

21. Richard O. Carlson, "Environmental Constraints and Organizational Consequences: The Public School and Its Clients," in Daniel E. Griffiths, ed., *Behavioral Science and Educational Administration* (Chicago: University of Chicago Press, 1964), pp. 263–76; Waller, *Sociology of Teaching*, pp. 10, 401–5; Charles E. Bidwell, "The School as a Formal Organization," in James March, ed., *Handbook of Organizations* (Chicago: Rand McNally, 1965), pp. 972–1022.

22. Charters, "Social Background of Teaching," pp. 746–52; Harmon Zeigler, *The Political Life of American Teachers* (Englewood Cliffs, N.J.: Prentice-Hall, 1967); Van Maanan, "Making of Policemen."

23. Howard S. Becker, "The Career of the Chicago Public Schoolteacher," *American Journal of Sociology* 57 (1952): 470–77; Daniel Griffiths, "Teacher Mobility in New York City," *Educational Administration Quarterly* 1 (1965): 15–31; William D. Greenfield, "Socialization Processes among Administrative Candidates in Public Schools" (Unpublished paper, Syracuse University, Syracuse, N.Y., 1975).

24. Fred C. Ayer, "The Duties of Public School Administrators," *American School Board Journal* 78 (Feb. 1929): 39–41 ff.; 80 (May 1930): 43–44; 78 (Apr. 1929): 52–53; 79 (Oct. 1929): 33–34, 136; 78 (June 1929): 60; William McAndrew, "The Plague of Personality," *School Review* 22 (1914): 315–25; NEA, Department of Superintendence, *Educational Leadership*, p. 176.

25. John Meyer and Brian Rowan, "Institutionalized Organizations: Formal Structures as Myth and Ceremony," *American Journal of Sociology* (1977): 340–63; Ayer, "Duties," 78 (Apr. 1929), 55, 50–54.

26. Esther Selke, "Is the Small Town Superintendency a Glorified Janitorship?," *School*

Executives Magazine 50 (1931): 412; Anon., "Why Superintendents Lose Their Jobs" and "Why I do Not Want to Be a Small Town Superintendent Again," *School Executives Magazine* 73 (1926): 52–53; J. H. Beveridge, "Hazards of the Superintendency and the Next Forward Steps in Reducing Them," *Addresses and Proceedings of the NEA, 1924,* pp. 864–69; H. E. Buchholz, "The Worst Job in the World," *American Mercury* 27 (1932): 315–22; George Henry, "Alas, the Poor School Superintendent," Harpers 193 (1946); G. H. Marshall, Clara W. Marshall, and W. W. Carpenter, *The Administrator's Wife* (Boston: Christopher Publishing House, 1941).

27. Bair, *Social Understandings,* p. 50; Neal Gross, *Who Runs Our Schools?* (New York: John Wiley, 1958); Clyde Morris, "The Careers of 554 Public School Superintendents in Eleven Midwest States," (Ph.D. diss., University of Wisconsin, 1957), p. 99; Robert K. Merton, *Social Theory and Social Structure,* rev. and enl. ed. (Glencoe, Ill: Free Press, 1957), chap. 10.

28. NEA, Department of Superintendence, *Educational Leadership,* pp. 176, 192.

29. AASA, *The American School Superintendency* (Washington, D.C.: AASA, 1952), p. 449; AASA and NEA Research Division, *Profile of the School Superintendent,* p. 74.

30. Cubberley, "Public School Administration"; Joel Spring, *Education and the Rise of the Corporate State* (Boston: Beacon Press, 1972); Tyack, *One Best System,* pt. 5.

31. Peter Schrag, *Village School Downtown* (Boston: Beacon Press, 1967), p. 55; Tyack, *One Best System,* pt. 4; Carlson, *School Superintendents,* chaps. 4–6; Joseph Cronin, *The Control of Urban Schools: Perspective on the Power of Educational Reformers* (New York: The Free Press, 1973); Arthur J. Vidich and Charles McReynolds, "Rhetoric versus Reality: A Study of New York City High School Principals," in Murray Wax, et al., *Anthropological Perspectives on Education* (New York: Basic Books, 1971), pp. 195–207; James Stephen Hazlett, "Crisis in School Government: An Administrative History of the Chicago Public Schools, 1933–1947," (Ph.D. diss., University of Chicago, 1968).

Section 13

1. Ella Flagg Young, as quoted in anonymous article, "The Highest Salaried Woman in the World," *Western Journal of Education* 14 (1909): 515; John T. McManis, *Ella Flagg Young and a Half-Century of the Chicago Public Schools* (Chicago: A. C. McClurg, 1916).

2. Young, "A Reply," *Addresses and Proceedings of the NEA, 1916,* p. 357.

3. Young as quoted in "Highest Salaried Woman," p. 516; Joan Smith, *Ella Flagg Young: Portrait of a Leader* (Ames, Iowa: Educational Studies Press, 1979).

4. David Tyack, *The One Best System: A History of American Urban Education* (Cambridge: Harvard University Press, 1974), pp. 59–65; Joan N. Burstyn, "Historical Perspectives on Women in Educational Leadership," in Sari Knopp Biklen and Marilyn B. Branigan, eds., *Women and Educational Leadership* (Lexington, Mass.: Lexington Books, 1980), pp. 65–75.

5. Louise Connolly, "Is There Room at the Top for Women Educators?" *The Woman Citizen,* 8 March 1919, p. 840.

6. Margaret Gribskov, "Feminism and the Woman School Administrator," in Biklen and Branigan, *Women and Educational Leadership,* pp. 77–91; Geraldine Clifford is currently exploring the relationship between teaching and various modes of feminist activism in "The Female Teacher and the Feminist Movement" (Unpublished paper, University of California, Berkeley, Calif.); and "Marry, Stitch, Die, or Do Worse," in Kantor and Tyack, eds., *Work, Youth and Schooling.*

7. Richard Jensen, "Family, Career, and Reform: Women Leaders of the Progressive Era," in Michael Gorden, ed., *The Family in Social-Historical Perspective* (New York: St. Martin's Press, 1973), p. 273; Burstyn, "Women in Educational Leadership"; Kathryn K. Sklar, *Catharine Beecher: A Study in American Domesticity* (New Haven: Yale University Press, 1973); Carl N. Degler, *At Odds: Women and the Family from the Revolution to the Present* (New York: Oxford University Press, 1980), chap. 13.

8. Grace Strachan, *Equal Pay for Equal Work: The Story of the Struggle for Justice Being Made by the Women Teachers of New York* (New York: B. F. Buck, 1910); Ralph Schmid, "A Study of the Organizational Structure of the National Education Association,

1884–1921," (Ph.D. diss., Washington University, 1963); Margaret Haley, "Why Teachers Should Organize," *Addresses and Proceedings of the NEA, 1904*, pp. 145–52.

9. *Addresses and Proceedings of the NEA, 1901*, pp. 64–67; Joan Smith, "The Changing of the Guard: Margaret A. Haley and the Rise of Democracy in the NEA," AERA Paper, 1978, ERIC ED 153 911, pp. 5–6; Haley, "Why Teachers Should Organize"; Upton Sinclair, *The Goslings: A Study of the American Schools* (Pasadena, Cal.: The Author, 1924), p. 241.

10. Smith, "Haley," p. 9; David Ricker, "The School-Teacher Unionized," *Educational Review* 30 (1905): 344–74; Schmid, "Organizational Structure," p. 99; Sinclair, *The Goslings*, pp. 243, 267; Smith, "Haley," p. 16; Haley, "Letter on the Educational Association," *Chicago Teachers' Federation Bulletin* 4 (1905): 1–3.

11. Charles Eliot to Irwin Shepard, 6 February 1911, as quoted in Gordon Seely, Jr., "Investigatory Committees of the National Educational Association: A History of the Years 1892–1918," (Ph.D. diss., Stanford University, 1963), p. 195; Editorial in *Educational Review* 54 (1917): 214.

12. Jacqueline Clement, *Sex Bias in School Leadership* (Evanston, Ill.: Integrated Education, 1975), comments on the persistence of this conspiracy of silence well into the computer age.

13. Edith A. Lathrop, *Teaching as a Vocation for College Women* (Washington, D.C.: National Council of Administrative Women in Education Monograph no. 3, 1922), pp. 3–4.

14. Connolly, "Room at the Top?" p. 841; Lathrop, *Teaching as a Vocation*, p. 3; Dennis H. Cooke, "Trend Is toward Smaller Turnover among City Superintendents," *Nation's Schools* 11 (1933): 25.

15. Lathrop, *Teaching as a Vocation*, p. 3; NEA, *Report on Salaries, 1905*, pp. 54–69; Patricia Schmuck, *Sex Differentiation in Public School Administration* (Washington, D.C.: National Council of Administrative Women in Education, 1976).

16. Connolly, "Room at the Top?" pp. 841–42, 843, 840.

17. NEA, Department of Elementary School Principals, *The Elementary School Principalship in 1968* (Washington, D.C.: NEA, 1968), p. 11.

18. Lathrop, *Teaching as a Vocation*, pp. 3–4; Gribskov, "Feminism."

19. Julian E. Butterworth, *The County Superintendent in the United States*, U.S. Office of Education Bulletin no. 6 (Washington, D.C.: GPO, 1932), pp. 18, 23–30.

20. All state superintendents of schools to 1969 are listed in Jim B. Pearson and Edgar Fuller, eds., *Education in the States: Historical Development and Outlook*, vol. 1 (Washington, D.C.: NEA, 1969); NEA, *Studies in State School Administration*, pp. 4, 45; Ward Reeder, "Re-Organizing the Office of the Chief State School Official," *American School Board Journal* 71 (1925): 43, 150; Ellwood P. Cubberley, *State School Administration* (Boston: Houghton Mifflin, 1927).

21. Andrew Fishel and Janice Pottker, "Performance of Women Principals: A Review of Behavior and Attitudinal Studies," in Fishel and Pottker, eds., *Sex Bias in the Schools: The Research Evidence* (Rutherford, N.J.: Fairleigh Dickinson University, 1977), pp. 289–99; Kimball Wiles and Hulda Grobman, "Principals as Leaders," *Nation's Schools* 56 (1955): 75; Hulda Grobman and Vynce A. Hines, "What Makes a Good Principal?" *National Association of Secondary School Principals' Bulletin* 40 (1956): 5–16; Neal Gross and Ann Trask, *Men and Women as Elementary School Principals* (Washington, D.C.: Cooperative Research, USOE, 1964); Anon., "How Do Women Rate?" *Nation's Schools* 37 (1946): 45; Mrs. Vern Vanderburgh, "Women as Administrators," *Nation's Schools* 37 (1946): 48.

22. Helen Davis, *Women's Professional Problems in the Field of Education: A Map of Needed Research*, mimeographed (n.p.: Pi Lamda Theta study, 1936), p. 16.

23. Charles S. Meek, "How Shall the Superintendent Spend His Time?" *Addresses and Proceedings of the NEA, 1921*, pp. 730–31.

24. David Tyack, "Pilgrim's Progress: Toward a Social History of the School Superintendency, 1860–1960," *History of Education Quarterly* 16 (1976); G. H. Marshall, Clara W. Marshall, and W. W. Carpenter, *The Administrator's Wife* (Boston: Christopher Publishing House, 1941).

25. John Folger and Charles Nam, *Education of the American Population* (Washington, D.C.: GPO, 1967), chap. 3; David Peters, *The Status of the Married Woman Teacher* (New York: Teachers College Press, 1934).

26. Davis, *Women's Professional Problems*, p. 17; for a perceptive linkage of family constraints to other barriers, see Sari Kopp Biklen, "Introduction: Barriers to Equity—Women, Educational Leadership, and Social Change," in Biklen and Brannigan, *Educational Leadership*, pp. 1-23.

27. Connolly, "Room at the Top?" p. 841.

28. Young, quoted in *Educational Review* 46 (1913): 540.

29. Schmid, "Organizational Structure," chaps. 5-6; Sinclair, *The Goslings*, chap. 54; Lorraine McDonnell, "The Control of Political Change with an Interest Group: The Case of the National Education Association" (Ph.D. diss., Stanford University, 1975), chap. 1.

30. Connolly, "Room at the Top?" p. 841.

31. James Burns, *Leadership* (New York: Harper & Row, 1978), p. 457; for short biographies of Young, see Edward T. James, ed., *Notable American Women*, 3 vols. (Cambridge: Harvard University Press, 1971), 3: 697-99; *National Cyclopedia of American Biography*, 9: 26-27; *Addresses and Proceedings of the NEA, 1918*, pp. 685-86.

32. Ella Flagg Young, "Democracy and Education" (a review of Dewey's book of that title), *Journal of Education* 84 (1916): 5-6; John T. McManis, *Ella Flagg Young and a Half-Century of the Chicago Public Schools* (Chicago: A. C. McClurg, 1916), chap. 2.

33. Young's "closing words to the newspapers" as quoted in McManis, *Young*, pp. 210-11.

34. Suzanne Estler, "Women as Leaders in Public Education," *Signs* 1 (1975): 363-86.

35. McManis, *Young*, pp. 16-17, 19, 72, 36; Rosemary Donatelli, "The Contributions of Ella Flagg Young to the Educational Enterprise" (Ph.D. diss., University of Chicago, 1971), chaps. 3-4.

36. On Dorsey, see biography in *Notable American Women*, 1: 506-8; on Jarrell, see biography in Barbara Sicherman and Carol Hurd Green, eds., *Notable American Women: The Modern Period* (Cambridge: Harvard University Press, 1980), pp. 375-77.

37. Donatelli, "Young," pp. 99-105; Joan E. Smith, *Ella Flagg Young: Portrait of a Leader* (Ames, Iowa: Educational Studies Press, 1979), pp. 32, 33, 35-36, 109.

38. George S. Counts, *School and Society in Chicago* (Chicago: University of Chicago Press, 1925), chap. 10; Smith, "Haley," pp. 16-19; McManis, *Young*, chap. 10.

39. Counts, *Chicago*, chap. 10; Mary Herrick, *The Chicago Schools: A Social and Political History* (Beverly Hills, Calif.: Sage Publications, 1971), pp. 114-15, 74.

40. Dewey quoted in McManis, *Young*, chaps. 3-6, pp. 120-22; Ella Flagg Young, "How to Teach Parents to Discriminate Between Good and Bad Teaching," *Addresses and Proceedings of the NEA, 1887*, pp. 245-49; Ella Flagg Young, "Grading and Classification," *Addresses and Proceedings of the NEA, 1893*, pp. 83-86.

41. Haley quoted in Joan Smith, "The Influence of Ella Flagg Young on John Dewey's Educational Thought," *Review Journal of Philosophy and Social Science* 2 (1977): 148, 143-54.

42. McManis, *Young*, pp. 85, 98; Donatelli, "Young," chap. 5.

43. Ella Flagg Young, *Isolation in the Schools* (Chicago: University of Chicago Press, 1906), p. 106; McManis, *Young*, pp. 60-61, chaps. 8-9, pp. 126, 127-28; Donatelli, "Young," chap. 7.

44. Young, "A Reply," pp. 356-59; McManis, *Young*, pp. 197-98, quoting from her superintendent's report for 1913-14.

45. McManis, *Young*, pp. 165, 167, 162-63; her views are well stated in her superintendent's reports and in "The Educational Progress of Two Years, 1905-1907," *Addresses and Proceedings of the NEA, 1907*, pp. 383-405, and "The Present Status of Education in America—In the Elementary Schools," *Addresses and Proceedings of the NEA, 1911*, 183-86; Donatelli, "Young," chaps. 9-10.

46. Young, "Reply to W. T. Harris," *Addresses and Proceedings of the NEA, 1901*, 364; Young, "Industrial Education," *Addresses and Proceedings of the NEA, 1915*, 125-26, 127.

47. Young, "Democracy and Education," p. 6.

Section 14

1. For analysis of the varieties of progressive thought and practice, see Lawrence Cremin, *The Transformation of the School: Progressivism in American Education* (New York: Alfred A. Knopf, 1961).

2. John Dewey, *The Educational Situation* (Chicago: University of Chicago Press, 1902), pp. 22–23.

3. Dewey, *The School and Society* (Chicago: University of Chicago Press, 1899), pp. 43–44; Dewey, *Democracy and Education* (New York: Macmillan, 1916), pp. 377, 89–90.

4. Dewey, "Progressive Education and the Science of Education," in *Dewey on Education,* ed. Martin Dworkin (New York: Teachers College Press, 1959), p. 119.

5. Jesse Newlon, *Educational Administration as Social Policy* (New York: Scribner's, 1934), p. 93.

6. George Counts, *Dare the School Build a New Social Order?* (New York: John Day, 1932); Norman Woelfel, *Molders of the American Mind* (New York: Columbia University Press, 1933); Merle Curti, *The Social Ideas of American Educators* (New York: Scribner's, 1935), George Counts, *School Boards and the Selective Character of American Secondary Education* (Chicago: University of Chicago Press, 1922); C. A. Bowers, *The Progressive Educator and the Depression: The Radical Years* (New York: Random House, 1969).

7. For example, see Charles Beard, *The Unique Function of Education in American Democracy* (Washington, D.C.: Educational Policies Commission, 1937), pp. 106–29.

8. In a current study, Paul Peterson and Ira Katznelson of the University of Chicago are investigating working-class responses to public education; George Counts, *School and Society in Chicago* (Chicago: University of Chicago Press, 1925); Diane Ravitch, *The Great School Wars* (New York: Basic Books, 1974); Walter Lippman, *American Inquisitors* (New York: Macmillan, 1928); for one instance of the older ethnocultural politics reasserting itself, see David Tyack, "The Perils of Pluralism," *American Historical Review* 74 (1968): 74–98.

9. Edith Waterfall, *The Day Continuation School in England—Its Functions and Future* (London: Allen and Unwin, 1923), pp. 154–55; Phillip Curoe, *Educational Attitudes and Policies of Organized Labor in the United States* (New York: Teachers College Press, 1926).

10. Ellwood P. Cubberley, *Changing Conceptions of Education* (Boston: Houghton Mifflin, 1909), pp. 53–54; it is important to remember, however, that "businessmen" did not always want the same things—London ("Business and the Chicago Public School System") points out that the policies desired by the business elite changed over time and educators were not in synchronization or necessarily in sympathy with these changes.

11. Ella Flagg Young, "A Reply," *Addresses and Proceedings of the NEA, 1916,* p. 357.

12. Dan Lortie in *Schoolteacher* (Chicago: University of Chicago Press, 1975) suggests that classrooms actually have had a "cellular" and detached character. Arthur Stinchcomb's notion that organizations continue to show the influence of their time of origin might suggest that such a "cellular" character stems from the time that teachers worked in one-room schools—see "Social Structure and Organizations," in James G. March, ed., *Handbook of Organizations* (Chicago: Rand McNally, 1965), pp. 142–93.

13. Robert Peebles, *Leonard Covello: A Study of an Immigrant's Contribution to New York City* (New York: Arno Press, 1978).

14. Leonard Covello, *The Heart Is the Teacher* (New York: McGraw-Hill, 1958), pp. 29–31, 47, 50–51, 60–62, 92–93.

15. Covello, *Teacher,* p. 130; Peebles, *Covello,* chap. 5.

16. Peebles, *Covello,* pp. 133, 129–35; Covello, *Teacher,* pp. 109, 131–37; Covello, *The Social Background of the Italo-American School Child* (Leiden, Holland: E. T. Brill, 1967).

17. Leonard Covello, "A High School and Its Immigrant Community," *Journal of Educational Sociology* 9 (1936): 331–46; Peebles, *Covello,* chap. 8; Covello, *Teacher,* pp. 158, 165.

18. Covello, "High School"; Peebles, *Covello,* chap. 9; Covello, *Teacher,* pp. 180–83, 185, 205–6, 216–19, 231.

19. Covello, *Teacher,* pp. 197–98; Peebles, *Covello,* pp. 213–30.

20. Covello, *Teacher*, pp. 240–41; Leonard Covello, "The School as a Center of Community Life," in *The Community School*, ed. Samuel Everett (New York: Appleton-Century, 1938), pp. 125–63.

PART III

Section 15

1. King, as quoted in Richard Kluger, *Simple Justice: The History of Brown v. Board of Education and Black America's Struggle for Equality* (New York: Vintage Books, 1977), pp. 757, 758.

2. Langston Hughes, *The Panther and the Lash* (New York: Alfred A. Knopf, 1951), p. 14. Reprinted by permission.

3. Gunnar Myrdal, *An American Dilemma: The Negro Problem and Modern Democracy* (1944; reprinted, New York: Pantheon, 1972).

4. Lewis Lomax, *The Negro Revolt* (New York: Harper & Row, 1962); Edith K. Mosher, Anne H. Hastings, and Jennings L. Wagoner, Jr., *Pursuing Equal Educational Opportunity: School Politics and the New Activists* (New York: ERIC Clearing House on Urban Education, 1979).

5. U.S. Bureau of the Census, *Historical Statistics of the United States, Colonial Times to 1970* (Washington, D.C.: GPO, 1975), 1: 373; Ray Rist and Ronald Anson, eds., *Education, Social Science and the Judicial Process* (New York: Teachers College Press, 1977).

6. Frederick M. Wirt, "Neoconservatism and National School Policy," *Educational Evaluation and Policy Analysis* 2 (1980): 5–18.

7. Ibid.; David Tyack, "Do Schools Make a Difference? A Reassessment," *Andover Review* 2 (1975): 2–9.

8. Charles Silberman, *Crisis in the Classroom: The Remaking of American Education* (New York: Random House, 1970), p. 10; Jonathan Kozol, *Death at an Early Age: The Destruction of the Hearts and Minds of Negro Children in the Boston Public Schools* (Boston: Houghton Mifflin, 1967).

Section 16

1. Keith Goldhammer, "Roles of the American School Superintendent," in Luvern L. Cunningham, Walter G. Hack, and Raphael O. Nystrand, eds., *Educational Administration: The Developing Decades* (Berkeley, Calif.: McCutchan, 1977), pp. 148, 150–51.

2. Edgar Wesley, *NEA: The First Hundred Years* (New York: Harper & Bros., 1957), p. 397; U.S. Bureau of the Census, *Historical Statistics of the United States, Colonial Times to 1970* (Washington, D.C.: GPO, 1975), 1: 368.

3. Goldhammer, "School Superintendent," pp. 150–51; Charles E. Lindblom, "The Science of Muddling Through," *Public Administration Review* 13 (1959): 79–88.

4. Stephen K. Bailey, "New Dimensions in School Board Leadership," in William E. Dickinson, ed., *New Dimensions in School Board Leadership: A Seminar Report and Workbook* (Evanston, Ill.: National School Boards Association, 1969), p. 97.

5. NEA, U.S. Department of Superintendence, *Educational Leadership: Programs and Possibilities* (Washington, D.C.: NEA, 1933), pp. 159, 278, 325–30, 334–35; AASA, *The American School Superintendency* (Washington, D.C.: AASA, 1952), pp. 63, 437, 444; Larry Cuban, *Urban School Chiefs under Fire* (Chicago: University of Chicago Press, 1976); Nelson B. Henry, ed., *Changing Conceptions of Educational Administration* (Chicago: University of Chicago Press, 1946).

6. William Johnston, "Trends in the Concerns of School Superintendents as Evidenced

by a Review of the Resolutions Enacted by the American Association of School Administrators in the Twentieth Century" (Ph.D. diss., University of Toledo, 1965), pp. 113, 146–47; for a sample of cold war pressures on the schools, see the articles by Morris Mitchell, Goodwin Watson, J. Austin Burkhart, Jerome Nathanson, Horace Bond, Morton Puner, Frederick McLaughlin, and Kenneth Benne in *Nation* 173 (1951): 344–48, 371–74, 400–2, 423–25, 446–49, 470–72, 495–98.

7. For a sampling of such articles, strongly reminiscent of recent pressures for the 3 Rs, see *U.S. News and World Report,* 30 November 1956, pp. 68–69, 24 January 1958, pp. 68–80; *Time,* 7 September 1953, p. 68, 16 November 1953, p. 65; *Colliers,* 5 February 1954, pp. 23–28, 19 March 1954, pp. 34–40; *Life,* 24 March 1958, pp. 25–33; *Reporter,* 20 February 1958, pp. 8–14.

8. Arthur Bestor, *Educational Wastelands: The Retreat From Learning in Our Public Schools* (Urbana: University of Illinois Press, 1953); Archibald Anderson, "The Cloak of Respectability: The Attackers and Their Methods," *Progressive Education* 29 (1951–52): 69–70.

9. Joel Spring, *The Sorting Machine: National Educational Policy Since 1945* (New York: David McKay, 1976).

10. James Bryant Conant, *The American High School Today* (New York: McGraw-Hill, 1959); Conant, *My Several Lives: Memoirs of a Social Inventor* (New York: Harper & Row, 1970); Thomas Grissom, "Education and the Cold War: The Role of James B. Conant," in Clarence Karier, Paul Violas, and Joel Spring, *Roots of Crisis* (Chicago: Rand McNally, 1973), pp. 177–98.

11. For an overview of conflicts, see articles cited in *Nation* in n. 6; for an excellent review of the early and recent literature on school governance, on which we have drawn substantially, see William L. Boyd, "The Public, the Professionals, and Educational Policy Making: Who Governs?" *Teachers College Record* 77 (1976): 539–77.

12. James S. Coleman, "The Struggle for Control of Education," ERIC Report résumé ED 015 158, 7 October 1967, pp. 5–6, 7, 8.

13. W. Lloyd Warner, *Democracy in Jonesville* (New York: Harper, 1949), p. 198; L. Harmon Ziegler and M. Kent Jennings, *Governing American Schools* (North Scituate, Mass.: Duxbury Press, 1974); L. Harmon Ziegler, "Creating Responsive Schools," *Urban Review* 6 (1973): 28–44.

14. Boyd, "Who Governs?"; Lawrence Iannaccone and Frank W. Lutz, *Politics, Power and Policy: The Governing of Local School Districts* (Columbus, Ohio: Charles Merrill, 1970).

15. W. W. Charters, Jr., "Social Class Analysis and the Control of Public Education," *Harvard Educational Review* 24 (1953): 268–70; Peter Bachrach and Morton S. Baratz, "Two Faces of Power," *American Political Science Review* 56 (1962): 947–52; Frederick M. Wirt and Michael W. Kirst, *The Political Web of American Schools* (Boston: Little, Brown, 1972), pp. 109–10.

Section 17

1. Frances Piven and Richard Cloward, *Poor Peoples' Movements: Why They Succeed, How They Fail* (New York: Pantheon, 1977); Joseph Gusfield, ed., *Protest, Reform, and Revolt: A Reader in Social Movements* (New York: John Wiley, 1970); Bruce Miroff, "Presidential Leverage over Social Movements: The Johnson White House and Civil Rights," *The Journal of Politics* 43 (1981): 2–23; Andrew S. McFarland, "Recent Social Movements and Theories of Power in America" (Paper delivered at the Annual Meeting of the American Political Science Association, Washington, D.C., September, 1979—we are indebted to Paul Peterson for calling this paper to our attention).

2. Gunnar Myrdal, *An American Dilemma: The Negro Problem and Modern Democracy* (1944; reprinted, New York: Pantheon, 1972), p. 2; David Kirp, *Just Schools* (Berkeley: University of California Press, forthcoming).

3. Robert G. Newby and David Tyack, "Victims Without 'Crimes': Some Historical Perspectives on Black Education," *Journal of Negro Education* 40 (1971): 192–206.

4. The current "Moral Majority" constitutes such a conservative social movement—see

Frances Fitzgerald, "A Disciplined, Charging Army," *New Yorker*, 18 May 1981, pp. 53–141.

5. Richard Kluger, *Simple Justice: The History of Brown v. Board of Education and Black America's Struggle for Equality* (New York: Vintage Books, 1977); Martin Luther King, Jr., *Why We Can't Wait* (New York: Harper & Row, 1964).

6. Larry Cuban, *Urban School Chiefs under Fire* (Chicago: University of Chicago Press, 1976).

7. Robert L. Crain and David Street, "School Desegregation and School Decision Making," *Urban Affairs Quarterly* 2 (1967): 68, 70.

8. Piven and Cloward, *Poor People's Movements*, p. 12; Vincent Harding, "The Black Wedge in America: Struggle, Crisis, and Hope, 1955–1975," *Black Scholar* 7 (1975): 33.

9. Anthony Obershall, *Social Conflict and Social Movements* (Englewood Cliffs, N.J.: Prentice-Hall, 1973), pp. 209–10, 221; Franklin Frazier, *The Negro Church in America* (New York: Schocken Books, 1966), pp. 32, 43–44.

10. Harding, "Black Wedge," p. 32.

11. Ibid., pp. 30, 46; Obershall, "Social Conflict," pp. 224–25; for an excellent set of readings on desegregation, see Meyer Weinberg, *Integrated Education: A Reader* (Beverly Hills, Calif.: Glencoe Press, 1967).

12. Lewis Lomax, *The Negro Revolt* (New York: Harper & Row, 1962), pp. 194–96; Newby and Tyack, "Victims."

13. J. Harvie Wilkinson, III, *From Brown to Bakke: The Supreme Court and School Integration, 1954–1978* (New York: Oxford University Press, 1979), pp. 102, 105, 107, 121.

14. Howe quoted in Wilkinson, *Brown to Bakke*, p. 105; Obershall, *Social Conflict*, p. 233.

15. Harding, "Black Wedge," p. 39; Stokely Carmichael and Charles Hamilton, *Black Power: The Politics of Liberation in America* (New York: Random House, 1967).

16. U. S. Riot Commission (Koerner Commission), *Report of the National Advisory Commission on Civil Disorder* (New York: Bantam Books, 1968); Rustin quoted in Obershall, *Social Conflict*, pp. 233, 230–35.

17. Harding, "Black Wedge," pp. 39–40.

18. Edith K. Mosher, Anne H. Hastings, and Jennings L. Wagoner, Jr., *Pursuing Equal Educational Opportunity: School Politics and the New Activists* (New York: ERIC Clearing House on Urban Education, 1979); Anthony Downs, "Up and Down with Ecology—the Issue-Attention Cycle," *Public Interest*, no. 28 (1972): 38–50.

19. Robert Crain, *The Politics of School Desegregation* (Chicago: Aldine Publishing Company, 1968); for an excellent review of the results of educational attacks on poverty, see Henry Levin, "A Decade of Policy Developments in Improving Education and Training for Low-Income Populations," in Robert H. Haveman, ed., *A Decade of Federal Antipoverty Programs* (New York: Academic Press, 1977), pp. 123–88.

20. On role conflicts among black administr ators, see Rosie Doughty, "An Exploration of Some Associations Between Student-Community Unrest and the Promotion of Black Administrators in Public Schools" (Ph.D. diss., Ohio State University, 1974); Charles D. Moody, "The Black Superintendent," *School Review* 81 (1973): 375–82; Alonzo Crim, article on Atlanta public schools, *Daedalus* 110 (Fall 1981, in press).

21. Lorraine Collins, "About those Few Females Who Scale the Heights of School Management," *American School Board Journal* 163 (1976): 27; Glenda Lee Landon, "Perceptions of Sex Role Stereotyping and Women Teachers' Career Aspirations" (Ph.D. diss., University of Wisconsin, 1975), app. E, p. 190; Jacqueline Clement, *Sex Bias in School Administration* (Evanston, Ill.: Integrated Education Associates, 1975).

22. Frederick M. Wirt, "Neoconservatism and National School Policy," *Educational Evaluation and Policy Analysis* 2 (1980), gives a useful survey of recent studies.

23. Henry Resnik, *Turning on the System* (New York: Pantheon, 1970).

24. Marcus Foster, *Making Urban Schools Work: Strategies for Changing Education* (Philadelphia: Westminster, 1971), p. 151; Jesse McCorry, *Marcus Foster and the Oakland Public Schools: Leadership in an Urban Bureaucracy* (Berkeley: University of California Press, 1978), chaps. 2–3.

25. Foster, *Urban Schools*, p. 19; Rosemary Hallum with Albertine Foster, *Dr. Marcus A. Foster: A Man for All People* (Hayward, Calif.: Alameda County School Department, n.d.); Marcus Foster, "Grand Jury's Report: We Can Learn from its Analysis and Perspec-

tive," *Superintendent's Bulletin, Oakland Unified Public School District, Sept.–Oct. 1973*, p. 11.

26. Foster, *Urban Schools*, p. 19, chap. 8.

27. Ibid., p. 19, chap. 4.

28. Ibid., pp. 105, 109.

29. Ibid., pp. 111, 109, chap. 10.

30. Resnik, *Turning on the System*, pp. 131, 121–39.

31. Foster, *Urban Schools*, p. 144, chap. 11; Resnik, *Turning on the System*, pp. 137–39.

32. Tribute to Foster by Mayor John Reading, in "Dr. Marcus A. Foster, Superintendent of Schools," *Superintendent's Bulletin, Oakland Unified Public School District, Nov.–Dec., 1973*, p. 11.

Section 18

1. Gene I. Maeroff, "Harried School Leaders See Their Role Waning," *New York Times*, 5 March 1974, pp. 1, 29; professor as quoted in Michael W. Kirst, *Governance of Elementary and Secondary Education* (Palo Alto, Calif.: Aspen Institute for Humanistic Studies, 1976), pp. 19–20.

2. Arthur J. Vidich and Charles McReynolds, "Rhetoric versus Reality: A Study of New York City High School Principals," in Murray Wax, Stanley Diamond, and Fred O. Gearing, eds., *Anthropological Perspectives on Education* (New York: Basic Books, 1971), pp. 195, 198, 200, 202.

3. David Tyack, Michael Kirst, and Elisabeth Hansot, "Educational Reform: Retrospect and Prospect," *Teachers College Record* 81 (1980): 253–69.

4. Robert J. Havighurst, "Educational Leadership for the Seventies," *Phi Delta Kappan* 63 (1972): 403–6; Joseph M. Cronin, "The School Superintendent in the Crucible of Urban Politics," in Frank W. Lutz, ed., *Toward Improved Urban Education* (Worthington, Ohio: Charles A. Jones, 1973), pp. 145–75; Roald F. Campbell, "The Superintendent—His Role and Professional Status," *Teachers College Record* 65 (1964): 671–79; H. Thomas James, "Educational Administration: A Forty-Year Perspective" (*Division A* Invited Address, AERA Convention, New York, April, 1981); in other studies James and his colleagues note ways in which socioeconomic environments of school districts affect fiscal and other policy making: H. Thomas James, "Politics and Community Decision Making in Education," *Review of Educational Research* 37 (1967): 377–86, and H. Thomas James, James A. Kelly, and Walter I. Garms, *Determinants of Educational Expenditures in Large Cities of the United States*, College of Education, Stanford University, Report of Cooperative Research Project no. 2389 (Stanford, Calif., 1966); see also Thomas R. Dye, "Governmental Structure, Urban Environment, and Educational Policy," *Midwest Journal of Political Science* 11 (1967): 353–80.

5. Myron Lieberman, *The Future of Public Education* (Chicago: University of Chicago Press, 1960), pp. 34–36.

6. Lorraine H. McDonnell and Anthony Pascal, "National Trends in Collective Bargaining," *Education and Urban Society* 11 (1979): 124–51.

7. Marshall O. Donley, Jr., *Power to the Teacher: How America's Educators Became Militant* (Bloomington: Indiana University Press, 1976), chap. 13; Lorraine McDonnell, "The Control of Political Change within an Interest Group: The Case of the National Education Association" (Ph.D. diss., Stanford University, 1975), pp. 33–55; on the processes of internal change in organizations, see Mayer N. Zald and Michael Berger, "Social Movements in Organizations: Coup d'Etat, Insurgency, and Mass Movements," *American Journal of Sociology* 83 (1978): 823–61.

8. William L. Boyd, "The Public, the Professionals, and Educational Policy Making: Who Governs?" *Teachers College Record* 77 (1976): 573; Michael W. Kirst and Walter I. Garms, "The Demographic, Fiscal, and Political Environment of Public School Finance in the 1980s (Stanford, Calif.: Institute for Research on Educational Finance and Governance, 1980), pp. 33–35; Kirst, *Governance*, pp. 20–21, 24.

9. Stephen K. Bailey and Edith K. Mosher, *ESEA: The Office of Education Administers a Law* (Syracuse, N.Y.: Syracuse University Press, 1968), chaps. 1–3.

10. In some respects the vocational education programs prefigured the new categorical programs.

11. David Tyack, "The High School as a Social Service Agency: Historical Perspectives on Current Policy Issues," *Education Evaluation and Policy Analysis* 1 (1979): 45–57.

12. Brenda Turnbull, Marshall S. Smith, and Alan L. Ginsburg, "Issues for a New Department: The Federal Role in Education," (Unpublished paper, U.S. Office of Education, June, 1980), p. 4, n. 2.

13. John W. Meyer, "The Impact of the Centralization of Educational Funding and Control of State and Local Organizational Governance," Institute for Research on Educational Finance and Governance, (Stanford University, Stanford, Calif., 1980).

14. Turnbull, Smith, and Ginsburg, "Federal Role," p. 16.

15. Meyer, "Educational Funding," pp. 6, 17.

16. Anon.,"Fragmented Centralization in American Public Schools," in Institute for Research on Educational Finance and Governance, Stanford University, *Policy Notes* 1 (1980): 1–7.

17. Michael W. Kirst, "The New Politics of State Education Finance," *Phi Delta Kappan* 60 (1979): 427–32; Leonard M. Cantor, "The Growing Role of the States in American Education," *Comparative Education* 16 (1980): 25–31.

18. Arthur Wise, *Legislated Learning: The Bureaucratization of the American Classroom* (Berkeley: University of California Press, 1979).

19. Michael Kirst, "Organizations in Shock and Overload: California's Public Schools, 1970–1980," *Educational Evaluation and Policy Analysis* 2 (1979): 27–30.

20. Virginia Davis Harding, "Educational Administration and the Courts, 1954–1974," in Cunningham, Hack, and Nystrand, eds., *Educational Administration*, pp. 95–118; Ray Rist and Ronald Anson, eds., *Education, Social Science and the Judicial Process* (New York: Teachers College Press, 1977), introduction.

21. David Kirp, "Law, Politics, and Equal Educational Opportunity: The Limits of Judicial Involvement," *Harvard Educational Review* 47 (1977): 117–37.

22. David K. Cohen, "Reforming School Politics," *Harvard Educational Review* 48 (1978): 431.

23. Gerald Benjamin, ed. *Private Philanthropy and Secondary Education* (n.p.: Proceedings of the Rockefeller Archive Center, 1980); Frances Fitzgerald, *America Revised: History Schoolbooks in the Twentieth Century* (Boston: Little, Brown, 1979); Michael S. Schudson, "Organizing the 'Meritocracy': A History of the College Entrance Examination Board," *Harvard Educational Review* 42 (1972): 34–60.

Section 19

1. Michael W. Kirst and Walter I. Garms, "The Demographic, Fiscal, and Political Environment of Public School Finance in the 1980s (Stanford, Calif.: Institute for Research on Educational Finance and Governance, 1980); National School Public Relations Association, *Declining Enrollment: Current Trends in School Policies and Programs* (Arlington, Va.: NSPRA, 1976); Michael W. Kirst, "A Tale of Two Networks: The School Finance Reform versus the Spending and Tax Litigation Lobby," Institute for Research on Educational Finance and Governance, Stanford University, Stanford, Calif., 1980; William L. Boyd, "Educational Policy Making in Declining Suburban School Districts: Some Preliminary Findings," *Education and Urban Society* 11 (1979): 333–66; for a useful set of papers on organizational decline and retrenchment in public organizations, see *Public Administration Review* 38 (1978): 315–57.

2. Daniel L. Duke and Adrienne M. Meckel, "The Slow Death of a Public High School," *Phi Delta Kappan* 61 (1980): 674–77.

3. Daniel L. Duke, Rosalyn Herman, and Jon S. Cohen, "Running Faster to Stay in Place: New York City Schools Face Retrenchment" (Unpublished paper, Stanford University, 1981), pp. 17–19.

4. Ibid., pp. 19, 20–30.

5. Paul Woodring, "Retrospect and Prospect," *Saturday Review,* 19 September 1970,

p. 66; David Tyack, "Formulating the Purposes of Public Education in an Era of Retrenchment," *Educational Studies* 11 (1980): 57–60.

6. Leonard Fein, *The Ecology of the Public Schools: An Inquiry into Community Control* (New York: Pegasus, 1971); Fred S. Coombs and Richard L. Merritt, "The Public's Role in Educational Policy-Making: An International View," *Education and Urban Society* 9 (1977): 167–96.

7. Arthur Wise, *Legislated Learning: The Bureaucratization of the American Classroom* (Berkeley: University of California Press, 1979); Paul Berman and Milbrey Wallin McLaughlin, *Federal Programs Supporting Educational Change: Implementing and Sustaining Innovations,* vol. 7 (Santa Monica, Calif.: Rand, 1978).

8. Brenda Turnbull, Marshall S. Smith, and Alan L. Ginsburg, "Issues for a New Department: The Federal Role in Education" (Unpublished paper, U.S. Office of Education, June, 1980), p. 20; J. Myron Atkin, "Government in the Classroom," *Daedalus* 109 (1980): 85–97; Michael Kirst, "The State Role in Education Policy Innovation," Institute for Research on Educational Finance and Government, Stanford University, Stanford, Calif., 1981; Jerome Murphey, "State Role in Education: Past Research and Future Directions," *Educational Evaluation and Policy Analysis* 2 (1980): 34–51.

9. Turnbull, Smith, and Ginsburg, "Federal Role," pp. 19–20; John Goodlad, "Can Our Schools Get Better?" *Phi Delta Kappan* 60 (1979): 342–47, and his forthcoming summary volumes of longitudinal study of effective schools; Ronald Edmonds, "Some Schools Work and More Can," *Social Policy* (March/April, 1979): 28–32; Michael Rutter et al., *Fifteen Thousand Hours: Secondary Schools and Their Effects on Children* (Cambridge: Harvard University Press, 1979); also see collection of articles on "The Search for Effective Schools," *Harvard Graduate School of Education Alumni Bulletin* 25 (1980): 1–39.

10. Phillip Selznick, *Leadership in Administration: A Sociological Perspective* (New York: Harper & Row, 1957), p. 151.

11. Norman Drachler, "Issues of Governance in Compensatory Education with Special Reference to Detroit, Michigan" (Unpublished paper, Stanford University, Palo Alto, Calif.), p. 35.

12. Arthur Newman, ed., *In Defense of the American Public School* (Berkeley, Calif.: McCutchan, 1978).

13. Charles Beard, *The Unique Function of Education in American Democracy* (Washington, D.C.: Educational Policies Commission, 1937); Educational Policies Commission, *Research Memorandum on Education during the Depression* (New York: Social Sciences Research Council, 1937); forthcoming study on educational policy making in the Depression by Robert Lowe, Elisabeth Hansot, and David Tyack.

14. "Gallup Poll," *Phi Delta Kappan* 61 (1980): 33–46; 1981 Gallup Poll results on parents reported in *Nevada State Journal,* 23 August 1981.

15. "Gallup Poll (1980)"; Hazel Erskine and Richard Siegel, "Civil Liberties and the American Public," *Journal of Social Issues* 31 (1975): 23.

16. Alonzo Crim, article on Atlanta public schools, *Daedalus* 110 (Fall, 1981, in press); R. Freeman Butts, "Public Education and Political Community," *History of Education Quarterly* 14(1974): 165–83.

17. Arnold Heidenheimer, Hugh Heclo, and Caroline Teich Adams, *Comparative Public Policy: The Politics of Social Choice in Europe and America* (New York: St. Martin's Press, 1975); Grace and Fred Heckinger, *Growing Up in America* (New York: McGraw-Hill, 1975).

18. John Dewey, *My Pedagogic Creed* (1897; reprint ed., Washington, D.C.: Progressive Education Association, 1929), p. 16.

Index

Index

Cohen, David, 9, 248
Coleman, James, 215, 221–23
Colorado, 213
Colorado State Teachers College, 121
Columbia University: Institute for Educational Research, 157; Teachers College, 98, 115–16, 120, 126, 130, 131, 134, 135, 137, 139–43, 145, 155, 161, 173, 192, 203, 204
Committee of Ten, 137, 138
Common School Advocate, 50
Common schools: capitalism and, 18, 22, 24, 28; class and, 21–22, 29, 32–33, 45, 56, 59, 73, 83; development of, 17–28; enrollment in, 31–33; ethnicity and, 23, 29, 73, 78–83; legislation for 39–40; millennialism and, 38, 94; ministers in, 48–49, 84; missionaries in, 39–44; movement for 3–4, 5, 7, 13, 59, 110, 225, 226, 239–40; national system of, 30, 34; need for, 38; plans for, 30; politics and, 10; promoters of, 45–48, 56–63; Protestantism and, 16, 19, 21, 23, 24, 30–31, 34–38, 45, 54, 71–72, 73–78, 83; race and, 29, 32–33, 83; regional differences in, 31–33, 83–93; of the Roman Catholic Church, 73; women in, 63–72
Commonwealth Fund, 133, 134, 156, 165
Communism, 150, 220–21
Competency, minimum, 246
Competition, 10, 184–201
Compulsory attendance, 31, 60, 101, 102–3
Conant, James Bryant, 221, 222
Condon, Randall, 141
Congregational Church, 34–35, 74
Congress of Racial Equality (CORE), 229
Connecticut, 161–62
Connolly, Louise, 184, 188, 192, 193
Consumerism, 5
"Continuation School," 111
Cooke, Jay, 36
Corporations: growth of, 6; as model for education, 107–8, 110, 112, 128, 141–42, 145, 157–60, 179, 181, 206, 240; *see also* Capitalism
Country School, The (play), 26
Counts, George, 9, 115, 204
Courtis, Stuart A., 154
Covello, Leonard, 207, 208–11, 236, 237, 255, 258
Crain, Robert L., 226
Crary, Isaac, 45
Cremin, Lawrence, 45, 264
Crim, Alonzo, 232, 260
CTF (Chicago Teachers Federation), 139, 185, 186, 196–97, 199–200
Cuban, Larry, 174, 225, 268
Cubberley, Ellwood Patterson, 11, 45, 103, 109, 112, 114, 115, 117, 118–19, 120, 121–28, 130, 131, 134, 140–44, 151, 157, 158, 164, 171, 204, 205, 218, 219
Culture, chauvinism of, 208, 209, 224–25
Cummings, Robert, 268
Curry, Jabez Lamar Monroe, 89, 90
Curti, Merle, 9, 53, 204

Dabney, Charles, 89, 90, 91
Darrow, Clarence, 76
Darwinism, 205
Davis, Helen, 190–91
Democracy, 128, 194–95, 197, 198–201, 202–4, 207
Democracy in Education (Dewey), 201
Democratic party, 102, 103
Denver (Colorado) Public Schools, 203
Departments of education (state), 5–6, 18, 34, 58–60, 219
Desegregation, 214, 224–31, 242; *see also* Civil-rights movement
Detroit (Michigan) Public Schools, 144–52, 206, 256
Dewey, Evelyn, 154
Dewey, Godfrey, 154
Dewey, John, 3, 114, 154, 181, 194, 197, 198–99, 201–4, 258, 262
Dies, Martin, 150
District of Columbia, 101
District schools, 29
Domhoff, William, 129
Donley, Jr., Marshall, 241
Dorsey, Susan, 196
Downs, Anthony, 231
Drachler, Norman, 256
Driver education, 243
Dropouts, 208, 218, 236
Drug-alcohol abuse prevention, 242–43
DuBois, W. E. B., 87
Duke, Daniel, 250, 251

Eaton, John, 43
Edmonds, Ronald, 255
Education: corporate model in, 107–8, 110, 112, 128, 141–42, 145, 157–60, 179, 181, 206, 240; equality of, 111; public v. private, 29–30; regional differences in, 31–32, 83–85; social evolution and, 116–17
Educational Administration as Social Policy (Newlon), 203
Educational associations, 43, 49–50, 65–66, 139–40
Educational Policies Commission, 135, 219, 258
Educational psychology, 118
Educational Research Association, 156
Educational revival agencies, 48–49

305

Index

Index

New York University, 139
Noble, David, 157, 267
Normal schools, 18, 31, 66, 146, 196, 199
Norms, educational, 152–60
North American College (Rome), 173
North Carolina, 32, 46, 83, 90
North Dakota, 187

Occupation, testing and, 156
Ogden, Robert, 90, 91
Ohio, 22, 70, 75, 206
Ohio State University, 143
Ohles, John, 45
Ohrenberger, William H., 179
Oklahoma, 164–65
One Best System, The (Tyack), 267
Opportunity, equality of, 111
Oregon, 25–28, 39–44, 79, 162
Our Country (Strong), 116

Pan-Protestantism, 34–38, 43, 61, 73–74, 78, 94, 179
Parker, Francis, 96, 199
Parker, Theodore, 62
Parks, Rosa, 214
Parochial schools, 22, 23, 30, 42, 112; enrollment in, 78; ethnicity and, 80–83; funds for, 77, 78
Parsons, Francis, 46
Payne, Bruce, 115, 131
Peabody Education Fund, 89
Peck, George, 82
Peck's Bad Boy (Peck), 82
Pedagogy, 98–100
Pennsylvania, 234–37
Peterson, Paul, 267
Philadelphia (Pennsylvania) Public Schools, 234–37
Philanthropists, 90–91, 93; *see also specific foundations*
Philbrick, John, 160
Physical education, 153, 155, 243
Pickard, Josiah, 197
Pierce, John, 45
Pietism, 74; small-town, 114–19
Pilgrim's Progress, The (Bunyan), 16
Piven, Frances Fox, 227
Placement, sponsorship and, 125, 135, 138, 140–44
Playground, 106
Plea for the West (Beecher), 71
Plunkett, George Washington, 144
Politics, 30, 38, 54, 59–62, 107–8, 112, 123, 129, 133–52, 205, 221–22, 238–39, 240; administrative decisions and, 7, 8; common schools and, 10; private groups and, 248; women and, 68

Portland (Oregon) Public Schools, 162
Power: administrative, 6–7; networks of, 129–40
Presbyterian Church, 116
Pressey, Sydney, 115
Principals, 176; blacks as, 235–37; minority, 232–33; as teachers, 255–56; urban high school, 238–39; women as, 183, 189, 199
Pritchett, Henry, 164
Private schools: affirmative action and, 216; nineteenth-century, 29, 31, 32; in the South, 83, 87; vouchers/tax credits for, 250
Professional associations, 136, 146, 248
Professionalism, 193; of administrators, 106–8, 112, 226; sexism and, 187
Professionalization, 6, 18, 31, 118–20, 121, 153, 226; National Education Association and, 138; surveys and, 161
Professors: in networks, 131, 132; sponsorship of, 141
Progressives, administrative, *see* Administrative progressives
Progressive education, 220
Progressive era, 3, 10
Proposition 13, 246, 250
Protestantism, 5, 10, 55–56, 73–74, 115, 116, 169–70; American Sunday School Union and, 35–38; in common schools, 16, 19, 23, 24, 30–31, 34–38, 54, 71–72; pan-, 34–38, 43, 61, 73–74, 76, 78, 94, 179; Southern, 85–93
Protestant-republican ideology, 13, 18, 21, 54, 73, 95, 107, 121, 266
"Psalm of Life" (Longfellow), 16
Psychologists, 118; networks of, 131; tests and, 159
Public Education in the United States (Cubberley), 127
Public School Administration (Cubberley), 123
Public schools: early importance of, 3; growth of, 30; *see also* Common schools
Pupil accounting, 153, 243–46

Quandt, Jean, 116

Race: common schools and, 29, 32–33, 83; equity and, 214, 261; National Education Association and, 136; racism and, 9, 127, 204, 213–17; of superintendents, 169; *see also* Civil-rights movement
Reagan, Ronald, 233
Reavis, William C., 142
Reconstruction, 85–93
Recordkeeping/forms, 159

Index

"Relative Frequency of English Speech Sounds" (Dewey), 154

Religion, 10, 29, 112, 168, 202; common schools and, 21, 45, 73–78, 83; reading of Bibles and, 22, 30, 73–74, 75–76; of superintendents, 168, 169

Republican party, 101–3, 168–69

Research, 206; in administration, 152–60; in universities, 129; taxes and, 155; *see also* Surveys

Resnick, Henry, 236

Retrenchment, 249–53, 257–58

Revisionism, 8–9, 11–12, 249, 264

Revivalism, Southern, 83–93

Rice, Joseph Meyer, 160

Rickover, Hyman, 220

Rigler, Frank, 162

Riles, Wilson, 255

Rockefeller, John D., 37, 90, 91, 156

Rodgers, Daniel, 109, 266, 268

Roman Catholic Church, 11, 23, 41, 71, 74–77, 169; common schools of, 73; Evangelicalism and, 78; schools of, 22, 30, 42, 112

Roosevelt, Theodore, 119, 123, 198

Rose, Robert, 141, 142

Rosenberg, Bella, 9

Rosenwald, Julius, 91

Ross, Dorothy, 120

Rowan, Brian, 177

Rural areas, 4, 32–33, 114–19, 170, 171–72; enrollment in, 33; female superintendents in, 188; missionaries in, 39–44; in the nineteenth-century, 17, 25–28; surveys of, 165

Russell, James, 126, 137

Russell Sage Foundation, 131, 156, 163–64

Rustin, Bayard, 231

Rutter, Michael, 255

Sadler, Michael, 3, 258

Salaries, 186, 187; of superintendents, 189–90; of teachers, 241

Scholarships, 29

School and Society (Dewey), 198

School boards, 96–97, 148; appointment of administrators, 190; autonomy of, 218–19; elites and, 204, 221–23; local superintendents and, 167, 170; roles of, 96, 107, 122–23

School Executives Magazine, 121, 177

School lunch programs, 106

Schrag, Peter, 179

Schultz, Stanley, 95

Schurz, Carl, 19

Science of education, 6–7, 98, 107–8, 110, 112–13, 119–20, 145, 202, 206–7, 240; research and, 152–60; surveys and, 160–67

SCLC (Southern Christian Leadership Council), 229, 230

Scott, Anne Firor, 66

Sears, Barnas, 89

Sears, Jesse, 119, 126, 158

Segregation, racial, 127, 226–31

Selznick, Philip, 255

Seminaries, female, 66–67, 69–72

Separatism, 23, 28

Sex education, 204, 221

Sex (gender), 29, 32, 261; equity and, 214; National Education Association and, 64, 136, 138, 180, 185, 192–93, 197, 233; school roles and, 63–64, 67–72, 168, 170, 180–201, 231–32

Sexism, 9, 187, 190; *see also* Feminism

Shakespeare, William, 26

Shedd, Mark, 235

Silberman, Charles, 216

Siljestrom, Per Adam, 19, 20, 72

Sinclair, Upton, 129, 137

Singleton, Gregory, 103

Sklar, Kathryn Kish, 68, 69, 70, 72

Slade, William, 71

Slater, John F., 91

Slavery, 85–86

Smith, Glenn, 137

Smith, Marshall, 244

Smith, Timothy, 266

Smith-Hughes Act of 1917, 243

Snedden, David, 131, 152

Social Frontier, The, 204

Socialism, 204

Socialization: male v. female, 190–91; occupational, 172–80; schools and, 117; of superintendents, 172–80; of teachers, 174–76

Social movements, as concept, 44, 266; nineteenth century, 44–56; recent, 213–14, 225–34

Social workers, 155

Sociology of Teaching, The (Waller), 172

Southern Christian Leadership Council (SCLC), 229, 230

Southern Education Board, 90–91; Bureau of Information and Advice on Legislation and School Organization, 91–92

Spargo, John, 126

Spaulding, Frank E., 117–18, 131, 133, 141, 155, 157, 166, 205

Special education, 153

Specialization, 124–25, 155, 200; in school bureaucracy, 159

Spencer, Herbert, 97

Sponsorship: administrative progressives and, 140–44; placement and, 125, 135, 138, 140–44; of professors, 141; of superintendents, 141–44, 173, 192; of women, 197

Standardization, 160, 167; of American Sun-

Index